CONNECTING YOUNG ADULTS AND LIBRARIES

SECOND EDITION

A How-To-Do-It Manual

Patrick Jones

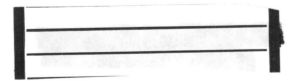

HOW-TO-DO-IT MANUALS FOR LIBRARIANS

NUMBER 59

NEAL-SCHUMAN PUBLISHERS, INC.
New York, London

Published by Neal-Schuman Publishers, Inc.
100 Varick Street
New York, NY 10013

Printed and bound in the United States of America.

Second impression⸴ 1999

Library of Congress Cataloging-in-Publication Data

Jones, Patrick.
    Connecting young adults and libraries : a how-to-do-it manual / Patrick Jones.—2nd ed.
        p. cm.—(How-to-do-it manuals for librarians ; no. 59)
Includes bibliographical references and index.
    ISBN 1–55570–315–1
    1. Young adults' libraries—Administration—Handbooks, manuals, etc.
2. Young adults—Books and reading—Handbooks, manuals, etc. I. Title.
II. Series: How-to-do-it manuals for libraries ; no. 59.
Z718.5.J66   1998
025.5'6—dc21   97–37124
                                                CIP

DEDICATION

To my mother, Betty Jones, and in memory of my father, Vaughn P. Jones.

CONTENTS

Dedication	iii
Quick Guide to Bib Squibs, Figures, and Other Good Stuff	ix
Acknowledgments	xv
Introduction	xvii
The YA Librarian's Planning Calendar	xix
August	1
September	23
October	65
November	93
December	175
Year-End Review: YA Bests	177
January	241
February	275
March	313
April	331
May	373
June	401
July	453

PART I: WHERE YA?		3
1	Trends in YA Services	5
PART II: WHO YA?		23
2	Investigating the Audience	25
2.1	Contradictions/Stereotypes	25
2.2	Developmental Tasks	30
2.3	Works in Progress	38
2.4	Opposites Attract	46
2.5	YA Lives and Times	53
PART III: WHY YA?		67
3	Making the Case	69
3.1	Why Kids Need Libraries	70
3.2	Why Libraries Need Kids	72
3.3	Creating Support	75
3.4	Fulfilling the Roles	79

3.5	Service Plans	84
3.6	Changing the Question/Developing a Vision	86
PART IV: WHAT YA?		**95**
4	YA Collections	97
4.1	YA Literature	97
4.2	Reading Research	100
4.3	Reading Interests	106
4.4	Collection Questions	108
4.5	Setting Priorities	112
4.6	Fiction	114
4.7	Nonfiction	132
4.8	Periodicals	138
4.9	Music	151
4.10	Nonprint Collections	153
4.11	Technology	156
4.12	Selection Tools	159
4.13	Collection Concerns	160
4.14	Reaching Reluctant Readers	168
5	Reference, Readers' Advisory, and Instruction	179
5.1	Qualities for Quality Service	179
5.2	Reference Services	186
5.3	Readers' Advisory Services	195
5.4	Library Instruction and Orientation	206
5.5	Schools and Library Cooperation	223
6	Booktalking: Don't Tell, Sell	243
6.1	Research	243
6.2	Rules	245
6.3	Hooks	253
6.4	Shows	260
6.5	Booktalk Examples	266
PART V: HOW YA?		**277**
7	Surveying the Field	279
7.1	Short History	279
7.2	By the Numbers	281
7.3	By the Books	300
7.4	Marketing to Young Adults	303
7.5	Measurement and Evaluation	307

8	Issues in YA Services	315
8.1	Access	315
8.2	Confidentiality	316
8.3	Privacy	317
8.4	Social Responsibilities of Libraries and Librarians	318
8.5	Censorship	319
8.6	Restricted Access to Services	321
8.7	Latchkey/Homeless	323
8.8	Out-of-School and Non-College Bound YAs	324
8.9	Lack of Diversity in the Literature	325
8.10	Defining YA Services	326
9	High-Speed Connections: YAs and the Internet	333
9.1	Youth, the Internet, and Library Policy	333
9.2	Applying the Policy	342
9.3	Alphabet of Criteria	345
9.4	Public Library YA Web Sites	348
9.5	The YA Librarian's Help/Home Page	354
9.6	Annotated Best Sites	357
10	YA Training	375
10.1	The Need for Training	375
10.2	The Goals of Training	376
10.3	Tips and Tools for Training	377
10.4	Training Exercises	380
10.5	A Training Checklist	396
APPENDIXES		
A.	YA Publishers Directory	403
B.	YA Magazines Directory	413
C.	YA Professional Periodicals Directory	417
Bibliography		419
Index		455
About the Author		461

QUICK GUIDE TO BIB SQUIBS, FIGURES, AND OTHER GOOD STUFF

BIB SQUIBS

Books about Body Image (Mostly Fiction)	124
Books about Death and Dying (Mostly Fiction)	123
Books about Life and Death	123
Books about Sex and Sexuality (Mostly Fiction)	120
Books about Substance Abuse (Mostly Fiction)	121
Books about Death and Dying (Mostly Fiction)	123
Comic Novels	126
Fun Fast Facts	196
Genre of Style	131
Historical Fiction	125
Informational Nonfiction: 15 Top Titles	134
Mysteries and Thrillers	124
Parenting YAs	42
Romances	125
Social Issues Fiction	122
Top 10 Horror Titles (by Author)	119
Top Training Tools	380
Underground Classics	130
YA Lives and Times	59
YA Programming	35
YA Readers Advisory Tools	200
Young Adult Literature	98
Youth Participation	33

FIGURES LISTED BY FIGURE NUMBER

2–1	What Teenagers Want to Be Called	54
2–2	How Old Teens Want to Be	55
2–3	Leisure-Time Activities of Teens	56–57
2–4	Where Teens Prefer to Spend Their Leisure Time	58
2–5	What Teens Like Most about Being Teens	59
2–6	What Teens Dislike Most about Being Teens	60
2–7	Biggest Adult Misconceptions about Teens	61

3–1	The White House Conference on Libraries Position Paper	71
3–2	YA User Survey	85–86
3–3	A Self-Evaluation Survey	87
4–1	The Reading Interest Survey	107
4–2	Setting Your YA Collection Priorities	113
4–3	Favorite Magazines by Gender	144
4–4	Most Popular Magazines According to Librarians	146
5–1	What Attracts Teens to Advertisements	182
5–2	Personal Bibliography Card	199
5–3	A Form for Preparing a Booklist	203
5–4	Library Orientation: An Evaluation Form for Students	213
5–5	Library Orientation: A Teacher Evaluation Form	214
5–6	A Sample Reporting Form	215
5–7	The Big Six in Action	219–221
5–8	Teacher Postcard	227
5–9	Assignment Alert Form	228
5–10	A Sample Teacher Letter	229
5–11	Materials Unavailable Card	230
5–12	A School Planning Form	234–235
6–1	A Booktalk Card	250
6–2	A Booktalk Evaluation Form for Students	263
6–3	Booktalking: Teacher Evaluation	264
6–4	Reporting Form for Booktalking	265
7–1	YA Statistics	280
7–2	Results of Staffing Survey	285
7–3	Results of Youth Survey	286
7–4	Percent of public libraries indicating . . . a reason or the primary reason that some young adults . . . do not use the public library, by library characteristics	287–288
7–5	Percent of public libraries, by frequency	289
7–6	Percent of public libraries indicating . . . internal barriers to increasing services and resources to young adults	290
7–7	Percent of public libraries indicating various ways they serve young adults as a distinct user group . . .	291
7–8	Percent of public libraries that mention a distinct young adult collection . . .	292
7–9	Percent of public libraries indicating being engaged in cooperative activities with local schools . . .	293
7–10	Availability of various public library services and their usage by young adults . . .	294
7–11	Percentage of public libraries reporting how the ethnic diversity . . . has changed . . .	295
7–12	Differences between Libraries with/without a YA Librarian	297
7–13	YA Marketing Plan	308
8–1	Self-Evaluation for Restricted Access	322

8–2	Where's a YA?	328
9–1	Directory of Model Public Library YA Pages	349–351
10–1	Family Feud Overheads	385
10–2	Tasks for Tasks Handouts	385
10–3	That Was Then, This Is Now (Adult)	387
10–4	That Was Then, This Is Now (Teen)	388
10–5	A Day in the Life [of a YA]	389
10–6	Building the Perfect YA Librarian	390
10–7	Meeting the Needs of YAs through Fiction	391
10–8	Blame the Victim	395
10–9	Programming Tapestry	397

OTHER GOOD STUFF

BOOK LISTS AND OTHER RESOURCES

10 "Big Ones"	201
100 Best Books	129
Annual Lists	161
Adult Authors for Rampant Readers	167
Best of the Best of the Best: Margaret Edwards Award Winners	128
Best-Selling YA Magazines to Middle and High School Libraries	145
Bodart Booktalking Resources	244
Capsule History of YA Services	301
Current YA Series	117
Directory of Model Public Library YA Pages [Internet]	349–351
Favorite Magazines by Gender	144
Lists from *Booklist* (1990-1996)	162
Magazines Aimed at Adults, Popular with YAs	147
Most Popular Magazines According to Librarians	146
Other "Best" Lists	163
Picture Books for YAs: Top 10 Titles	170
Publications and Reports from the Carnegie Council	40
Selection Tools: Reference Books	164
Top 30 YA Authors (A Personal Opinion)	115
Top-Selling Magazines to School and Public Libraries	145
Winners of the Delacorte Best First YA Novel Contest	132
YA Review Sources	160
Year-End Review: YA Bests	177

COMMON MYTHS AND TRUTHS ABOUT YOUNG ADULTS

Biggest Adult Misconceptions about Teens	61
Essential Requirements for Healthy Adolescents	29
How Do YAs Choose Books?	105
How Do YAs Find Out about New Books?	105–106
How Old Teens Want to Be	55
Leisure Time Activities of Teens	56–57
Meeting the Needs of Independent YA Learners:	
An Alphabet of Ideas and Questions	82
Milestones of Early Adolescence (11 to 14)	30
Milestones of Middle Adolescence (15-16)	31
Milestones of Late Adolescence (17 to 18)	31
Myths and Facts	28
What Are YA Attitudes about Reading?	106
What Are YAs Reading?	102–105
What Attracts Teens to Advertisements?	182
What Do YAs Like?	101
What Generalists Need to Know about YA Psychology	377
What Makes Readers Reluctant?	168
What YAs Need and Want from Libraries	84
What Teenagers Want to Be Called	54
What Teens Like Most about Being Teens	59
What Teens Dislike Most about Being Teens	60
Where Teens Prefer to Spend Their Leisure Time	58
Who Is Reading?	102
Why YAs Are Important Customers	184

FACT SHEETS

Booktalking	246
Homework Collection	193
Library Orientation	210
Library Instruction	217

LIBRARY STAFF TRAINING RESOURCES

Blame the Victim	395
A Day in the Life [of a YA]	389
Effective Active Learning Approaches	382
Effective Closings	382
Effective Openings	380
Family Feud Overheads	383
Programming Tapestry	397
Tasks for Tasks Handouts [Form]	385
That Was Then, This Is Now (Adult)	387
That Was Then, This Is Now (Teen)	388
Training Tips and Strategies	381

PLANNING TIPS AND FORMS FOR YA SERVICES

Access to Electronic Information, Services, and Networks: Questions & Answers	341
Assignment Alert Form	228
Behaviors That Contribute to Successful Transactions	187
Best Reference Transactions	186
The Big Six [Instruction in Doing Research]	218
The Big Six in Action	219–221
Booktalk Card [Form]	250
Booktalk Evaluation Form for Students	263
Booktalking: Policies	247
Booktalking: Teacher Evaluation	264
Criteria for Evaluating Series Fiction	111
Critical Needs Facing Young Adult Librarians	299
Differences between Libraries with/without a YA Librarian	297
Do's and Don'ts of Booktalking	251
Form for Preparing a Booklist	203
Homework Centers: Elements of Success	194
How Does Series Fiction Meet the Needs of YAs?	112
How to Win Customers and Keep Them for Life	185
Library Orientation: An Evaluation Form for Students	213
Library Orientation: Planning	209
Library Orientation: Teacher Evaluation Form	214
Listserv [Definition]	15
Materials Unavailable Card [Form]	230
Meeting the Needs of YAs through Fiction	391
Merchandizing Plan	116
Original Alphabet of Hooks for Books	256
Output Measures and More Data Elements	300
Personal Bibliography Card [Form]	199
Planning Process: Booktalking	245
Reading Interest Survey [Form]	107
Reporting Form for Booktalking	265
Sample Reporting Form	215
Sample Teacher Letter	229
School Planning Form	234–235
Self-Evaluation for Restricted Access	322
Self-Evaluation Survey [Form]	87
Setting Your Collection Priorities	113
Teacher Postcard [Form]	227
Tips for Training Teen Volunteers	32
Web Sites Evaluating Web Sites/ Internet Information Sources	345
Why Hire a YA Specialist?	299
Worst Reference Transactions	186
YA Marketing Plan	308

YA Nonfiction Series: Evaluation Criteria   137
YA Space-Planning Questionnaire   89
YA User Survey [Form]   85–86

YA SERVICES STANDARDS AND GOALS STATEMENTS

Building the Perfect YA Librarian   390
Developmentally Based Performance Measures   309
Goals of the Young Adult Library Services Association   78
Illinois Goals for Youth Services   77
National Education Goals   74
New York Standards for YA Services   76
Public Library (PLA) Roles   79
Qualities for Quality Service   183
Service Plan Goal   88
Top Traits [of YA Librarians]   184
Traits of an Effective YA Librarian   183
What Is Excellence in Library Services to YAs?   180
White House Conference on Libraries Position Paper   71
Young Adult Library Services Association Vision Statement   90
Young Adults Deserve the Best   181

YA SURVEYS

Comparison of 1995 and 1988 NCES Surveys   298
Findings of the Carnegie Council   281
National Center for Education Statistics (NCES):
   "Services for Children and Young Adults in
   Public Libraries"   287–288
The Power of Reading   101
Results of Staffing Survey   285
Results of Youth Survey   286
Review of Reading Interest Surveys   100
Role of the Public Library: Results of a Gallup Poll   81
Role of the Public Library: Results of a Gallup Poll
   of Community Leaders   80
Summary of 1988 National Center for Education
   Statistics Report   296
Summary of *Youth Indicators 1996*   282
USA Today Surveys   284
Where's a YA?   328
YA Services in 1968   302
YA Services in 1979   302
YA Services in 1993 (Predicted)   303
YA Statistics   280
Youth Market   283

ACKNOWLEDGMENTS

I would like to thank the staff, faculty, administration, and students at Saint Agnes Academy (Houston, TX) who were all wonderfully supportive as I (once again) started a new job in a new city while finishing this book. I also would like to thank the folks back at the Allen County Public Library (Fort Wayne, IN), in particular Cindy Nolot, Michael Clegg, Jeff Krull, and Sarah Cornish, for their support during my time there. I'd also like to acknowledge Janet Dickey, Lynn Cockett, Jim Rosinia, and Stella Baker, my occasional writing/conference partners, and Dorothy Broderick, my more-than-occasional article editor, for their contributions to this book. In addition, I'm grateful to the Young Adult Library Services Association for providing me with so many opportunities and to all the people who organized and attended workshops I've presented over the past few years. Finally, on a professional level, I'm most grateful to Mary K. Chelton for "putting me over" with so many people, for her specific suggestions on improving this book, and for being an inspiration to anyone who works with young adults.

The author and publisher are immensely grateful to the following publications for granting us permission to adapt, revise, and reuse portions of many of the articles authored or coauthored by the author in this book: *American Libraries*, *The Book Report*, *The Booktalker's Companion*, *The Emergency Librarian: The Magazine for School Library Professionals*, *Journal of Youth Services in Libraries*, *Kliatt Paperback Book Guide*, *The New Booktalker*, *Noteworthy: The Econo-Clad Books Newsletter*, *School Library Journal*, and *Voice of Youth Advocates*. We also express gratitude to Stella Baker for permission to reuse the "YA 101" handout jointly prepared by the author and Ms. Baker.

On a personal note, I'd like to acknowledge my partner Erica Klein, who endured the past five years of my flying around and out of the country to do workshops, spending Sunday mornings building Web pages, and messing up the office while preparing presentations, writing articles, and working on this book.

INTRODUCTION

In 1995, the National Center for Education Statistics released a statistical report entitled *Services and Resources for Children & Young Adults in Public Libraries*.[1] Although the report was chock full of numbers, one factoid stands out—only 11 percent of public libraries have a YA (young adult) librarian. Sadly, this represents no change from the 1988 national survey of YA services in public libraries. This fact flies in the face of other facts found in both surveys, that libraries with YA librarians were more likely to

- Report heavier use by YAs
- Set up a separate budget for YA materials
- Maintain separate and diverse YA collections
- Collect statistics related to YA use
- Train other staff to serve YAs
- Collect CD-ROMs
- Offer programs
- Participate in information-sharing meetings with school staff
- Engage in cooperative automation projects or share resources online with schools

Although neither report said so explicitly, it seems implicit that YA patrons coming to a public library with a YA librarian will find both better and more services than they will find in a public library without a YA librarian.

The survey did document that use of public libraries by YAs was down slightly (23 percent compared to 25 percent in the 1988 survey). The survey also documented areas of critical need where the demand for services was high and the availability was low. If public libraries are, as their mission statements suggest, supposed to meet the needs of the public, it appears that in 89 percent of public libraries, that public does not include patrons between the ages of 12 and 18.

MEETING NEEDS

Connecting Young Adults and Libraries: A How-to-Do-It Manual, 2nd Edition, helps librarians meet the needs of their young adult patrons. YA librarians will find interesting information that enhances or justifies their current efforts. Libraries without YA professionals, which comprise the other 89 percent of libraries trying to provide some level of quality YA service, will find all sorts of resources in this book. The mission here is to impart knowledge, inspire attitudes, and improve skills to create better YA customer service.

Other groups who may find this manual useful are

1. New YA librarians who land in YA jobs often without any training
2. School librarians in senior high, junior high, and middle school media centers (although most of this book contains public library issues and examples)
3. Youth services coordinators and consultants or others responsible for training and managing as opposed to doing
4. Managers, administrators, and directors who shape policy and make decisions regarding allocation of resources. Most of these directors, let's assume, are not anti-YA, but rather have limited resources and need to set priorities. One of the goals of *Connecting Young Adults and Libraries*, 2nd Edition, is to try to move YA services up in the list of priorities so that it gets attention, nurturing, and resources. Although those directors may not read this book, if you are among those who provide and care about YA service, I suggest you share with them the information you find here.
5. Library school students who need a mix of information. Because many of the YA courses in library and information science graduate programs focus only on YA literature, this book provides students with some idea of the nuts and bolts of everyday YA work, found especially in public libraries.
6. Children's librarians. In many cases, the people responsible for serving YAs also wear the hat of children's librarian. Some might have the title "youth librarian," but most do not and end up doing YA by default. Many of the skills children's librarians possess—for example, storytelling, planning, and dealing with homework questions—will serve them well as YA librarians. As YA librarians, they also must learn how to transfer their other skills to serving teens.

This book, then, is a tool for building, fixing, or constructing YA services as needed. It is not a book about YA literature. Many fine tomes exist on that subject. This book focuses on managing the items that make up the core of YA work in public and school libraries, such as dealing with planning services, assisting with homework assignments, maintaining crowd control, grappling with technology, and having enough *Fear Street*s or John Grisham titles on the shelf. Librarians across the county spend more time rounding up information for homework and popular literature than they do rounding out individuals with YA literature.

This book is arranged so that you can choose the section that best fits your library's needs and level of commitment to YA services. Some libraries might want to provide only reference, and others may feel that reference is not enough. Regardless of the service (or budget) level of your library, you will find sample documents, forms, research reports, and lists in *Connecting Young Adults and Libraries*, 2nd Edition, ready for you to adapt and use to build and manage your own YA services.

THE YA LIBRARIAN'S PLANNING CALENDAR

Between chapters, you will find a calendar to help you in planning your YA services. This calendar gives you a crash course in developing, delivering, and creating support for serving young adults. These calendar sections offer practical advice and give you how-to information for managing proactive YA services.

Most importantly, this calendar shows, along with the rest of the book, the potential for serving young adults. If you are a generalist serving young adults, you know that it is a chore to keep up with all your other tasks while handling even minimal YA responsibilities. You are to be commended for taking on this task and doing it well. The calendar is designed to help you build on those responsibilities by taking steps to create support within the organization, the community, and eventually among the administration for a larger commitment to serving youth.

CREATING RAVING FANS

Since I completed the first edition of *Connecting Young Adults and Libraries*, I have spent most of my time working not as a YA librarian, but as a public library branch manager. Although I still did YA, my focus shifted more toward another passion: customer service. Because customer service is all about connecting patrons and services, I have added marketing and customer service materials to the YA framework of this book. This edition focuses on defining, designing, and delivering quality customer service to YAs. This book is based on the idea of turning teenagers not merely into library patrons but into raving fans—patrons who are enthusiastic and creative in their approach and reaction to YA services.

Ken Blanchard, a noted business writer and guru, speaks about the importance of considering what your patrons, or customers, want if your goal is to create raving fans:

> The customer service relationship goes far beyond your company's product. If you don't listen to your customer's thoughts to learn his needs and desires, you fail to give him what he needs as a product because you simply don't know what that need really is. Further, you reject him as a person. By not listening to him, you're saying his thoughts have no value.[2]

You can create raving fans of your YA services by

1. Developing a vision and plan for your YA services by asking "Where are we now?"[3]
2. Knowing the customer's wants and needs by asking "To whom and why are we providing YA services?"[4]
3. Delivering what you promise plus one percent more by asking "What services will we provide and how will we provide them?"[5]

Throughout this book, you will see this customer service strategy in action.

EXAMINING THE STRATEGY

This book is different in its organization and strategy than the first edition. Because I want to help you turn your teenaged patrons into raving fans of your YA services, this book looks at the basic issues involved in serving young adults, beginning with considering where YA services are today and where are they headed. In Part II, I help you identify your customer by learning about the young adults who come into your library. Part III answers the question "Why serve YAs?" Part IV contains chapters on the nuts and bolts of core services to young adults: developing collections, providing reference and readers' advisory services, and working with schools. Another core service is booktalking—a popular method of combining reactive readers' advisory services with a proactive service of outreach programming. Finally, Part V looks at how we provide services to young adults by looking at the things we do "off desk" to serve young adults. Chapters in this part contain information about the planning, evaluating, and marketing issues involved in serving YAs. This part also contains essential information on making high-speed connections with YAs via the Internet and connecting with other staff through training.

Noting the lack of YA librarians and the lack of training on YA issues, *Connecting Young Adults and Libraries*, 2nd Edition, comes with a training toolkit in Chapter 10. This chapter includes training tips and techniques, lots of road-proven training exercises, and a training checklist.

The appendix in this edition provides the addresses for YA publishers, YA magazines, and YA professional periodicals. The bibliography provides references you can use for more information about the topics and citations used throughout this book.

SPECIAL FEATURES IN THIS BOOK

Connecting Young Adults and Libraries, 2nd Edition, includes a number of special features that will help you get the most from the information in this book:

- The Planning Calendar, located between chapters throughout the book, helps you plan and make progress in implementing and improving YA services,
- Top ten buying lists in Chapter 4 enable you to find out about core collection information,
- Short bibliographies, called **Bib Squibs**, are provided throughout the book for easy access to references and resources,
- Training exercises to teach key concepts to other staff.
- Numerous sidebars are used to provide survey information, important findings, resources, and more.
- Figures give you ready-to-copy forms and handouts you can use as you streamline and strengthen your YA services.

DEVELOPING A YATTITUDE

In the time since the publication of the first edition, I have spent a great deal of time on the road speaking at conferences and presenting training sessions. In meeting people across the country, I learned a great deal about the state of YA services. I particularly was struck by the absolute conviction many people, most of them not YA librarians, have for serving this age group. Fortified by justifying their position repeatedly to managers and directors about spending time serving those "darn kids," their attitudes were inspiring.

Connecting Young Adults and Libraries, 2nd Edition, is a hybrid of experience, intuition, research, reading, and writing as a way of knowing. The book begins with a philosophy and an attitude: a YAttitude. A YAttitude recognizes the value of YAs, their right to quality library services, and the passion needed to serve them. Librarians without a YAttitude, after using this manual, might find themselves "converted." Perhaps those with the attitude will find this book a tool to move them into action. Either way, this information will help increase awareness of both the needs and wants of YAs and explore how libraries can respond. For those who have a passion for connecting young adults and libraries, the YAttitude and the tools are worth learning—not just because it is our job, but because it is an enjoyable, rewarding, and increasingly indispensable adventure.

ENDNOTES

1. *Services and Resources for Children and Young Adults in Public Libraries.* U.S. Dept. of Education, Office of Educational Research and Improvement, National Center for Education Statistics, 1995.
2. Ken Blanchard and Sheldon Bowles. *Raving Fans: A Revolutionary Approach to Customer Service.* New York: Morrow, 1992: 121.
3. "Young Adult Library Services Association Vision Statement," *Journal of Youth Services in Libraries* (Fall 1994): 108–109.
4. Peter Zollo, *Wise Up to Teens: Insight into Marketing and Advertising to Teenagers.* Ithaca, NY: New Strategist Publications, 1995.
5. Michael LeBoeuf, *How to Win Customers and Keep Them for Life.* New York: Berkley, 1987.

AUGUST

Goal: Gather and read documents that will provide you (and your director) with a philosophical basis for serving YAs.

1. **Read the core documents** (see 7.3) and then act upon them. In particular, focus on two documents:

   Directions for Library Service to Young Adults. Make it your bible: look at it, learn it, love it, and pass it on to others. Don't give it to your director to read, however; instead summarize key points and/or photocopy a few pages.

   Bare Bones: Young Adult Services Tips for Public Library Generalists. Circulate sections of it freely among other staff, in particular sections on "homework help" to anyone who does reference with YAs. More importantly, let your director know that *Bare Bones* is useful as a training manual for all staff.

2. **Find standards:** There are no national standards for serving YAs, but there might be local ones. Wisconsin, Illinois, New York, and New Jersey all have recently issued standards or goals for youth services (see 7.5). If you are not from those states, then what is going on in your state? Does your state library have a youth consultant at the state library? Libraries like comparing themselves to other libraries, so if there are no standards, then are there libraries within your state or region of similar size or funding that you could use for comparison? Like industry ratios, standards provide us with a benchmark for comparison and a basis for improvement.

3. **Visit the YALSA Web site** on the ALA Web page (http://www.ala.org/yalsa/) to find key documents from the leading professional association in the field. Find here not only lists you can use, but press releases about award opportunities. From the ALA site, you can keep up-to-date with actions and documents, like the ALA Council Resolution on Internet Filtering.

4. **Read the professional literature**, but not just *VOYA*. You must read *VOYA* (Subscribe today!) but does your director? Which journals does your director read? Find out and get on that route list. You need to know what she is thinking and what trends she is finding, based on what she is reading in the professional literature.

5. Make it a point to **sit down at Infotrac** or a similar index once a month and do a literature scan for YA issues, in particular those related to trends. Serving YAs does not happen in a vacuum, and you need to know the trends and issues affecting YAs. In

terms of books, the *VOYA* professional column is great for finding resources. Also, foundations, research centers, and government groups publish important documents also mentioned in *VOYA*.

6. **Read *Why Kids Need Libraries*** (see 3.1), prepared for the White Conference on Library and Information Science. Use it as a tool to fashion arguments on why your own library should support serving youth. This document thinks nationally, but you should use it locally.

PART I: WHERE YA?

1 TRENDS IN YA SERVICES

All you need to do is pick up a newspaper, read a magazine, or turn on a local TV news program to get the latest update on teens in trouble. The news story will roll off the latest statistics on drug use, pregnancy, violence, homicides, and guns. A sad, almost desperate picture will be painted, leading readers and viewers to think that all young adults are running "wild in the streets."[1] Even scholarly journals are calling to arms. An editorial in the *Journal of Research on Adolescence* states, concerning teens, that "there is nothing short of a generational time bomb" ticking.[2]

The crisis of youth was brought home to attendees at the 1994 American Library Association annual conference by speakers Deborah Prothrow-Stith, author of *Deadly Consequences*,[3] and Marian Wright Edelman, author of *Measure of Our Success*[4] and founder of the Children's Defense Fund. Youth issues were highly visible during the conference because the ALA President's program focused on customer service to YAs. This program coincided with the publication of the documents *Beyond Ephebiphobia*,[5] *Excellence in Library Services to Young Adults*[6] and the reprint edition of Margaret Edwards' *The Fair Garden and the Swarm of Beasts*.[7] With these documents and the awards for customer service,[8] the visibility of services to YAs was preeminent.

Yet, even all this visibility cannot blind us to the fact that in many libraries, especially public libraries, YAs are not served—they are tolerated. In these libraries, there are no YA librarians, no YA collections other than a rack of *Sweet Valley High* romances, and services provision falls to a generalist/adult/children's librarian without YA training. In some cases, having a YA librarian is worse than not having one. Then everyone else feels "off the hook" and doesn't provide good service to YAs because they feel that is "the YA librarian's job." In school media centers, librarians face daily demands to provide new technology while fighting for their very existence. Therefore, just because the spotlight is on YA services and in some ways all is bright, the real picture is considerably darker.

1.1 IN CRISIS IS OPPORTUNITY

The increased visibility of teen problems in society and the increased visibility of services to YAs in libraries are converging as we prepare to enter the next century. Libraries are not the sole answer to the "teen crisis," but they certainly can be part of the solution.

> 66 If libraries avoid serving YAs and funding agencies and administrators allow them to do so, the dangerous world that YAs live in can only increase. 99

President John Kennedy once said, "when written in Chinese the word 'crisis' is composed of two characters. One represents danger and the other represents opportunity." [9] Thus, this crisis mentality presents tremendous opportunities for those institutions willing to work with YAs. These opportunities fall into 10 themes and represent the trends shaping services to young adults in public libraries at the end of the 20th century:

1. Evaluating services
2. Changing demographics
3. Responding to "at-risk" YAs
4. Providing access to automation
5. Defending intellectual freedom
6. Involving youth in libraries
7. Serving younger young adults
8. Reaching out
9. Training generalists
10. Emphasizing education

The way in which libraries take advantage of these opportunities will depend, of course, on many factors, including the usual issues of staff, money, and space. Yet, the most important factor of all is the willingness to make serving YAs a priority. By doing so, libraries are helping to solve today's problems and building an investment for the future.

Although many of these trends were evident at the time I wrote the first edition of *Connecting Young Adults and Libraries*, all have become more visible in the past five years. These trends shape the way we serve young adults. They affect who we serve (middle school students) and who we don't serve (at-risk youth). They shape where kids find services (outreach) and who provides it (training generalists). They shape new issues brought on by technology (Internet access) and age-old, heated issues (intellectual freedom). They shape priorities (emphasizing education) and determine how we measure our success (evaluation). How well libraries respond to each of these trends, each of these challenges, each of these opportunities, will shape the course of the services to young adults in the future.

Predicting the future, however, is no easy trick. Recently, many leaders in youth services commented on the changing role of libraries and librarians.[10] None of them were doomsayers, but the emphasis was clear—technology, change, competition, and "information access" skills are the tools of tomorrow. Patty Campbell noted that 1960s' YA services leader Margaret Edwards viewed reference work as "the enemy." She quoted Edwards as saying, "I am upset by the library world's increasing absorption with the retrieval of information." [11]

Edwards' worst nightmare appears to be coming true: today there is more emphasis on information and less on literature. What drives the 10 opportunities we are discussing is technology pushing the information age. Calling "technology" a trend is to minimize its importance, however; quite simply, it has challenged and changed practically every working assumption and day-to-day reality of working with youth.

EVALUATING SERVICES

Three documents have been published that demonstrate the growing importance of measurement and evaluation in the YA field.

The recent publication of *Output Measures and More*[12] uses familiar measures but also introduces new measures aimed only at YAs. More than just numbers, *Output Measures and More* provides a rationale for providing quality service and gives you instruction on how to use qualitative evaluation tools to measure success. To seek funding for YA services, libraries must be able to state and then prove how they can affect the lives of young people.

The 1995 National Center for Education Statistics (NCES) survey helps libraries evaluate their strengths and weaknesses and provides them with benchmarks for comparison. Collecting national statistics like these should drive the need for local libraries to look at *what* they do as the first step in planning *how* to do it better.

A third document, *Public School Library Media Centers in 12 States,*[13] emerged from the combined efforts of the National Commission on Libraries and Information Science, ALA's Office of Research and Statistics, and the American Association of School Librarians. The statistics cover such topics as collection development, information technology, and funding. The conclusion drawn from this study was obvious: school libraries are not getting the resources they need to support the learning activities of students. Like the public library survey, the "bad news" presents libraries with solid information for comparison and case-making.

CHANGING DEMOGRAPHICS

A 1994 *Business Week* cover story spread the news: in the next few years, there will be more YAs than ever.[14] Although it is impossible to know whether more YAs means more teen library users, it is a fact that the pool of potential users will increase.

This pool will be much different, however, than it has been in the past. Perhaps the most striking change is the ethnic diversity. The next generation will be multicultural, not only in demographic make-up, but also in influence.[15] This change is a perfect fit, because youth librarians in the past few years have been increasingly sensitized to multicultural issues. Bibliographies, articles, and entire books have been published to provide libraries with the information they need in order to respond.[16] Thus, this diverse teen population should find libraries more inviting, more reflective, and more "in tune" to their needs.

Yet, as the NCES survey noted—multicultural materials represents one of the few areas where availability outweighs demand. Mary Kay Chelton suggested this disparity "raises the issue of more appropriate user needs assessment, collection promotion activities, or collection development for ethnic and cultural-minority communities." [17] Now that the materials are available, libraries need to start looking at services to promote and programs to deliver.

This ethnic diversity presents many challenges for libraries serving youth. First, most public libraries do not mirror their communities: they are managed and run by members of the white middle class. Given that fact, libraries, like businesses, need to realize that actively recruiting a more ethnically diverse staff is an advantage. Diversity training seems necessary, as does community involvement and outreach: for many youth we would like to serve, circumstances may hinder their ability to visit a public library, thus outreach programs or drop-off collections at community centers might be a first step into meeting these real needs.

Similarly, the diversity of formats collected for youth needs continued expansion: those learning English might find their needs better served by listening to a book than reading one or viewing a DK-type pictorial representation rather than a dense, text-heavy treatment of a subject. Finally, this diversity presents yet another reason for libraries to offer Internet access for youth. On the World Wide Web, youth can do their own collection development by choosing sites on the Web that interest them at their level.

In addition to an increased ethnic diversity, other demographic factors weigh into decisions about serving young adults. In many ways, this next generation of YAs will be "needier" than ever, yet conversely also more independent. More will be coming from single-parent homes where they often parent a younger sibling, more will spend their early adolescent years home alone, and more will work outside the home. YAs will be more adult and less "young." [18] But even though the demographics, dangers, and decisions are changing, there is a core part of adolescence that does not change: YAs today experience the same emotions, hurts, and conflicts that their parents, you, and I did.

RESPONDING TO "AT-RISK" YAs

"At-risk" teens are the focus of the Carnegie Council on Adolescent Development[19-21] and the earlier work from the Center for Early Adolescence.[22-24] The solutions they propose are no surprise: more programs, more services, more structure, and more access to caring adults. These things are what libraries can and do offer YAs. If libraries are willing to work within their community with other organizations to either set up cooperative programs and/or seek outside funding for such programs, then libraries can indeed, as a National Library Week slogan proclaimed, change lives. If at-risk YAs are walking a high wire, it seems natural that libraries and community-based organizations need to team up to provide a safe place for YAs to land.[25] A place that is safe and accessible is just one factor for successful after-school programs.

Many of the best programs in *Excellence* concerned at-risk youth. For example, the San Diego Public Library has

> [C]reated thirty-three homework centers for at-risk youth, both at library branches and at satellite sites in recreation centers, YMCAs, Boys and Girls Clubs, and housing complexes within the city, as part of a citywide Neighborhood Pride and Protection Program. The centers include study carrels, specialized juvenile reference collections and subject materials, and computer workstations loaded with relevant school-related software. Neighborhood based tutoring service, sponsored by local area agencies, are also available.[26]

A similar program began recently at the public library in Houston, Texas, called ASPIRE. In this program, branch libraries in neighborhoods with heavy at-risk youth populations provide after-school homework assistance through use of library materials, the Internet, as well as tutoring. Although both such programs are very ambitious, they represent just one way in which libraries are responding directly to at-risk teens. The key to both programs isn't funding alone; but rather building a network among libraries, schools, and neighborhood organizations to find solutions.

PROVIDING ACCESS TO AUTOMATION

All libraries are riding an ever-changing technology curve. The core issue for most of these technologies is access. For YAs, that relates to free and fair access, as stated in the Library Bill of Rights[27] and reinforced with the ALA's statement on electronic access.[28] How about this for a slogan: You don't need to be 16 to drive on the (information super) highway.

Technology presents libraries with many issues and decisions. More than ever, in this swirl of change, libraries need to hold on to their core values. The primary core value—access to library materials regardless of age—needs upholding now more than it ever has.

Yet access is just that: an opening. Access does not mean that youth (or adults for that matter) are capable of using the access successfully, in part because they lack skills to locate information. Even though computerizing just about every single information resource has its advantages, libraries need to be cognizant of the fact that lots of people, from age 16 to 61, are not comfortable using computers. And even so, what does that have to do with searching Infotrac or most any library online catalog? As Mary Kay Chelton points out,

> [A] small but growing body of research indicates that many children and young adults lack the cognitive skills necessary to navigate many of the systems public librarians and their technology vendors take for granted. Whether this is inadequate knowledge of the alphabet, underdeveloped motor skills, an inability to spell . . . or an inadequate hypothetical understanding of database construction, the assumption cannot be made that popularity automatically equals competence.[29]

Access is not real access unless we can develop user-friendly tools and provide continual training for staff and patrons. The concern of most people is not that youth can't find what they want; it is the fear of many that youth will find material libraries don't want them to access.

Of course, practical and community considerations come into play as well. Some libraries might not want to provide anyone with access to certain aspects of the Internet (such as alt.rec.sex.whatever) and that is, like so many choices we make, a selection decision. If libraries don't want Internet access terminals in children's and youth rooms, the same way many other items (*Value Line*) are left out, that is also a selection issue. If libraries have Internet access and make it available for adults, then it is not a "selection" issue if youth are denied access; it is, simply, a violation of a core professional value—namely, free access regardless of age.

This opportunity is real: libraries are providing more access to information for patrons than ever before. Librarians need to remember that youth patrons are patrons first and youth second, and they need the same access to information as adults. Still, access is not an easy issue, especially in school libraries, with so many competing interests. It is, as one of the best articles on the subject noted, "A Delicate Balance."[30] The issue is delicate for many reasons, but primarily because it pushes youth librarians between a rock and hard place trying to split lines between selection and censorship. The defeat of key parts of the Communications Decency Act was certainly a great victory for librarians, but then the spoils are local decisions about "sex, kids, and the public library,"[31] where in order to maintain support, some sort of compromise—normally in the name of filters—are under consideration. No doubt, the forces behind the failed CDA will attempt to do at the local level, in particular through library and school boards, what they couldn't achieve on a national level.

> " Librarians need to remember that youth patrons are patrons first and youth second, and they need the same access to information as adults. "

DEFENDING INTELLECTUAL FREEDOM

In addition to more information, libraries now provide more formats than ever before. A plethora of nonprint items now make up a good portion of the budget of any library and a higher percentage of library use. YAs, in particular, gravitate toward nonprint formats, seemingly living out the "MTV generation" stereotype.

Nonprint is a lightning rod for those who want to deny access to youth. Music, video, and video games in private industry all use parental advisory labels and/or have company rules about selling and/or renting materials to those under 18. But libraries have different missions and different values. Again, one of those core values is intellectual freedom. Yet, it seems that when the item in question is not a book—for example, a classic like *Catcher in the Rye* that everyone can rally behind—but a compact disc by the latest gangsta rap group, those voices for "intellectual freedom" grow silent. We live in an entertainment culture that brings forth works of commerce, representing values that seem in direct contradiction to the values of both people working in and supporting libraries. Yet as public libraries, we provide popular materials for all segments of the public, and popular materials center is a common public library role. Popular materials means just that: both John Grisham and Snoop Doggy Dog.

Yet, books still face challenges nationally with movements like Family Friendly Libraries and local efforts. For this reason, a new version of *Hit List II*[32] from YALSA has been published. In this document, readers will find information about challenged titles to help them make their defensive plans. For the included titles, *Hit List II* provides information on reviews of the works, plot summary, and other vital information compiled all in one place for when the censor arrives. The opportunity to defend intellectual freedom is one which librarians will hear knocking constantly in the coming years.

As we fulfill one of these trends (providing access to automation), it interlocks with another—defending intellectual freedom. A great deal of our patrons don't know anything about the Internet other than that youth can access pornography. Libraries need to do a much better job of getting the "good word" out about youth and the Internet. In battles over intellectual freedom, there will always be two sides: librarians defending it and a small yet vocal group attacking it. In the middle are many people—friends, board members, and patrons—who might go either way. If we are going to defend intellectual freedom, we need to be on the offensive about the importance of the concept *and* the practice.

INVOLVING YOUTH IN LIBRARIES

One of the findings of the Carnegie Council was that programs where youth had some input into the planning were very successful. Librarians working with YAs have long known the value of youth participation. This value comes to the forefront in four ways. First, the YALSA President's program at the 1995 ALA annual conference was called "Youth Participation: It Works." Second, as part of this program, the document *Youth Participation in Libraries*[33] was showcased. This document combines the best from two older publications[34-35] along with new information. This document also contains a directory of libraries with strong youth participation programs. Third, the inclusion of a youth participation measure in *Output Measures and More* underscores the importance of this idea. Finally, YALSA has allowed avenues for YAs to participate in the Best Books and Quick Picks selection committees. By involving youth, libraries provide kids with an opportunity to grow, and libraries grow along with them.

One example of this is in the creation of public library YA home pages. Many libraries have involved existing youth groups or created new ones to provide input into selecting sites. Some, such as the Internet Public Library's Teen Division and the Boulder (CO) Public Library, have, for the most part, given over this responsibility totally to teenagers. Although librarians should continue to play a strong role, in particular in identifying reference and informational sites, it would seem that teens know best for recreational and informational sites. Although many a director might express concern, this type of youth involvement represents a most positive image for the library in the community as well as for teenagers. When most of the general public seems to believe that public libraries are turning into peep shows for adolescent boys, this type of youth involvement demonstrates the opposite. By involving youth, we help teach them responsibility with great benefit to the library. It's a win-win arrangement.

SERVING "YOUNGER" YAs

For many years, serving YAs meant serving high school students. Yet, some of the hottest action is even lower, at the middle-grade level, where 5th and 6th graders resemble very much their teen brothers and sisters. Middle-grade students are not old children, but young YAs. Many statewide programs have recognized this fact and have responded. In Indiana, the Lilly Foundation recently funded a program called "Opening Doors for Middle Grade Readers."[36] This program provided public libraries with paperback books for middle-grade readers and professional materials to use for selection. They also sponsored workshops and programs at Indiana Library Federation conferences. In Wisconsin, the Youth Services Section of the Wisconsin Library Association produced a document called *Middle Readers Handbook*,[37] containing program ideas, recommended reading, and other valuable information reaching that age group.

For libraries, this phenomenon presents several opportunities. First, we need to resolve to work better and cooperatively within our own libraries to serve this age. Technically, in most systems, 5th and 6th graders fall under the purview of juvenile departments, yet the materials (in particular, the recreational reading materials) those kids are interested in reading hang in YA collections. Second, as schools reconfigure to "isolate" middle graders, libraries need to recognize that these years are now the "years of decision" for students about many things, including library use and/or reading. Instruction, booktalking, or even just improved collections for this age group will help hook them into libraries for years to come. Finally, the declining age of YAs means this is a huge consumer market. As such, middle-schoolers will be responding to the marketplace, following fads and fashions in entertainment and information gathering; therefore a collection of Newbery award winners won't do much to meet their recreational needs.

The middle-grade market is untapped in most libraries and presents not just an opportunity, but an explosion of possibilities to make a real difference at this critical time in a young person's life. The downside, however, is that because libraries have limited resources, if publishers are placing emphasis on middle-school services, less emphasis is being placed on services for older readers.

An outgrowth of this trend seems to be that many YAs are approaching adult books at an earlier age. It seems common to see a 9th grader reading John Grisham as opposed to Richard Peck. YA literature is still serving as a transition, but this trend shows that transition happening at an earlier age, partly because teenagers are wanting to act or be perceived as older than they really are and partly due to a natural phenomenon best demonstrated within the horror genre.

Stephen King is an adult horror writer with great appeal to teenagers. For years, older teens—juniors and seniors—were a large part of King's audience. Younger teens are now becoming King readers. Thus, horror written for 9th and 10th graders by authors like Christopher Pike or L.J. Smith is read by junior high students. Books for junior high students, like R.L. Stine's *Fear Street*, get read by 5th and 6th graders, causing Stine's younger series *Goosebumps* to be read increasingly by 3rd and 4th graders, while even younger kids want to buy the books. The positive aspect of this trend is an upswing, represented by authors like Rob Thomas,[38] of YA authors writing a harder-edged fiction trying to win back the high school crowd for young adult literature.

REACHING OUT

One avenue to make such a difference is by providing outreach services to YAs who, for a variety of reasons, are not able to visit libraries. Many of the programs outlined in *Excellence* were outreach programs aimed at such youth. One example is Cuyahoga County

(OH) Public Library's "Leap" program.[39] Under this program, the library gathered kits about topics of interest to YAs, such as AIDS, parenting, relationships, etc. In each kit were books (fiction and nonfiction), videos, posters, booklists, and other items. These kits went out to institutionalized teens in homeless shelters, correctional facilities, etc. Other programs in *Excellence* and elsewhere[40] are attempting to reach the same goal. Related is an effort for libraries to reach out to gay and lesbian youth.[41] This type of concern is indicative of proactive YA library services—reaching out to those who might seem on the fringes. When librarians reach out to YAs, they often find YAs reaching out to libraries as a safe haven.

At the same time, outreach shouldn't be categorized only as programs for at-risk youth. Outreach programs such as booktalking, instruction, storytelling, and the like can benefit all. In addition, the disadvantage to outreach is that when most librarians inquire about conducting such outreach, they hear the ominous phrase, "we need you on the desk." Yes, reference and public service desks do need to be covered and yes, we should make sure we are doing an adequate job of serving the patrons we already have before we embark on outreach. But we don't do outreach for the sake of doing—we do it because that time "off the desk" benefits time "on desk." For example, time spent booktalking represents a proactive readers' advisory service and it might actually reduce the time spent on desk. The same holds true for library instruction. Although "on the desk" is necessary, librarians wanting to improve and/or increase services to teenagers can meet many more teenagers in a day of outreach (maybe 300 or more) than they would sitting at the desk from 9:00 a.m. to 3:00 p.m. (perhaps zero).

> "Although "on the desk" is necessary, librarians wanting to improve and/ or increase services to teenagers can meet many more teenagers in a day of outreach (maybe 300 or more) than they would sitting at the desk from 9:00 a.m. to 3:00 p.m. (perhaps zero)."

TRAINING GENERALISTS

YA librarians have not only been reaching out to YAs, but to other librarians. Stymied by the inability of public libraries to create YA services departments, YA leaders begin to take a different track to focus on serving YAs rather than YA services. *Bare Bones* is an example of this: there is nothing in this title an experienced YA librarian would not know, but just about everything a non-YA librarian would need to know about serving YAs. Although I am not meaning to discount the job that generalists do, as Mary K. Chelton noted, the concern is more "what, if any, youth-services training these staff have had, the sources they use, and their level of motivation as regards continuing to learn how to better serve their youth clientele."[42] A welltrained or experienced nonprofessional might be able to provide the same quality of reference service as an MLS librarian, but the nonprofessional might not be aware of the possibilities of service. A trained YA librarian can provide a range of services and responses unavailable to a generalist. Knowing the "bare bones" is necessary, but YA librarians understand the muscle and the flesh of the service as well.

Bare Bones leads indirectly to two "Serving the Underserved" workshops. These two-day seminars occurred before the 1994 annual ALA conference and again before the 1996 midwinter conference. Using a "train the trainer" model, these workshops provided YA librarian leaders with information on how to train generalists to provide basic YA services. Each of the seminar participants committed to providing at least one training of generalists. A listserv was developed to track progress and trade ideas. [43-44]

Independent of this, other library agencies are realizing that the need for YA services coupled with the lack of YA librarians means training for generalists. The Pioneer Library System in New York developed one such program using an LSCA grant. Like "Serving the Underserved," this conference trained YA specialists to train generalists at regional workshops. In addition, the workshop participants working in small groups wrote training exercises and a core curriculum. In Florida, a similar series of workshops was developed. Other states have undertaken similar efforts to provide "bare bones" style information aimed at generalists either by producing manuals or developing standards. [45-48] The recognition is that YAs are underserved and YA librarians are underrepresented; therefore, the only available opportunity to improve services is to train generalists.

EMPHASIZING EDUCATION

The most often-asked questions of librarians by YAs do not involve library programs, YA literature, or even recreational reading, but rather homework. Many libraries and communities are responding by developing homework resources. Homework resources take many forms—from a collection of YA nonfiction "hot topic" series books to more in-depth collections like Student Express at Enoch Pratt Library in Baltimore, Maryland, to full-blown homework centers complete with tutoring, like those in San Diego, California, Austin, Texas, and Lincoln, Nebraska. [49]

Such centers develop from local circumstances and needs, but perhaps the future will see more funding from states and the federal government. At the federal level, the National Education Goals remains a top priority in Department of Education's Office of Library Programs. Each goal presents libraries with tremendous opportunities for innovative programs and services. [50] Each goal also has a strong YA component. These goals offer public libraries a tremendous opportunity to establish themselves as educational partners in communities. For media centers, these goals could provide the wedge to drive home the importance of information literacy and the need for the media center to be the heart of every school.

A **listserv** is a specific program often used to define mailing lists. Users subscribe to a mailing list where they post and then receive messages. Users may get messages on an individual basis or as a digest. Two listservs popular with YA librarians are PUBYAC (Public Library Young Adults and Children) and LM_NET (Library Media Specialists Network).

> ❝ The recognition is that YAs are underserved and YA librarians are underrepresented; therefore, the only available opportunity to improve services is to train generalists. ❞

Another national program shaping the future of libraries and education is the Library Power Program.[51] Funded by the DeWitt Wallace-Reader's Digest Fund, Library Power has provided participating school libraries with funds for resources and mini-grants for special projects and continuing education. Under Library Power, school libraries are becoming the agents of change in schools moving toward the "information age" rather than merely reacting to change. Library Power has "turned libraries into dynamic media centers where students are helped to be effective learners and where teachers, administrators, and library media specialists work together to develop high-quality lessons for students."[52] In addition to affecting directly the quality of work being produced by students, Library Power has been a tremendous boon to the image of school libraries, necessary in an age when media centers are being closed left and right. Because of Library Power, one principal noted, "teachers no longer see librarians as book exchangers. Librarians have become part of the team. In fact, the library has become the center of the school."[53]

1.2 WHERE'S THE CRISIS?

In both libraries and society, the spotlight is on YAs. Librarians have the tools to plan, implement, and evaluate services. They know the needs and the problems, and they know they can help with the solution. If there is a crisis in service to YAs in libraries, it is not at the reference desk, but in the administrators' office. The crisis, like that facing many YAs, is brought on by neglect. In some cases it is deliberate, but in other cases the neglect is more benign—the failure to see serving YAs as a priority.

In the past few years, our profession has adopted an "advocacy now" campaign. This campaign encourages libraries to "get the word out" about all the good things libraries do in their communities. Yet, 89 percent of those public libraries are not doing their job of serving YAs. Library leaders grandly join an ALA President's "Kids Can't Wait"[54–55] campaign while making the kids back in their own libraries wait for quality services.

Administrators should already know that "Kids Need Libraries" and that "Kids Can't Wait," but maybe they need to remember that libraries need kids. If libraries want to remain relevant, it is not only a matter of providing the hottest technology but also of recognizing the future of libraries. Our future isn't in machines but in patrons; our patrons tomorrow are needing our help today.

> " If there is a crisis in service to YAs in libraries, it is not at the reference desk, but in the administrator's office. "

ENDNOTES

1. Barbara Kantrowitz, "Wild in the Streets," *Newsweek* (August 2, 1993): 45.
2. Richard Lerner, Doris Entwisle, and Stuart Hauser, "The Crisis among Contemporary American Adolescents: A Call for Integration of Research, Policies, and Programs," *Journal of Research on Adolescence.* no. 4 (1994): 1–4.
3. Deborah Prothrow-Stith, *Deadly Consequences: How Violence Is Destroying Our Teenage Population and a Plan to Begin Solving the Problem.* New York: HarperCollins, 1991.
4. Marion Wright Edelman, *The Measure of Our Success.* Boston: Beacon Press, 1992.
5. *Beyond Ephebiphobia: A Tool Chest for Customer Service to Young Adults.* American Library Association, 1994.
6. *Excellence in Library Services to Young Adults: The Nation's Top Programs.* Mary Kay Chelton, ed., American Library Association, 1994.
7. Margaret A. Edwards, *The Fair Garden and the Swarm of Beasts: The Library and The Young Adult.* Reprint ed. Commentary by Patty Campbell. American Library Association, 1994.
8. "President Franklin Recognizes Outstanding Youth Programs," *American Libraries* (April 1994): 370.
9. John Kennedy from a speech in Indianapolis, IN (April 12, 1959), quoted in *Columbia Dictionary of Quotations.* New York: Columbia University Press, 1993.
10. "In Service to Youth: Reflections on the Past; Goals for the Future," *School Library Journal* (July 1994): 23–29.
11. Patty Campbell, "Reconsidering Margaret Edwards." *Wilson Library Bulletin* (June 1994): 40.
12. Virginia A. Walter, *Output Measures and More: Planning and Evaluating Public Library Services for Young Adults.* American Library Association, 1995.
13. *Public School Library Media Centers in 12 States: Report of the NCLIS/ALA Survey.* U.S. National Commission on Libraries and Information Science, 1994.
14. Laura Zinn, "Teens: They're Back," *Business Week* (April 11, 1994): 1+.
15. Beth Howard, "Class of 2001," *Omni* (September 1992): 34–39.
16. Hazel Rochman, *Against Borders.* American Library Association, 1993.
17. Mary Kay Chelton, "Three in Five Public Library Users Are Youth," *Public Libraries* (March/April 1997): 107.

18. *Youth Indicators 1996: Trends in the Well-Being of American Youth.* National Center for Education Statistics, 1996.
19. Carnegie Council on Adolescent Development: Task Force on Youth Development and Community Programs, *A Matter of Time: Risk and Opportunities in the Nonschool Hours.* Carnegie Corporation, 1992.
20. Carnegie Council on Adolescent Development: Task Force on Youth Development and Community Programs, *Great Transitions: Preparing Adolescents for a New Century.* Carnegie Corporation, 1995.
21. Carnegie Council on Adolescent Development, *Consultation on Afterschool Programs.* Carnegie Corporation, 1994.
22. Peter Scales, *A Portrait of Young Adolescents in the 1990's: Implications for Promoting Healthy Growth and Development.* Center for Early Adolescence, 1991.
23. Leah Lefstein and Joan Lipsitz, *3:00 to 6:00 PM: Programs for Young Adolescents.* 2nd ed. Center for Early Adolescence, 1986.
24. Joan Lipsitz, *After School: Young Adolescents on Their Own.* Center for Early Adolescence, 1986.
25. Stan Weisner, *Information in Empowering: Developing Public Library Services for Youth at Risk,* 2nd ed. Bay Area Library and Information System, 1992.
26. Chelton, p. 105.
27. "Library Bill of Rights," American Library Association, 1991.
28. "Access to Electronic Information, Services and Networks," American Library Association, 1997.
29. Chelton, p. 107.
30. Bruce Flanders, "A Delicate Balance: Student Access to the Internet," *School Library Journal* (October 1994): 32–35.
31. Marilyn Gell Mason, "Sex, Kids, and the Public Library," *American Libraries* (June/July 1997): 104–106.
32. Intellectual Freedom Committee, Young Adult Library Services Association, *Hit List II: Frequently Challenged Books for YAs.* American Library Association, 1996.
33. Caroline A. Caywood, Young Adult Library Services Association, *Youth Participation in School and Public Libraries.* American Library Association, 1995.
34. *Youth Participation in Libraries: A Training Manual.* American Library Association, 1991.
35. *Youth Participation in School and Public Libraries.* National Commission on Resources for Youth with the Young Adult Library Services Association. American Library Association, 1983.
36. *Opening Doors for Middle-Grades Readers.* Indiana Library Federation, 1990.

37. Youth Services Section, Wisconsin Library Association, *Middle Readers Handbook*. Wisconsin Library Association, 1993.
38. Joel Schumacher, "Rats Draw Rob: An Interview with Rob Thomas," *Voice of Youth Advocates* (June 1997): 88–91.
39. Cynthia Glunt, "Guidance to Go," *School Library Journal* (Oct. 1995): 56.
40. Pam Carlson, "Books, Books, Books—Let Us Read: A Library Serving Sheltered and Incarcerated Youth," *Voice of Youth Advocates* (August 1994): 137–139.
41. Helma Hawkins, "Opening the Closet Door: Public Library Services for Gay, Lesbian, & Bisexual Teens," *Colorado Libraries* (Spring 1994): 28–31.
42. Chelton, p. 106.
43. Karen Sipos, "Training Trainers in Teen Service," *American Libraries* (November 1996): 54.
44. C. Allen Nichols, "Get on Board the YA Train," *Voice of Youth Advocates* (February 1995): 333–335.
45. *Developing Public Library Services for Young Adults*. Division of Library and Information Services, Florida Dept. of State Libraries, 1994.
46. *Bridging the Gap: Young Adult Services in the Library*. Missouri State Library, 1992.
47. *Book Beat, a YA Services Manual for Louisiana's Libraries*. State Library of Louisiana, 1992.
48. *Wisconsin Public Library Youth Services Guidelines*. Youth Service Section, Wisconsin Library Association, 1995.
49. *Excellence*, pp. 31–34.
50. Barbara Stripling, *Libraries for the National Education Goals*. ERIC, 1992.
51. Michael Sadowski, "The Power to Grow: Success Stories from the National Library Power Program," *School Library Journal* (July 1994): 30–35.
52. "Professional Communities Grow in Library Power Schools," *Library Power* (Summer 1997): 1.
53. "Professional Communities," p. 8.
54. Mary Somerville, "Kids Can't Wait," *American Libraries* (September 1996): 32.
55. Mary Somerville, "Thanks to You, Fewer Kids Are Waiting," *American Libraries* (June/July 1997): 50.

SEPTEMBER

Goal: To gather statistics and data on YAs and YA services.

1. **Gather all available statistics from your own library:** Every planning process begins with the question "Where are we now?" Answer it with facts, not assumptions or agendas. Collect all the hard data your library system has available, which might include

   - Circulation of materials by YAs
   - Circulation of materials for YAs
   - Reference transactions
   - Budgets
   - Program attendance
   - Class visits to/from library
   - Library card registrations
   - Volunteer hours
   - Staffing
   - Square feet per department

   If your library does not collect this data, you need to be proactive about getting it. Maybe one of the best things you can do for the YA cause is get on your library's automation planning committee to ensure that everything your library counts, counts also for YAs.

2. **Know thy community:** The first rule of public librarianship is also the first rule of serving YAs. Gather information and statistics about YAs, including

   - Census and demographic data
   - Forthcoming population trends (how many 7 to 9 year olds?)
   - School registration and trends
   - Drop-out rate
   - Number of schools that serve young adults
   - Number of other youth-serving agencies
   - Number of home-schooled secondary students

3. **Learn thy community:** Put together a simple survey to distribute at schools. (See 7.4) Distributing it at the library defeats the purpose because part of the data you want to collect is on nonusers. Get YA volunteers to help compile the results you'll share widely.

4. **Compare stats, externally:** The 1995 NCES survey should be a benchmark to use to compare your library's services—how do

you compare? (See 7.2) Fill out the survey for your own library and then compare with the national findings. The fact that almost 25 percent of library patrons are YAs is the most important statistic. Everyone else working in the building needs to know that fact—not to "shame" your director, but so that you can compare what you do with what happens nationally.

5. **Compare stats, internally:** How does YA stand up against other services in the library? Looking at circulation it will be the least—there are more adult and children's materials circulated—but what would your YA services look like if you compared those numbers with other numbers, such as

- Percentage of budget/circulation. Let's say the budget for children's materials is $20,000 and they circulate 80,000 items; but if your YA materials budget is $5,000 and you circulate 30,000 items, then YA has the higher circulation-per-dollar ratio.
- Square-feet-per-circulation. Managers at chain bookstores rate by profit per square foot. Same idea as before—compare space available with circulation.
- Staffing-per-circulation. Same idea, using amount of staff-per-checkout.
- Turnover rate, fill rate, or other output measures.
- Percentage increases in circulation, reference, etc.

Just looking at the hard numbers, services to YAs will come up short. But, when you create ratios using other data, it should be obvious that YA gives the most "bang for the buck."

PART II: WHO YA?

2 INVESTIGATING THE AUDIENCE

Serving YAs is a unique job because teenagers are unique people. This understanding is crucial because often the problems libraries have in serving YAs (and the reasons they give for not serving them) stem from misunderstanding and misinformation. Too often libraries allow the few "problem patron" teens to become the image of how all YAs use or misuse libraries. Many of the behaviors librarians have always found annoying among YAs—mainly loudness and rudeness—are directly related to the physical and psychological changes taking place in a YA's life.

What is much different today is the severity of those changes, the risk factors with which many YAs live, and the age at which young adults are now making hard decisions—earlier and earlier in each generation. A report from the Carnegie Council on Adolescent Development says that the real "problem" among teens, especially those aged 10 to 15, is simply having too much free time and too little to do:

> Each day America's 20 million young adolescents decide how they will spend at least five (40 percent) of their waking hours when not in school. For many, these hours harbor both risk and opportunity... Time spent alone is not the crucial contribution to high risk. Rather it is what young people do during that time, where they do it, and with whom that lead to positive or negative consequences.[1]

Libraries need to present themselves as a real alternative—a positive choice for young (and old) adolescents. Research done by businesses and social institutions allows us to better understand teens. We need to use this research to identify our customers and evaluate our attitudes and actions with an eye toward improving the library service we provide YAs.

2.1 CONTRADICTIONS/STEREOTYPES

Chances are, if you are reading this book, you already are a YA advocate. That's one contradiction, because most libraries do not have YA advocates and do not feel they need one. Instead, because they have a rack of *Sweet Valley High*s and a four-year-old electronic encyclopedia, they think they *are* serving YAs. That is not a level of service that makes a difference.

This book shows you how to provide library services in such a way that not only will the YAs currently using your library have a positive library experience, but your quality service will create more of a demand. A positive library experience means that YAs find what they need, do not feel frustrated, feel they have been helped and not hindered, and want to come back. They want to come back not only tomorrow, but next year and for years to come. Every encounter you have with a YA is a moment of opportunity to create a customer for life.

Many staff members think there already are too many YAs in the library. They refer to them as "those kids" (if not worse). You may be using this manual to learn how your library can serve YAs; but because it is *your* task, everyone else feels relieved because now the YAs are your "problem." YAs are nobody's problem; they are everyone's responsibility.

Let's look at some contradictions between libraries and young adults:

> **"Every encounter you have with a YA is a moment of opportunity to create a customer for life."**

1. Libraries' first priority is promoting reading, but the YA years are when many individuals either stop reading for pleasure or assign it a lower priority.
2. Libraries are about research, but for many YAs, doing research for their high school term papers is not enjoyable. Many YAs associate libraries with a negative rather than a positive experience.
3. Libraries are about programs, but as the 1995 NCES report indicated, the main barrier for most YAs is competition with other programs or activities.
4. Libraries are like school—run by adults with lots of rules—but the school experience is not pleasant for many YAs. Adults and their rules are two root causes of YA dissatisfaction.
5. Libraries are still about books—we call school libraries *media centers* and we are loaded with technology, but we are still primarily in the book business. Many YAs are not in that business. Their sources of information are different and their recreational needs are satisfied elsewhere.
6. Libraries are still libraries—library automation bloomed in the past few years and more teenagers have experience using computers than they did five years ago. These facts do not complement, however; they clash. You automate a card catalog, but it is still a catalog. Users still need to know how to search, how to interpret search results, and then how to find the materials: this has nothing to do with the computer skills that many YAs have.
7. Libraries are about limits—we claim to provide access, but to

many YAs, libraries are in the limiting business. We limit which books people can check out, the number they can take, how they can behave in the building, how many people can sit at one table, etc. Libraries set limits and the essence of the YA experience is testing limits.

Libraries could not function without rules, limits, and organization. This certainly is not a call for bibliotech rebellion, but rather a reminder that the reason we talk about "connecting" YAs and libraries is that the nature of both beasts keeps them apart. Thus, the very group we want to serve, in many cases and for many reasons does not want our attention. However, as the NCES report indicated, many YAs in libraries are using school assignment assistance and checking out materials. Thus, the final contradiction: Lots of teens need to use libraries but often do not find either the materials they need or the service they deserve, and there are even more teens who don't use libraries but could and would, if they saw them as important and inviting.

MOVING IN STEREO

The contradictions emerge from some rather broad generalizations about libraries and YAs. Each group has its own set of priorities, based on its owns needs and wants. What kind of stereotypes do librarians have about YAs?

Stereotypes of YAs Held by Librarians

1. Loud and obnoxious
2. Full of energy
3. Rushed
4. Disorganized and chaotic
5. Emotional
6. Flip and disrespectful
7. Unpredictable
8. Physical/sexual
9. Concerned with "hip"
10. Care only about appearance
11. Tuned into non-print
12. Travel in packs
13. Destructive
14. Dangerous
15. Weird looking
16. Smart-alecks
17. Pressured
18. Not interested in libraries

Myths and Facts

Myth: Adolescents are a monolithic homogeneous group.
Fact: Adolescents vary greatly in their physical development, life experiences, values, and aspirations. Individuals of the same age differ enormously in their growth patterns, personality, aptitudes, and coping skills.

Myth: "Raging hormones" make adolescents difficult to control and influence.
Fact: Although hormonal changes do have a profound effect, these changes do not mean that adolescents are inherently difficult, contrary, or uneducable. The effects of these changes are influenced highly by social and interpersonal factors. When such influences are positive, the biological transition goes more smoothly.

Myth: Youth culture is in direct opposition to adult values.
Fact: The social organization of adolescence is distinct from that of the child or the adult, with its own music, heroes and heroines, language, and styles. Within this society, there are adolescent subgroups, each emphasizing particular interests, attitudes, and values. But youth culture is not essentially oppositional or hostile to adults. Although tensions are inevitable in this time of major transition, only a minority of teenagers engages in rebellion against their parents as they seek to establish a sense of autonomy and a separate identity.

Myth: Peer influence is negative.
Fact: Despite negative stereotypes, the influence of peers often is beneficial to adolescents. In favorable circumstances, adolescents feel secure with their friends, find joy in groups, and acquire a basis for hope. Peers can contribute to a young person's self-esteem, sense of identity, and achievement.

Myth: Adolescents just act; they don't think.
Fact: Adolescents are capable of complex reason, including the weight of consequences. Research has shown that capacity for critical thinking and for competent decision making is achieved by early to middle adolescence.

Adapted from *Great Transitions: Preparing Adolescents for a New Century.* Carnegie Corporation, 1995.

Of course, YAs have stereotypes of their own, as the following list shows.

Stereotypes of Librarians Held by YAs

1. Obsessed with quiet
2. Dull and staid
3. Slow people, computers, systems
4. Anal-retentive detail freaks
5. Cold and uncaring
6. Solemn
7. Rigid
8. Intellectual/neutered
9. Out of touch with the times
10. Boring
11. Bookworm
12. Can't deal with more than one person at a time
13. Overprotective
14. Weaklings
15. Bad hair, ugly shoes
16. Serious
17. Read all day
18. Not interested in teenagers

Even without pairing these stereotypes up side by side, it is obvious that libraries and YAs share some sort of "evil twin" relationship. Whenever you deal with stereotypes, the best course of action is to replace images with facts and look at the positive attributes of an age group. The Myths and Facts on this page give you the data so you can balance the stereotypes with reality.

The Carnegie Council on Adolescent Development, which provided the data for the Myths and Facts and the "Essential Requirements for Healthy Adolescents," reports:

> To help adolescents meet the challenges of adulthood in a changing world that is growing ever more complex, adults in key institutions must respond to make the best use of these positive and adaptive qualities of adolescents . . . Small steps taken at this critical time of life can make a big difference in determining an adolescent's life chances.[2]

Essential Requirements for Healthy Adolescents

- Find a valued place in a constructive group
- Learn how to form close, durable human relationships
- Feel a sense of worth as a person
- Achieve a reliable basis for making informed choices
- Know how to use the support systems available to them
- Express constructive curiosity and exploratory behavior
- Find ways of being useful to others
- Believe in a promising future with real opportunity
- Master social skills, including the ability to manage conflict peacefully
- Cultivate the inquiring and problem-solving habits for lifelong learning
- Acquire the technical and analytical capabilities to participate in a world class economy
- Become an ethical person
- Learn the requirement of responsible citizenship
- Respect diversity in our pluralistic society

Adapted from *Great Transitions: Preparing Adolescents for a New Century*. Carnegie Corporation, 1995.

Yet, even small steps can be difficult because of the differences between what YAs want and need and what libraries can provide. Even for a staff with a good YAttitude, these barriers must be overcome. We are not talking simply about two different sets of perceptions, but two totally different worlds. Because they inhabit different worlds, libraries and YAs have different sets of values, priorities, norms, and even to some degree, a different language.

So, where is the common ground? If the worlds are so different, why do they interact? Simple necessity is the answer. We have a resource called *information*. We have it, control it, and provide access to it; and YAs need it. Sometimes they need it to do their jobs, sometimes to kill some time, and sometimes to save their lives. Being the keepers of information adds another element to this relationship, and that element is power. Because we have information they need and they have to go through us to get to it, libraries have some measure of power over YAs. That is part of the contradiction.

Many YAs don't want to be in libraries. They are there because they have to be: it is not a matter of choice on their part. They have to come to the library to find information they aren't interested in to write a paper they don't want to write so they can hand it in to a teacher they don't like to get a grade in a class they can't stand so they can graduate from the school they loathe so they can get away from their parents who don't have a clue.

YAs come to the library as the first step, with more than just a notebook and pencil (which many will forget and ask you for): many YAs come to the library with an attitude. You know the attitude: it's the one people bring with them when they are someplace they really do not want to be. In the summer or after school, the YAs hanging out in groups looking at library magazines are not always there because they want to be, but because they don't have any other place to go.

Thus, many YAs come to us out of burden and boredom, which are not the best motivators for a successful relationship. And when they get to the library, what do they find? Normally, they find an overworked staff without the resources to do their jobs well, feeling underappreciated and underpaid, feeling overwhelmed in an environment of rapid technological improvement that does not make things better, and feeling like none of these things are about to change in the near future. And in walks the 16–year-old, with everything showing pierced at least once, 30 minutes before closing. He would rather be anywhere else in the world but needs by tomorrow a paper on symbolism in the plays of Arthur Miller. He can't figure out how the computer catalog works, but still he and his friends have a good time laughing about it. Fifteen minutes before closing he comes up to the desk and mumbles something that sounds like a reference question. Not exactly a success story in the making, is it?

2.2 DEVELOPMENTAL TASKS

Of course, the preceding scenario wouldn't happen if the YA behaved differently, but there are a number of "ifs" involved:

- *If* he had come in not just before closing,
- *If* he had not waited until the night before the paper was due,
- *If* he had asked for help earlier,
- *If* he had come alone instead of with his peers, and
- *If* he would have spent less time yukking it up and more time concentrating on finding information, his experience at the library might be a more pleasant and productive one.

Those "ifs" are part of normal YA life. Most of the behaviors that drive us crazy (and make us like) YAs stem from the developmental tasks and milestones of the YA. Developmental tasks are those emotional, social, sexual, intellectual, and psychological changes that make up adolescence.

Different writers define these milestones in different ways. One of the better recent presentations appeared in *Adolescence* by Elizabeth Fenwick and Dr. Tony Smith. In this unique book, Fenwick and Smith explore the behaviors of adolescents and suggest techniques for parents in dealing with these behaviors. I've adapted their detailed discussion of developmental milestones into three simple lists: early adolescence, middle adolescence, and late adolescence. These lists are provided in the margins of this page and subsequent pages in this section.

Each grouping is unique, but you find four common goals in each developmental stage: independence, excitement, identity, and acceptance. This section explores each of these stages and gives you ideas about how your library can best respond to these normal YA developmental tasks.

Gaining Independence: From birth, children learn to be dependent upon their parents. During the YA years, this basic relationship changes as teens learn to do things on their own. Each step is a step away from dependence toward independence: From their first time staying home alone to their first dates; from the first time driving mom's car to buying their own cars. As they move toward independence, they are learning about responsibility, discovering how to make decisions, and trying out various acts of petty rebellion.

Milestones of Early Adolescence (11 to 14)
Concern about appearance increases
Independence from family becomes more important
Rebellious/defiant behaviors may appear
Importance of friends increases
Peer group dominates
Ego dominates viewing of all issues
Adapted from Elizabeth Fenwick and Tony Smith. *Adolescence.* DK Publishing, 1994.

Milestones of Middle Adolescence (15 to 16)
Becomes less self-absorbed
Makes own decisions
Experiments with self image
Takes risks and seeks new experiences
Develops a sense of values and morality
Begins to make lasting relationships
Becomes sexually aware
Increases intellectual awareness
Interests and skills mature
Seeks out "adventures"
Adapted from Elizabeth Fenwick and Tony Smith. *Adolescence.* DK Publishing, 1994

Milestones of Late Adolescence (17 to 18)
Views world idealistically
Becomes involved with world outside of home and school
Sets goals
Relationships stabilize
Sees adults as "equals"
Seeks to establish independence firmly
Adapted from Elizabeth Fenwick and Tony Smith. *Adolescence.* DK Publishing, 1994.

Library responses:

1. *Library cards:* YAs should have their own cards so they can check out materials independent of their parents and learn the responsibility that involves. Schools and libraries should wage campaigns to get every YA registered for a card at the beginning of each school year. The issue of giving every YA a library card brings with it several caveats: Many libraries are struggling with library card issues, such as minors' access to videos and debating confidentiality of records balanced against a parent's "right to know." An increase in YA library cards will create more lost cards, more problems at the circ desk, and more headaches. But the gain is great: if libraries want YAs to feel welcome, we cannot deny them the ability to access materials. With more and more noncirculation functions in libraries requiring a card, it is vital that YAs not be without access. If teens don't have library cards and they want books they won't ask mom to check out for them (maybe a novel like *Crosses* or a nonfiction book about sexual orientation), they are either going to steal the book (we lose) or not take it (we both lose).

2. *Library instruction:* By teaching YAs how to use our resources effectively, we allow them to work independently. Instruction can help YAs learn about the information gathering and evaluating process, develop critical-thinking and decision-making skills, plus teach them time management. For libraries, instruction *is* time management; it is certainly more efficient to provide YAs with instruction in a controlled setting than give the same instruction in the more frantic, over-the-desk routine. In school libraries, instruction is one of the most important, if not *the* most important role. Although there are a variety of schools of thought on how to teach library skills, one currently in vogue is the "Big Six." [3] (You can read more about the Big Six method in Chapter 5.)

3. *Volunteerism:* Teen volunteer programs give YAs a chance to experience independence and responsibility. Many teens have time and energy and are waiting for a chance to contribute while librarians belabor the fact that they are short-staffed. Training, supervising, and encouraging volunteers takes up-front time and effort, but has a huge payoff for the library. Chelton wrote about teens needing positive interaction with adults and a teen volunteer program punches that ticket. Although not a lot of research has been done, there is plenty of anecdotal evidence documenting how well YA volunteers work in libraries.

4. *Advisory groups:* Advisory groups provide teens with a forum to learn decision-making skills, take on new responsibilities, and

Tips for Training Teen Volunteers

Volunteers need

1. Job descriptions and skill assessment
2. Schedules and planning
3. Communication and information
4. Rewards and recognition
5. Motivation
6. Attention
7. Variety
8. Responsibility
9. Ownership and pride
10. Evaluation

Libraries may need help with

1. Circulation routines
2. Children's services and programs
3. Displays
4. Preventative book maintenance
5. Catalogs, pamphlets, etc.
6. Straightening; basic shelving
7. Typing and addressing
8. Selecting and advising materials
9. Inventory—collection maintenance
10. Weeding
11. Shelf reading
12. Copying and collating
13. Decorating

Training Teen Volunteers: Bib Squib

Baldwin, Liz. "A Summer Lesson in Service," *School Library Journal* (May 1993): 40.

Clarke, Susan. "A Strategy for Happy Endings," *Book Report* (November/December 1992):14–17.

Eisenhut, Lynn. "Teen Volunteers," *Voice of Youth Advocates* (June 1988): 65–70

Finney, Kay. "Teenagers Work Well in the Berkeley Public Library," *Voice of Youth Advocates* (April 1994): 11–16.

Houghton, Rita and Pamela W. Federspiel. "Volunteer Programs for Young Readers in Southeast Indiana," *Indiana Libraries* (Volume 8: no 2):16–19.

Lipper, Lucretia. "YAs Need TLC . . . Especially in the Summer," *Voice of Youth Advocates* (June 1993): 76–78.

McGrath, Marsha and Jana R. Fine. "Teen Volunteers in the Library," *Public Libraries* (January/February 1990): 24–28.

Morris, Betty. "Organizing Volunteers," *Book Report* (November/December 1992): 17.

Nyfeler, Susan. "Stuff for Kids to Do Besides Shelving Books When They Volunteer in the Summer," *Unabashed Librarian* (Number 73): 9–10.

"A Season for Service," *Public Libraries* (May/June 1993): 135–141.

Strickland, Charlene. "Library Volunteers and You," *Wilson Library Bulletin* (November 1989): 72+.

"Supervising Teens," *Unabashed Librarian* (Number 80): 14.

---

participate in different programs and projects. Again, not much research, but plenty of publications showing why organized and structured youth participation benefits everyone. In successful youth programs, adults do the following:

> [L]isten to the views of young adolescents and involve them directly in planning programs. Young people respond with enthusiasm to programs that reflect their input; they may shun programs that adults plan without them.[4]

5. *Music collection:* Rap music isn't popular just because of the booming tracks. For many suburban YAs, few things are as "cool" to them as driving around with the volume and bass cranked up. In addition, listening to rap is wearing a rebellion badge—similar to the way Elvis, the Beatles, or the Sex Pistols

---

> **Youth Participation: Bib Squib**
>
> Bern, Alan. "What We Did Together over Their Summer Vacation," *Voice of Youth Advocates* (February 1996): 357+.
> Dunn MacRae, Cathi. "Watch Out for 'Don't Read This'," *Voice of Youth Advocates* (June 1995): 80+.
> Maggio, Mary. "Romancing the Young Teen," *Voice of Youth Advocates* (February 1996): 360+.
> Rosenzweig, Susan. "Books that Hooked 'em: Reluctant Readers Shine as Critics," *American Libraries* (June 1996): 74.
> Sprince, Leila. "For Young Adults Only: Tried and True Youth Participation Manual," *Voice of Youth Advocates* (October 1994): 197+.
> "YALSA and FOLUSA announce collaboration," *American Libraries* (November 1996): 6.
> *Youth Participation in School and Public Libraries: It Works*, edited by Caroline A. Caywood, Young Adult Library Services Association, 1995.

were in your home when you were a teenager. That's nothing new: music has been a channel for teen rebellion for years. The change in the 1990s, however, is that music has become more controversial and more extreme. Few things are as important to YAs as music, as teen marketing guru Peter Zollo writes:

> [M]usic is probably the most influential and pervasive medium in teenage lives. It can reflect a teen's own personal experiences, and it unites teens into collective whole. But music not only reflects the teen experience, it also defines it.[5]

A music collection becomes a prime opportunity to connect with YAs. Allowing YAs to choose the music for a library demonstrates a perfect example of something that requires minimal cost but offers maximum impact on teens. They get to make choices (independence), they get to pick out music (excitement), they get to choose the genres they like (identity), and they get to see their opinions valued (acceptance). That's definitely a win-win solution.

Managing Excitement: Because everything changes, everything is possible. Physical changes have wrought emotional changes for YAs and now the world is a more exciting (and scary) place with many more possibilities, opportunities, and dangers. Excitement manifests itself in abundance of energy, wild enthusiasm, good humor, bad pranks, vandalism, and the desire not to let the body or the mind be still for too long.

Library responses:

1. *Programming:* Programs can offer teens a chance to participate actively rather than react passively. They can generate enthusiasm and channel energy into productive pursuits. Although this book does not address programming, plenty of excellent literature describing successful programs or programming processes is available. Although they were not intended for the library audience, the Carnegie Council presented the following findings on elements of effective youth programs. (*Note:* The information that follows was adapted from *A Matter of Time: Risk and Opportunity in the Nonschool Hours*, Carnegie Corporation, 1982.)

   Successful programs are those which offer the following:

   - Opportunities to form secure and stable relationship with peers and caring adults
   - Safe and attractive places to relax
   - Opportunities to develop relevant life skills
   - Opportunities to contribute to their communities
   - Opportunities to feel competent

   Programs will be successful, therefore, if they are

   - Safe and accessible
   - Tailored in content and methods to the characteristics, interests, developmental needs, and diversity of young adolescents
   - Planned and executed with other community organizations and government agencies
   - Designed for youth participation
   - Reaching out to families, school, and other partners
   - Identifying and measuring outcomes
   - Advocating vigorously for youth
   - Establishing strong youth-serving organizations
   - Strengthening research
   - Helping develop youth leaders

2. *A YA Area:* Not only does having a YA area answer teens' need for independence (their own room), but it also can be the place where exciting things happen. Better, from most staff's perspective, a YA area means YAs will congregate there rather than spreading their (potentially disruptive) energy through the en-

---

YA Programming: Bib Squib

Black, Nancy E. "Lasers in the Jungle: Programming Tips, Techniques and Ideas for Young Adults," *Emergency Librarian,* v. 19 (May/June 1992): 16–19.

Excellence in Library Services to Young Adults: The Nation's Top 50 programs. Mary K. Chelton, ed. American Library Association, 1994.

"Focus on Young Adult Programming," *Journal of Youth Services in Libraries* (Summer 1996): 378+.

"Need a Program Idea? Try These . . . ," *Voice of Youth Advocates* (April 1995): 19+.

Shaevel, Evelyn and Peggy O'Donnell. *Courtly Love in the Shopping Mall.* American Library Association, 1991.

Wallace, Mildred. "Tips for Successful YA Programming," *Journal of Youth Services in Libraries* (Summer 1993): 387+.

Wisconsin Library Association, Children's and Young Adult Services Section. YA Task Force. *Young Adult Program Idea Booklet.* Wisconsin Library Association, 1991.

tire building. This YA area needs materials, comfortable chairs organized so socializing can occur, and an ambience created by posters or other decorations.

3. *Magazines:* Because the YA attention span is short, magazines are a desired reading format. In addition, make sure that magazines are current so they cover "hot topics"; they also should be full of photos. For a fuller discussion of magazines, see "Periodicals," in Chapter 4, and also "Sex, Thugs and Rock N Roll" in *Young Adults and Public Libraries.*[6] Magazines give libraries a chance to provide something YAs will really like. How important are magazines to YAs, especially to our main YA audience—teenage girls? According to Zollo:

> [T]here is no medium as intimate or directly relevant to teenager girls as magazines. . . . With the exception of friends, magazines are the place where teen girls say they find out about the latest trends.[7]

4. *Games:* YA areas should have board games and/or computer games available. Games speak to the YA need "to do." Games are social in nature, require mind energy, and are a launching pad for laughs. The downside is that with the excitement comes noise. A computer with games or Internet access to MUDS is

not going to be a silent place. YAs are going to be excitable, which means you need to set up functions to channel that energy. Part of preparing for handling the excitement games bring is to adjust your library's expectations.

5. *Adjust expectations*: You cannot expect a group of YAs full of energy stored up from a day of school to walk into the library and be perfectly quiet. You must have both limits and realistic expectations for your YAs. If your expectations resist flexibility, you are going to create an impossible situation both for you and your YAs.

Developing Identity: "Who am I?" is the basic YA question. Teens define themselves in many ways: some try to be as similar to everyone else as possible; some attempt to be as unique as possible. Most teens are somewhere in-between. The search for identity brings on even more changes as YAs attempt to say, scream, or whisper in what they say, wear, do, and read this question of "Who am I?"

Library responses:

1. *Readers' advisory:* What people read helps define them. When you help YAs choose materials by matching their interests with the library's collections, you are helping them establish an identity. Although I do believe that a collection should serve a mass YA audience—providing lots of series, comic books, books about music—there is a need for some balance. Kids not interested in "what's hot" need materials reflecting their interests as well, whether it be fantasy, science fiction, or the novels of Cynthia Voigt.

2. *Share an interest*: Not everything YAs care about will be totally alien to you. Many times YAs feel real doubts about the things they like or do not like, especially if it is outside the YA mainstream. For example, if you have an appreciation for classical music and you find that a YA does as well, encourage the YA to explore classical further. Depending on how well they know you, you are a role model for some of these YAs. [8] My example is a group of girls who surfed the Internet for Monty Python sites and found it amazing that I could quote huge chunks of dialog from the film *Monty Python and the Holy Grail*.

3. *Writer's programs*: Offering YAs an opportunity to express themselves creatively is a fantastic way to meet this developmental task. Through writing, YAs explore themselves. You will be amazed, even shocked, at the things they come up with, because many YAs find their "dark side" when they pick up a pen. Producing a literary magazine[9] or e-zine is a low-cost program a

> " Sometimes you will find the kids who are library regulars are having trouble forming an identity: they do not fit in with the other kids and seek refuge at the library. By sharing a little of yourself, you can make a huge impact. "

library can do that benefits teens, cooperates with schools, and thus profits the library.

4. *Artist's programs:* Working with schools to develop a student art show to showcase YA expression might involve more YAs than a writer's program. Art, however, needs to include all the kinds of arts YAs like and use to define themselves: comics, cartoons, album cover design, fashion, graffiti, video, collages, computer-generated art, Web page design, even skateboard decoration.

5. *Individualize:* Because YAs often travel in packs, it is hard to get to know individuals. Some YAs will respond to you immediately, while others might be harder to reach. During a reference interview, there is no time to learn anything, except perhaps a name. But that's a big thing. Learning the names of various YAs who frequent your building is an important first step. By getting to know names, faces, and personalities of even a few YAs, you will find it more difficult to stereotype and much easier to accept them. When business librarians finish a reference interview with an adult patron, many librarians hand one of their cards to the patron; why don't we do the same for teens?

Seeking Acceptance: Because the YA seeks independence, looks for excitement but sometimes finds only trouble, and tries to develop an identity, the last developmental theme is, not surprisingly, acceptance. Because as teens are doing all these things and redefining themselves and their relationships, they make mistakes. YAs make a lot of mistakes—most of them small, a few of them big. Because they try too hard to develop and carry off a self, it is a fragile thing: under constant attack from outside and inside.

Library responses:

1. *Space:* YAs need not so much physical space, as psychological space. The most basic thing any library can provide is a place for people to sit and think. Sometimes that is all a YA really needs and wants from us—a place for alone time. Not only do we provide the space, we must be careful not to invade it.

2. *Positive experience:* A YA who comes to the library and finds unfriendly service, no information for schoolwork, and frustrating technology will have a negative library experience. The tone needs setting for all patrons, but especially for YAs, that the library is a place where they can "win." The library should be an inviting place with helpful people. YAs are so self-conscious that they take any sort of rudeness very personally. They will also think the situation is somehow their fault. Because the

YA ego is fragile, it displays itself with macho bravado or extreme shyness—neither of these traits is the easiest to work with in a reference interview.

3. *"Deal with it"*: YAs will hurl chess pieces across the room and they will rip pictures from magazines. The behavior is unacceptable. That should be the message conveyed—not that the teens are unacceptable. Correct the behavior and not the person; practice discipline with dignity.[10]

4. *Outreach:* Lots of YAs never come into a library, or if they do, they escape notice. They are the YAs who do not get into the honors' class, do not write or draw, and do not hang out in front of the building smoking. The only way to meet this large group is to get into the schools or get the schools into our libraries. We need to tell these YAs about what we do and what we have and welcome them.

5. *Meeting special needs:* Everyone is accepted: YAs who cannot read are welcomed into the library, as are YAs who do not speak English or cannot speak at all. Those serving YAs need to be always conscious of the fact there is no average YA. If the library cannot answer these needs, it must be aware of the resources in the community that can assist these teens.

Meeting these development needs is an example of the raving fans approach to offering YA services. Creating raving fans involves deciding on a vision (a library that provides opportunities for YAs to be YAs), knowing the customers (understanding the tasks), and then delivering the programs and services outlined here. You can go that extra step and provide the "one percent more" by making sure teens can expect that same service from everyone in the building. In a time when YAs are under pressure and, as a group, under great suspicion, libraries can be a positive force in their lives, which creates another win-win situation.

2.3 WORKS IN PROGRESS

If you commute to work in a city of any size, you know about sitting in traffic during road construction. It is one of the most stressful of all activities. The area is messy and disorganized; everyone is short-tempered. You try to remember that it is a work in progress—when the construction is completed, things will look and work a whole lot better. That is also what a YA is—a work in progress.

When your library became automated, hopefully some thought went into implementing the change. For everyone on the staff, automation meant some kind of change. During the automation process, the staff probably behaved differently. There might have been a higher level of stress, probably some impatience, and maybe even hostility. Change does that to people.

Now imagine your entire world changing. Everything—all of your relationships, your body, your voice, your sexuality, everything. Imagine waking up in the morning to find hair growing on parts of your body that never had hair before. That's adolescence. The one common theme of adolescence is change. But in the 1990s, YAs are undergoing change while facing more roadblocks and dangerous detours.

The Carnegie Council on Adolescent Development conducted a decade-long study of issues facing teenagers, in particular early adolescents. From the study, a series of reports were published looking at what it was like to be 13. With one exception,[11] there has been nothing written about these reports in the library literature, which is a shame because the research is so solid and the recommendations so important.

The executive summary of the concluding document *Great Transitions* states:

> Adolescence is one of the most fascinating and complex transitions in the life span: a time of accelerated growth and change second only to infancy; a time of expanding horizons, self discovery and emerging independence; a time of metamorphosis from childhood to adulthood. . . . The events of this crucially formative phase can shape an individual life course and thus the future of the whole society.[12]

In a sense, this statement has been true since adolescence has been recognized as a distinct phase of life. There are other definitions, from those in the dictionary to classical social sciences definitions along the lines of "a person not yet an adult, yet no longer considered a child." As stated, YAs are a work in progress. Like road construction, YAs are in a building process—you can see the potential of the beauty, yet are frustrated by the aggravation the progress brings.

The difference, of course, is that the setting for this work in progress has changed rapidly during the past decade, as noted by the Carnegie Council:

> [A]dolescents are confronting pressures to use alcohol, cigarettes, or other drugs and to have sex at earlier ages. Many are depressed: about a third of adolescents report they have contemplated suicide. Others are growing up lacking the competence to handle interpersonal conflicts without resorting to violence. By age seventeen, about

Publications and Reports from the Carnegie Council
{The first three may be ordered by sending the amount indicated to CCAD, P. O. Box 753, Waldorf, MD 20604.}

Reports
Great Transitions: Preparing Adolescents for a New Century, concluding report of the council ($10.00).
A Matter of Time:Risk and Opportunity in the Nonschool Hours, report of the Task Force on Youth Development and Community Programs ($13.00).
Turning Points:Preparing American Youth for the 21st Century, report of the Task Force on Education of Youth Adolescents ($9.95).
Fateful Choices: Healthy Youth for the 21st Century, by Fred Hechinger. ($18.50 hardcover, $8.00 softcover). The report is available from Hill and Wang.

Books
Preparing Adolescents for the 21st Century: Challenges Facing Europe and the United States. R. Takanishi and D. Hamburg, eds. (Forthcoming). New York: Cambridge University Press.
Adolescence in the 1990s: Risk and Opportunity. R. Takanishi, ed. New York: Teachers College Press.
Promoting the Health of Adolescents: New Directions for the Twenty-first Century, Susan G. Millstein, Anne C. Petersen, and Elena O. Nightingale, eds. New York: Oxford University Press.
At the Threshold: The Developing Adolescent. S. S. Feldman and G.R. Elliott, eds. Cambridge, MA: Harvard University Press.

Working Papers
The following working papers of the council are available from ERIC (Educational Resources Information Center) at (800) 442–3742:

Schooling for the Middle Years: Developments in Eight European Countries by David Hirsch (December 1994).
Consultation on Afterschool Programs, Carnegie Council on Adolescent Development (September 1994).
Promoting Adolescent Health: Third Symposium on Research Opportunities in Adolescence, Carnegie Council on Adolescent Development (June 1993).
Depression in Adolescence:Current Knowledge, Research Directions, and Implications for Programs and Policy, by Anne C. Petersen, Bruce E. Compas, and Jeanne Brooks-Gunn (November 1992).
Violence Prevention for Young Adolescents: A Survey of the State of the Art, by Renée Wilson-Brewer, Stu Cohen, Lydia O'Donnell, and Irene F. Goodman (September 1991).
Violence Prevention for Young Adolescents: The State of the Art of Program Evaluation, by Stu Cohen and Renée Wilson-Brewer (September 1991).
Adolescent Health Care Decision Making: The Law and Public Policy, by Josephine Gittler, Mary Quigley-Rick, and Michael J. Saks (June 1990).
Risk Taking in Adolescence: A Decision-Making Perspective, by Lita Furby and Ruth Beyth-Marom (June 1990).
Life Skills Training: Preventive Interventions for Young Adolescents, by Beatrix A. Hamburg (April 1990).
School and Community Support Programs that Enhance Adolescent Health and Education, by Richard H. Price, Madalyn Cioci, Wendy Penner, and Barbara Trautlein (April 1990).
Strategies for Enhancing Adolescents' Health through Music Media, by June A. Flora (February 1990).
Popular Music in Early Adolescence, by Peter G. Christenson and Donald E. Roberts (January 1990).
Preventive Programs that Support Families with Adolescents, by Stephen A. Small (January 1990).
Young Adolescents and Community Service, by Joan Schine (June 1989).
Teaching Decision Making to Adolescents: A Critical Review, by Ruth Beyth-Marom, Baruch Fischoff, Marilyn Jacobs, and Lita Furby (March 1989).
Adolescent Rolelessness in Modern Society, by Elena O. Nightingale and Lisa Wolverton (September 1988).
The Potential of School-Linked Centers to Promote Adolescent Health and Development, by Susan G. Millstein (September 1988).

a quarter of all adolescents have engaged in behaviors that are harmful or dangerous to themselves and others. Altogether nearly half of American adolescents are at high or moderate risk of seriously damaging their life chances.[13]

Going further, the Carnegie Council's final report outlines the essential requirements for healthy adolescent development in today's society. More importantly, in many ways, the teen years are the "last chance" for institutions, such as libraries, to have reasonable easy access to groups and thus make a difference in the life of YAs. Considering these findings, the following recommendations emerged from the Carnegie Council:

- Re-engage families with their adolescent children
- Create developmentally appropriate schools for adolescents
- Develop health promotion strategies for young adolescents
- Strengthen communities with young adolescents
- Promote constructive potential of the media [14]

As with the development tasks, let's look at some practical applications for libraries:

Re-Engaging Families: The following ideas help libraries respond to the task of re-engaging families:

1. *Conduct workshops for parents about library resources for YAs.* Libraries have changed dramatically since most parents attended college. A reintroduction to libraries would help parents get involved with their children's schoolwork.
2. *Work with community organizations to sponsor programs or information packs on parenting adolescents.* Books about parenting teenagers have certainly been a growth industry and libraries should make an effort to collect in this area. For most parents, the early years of adolescence are among the most difficult. Again the lowest level of activity would be to buy the materials, next would be to set them aside in a special and well-defined collection, and then finally to program or promote parenting programs.
3. *Consider parents' schedules.* From an administrative standpoint, libraries need to consider flexible scheduling for parents of adolescents to attend school and after-school functions.
4. *Intergenerational programming.* Although I myself have no experience in this area, a body of professional literature, including a well-received book,[15] is available on this subject.

Creating Developmentally Appropriate Schools: The following steps help libraries respond to the need for developmentally appropriate schools:

1. *Support new or transformed middle schools.* Because some of the hallmarks of such schools are cooperative learning, analytical problem-solving, and intellectual stimulation, the range of services libraries can offer is tremendous. It seems ironic that communities would build new schools around this model, saying, "This age group is important and we want to nurture them," and for the public library to not support the effort by providing staff to work with such schools. There is a tremendous opportunity for libraries to come forward openly and announce they

---

Parenting YAs: Bib Squib

Bingham, Mindy. *Things Will Be Different for My Daughter: A Practical Guide to Building Her Self-Esteem and Self-Reliance.* New York: Penguin USA , 1995.

Dobson, Dr. James. *Life on the Edge.* Irving, TX: Word Books, 1995.

Eagle, Carol J. *All That She Can Be: Helping Your Daughter Maintain Her Self-Esteem.* New York: Fireside, 1994.

Elkind, David. *Parenting Your Teenager in the 1990s.* New York: Ballantine Books, 1994.

Fenwick, Elizabeth and Tony Smith. *Adolescence: The Survival Guide for Parents and Teenagers.* DK Publishing, 1994.

Gallup, George H. and Wendy Plump. *Growing Up Scared in America: And What the Experts Say Parents Can Do About It.* Ridgefield, CT: Morehouse Pub Co, 1996.

Orenstein, Peggy. *Schoolgirls: Young Women, Self-Esteem, and the Confidence Gap.* Landover Hills, MD: Anchor Books, 1995.

Pipher, Mary. *Reviving Ophelia: Saving the Selves of Adolescent Girls.* New York: Putnam Pub Group, 1994.

Steinberg, Dr. Laurence and Ann Levine. *You and Your Adolescent: A Parent's Guide for Ages 10 to 20.* New York: HarperCollins, April 1991.

Youngs, Bettie B. *Safeguarding Your Teenager from the Dragons of Life: A Parent's Guide to the Adolescent Years.* Deerfield Beach, FL: Health Communications, 1993.

want to join forces with the schools in meeting the needs of this age group by hiring a YA librarian to coordinate library materials, programs, and services to middle-school students.

2. *Serve middle-school students by working cooperatively within libraries.* Because these kids are on the disputed border of youth librarianship—both children's and YA librarians claim them as their own—libraries must organize their own thinking on the best way to serve middle-schoolers.

Developing Health Promotion Strategies: YA services can help promote healthy adolescent development by using these ideas:

1. *The core part of this recommendation deals with "instilling in adolescents the knowledge . . . that fosters physical and mental health."* Stephanie Zvirin's *Best Years of Their Lives*[16] presents libraries with a buying guide to self-help materials. In addition to giving teens what they want, libraries can help foster healthy adolescent development by also giving them what they need. Earlier we talked about measuring success, and in this area, it is quite easy to do. Simply count the number of sex instruction books on the shelf before a junior high class visit and the number after the visit. They will not be checked out; instead, they get stashed in the biographies. Sure, the kids are looking at the pictures, but mostly they are seeking out information, not for homework, but for lifework. Libraries need to make a commitment to purchasing teen self-help and health titles.

2. *Mimicking the success of* Sweet Valley High *and* Fear Street, *publishers are using "brands" or series.* Because of this, the books are more identifiable to teens (and to librarians) either by a series name or certain look. Even in this area, the look of a book is important. Not only the cover, but also the inside. A teen seeking information might do better with a book loaded with lists, charts, and first-person case studies than a book with a more traditional approach. Photos, lots of white space, and suggested readings or sources for more information (including 800 numbers and Web sites) make the book more appealing to YAs. Inside, the book should be you-directed, speaking to the reader rather than discussing the "problem" in some generalized way. Finally, the point of view needs to offer teens hope and the message that they have the power to affect their lives in a positive way.

3. *More than just buying these titles and making them available, we should look for ways to make them more accessible.* We need to shelve books where they are easy for YAs to find and close to a place where YAs can read privately. We can mention them in

booktalks or show them during class visits and tours. We can include them on booklists and promote them to community service workers and school counselors.

4. *One way to make sure YAs get this information and do it cheaply is to provide the information in the desired YA format of paperbacks.* Although this format is most often considered for fiction, increasingly YA nonfiction titles are published in both trade and mass market size paperback. Much of this nonfiction is educational or recreational in nature, yet informational books are gaining in popularity. Logs of reference questions would not document this because YAs are reluctant to seek assistance in finding books that will assist them solving a problem or dealing with a crisis. If the motto of high demand/heavy paperback collection development is "give them what they want," the amendment for informational paperback nonfiction should be " . . . but will not ask for."

5. *YAs are reluctant to seek assistance in finding materials for many reasons.* Because the YA years are a time of building self-esteem and establishing independence, asking for assistance is contradictory to those developmental tasks. That is true for YAs working on a homework problem, but it is even more so for those working on a personal problem. Being ego driven, teens are easily embarrassed and uncomfortable by the changes taking place in their lives and their bodies. It is safe to say that every YA has questions and, therefore, that every library should have books with the answers from a variety of viewpoints. Christian publishers and small presses like Free Spirit and Morning Glory are producing some of the best original paperbacks in this field.

Strengthening Communities: The library can be a part of a community strengthening commitment by putting a few ideas in action:

1. *Libraries are only one of many organizations that can provide some structure for YAs.* On the most basic level, just providing YAs with an area in a library that houses materials they are interested in provides one alternative, albeit small, and represents the library's commitment to serving youth.

2. *Coordinate efforts in planning YA activities.* All the Carnegie Council documents repeatedly stress that any institution involved with youth needs to cooperate in planning activities. For libraries, becoming involved in youth networks is a necessary first step to strengthening YA communities.

3. *Focus on the individual, not the group.* Although the Carnegie report deals with large societal changes that need to take place, it is a given that YAs gain strength one "raving fan" at a time.

By treating YAs with respect and being responsive to their information needs, libraries daily can make a difference.

Promoting Constructive Media Use: A tremendous potential exists for the use of media in libraries. YA services can create raving fans by enlisting YAs in their media strategies:

1. *Involve youth in building media for libraries.* The World Wide Web is the media of the 1990s; allow youth to become involved. Pages created by youth abound on the Internet and public libraries should embrace this trend. Libraries having difficulty in forming or maintaining youth advisory boards should see this as an excellent opportunity to provide YAs with a chance to participate.
2. *Help youth learn about media.* One part of this recommendation is to help young people become more media literate. Book discussion groups provide librarians with an opportunity to help YAs look at popular literature critically. In addition, such groups should demonstrate to librarians that YAs know the difference between what is real and unreal. Listening to a group of kids talk about scary books as mindless entertainment, not as how-to tomes, would easily dismay that genre's critics.

Here is another example of raving fans in action. The vision is a library geared toward promoting healthy adolescents. The Carnegie documents help us learn about needs and methods. Then we deliver. The Carnegie Council report concludes:

Much of the current spending for adolescents could achieve better results if it were redirected toward fundamental, comprehensive approaches. Preventing much of the damage now occurring would have a powerful social and economic impact, including higher productivity, lower health costs, lowered prison costs, and improved human welfare. . . . In an era when there is much well-founded concern about losing a vital sense of community, these initiatives on behalf of all our children can have profound collateral benefits of building solidarity, mutual aid, civility, and a reasonable basis for hope. [17]

But more importantly, promoting healthy adolescents should be not a short-term commitment—get a grant; do a project commitment—but rather a priority that is planned and integrated into the structure of the organization, like a reference, genealogy, or children's department. Not a personal commitment, but an institutional one, as the following text describes:

[A] key lesson learned . . . is the importance of serious, careful examination of the facts, nonpartisan analysis, broad dissemination with involvement of key sectors and *sustained commitment over a period of years* (emphasis mine). Above all, a long-term view is essential to bring about the difficult, indeed fundamental, changes necessary in modern society to improve the life chances of all our children. [18]

> 66 YAs are loud and libraries are quiet, and opposites attract. 99

2.4 OPPOSITES ATTRACT

The problem in libraries, however, is that although phrases like "investing in our future" sound good on paper, they really do not help when libraries are faced daily with a group of loud, disruptive, and potentially rowdy middle-school students who invade the library after school. Nor do they help in libraries in communities with serious gang, crime, and/or vandalism problems. Teens have been demonized; ads for almost every candidate for every office in the 1996 elections connected getting tough on crime as cracking down on teens. In the media, with few exceptions, teens are hoodlums and psychopaths. Films like *The Substitute* and *Dangerous Minds* show high schools as war zones (just as the film *Blackboard Jungle* did in the 1950s), where most of the adults, except those who know martial arts, quiver in terror. In the 1990s, it seems as though teenagers have replaced the Soviets as public enemy number one in the media and political discourse.

Librarians carry that package as well and respond in kind. After story time, a group of toddlers comes running and screeching like mad around the library and no one says anything. Two senior citizens loudly discuss medical bills while standing at the copier and no staff member asks them to be quiet. A "regular" patron's long-winded and full-voiced discussion of the latest best-seller goes on without a "Shhh!" Or groups of six adults having left a library program stand in front of the circulation desk discussing it and no one says anything to them. And loudness never seems to be an issue when something important is being discussed by staff—like where to go to lunch. But at 2:30, when two YAs enter the building talking and on occasion laughing, it is somehow the end of the library world as we know it, prompting the "Sshhhh!" response from the nearest library employee. Some YAs laugh it off, some ignore it, and some just turn around and leave, wondering what our problem is. Some staff seem to think that the sole goal of many YAs is to disrupt the quiet of a peaceful library setting (the swarm of beasts invading the fair garden). Both assumptions here are wrong, but follow logically given the contrasts between YAs and libraries. YAs are loud and libraries are quiet, and opposites attract.

The focus here is on YAs as real and perceived problem patrons and developing strategies to correct the inappropriate behavior that often ensues when YAs congregate in libraries. Issues like youth gangs are not YA problems, but a criminal-behavior-in-the-library problem. The library cannot solve the gang problem—that is an issue for the community. Similarly, these are not strategies for latchkey children—that is a circumstance that leads often to disruptive behavior, but is not itself disruptive. Our concern is with behavior, not circumstances, and with gangs of YAs rather than YAs in gangs.

YAs congregate in libraries for a variety of reasons. The most obvious reason is the same reason others do—because they have an information need that the library can meet. Sometimes this information need is school-related, other times not. For younger teens, libraries are a place they often feel comfortable in a world they are growing more confused about every day. Libraries also serve as an after-school social center. In many communities, once school is over, there are not locations for YAs to gather except their local public libraries. The library is free, easily accessible, and known. It is also an acceptable place for parents to send their YAs: libraries are thought of as safe havens. Libraries are, normally, easy to get to, close to schools or other institutions, and have chairs much more comfortable than those at McDonalds.

The congregation aspect—the swarm of beasts—causes the most problems for libraries. In some libraries, this is just a numbers problem. For those libraries located near schools, the crowd that gathers around 2:30 can be intimidating for no other reason than its bulk. This scenario requires leadership: a single librarian cannot be the answer to serving or policing 75 YAs at once.

The person in charge of the library must set the tone and, working with the YA librarian, develop the strategy for all staff. If during this time, library staff is merely acting as security guards, perhaps the better use of library resources would be just to hire one rather than using staff in that capacity. Security guards are, in many libraries, unavoidable—YAs want to feel as safe in the library as you do. Yet within that group of 75, many need library help, and it makes good sense for people trained to do that to do that. Following your directions, let security handle keeping the peace. That is a short-term solution; long term the staff should be working with schools to develop after-school programs, working within the community to find recreational alternatives, and finally working within the library to train staff on serving YAs.

If a group of 75 adults or preschoolers emerged in the library at one time, there would be noise. Developing realistic expectations of behavior is the first step to solving the YA problem-patron challenge.

WHAT IS DISRUPTIVE?

YAs are in a day-to-day learning process about accepting responsibility. Told what to do as children, they are now facing choices despite not having clear ideas on what the limits are for them. Thus, they test the limits. Confrontations between librarians and YAs often revolve around this very issue: how much is allowed and who decides. This task explains the contempt YAs hold for adults, especially those connected with institutions like libraries. It explains why some YAs often talk back and challenge authority. Finally, it should explain why librarians should always be sure to correct inappropriate behavior in terms of the behavior rather than the person.

Consider how you feel when you are learning a new job. Did you want to be attacked and made to feel stupid? Or did you want to discover what you did wrong and learn how to do it better next time? That is what YAs are doing every day, learning a new job—how to be a person in society. It is on-the-job training with no pull-down help menus.

Trying to remember this in the abstract is difficult when you are confronted with a group of boys cursing loudly in the reference area or a group of girls shouting in front of the front door of the library. In both cases, it is clear that the behavior is inappropriate because it disrupts others. That of course is the litmus test. If a class is at the library to work on homework and several boys are passing around the *Sports Illustrated* swimsuit issue, the situation might be annoying but it is not inappropriate because it does not disrupt others. Or if a group of YAs plop down their textbooks and then proceed to spend three hours talking in normal library hushed tones (okay, with an outburst or two), gossiping rather than doing homework, that is not disruptive, either. The real question with YAs and librarians is getting the correct answer to the question: Who has the problem? Clearly, when YAs are talking but not disrupting others, the problem is our reaction, not their action.

STRATEGIES FOR HANDLING DISRUPTIVE BEHAVIOR

How then to deal with the reality of disruptive behavior among YAs? In addition to understanding why YAs behave the way they do, some strategies also are in order. These strategies revolve around four R's: relationships, rules, and reactions are the first three. The final "r" is the most basic and most important of all: respect. Some librarians just don't like YAs and no matter what, that is not going to change. No one requires libraries to like the people they serve. The key is respecting YAs as library patrons first. Not just characterizing all of them as "loud kids" or the YA librarian's problem, but as patrons who demand, require, and deserve our respect. If we don't see them that way, then we are the real disruptive element, not the YAs.

Forming Relationships. Use the following guidelines to focus on relationships with each of these important groups:

1. *With YAs:* Because YAs are group animals, it is important to identify the groups and their leaders. Direct your energies toward meeting these leaders—getting to know their names, their likes, and their dislikes. You want the leader working with you, not against you. It is much better if the peer groups themselves work to keep things cool. Librarians need to be more than the "quiet police." What if teens saw the librarian in a different role? What if they saw a librarian as someone who came into their classroom to tell them about library materials or as someone who helped them learn how to use the library to get their report done? Instead of the quiet cop, they could see you as a person who helps them find sites on the Internet or insert graphics into papers they are writing on the library's computer. YAs then have a different relationship with the library than they had before they connected library experience with a name or a friendly face.

2. *With staff:* No one can do YA work alone and everyone has to be on board. If you are serious about solving problems, you cannot have others working against you. All staff members, not just whoever bears the brunt of serving YAs, need information and education about redirecting behavior. No one is well served if the YA librarian busts tail to improve relationships and the clerk at the checkout desk is being rude and insulting. Not everyone on staff can or will be a YA advocate, but again, everyone must understand that YAs are patrons first, just like anyone else who walks through the door.

3. *Relationships outside the library:* Who else in the community serves YAs? Network with schools, youth groups, churches, human service agencies, and other groups in your community working with YAs. What about working with the Chamber of Commerce or businesses that cater to teens and perhaps face some of the same problems? A relationship with the police department also is essential. Sometimes YAs—like other patrons—do get out of hand and you might need some help. But, you need to know your expectations. Do you want the police officer to just show the badge, or is the library willing to follow through prosecuting patrons who engage in criminal behavior? If disruptive patrons refuse to correct the behavior after reasonable attempts on the part of staff, then it is no longer a library problem, but a criminal one.

4. *Relationships with a YA:* Get to know one teen. You might even like him or her. Once you get to know YAs as people, it becomes harder to stereotype them. In addition, you want to nur-

ture a relationship that encourages YAs to develop responsible behavior. Put the onus on the YA or YAs behaving inappropriately. Make it their choice: "Look, your behavior is inappropriate because it is disrupting others. If you choose to behave this way, then you are choosing to leave. If you wish to stay, then you must be less disruptive. You decide."

5. *Relationship with yourself:* Not to launch into a self-esteem building course, but it is important to be confident when dealing with YAs. It takes a degree of toughness to deal with YAs, even if you understand why they do the things they do. If they cut you down, it is just to make themselves feel bigger because feeling bigger and better is what they are trying to do all the time. Self-esteem is a YA's daily concern.

Setting Rules. These guidelines help you set rules that add realistic structure to your YA services:

1. *Think carefully about written rules.* YAs have a knack for finding loopholes in rules. The simple, posted rule "No gum allowed" seems clear, but YAs could engage you for heated minutes with retorts of "It says no *gum*, not *no chewing gum*!" or "It says nothing about chewing tobacco," etc. Although we might feel safer with written rules of conduct, unless you allow the YAs to develop the rules themselves, written rules can be trouble waiting to happen. There are, admittedly, many valid reasons, some of them legal, for having such rules—so this may not be negotiable. Any written rules of conduct should not be only YA directed, however. An abundance of literature is available on dealing with problem patrons and situations in libraries[19–20] and you need to fit YAs into that context when developing rules and policies.

2. *Know the difference between noise and disruptive behavior:* Even without posted rules for using the library, there is one overriding rule and it applies to everyone: if your behavior disrupts others, that behavior is inappropriate and you must stop it or leave the building. This is a fine line, especially with YAs who tend to get carried away. A small group studying quietly can get very loud very quick. But are they being consistently disruptive? Probably not, but things just got out of hand for a moment of two. Maintaining eye contact (but not the "evil eye," for goodness sake) with the perceived leader at the table might help teens keep things calm.

3. *Be fair, firm, and consistent:* You can't treat the honor students and the shop students differently—there is no playing favorites in the YA world. Approaches to YAs must be firm: no snooping

around or meekly suggesting "Gee whiz, can you please not be so loud?" Instead, make a firm statement that the behavior is inappropriate and cannot continue. Present YAs with a choice to modify the behavior or leave. This must be as consistent as possible among all staff members. The rules can't change from day-to-day because that confuses the YAs and creates many problems for everyone. If your application of discipline is not fair, don't expect the results you want. Further, YAs have a sharp sense of injustice. If they get their heads knocked for being loud only to witness a group of staff people talking at a high volume, they will make a stink about it. We need to practice what we preach and live within the rules we set and enforce. Add another "r" for *role model.*

4. *Be aware of hidden agendas:* Librarianship is a female-dominated profession and the job of YA hellraiser is a male-dominated one. Add another contradiction and obstacle to the list. Related, in many libraries it is also a race issue as well—in most urban public libraries, the staff is not a mirror of the community it serves. Some additional training from outside the library might help staff handle situations with these hidden agendas and challenges. Sometimes the real issue is not YAs, but dealing with diversity of our users.

5. *Enforce the rules:* You cannot threaten to throw YAs out eight or nine times, nor can you just ignore them and hope they go away. If you are going to intervene, you must prepare to follow through with that action. If you follow through, and the behavior continues, seek assistance in enforcing. If YAs realize you are all bark and no bite, they might just sit around the table figuring out what to try next.

6. *Draw the line:* If a particular YA is a constant problem, then don't allow him or her back. If that person is a negative example peer leader, the best thing you might do for all YAs is to rid your library of that person. If your goal is a better environment for all YAs and to give your staff a positive image of this age group, then ridding the library and yourself of a constant negative seems an unfortunate but necessary choice.

7. *Don't escalate:* When you enforce your rules, YAs will often challenge them. They will want to ask you questions or say things like, "This is a public library, so I'm allowed here." You merely need to restate your position: correct the behavior or leave. Discussions often lead to debates, which lead to shouting matches. In addition to having a nasty scene in front of other patrons, if the YAs "get to you" once, they will try to do it again. You probably can't avoid confrontations, but you can derail heated conflict.

Controlling Your Reactions. The way in which you respond to YAs greatly affects how they respond to the library. Use these guidelines to consider your reactions:

1. *Don't power trip:* One of the reasons librarians have a bad image with YAs is that they see us as mean and controlling, thinking it is "our" library when really the library belongs to the public, even to YAs. This power can also manifest itself in controlling problem situations. If you abuse your power, you are setting up a dangerous situation. If you humiliate, embarrass, or humble a YA, that young person will remember it—and then in winning, you have really lost.

2. *Keep cool:* If you lose your cool or become rattled, YAs get the reaction they want and a payoff for inappropriate behavior. The task is a hard one, but you need to stay within yourself and just let it bounce off you. YAs will test you like they do a new teacher or a substitute.

3. *Remember that it is not personal:* If YAs call you a name, it is because they feel a need to test you or maybe to strike out at you as an authoritarian figure. They are not attacking you personally. Certainly there are limits here—racist, homophobic, sexist, or sexually harassing tirades should not be tolerated from YAs any more than they would be from any other patron.

4. *Lighten up:* YAs makes mistakes because they are YAs learning this new job. Most of the mistakes are not the end of the world or even the Dewey Decimal system. If we constantly overreact to everything, real connections are hard to make. All that stress we feel from YAs often is not from them, but from ourselves. We need to develop realistic expectations and remember that what YAs appreciate most is someone with a sense of humor.

5. *Project and remember:* Before you react to a YA, take a moment to remember being a YA. Summon up all those feelings of insecurity and confusion, and then project them on that YA who is causing us a problem. Those YAs are going through the same sorts of emotions you were as a teen. If we can remember that, our reactions to YAs might be more satisfying and less stressful for both groups.

> “ We need to develop realistic expectations and remember that what YAs appreciate most is someone with a sense of humor. ”

Remembering Respect: Respect is the foundation on which all the rest of these strategies rest. None of the strategies discussed in this section is fool-proof. Like all problem-patron situations, responding to behaviors takes a large dosage of good judgment, timing, and people skills.

Despite the contradiction of libraries and YAs, we have some things in common on which we can base mutual respect. Our emotional make-up is often the same: librarians, like YAs, often feel unloved, underappreciated, and desperate for attention. We do not get the respect we have earned. Libraries and YAs are also opposites in many ways, but we share the same ground and should learn to live with each other.

The fact of the matter is that we, as librarians, have more to lose if this relationship fails. The YA can always use a school library, send in a parent or friend, buy materials, or just ignore libraries all together. By losing the YA patron, libraries lose big. We lose not only a future user and potential supporter, but we also lose the child we have been encouraging to use libraries for the past 12 years.

2.5 YA LIVES AND TIMES

Like most failed relationships, the one between libraries and YAs deals with misunderstanding and lack of communication. Although librarians with teenage children certainly know something about their own kids and their kids' friends, to serve teens it is important to know what is important to them. Unfortunately, chances are that your child and his or her friends are not a "representative sample" of the teen population.

Peter Zollo is the president of Teenage Research Unlimited and he has been collecting research from representative samples of the teen population for some time. He has collected his findings in the book *Wise Up to Teens: Insights into Marketing and Advertising to Teenagers.* Although aimed at businesses, the research is dynamite and the library applications are obvious. Zollo could be a YA librarian when he writes:

> [T]here are two keys to success in (the YA market): first, acknowledging the importance of teenagers as consumers; and second, recognizing their uniqueness.[21]

Let's look at just a few of the facts revealed in this book about teen lives and times. One of the more interesting facts reported in the last NCES survey was that *young adult* is defined as ages 12–18. Zollo found that *young adult* is also the term that people in this age group prefer as a label (see Figure 2–1). He also found, however, that they really don't want to be young: all YAs want to be older (see Figure 2–2). Both of these surveys have tremendous implications for librarians in naming areas, publications, and even booklists. They have implications for purchasing and shelving materials—maybe you think an 18–

Figure 2-1 What Teenagers Want to Be Called

Teens prefer to be called "young" more than "teen" or "teenager."

(percent of teens citing label preference, 1992)

	percent
Young men/women	62%
Young adults	59
Teenagers	43
Teens	42
Students	31
Boys/girls	14
Kids	9

Source: TRU *Teenage Marketing & Lifestyle Study*

Reprinted, with permission, from Peter Zollo, *Wise Up to Teens.* New Strategist Publications, 1995: 43.

year-old should have access to *The Joy of Gay Sex*, but putting it in the YA area means the 18–year-old won't find it, but the 12–year-old will. Further, it shows that booktalking or promoting YA fiction to older kids is a tough row because they are interested in protagonists older than those in most YA novels are.

It's no big surprise that reading YA novels is not number one on the teen list of leisure time activities (see Figure 2–3). Reading is number 16, and going to the library is down there between working and computer games. Libraries rate higher than computer games? My guess is that perhaps the high percentage of boys using computer games are balanced out by fewer girls participating in this activity, but then the "girl games" movement is just starting off. [22] But of items in the top 20, there are lots of library tie-ins: listening to music (we have that), reading newspapers (we've got those too), reading magazines for pleasure (ditto), and even reading books for pleasure (we've still got those as well). Libraries, however, rate no mention as a place where teens spend leisure time (see Figure 2–4).

Although there is not a direct connection, it is certainly noteworthy both what teens like most about being a teen (see Figure 2–5) and what they like least (see Figure 2–6). "Lack of respect" counts rather high on the list and seems directly related to teens' feelings about the most common misconceptions that adults have about them (see Figure 2–7). Of course, the way to relieve misconceptions is to replace

---

Figure 2-2 How Old Teens Want to Be

On average, 12-year-olds want to be 17, literally skipping over most of their teen years.

(teens' actual age and the age they aspire to, in years, 1992)

actual age	aspired age	gap in years
12	17	5
13	18	5
14	18	4
15	18	3
16	19	3
17	20	3
18	20	2
19	20	1

Source: TRU *Teenage Marketing & Lifestyle Study*

Reprinted, with permission, from Peter Zollo, *Wise Up to Teens*. New Strategist Publications, 1995: 185.

them with facts. The past few years have seen lots of "pop culture" books about teenagers that give great insights into teen lives and times.

We have gone full circle. We started this chapter talking about contradictions between teens and libraries, noting that stereotypes play a big role. We have ended with teens noting the stereotypes they think adults have about them. The only way to connect YAs and libraries is to look beyond stereotypes, realize misconceptions, and begin looking at teens not as problems, but as Zollo points out, as important customers with unique needs.

Figure 2-3 Leisure-Time Activities of Teens

Many teen leisure-time activities are also those enjoyed by the rest of the population.

(percentage of teenagers participating in selected activities during the past week, and number of hours teens spent participating in the activity, 1994)

	percent participating	number of hours
Watching TV	89%	11.5
Listening to FM radio	95	10.3
Listening to CDs, tapes, records	93	9.6
Talking on phone (local calls)	81	6.2
"Hanging out" with friends	80	8.0
Using a microwave oven	80	4.7
Eating fast food	79	3.9
Reading newspapers	76	2.8
Playing sports	75	6.6
Reading magazines for pleasure	73	2.7
Exercising/working out	72	5.0
Cleaning the house	72	3.6
Cooking/preparing meals for self	71	2.9
Watching rented videos	69	4.2
Shopping for self	62	3.0
Reading books for pleasure	60	4.5
Caring for/playing with children	58	4.2
Working on a hobby	56	3.6
Studying	55	3.8
"Cruising" in car	53	3.9
Running errands for family	52	2.3
Doing laundry	51	2.3
Shopping at/hanging out at mall	50	2.7
Going to parties	49	3.2
Driving a car	49	4.3
Going to religious functions	48	2.6
Dating/being with boyfriend/girlfriend	48	5.0
Going to movie theaters	48	2.2
Cooking/preparing meals for family	47	2.1
Playing home videogames	46	3.0
Talking on phone (long distance)	45	2.1
Grocery shopping for family	44	1.9
Going to sports events	41	2.5
Baking	37	1.6

Figure 2-3 (cont.)		
Using a computer at home	37	2.3
Using a computer at school/elsewhere	36	1.9
Working at a regular paid job	34	5.1
Going to a library/museum/gallery	33	1.4
Playing computer games	33	1.7
Going to amusement/theme park	32	2.1
Playing board games	31	1.2
Going dancing	29	1.5
Playing a musical instrument	27	2.0
Doing volunteer work	24	1.3
Playing arcade videogames	24	1.2
Reading magazines for school	22	0.8
Listening to AM radio	20	1.0
Going to concerts	20	1.1
Working on a car/truck/motorcycle	17	1.1
Going to community centers/YMCA	15	1.0
Using an on-line computer service	12	0.6

Source: TRU *Teenage Marketing & Lifestyle Study*

Reprinted, with permission, from Peter Zollo, *Wise Up to Teens*. New Strategist Publications, 1995: 88.

Figure 2-4 Where Teens Prefer to Spend Their Leisure Time

Nearly two-thirds of teens prefer to spend their free time after school at home.

(percent of teens saying they prefer to spend their leisure time at selected places after school, on weekends, and on a date; respondents could pick up to three places, 1994)

prefer to spend leisure time

	after school	weekend	on a date*
Home	63%	30%	6%
Friend's house	55	52	6
School/around school	30	7	2
Sporting facility	28	25	4
Boyfriend's/girlfriend's house	26	34	36
School dances	18	20	17
Mall	17	44	11
Downtown/uptown/city	17	32	14
Video arcade	16	23	4
Restaurant	16	32	36
Park	15	28	17
Party	8	48	26
Bowling alley	8	22	9
Movie theater	8	43	55
Church/place of worship	8	36	2
Roller rink	7	24	9
Teen/dance clubs	7	23	15
Beach	7	39	13
Concerts	4	26	18

*those who said they date/get together with their boyfriend or girlfriend at least once a week

Source: TRU *Teenage Marketing & Lifestyle Study*

Reprinted, with permission, from Peter Zollo, *Wise Up to Teens*. New Strategist Publications, 1995: 96.

Figure 2-5 What Teens Like Most about Being Teens

Teens cite close friends and having a boyfriend/girlfriend as what they most like about being teens.

(percent of teens citing factor as what they like about being teen, 1993)

	percent
Close friends	32%
Boyfriend/girlfriend	25
Freedom	24
Partying	24
Not getting caught	19
Able to drive	17
No adult responsibility	14
Dating	14
School events	13
Going to school	9
Few worries	8
Few expectations	6

Source: TRU *Teenage Marketing & Lifestyle Study*

Reprinted, with permission, from Peter Zollo, *Wise Up to Teens*. New Strategist Publications, 1995: 188.

YA Lives and Times: Bib Squib

French, Thomas. *South of Heaven: Welcome to High School at the End of the Twentieth Century.* New York: Pocket Books, 1996.

Gaines, Donna. *Teenage Wasteland: Suburbia's Dead End Kids.* New York: HarperPerennial Library, 1992.

Howe, Neil and Bill Strauss. *13th Gen: Abort, Retry, Ignore, Fail?* New York: Vintage Books, 1993.

Israeloff, Roberta. *Lost and Found: A Woman Revisits Eighth Grade.* New York: Simon & Schuster, 1996.

Meyer, Linda. *Teenspeak! A Bewildered Parent's Guide to Teenagers.* Princeton, NJ: Peterson's Guides, 1994.

Palladin, Grace. *Teenagers: An American History.* New York: Basic Books, 1996.

Pratt, Jane and Kelli Pryor. *For Real: The Uncensored Truth about America's Teenagers.* New York: Disney Press, 1995.

Rubin, Nancy J. *Ask Me If I Care: Voices from an American High School.* Berkeley, CA: Ten Speed Press, 1994.

Salinger, Adrienne and Tobias Wolff. *In My Room: Teenagers in Their Bedrooms.* San Francisco: Chronicle Books, 1995.

Figure 2-6 What Teens Dislike Most about Being Teens

More teens name "peer pressure" than anything else.

(percent of teens citing factor as what they dislike about being teens, 1993)

	percent
Peer pressure	33%
Not taken seriously	23
Not enough money	21
Age restrictions	19
Parent pressures	19
Lack of respect	17
Grades	15
Curfew	14
Going to school	13
Parent hassles	12
Physical changes	11
Worrying about fitting in	11
Standardized tests	9
Too much responsibility	7
Trends change fast	6
Treated badly at stores	5

Source: TRU *Teenage Marketing & Lifestyle Study*

Reprinted, with permission, from Peter Zollo, *Wise Up to Teens*. New Strategist Publications, 1995: 193.

Figure 2-7 Biggest Adult Misconceptions about Teens

According to teens, the biggest misconception adults have about people their age is that they are not mature enough to handle responsibility.

(percent of teens citing factor as a big adult misconception about teens, 1994)

	percent
Not mature enough	52%
Cause trouble	47
Lazy	35
No problems/worries	29
Take drugs	25
Not intelligent	24
Lack commitment	23
Watch too much TV	22
Don't strive	22
Sexually active	21
Bad drivers	21
Unconcerned about world	20
In gangs	19
Drink alcohol	16

Source: TRU *Teenage Marketing & Lifestyle Study*

Reprinted, with permission, from Peter Zollo, *Wise Up to Teens*. New Strategist Publications, 1995: 202.

ENDNOTES

1. Carnegie Council on Adolescent Development: Task Force on Youth Development and Community Programs. *A Matter of Time: Risk and Opportunities in the Nonschool Hours* (abridged version) Carnegie Corporation, 1991: 6.
2. Carnegie Council on Adolescent Development, Task Force on Youth Development and Community Programs. *Great Transitions: Preparing Adolescents for a New Century.* Carnegie Corporation, 1995: 30.
3. Michael B. Eisenberg and Robert E. Berkowitz, "The Six Habits of Highly Effective Students; Using the Big Six to Link Parents, Students, and Homework," *School Library Journal* (August 1995): 22–25.
4. *Great Transitions*, p. 107.
5. Peter Zollo. *Wise Up to Teens*. Ithaca, NY: New Strategist Press, 1995: 85.
6. Patrick Jones, "Sex, Thugs and Rock N Roll" in *Young Adults and Libraries*. Melanie Myers and C. Allen Nichols, eds. Greenwood Press, 1998 (scheduled).
7. Zollo, p. 70.
8. Sue Rosenzweig, "Leading by Example," *School Library Journal* (October 1995): 58.
9. Janet Dickey and Jean Delany, "Teen Reflections," *School Library Journal* (June 1988): 60.
10. Richard Curwin, *Discipline with Dignity*. Association for Supervision and Curriculum Development, 1988.
11. Jane Quinn, "A Matter of Time: An Overview of Themes from the Carnegie Report," *Voice of Youth Advocates* (October 1994): 192–195.
12. *Great Transitions*, p. 9.
13. *Great Transitions*, p. 10.
14. *Great Transitions*, p. 12.
15. Rhea Joyce Rubin, *Intergenerational Programming: A How-To-Do-It Manual*. New York: Neal-Schuman, 1992.
16. Stephanie Zvirin. *The Best Years of Their Lives*, 2nd Edition. American Library Association, 1995.
17. *Great Transitions*, p. 15
18. *Ibid.*
19. *Patron Behavior in Libraries: A Handbook of Positive Approaches to Negative Situations*. Beth McNeil and Denise Johnson, eds. American Library Association, 1996.
20. Tom Arterburn, "Librarians: Caretakers or Crimefighters?" *American Libraries* (August 1996): 32–34.

21. Zollo, p. 6.
22. "Great Games for Girls," *U.S. News and World Report* (November 25, 1996): 108.

OCTOBER

Goal: To create increased awareness of YAs and services to YAs within the organization.

1. **Start a newsletter:** In case you haven't noticed, you are gathering a lot of information. You either can distribute this information via memos every other day, or organize it all into a newsletter. In addition to providing info about serving YAs, the newsletter might also contain references to new books, articles in popular or professional magazines, statistics from *USA Today*, etc. Distribute this newsletter widely, with one copy to the director, maybe a copy to the President of the Friends, and maybe one to members of the Board, if such direct communication occurs. The newsletter does not need to be fancy or become a major chore, but it is important and you must take time to do it. No time? Maybe there is a YA in your community who would love the chance to assist putting it together. Letting other people know what is going on increases awareness, and that is vital to creating support.

   As an alternative, you can put together a collection of information instead of a newsletter: gather everything into a three-ring binder and put it where people can find it. Copy articles, charts, plus memos and other internal documents should go in the binder. Put booklists, reviews and the like in there too and ask everyone to glance at it. Keep the information weeded and ask others to contribute.

2. **Find allies:** Listen for any positive feedback and comments about YAs and (nicely) pounce upon the speaker. There might be YA advocates hidden all around your library. Get them involved in simple ways—ask them to review a book for your newsletter, or do a top ten list. If they help you, let them and everyone else know you appreciate it.

3. **Recognize superior service:** Libraries do not give out bonuses or raises based on performance. Often we do not do anything at all to recognize superior service. Provide recognition for those in your library who provide quality service—from pages to reference librarians to administrators. Give them a gold star or a certificate, a memo to their supervisor, put their name on a poster in the break room, or purchase some goofy yet memorable items to give as incentives. Don't kid yourself by thinking staff is going to fall over themselves to win your award, but given the lack of positive reinforcement in most libraries, a little subtle peer competition to earn that recognition might result in better

service. Like YAs, librarians feel ignored, underappreciated, and in need of praise.

4. **Share information about assignments:** All of this is well and good, but the reference staff might not remember any of it. They will, however, remember the kid who came in five minutes before closing needing three newspaper articles about Chaucer. These types of assignments are the bulk of a reference staff's interaction with YAs and require attention. If not, they will create frustration and problems, not support. (See 5.5) Be both proactive and reactive: try to get info about assignments beforehand or gather it after the fact. Keep a notebook or clipboard with a copy of the assignment and list possible sources.

5. **Perception is reality:** Everything to this point has been making a case for why libraries should serve YAs, but the case is building against you because of the three kids who stand in front of the library spitting, smoking, and swearing. Forget that anything else you do will make a difference, because chances are, this is the YA reality to most of the staff. Thus, their whole perception of YAs emerges not on all the stats you've been gathering and articles you've been routing, but on these three kids. Well, we don't make rules for three people and we don't sacrifice the whole for a very, very, very few. Not only are those few turning off the staff, but they are also turning off other YAs. Make an effort to reach everyone, but be smart and tough enough to know when the behavior of a few is creating a poor perception of the many, and do something about it. Like it or not, part of the role of people serving young adults is redirecting behavior.

PART III: WHY YA?

3 MAKING THE CASE

If you work in a public library, you know the scenario: You can hear them coming before they actually hit the door. They travel in duos or groups—perhaps better called *packs*—and they bring their noise and chatter with them. Once inside the library, they are a challenge to all. At the reference desk, they ask demanding questions that require constant follow-up. They have very specific needs, as though there is only one answer to their question and it is some kind of test for you to find it. Even worse are those who ask the same simple questions requiring repeatedly the same sources, year after year. Some are adept at computers and microfilm machines, but most are not. They also may dress funny and behave oddly. Disorganization rules as they spread out their mounds of paper until they've buried an entire table (or tables). They rarely say "Thank you." To the nonreference staff, they are pestering—needing change for the copier, wanting special favors because they are "regulars," and often leaving a mess of crumbled paper and food crumbs behind them. Because of this pestering, and also because they are loud, disorganized, messy, and difficult, most staff consider them obnoxious and are happy to see them go away or find a specialist to help them. They are a difficult user group indeed.

But enough about genealogists; this is a book about young adults.

In many ways, these two user groups are similar in personality. They are similar too in their library needs and in the reaction library staff have towards them. I freely admit that I hate serving genealogists because I don't understand them. I don't "get it"; I can't comprehend what drives them; I am frustrated by their information needs and find them akin to visiting aliens. There is no term for a fear and loathing of genealogists, but *ephebiphobia* means a fear and loathing of youth.[1] Many library staffs contain members, from directors to librarians to the maintenance crew, who suffer from ephebiphobia. This, of course, negatively impacts YA services. It will impact daily "at-the desk" interaction, yearly planning, and long-term goal setting. The impact is evident when YAs are classified as a "special user group," thus making those who want to serve the group develop rationalizations and make a case. Once you brush aside any user group as "special," the status quo is to exclude them, putting the onus on those who want to include them to create support.

Even in libraries not overrun by ephebiphobia, YA services are not running rampant. The 1995 NCES survey documented that 89 percent of public libraries don't have a YA librarian.[2] The reasons are the usual suspects:

- Not enough money
- Not enough staff
- Not enough space

Yet, these are not obstacles; they are perceptions. If a library can afford to open its doors and pay its bills, it has the resources to serve young adults. The problem is that those resources are being spent on something else. Let's say that we decide to eliminate purchasing just one shelf-sucking reference tool (*Thomas Register*, for example); then we would have a down payment to invest in materials for YAs. But wait—you say—people need resources like the *Thomas Register*; well, yes, they do, but YAs also need the materials you could buy with that wad-o-cash you used on *Thomas*. In a year in most public libraries, especially branch libraries, which would get more use—a directory of manufacturers or a collection of YA paperbacks? Yet we've all been conditioned that a source like *Thomas Register* is standard, a real "meat-and-potatoes-staple" and we must have it, regardless of cost, while YA recreational reading is considered gravy. You suggest in your public library that people needing information about manufacturers are a "special user group" and people will think you are akin to a space alien. The problem is not a lack of resources, but a lack of placing young adults as a priority. These priorities come out when making both macro (setting up budget lines) and micro (buying just one less of every adult best-seller and putting that $20 into YA materials) resource allocation decisions. Sure, adults need their libraries to house information about manufacturing, but kids need libraries too. We need to manufacture a case for serving young adults in libraries.

> " If a library can afford to open its doors and pay its bills, it has the resources to serve young adults. The problem is that those resources are being spent on something else. "

3.1 WHY KIDS NEED LIBRARIES

Why YA? It is odd that years after establishing the distinctive nature and large numbers of YA patrons, there is still a question about serving them. This type of question is not posed when other segments of the library market are being discussed. There are no workshops called "Why Business Patrons?" or "Genealogists: To Serve or Not to Serve?" Yet I've done more than one "Why YA?" justification festival workshop. At one of these workshops, we were listing reasons why libraries do not do a good job serving YAs. One response, which seemed to strike a chord with everyone who was thinking about "those people" back at their library who were happy that they didn't have to attend, was this answer: "Because librarians don't like them." A simple answer, but one with more than a little truth. If that is the case—think of where you work or have worked—then that really opens up a revolutionary concept in delivering library service: only those we like need apply. Imagine the cost savings to the taxpayers under this brave new plan if we only served groups we liked.

> **" In every community, now more than ever, kids need libraries. "**

A better plan would be for libraries to meet the needs of their communities. In every community, now more than ever, kids need libraries. In preparation for the second White House Conference on Libraries, a position paper explained the immediacy of the need (see Figure 3–1). Youth have many problems and dangers and libraries offer many solutions and successes.

Figure 3–1 The White House Conference on Libraries Position Paper

Kids Need Libraries—Now More than Ever
Children and youth are the future of this nation, yet:

- 50 percent of youth in this country are at risk
- More than half of our young people leave school without the knowledge or the foundation required to find and hold a good job

To Succeed, Kids Must Have

- The ability to listen, speak, and write effectively
- The ability to use modern technology to locate information
- The desire to become lifelong learners
- Respect for the rights and dignity of all people
- Self-confidence to believe they can create a better world

Libraries and Librarians Help Kids Succeed with

- Skilled instruction in using different types of information resources
- Enriching experiences, such as booktalks
- A supportive atmosphere to explore the world in which we live

Research Shows

- Access to and the amount spent for school libraries are the best predictors of students achievement
- Students who score higher on standardized tests tend to come from schools that spend money on school libraries
- 88 percent of the general public believes that public libraries should be an educational support center for students of all ages

Inadequate Library Funding Compromises Our Nation's Future

- Children and youth in all parts of the country need quality library services, but great funding disparity exists from school to school, town to town, and state to state.
- Libraries and librarians are the keys to educational success. They can make a difference but only if adequate funding exists.

Adapted from *Kids Need Libraries: School and Public Libraries Preparing the Youth of Today for the World of Tomorrow* (pamphlet prepared for the Second White House Conference on Library and Information Services). American Library Association, 1990.

YAs are at a risk for many reasons, but one of them is simply lack of information/knowledge. That seems a vacuum that libraries can help fill. Mary K. Chelton lists seven basic services libraries can offer to decrease risk:

- Assuring access to caring adults
- Assuring equitable access
- Assuring access to recorded information
- Assuring access to parent education
- Assuring access to information literacy instruction
- Assuring access to opportunities for learning/youth participation
- Assuring access to helping networks[3]

Although not all these services are available for every library, the idea behind each of them—that kids need libraries to provide them with access—is fundamental. Libraries are about opening doors, yet too few libraries are willing to open the door more than a crack.

3.2 WHY LIBRARIES NEED KIDS

For many directors and decision-makers, the question remains: why YA? Hidden behind this is the real question "What's in YA for us?" Simply put, libraries should serve YAs because serving YAs is good for the library. What does the public think we should do? Two recent Gallup polls[4-5] found that helping patrons support their formal education is the number one role—that's a YA role. Most libraries want to increase use and circulation—that's a YA opportunity because YA collections can give directors the most bang for the buck. Most libraries want to avoid chaos and disruption, so by serving YAs positively rather than merely reacting with rules, hostility, and security guards, YA services make things better for the library. Finally, every public library decision begins with the assumption of serving the needs of the community. In serving these needs, however, libraries also are serving themselves by making the institution look good, feel good, and be a better place.

The second set of reasons libraries need kids is more philosophical. A program of YA service is an effective and efficient use of resources that serves to position the library positively in the community. Here are 18 reasons why serving those under 18 is good for the library:

1. Today's patrons are tomorrow's voters and taxpayers.
2. Individuals continue their "library habits" from childhood through adulthood.
3. If patrons are "lost" during their YA years, they often do not return.
4. As YAs define themselves, libraries support them in establishing an identity as reader and library user.
5. By supplementing educational institutions, libraries become part of the education structure of the community.
6. By supplementing cultural institutions, libraries become part of the cultural structure of the community.
7. Libraries have the opportunity to be a "youth door to learning," not just a door for preschoolers.
8. YA services reduce stress in the library by serving YAs, rather than "tolerating" them.
9. Providing YA services enables libraries to act rather than react to situations involving teenagers.
10. YA services use the vast resources purchased in libraries for students with homework assignments.
11. Libraries can form community partnerships and develop cooperative relationships to serve underserved age groups.
12. Libraries can help their nation and/or city achieve National Education Goals by supporting YA educational needs.
13. Libraries can become a positive force for battling youth-related problems such as violence, at-risk behavior, etc.
14. YA services educate youth to become lifelong library users.
15. Libraries can defend the professional ethic of equal access regardless of age.
16. Libraries can keep the momentum for library use by children going: protect the investment.
17. YA services provide youth access to resources not available elsewhere.
18. Young adults need us.

Notice that the last reason here mirrors the first: because YAs need us and we need them—both now and years down the road.

Again, the research is clear: today's YAs are in trouble.[6] All the negative indicators are up[7] and not a day goes by without a negative news story regaling the latest atrocity by or upon an adolescent. The nation's youth policy is, for the most part, also its criminal justice policy.[8] People's patience is wearing out—not because YAs are at risk, but because they feel YAs are putting *them* at risk. The answer, they think, is more limits: curfews and get-tough policies. Thus, a public library or public school, as a tax-supported institution, has some level of responsibility to do something about this problem. As we said in the

NATIONAL EDUCATION GOALS

(1) SCHOOL READINESS
By the year 2000, all children in America will start school ready to learn.

(2) SCHOOL COMPLETION
By the year 2000, the high school graduation rate will increase to at least 90 percent.

(3) STUDENT ACHIEVEMENT AND CITIZENSHIP
By the year 2000, all students will leave grades 4, 8, and 12 having demonstrated competency over challenging subject matter including English, mathematics, science, foreign languages, civics and government, economics, arts, history, and geography, and every school in America will ensure that all students learn to use their minds well, so they may be prepared for responsible citizenship, further learning, and productive employment in our Nation's modern economy.

(4) TEACHER EDUCATION AND PROFESSIONAL DEVELOPMENT.—
By the year 2000, the Nation's teaching force will have access to programs for the continued improvement of their professional skills and the opportunity to acquire the knowledge and skills needed to instruct and prepare all American students for the next century.

(5) MATHEMATICS AND SCIENCE
By the year 2000, United States students will be first in the world in mathematics and science achievement.

(6) ADULT LITERACY AND LIFELONG LEARNING
By the year 2000, every adult American will be literate and will possess the knowledge and skills necessary to compete in a global economy and exercise the rights and responsibilities of citizenship.

(7) SAFE, DISCIPLINED, AND ALCOHOL- AND DRUG-FREE SCHOOLS
By the year 2000, every school in the United States will be free of drugs, violence, and the unauthorized presence of firearms and alcohol and will offer a disciplined environment conducive to learning.

(8) PARENTAL PARTICIPATION
By the year 2000, every school will promote partnerships that will increase parental involvement and participation in promoting the social, emotional, and academic growth of children.

Reprinted from "The National Education Goals," available on the U.S. Department of Education's Web site at http://www.ed.gov/pubs/goals/summary/goals.html.

60s, you are either part of the problem or part of the solution. Libraries should always be about problem-solving.

Yet for many librarians committed to serving youth, the first problem to solve is persuading reluctant administrators to make a commitment to YAs. What *commitment* means depends upon the resources available. A real commitment, of course, would be a separate YA department on the organizational chart and a separate YA room in the physical library, staffed with trained YA librarians who have an adequate materials budget and time off the desk to actually do stuff. Such a commitment is found in the library standards of New York and implied in the standards and goals for Illinois. Both documents explain the core concepts of YA commitment: equal access, adequate resource allocation, and responsive service from a trained staff. A similar statement of commitment can be found in the Young Adult Library Services Association's goals statement, spelling out the uniqueness of YA services and their importance.

No one wants a special commitment: YA librarians and advocates just want equally proportional resources dedicated to their user group as those found for other age level services. It seems, however, that reference staff, children's librarians, and sometimes even generalists don't have to work at creating support—it is implied.

" No one wants a special commitment: YA librarians and advocates just want equally proportional resources dedicated to thoir uocr group as those found for other age level services. It seems, however, that reference staff, children's librarians, and sometimes even generalists don't have to work at creating support—it is implied. "

3.3 CREATING SUPPORT

Like YA reluctant readers, library directors might be more interested in "reading" young adult services if they found the right book. That book might contain some of the following chapters:

Set goals: As Joe Jackson (the 1980s new wave/pop star, not the disgraced baseball player) once sang, "You can't get what you want until you know what your want." [9] I'm amazed when I speak with people at conferences who tell me they want to do something for YAs, but their director shows no interest. I ask "If your director made a commitment of resources, what would you want to do?" Their reply slugs out mushily along the lines of "You know, something for the kids." Even though you may arm yourself with lots of philosophical reasons for providing services, that needs backing up with a vision of service and a practical plan of attack.

Determine your director's purpose: It is a basic question, but an important one. If your library has a mission statement and a vision, everything you say about YAs has to fit within that framework. How can you attempt to persuade your director to do something, when you are not aware of what matters to the director or to the organization? What moves your director? What impresses her? What is supported and why? Draw logical parallels between services that currently get support and what you want to do in serving YAs.

Fit into plans: Related, what is your library trying to do? If your library has a five-year strategic plan, where do YAs services fit? Where does YA fit into the yearly goals and objectives? You want to work within the structure and turn it to your advantage. If one of the library's goals is to increase circulation overall, then push the YA agenda as a proven way to do just that. Does your director have a vision of where the library will be when all those YAs emerge in the next few years? Does your library have a customer service philosophy or any sort of "prime directive" on which to hitch your wagon? Finally, if your library allocates resources based on roles, then skip to the section "Ful-

New York Standards for YA Services

1. The public library should have a written selection policy which defines the purpose of the YA collection and delineates criteria for choosing materials.
2. A minimum of 15% of the library's total materials budget should be specifically designated for YA print materials
3. The YA materials collection should meet the current and potential needs of the community adolescents, providing a balanced collection of subjects in a variety of formats at various levels of comprehension.
4. All YA in the community must have equal and unrestricted access to the entire range of library services.
5. In response to the needs of the community, every library should regularly schedule programs for YAs, their parents, and others working with YAs.
6. A specific budget sufficient to plan, present, and publicize YA programs should be designated.
7. The public library collaborates with the local school in its service area in order to meet the informational and recreational needs of YAs and to create lifelong learners.
8. The YA services librarian establishes communication and cooperative relationships with social service agencies, recreation providers, local government, and community associations and organizations that serve youth.
9. The library's plan of service for YA should include a well-planned and coordinated publicity program
10. Every public library should have a clearly identified separate area designated for YAs.

Reprinted, with permission, from *The Key to the Future: Revised Minimum Standards for Youth Services in Pubic Libraries of New York State*. New York Library Association, 1994.

filling the Roles," and also see the first chapter of *Output Measures and More: Planning and Evaluating Public Library Services for Young Adults*. [10]

Establish proof: How can you improve anything unless you first prove it? If you have ever done a Myers-Briggs test, [11] you know a division exists between thinkers and feelers, and another between sensors (facts) and intuitives (philosophers). Librarians fit the model well, as it seems (an assumption based on my experience) most directors are thinkers/sensors, while most youth librarians tend to be feelers/intuitives. When speaking with your director, don't start sentences with "I feel" or "Don't you believe," but with "I know," "I can prove," and "I can document." Speak in terms of numbers and items you can measure, because, as Mary K. Chelton wrote:

[T]he main reason we evaluate is to make the invisible visible so that our decisions can be informed rather than intuitive and because no one is going to do it for us.[12]

Your case needs a numbers base, not nice thoughts about how things should be. State how things are and what improvements are possible. Most people dislike change; most directors like improvement. How can you improve unless you first learn how to prove?

Be proactive: When Chelton writes that "no one is going to do it for us," she is advocating a proactive approach. Don't think any director is going to ask for a plan on serving YAs; instead, you need to push the agenda. Offering YA services, like YAs themselves, calls attention to itself and is, on occasion, risk-taking.

Be persistent but have patience: Persistence and patience are called for repeatedly in serving YAs, and they are virtues when creating sup-

Illinois Goals for Youth Services

1. Enhance the influence of youth service librarians on public policy and decisions that affect the educational, information, literary, and literacy concerns of youth.
2. Guarantee that youth receive full and equal intellectual and physical access to all library resources, and full and equal protection of their confidentiality rights under the law.
3. Provide youth and youth services staff with opportunities to use the full range of library related information technology.
4. Encourage understanding and respect among people in our democratic society by providing diversity in public library services, materials and staffing for youth.
5. Improve the ability of libraries to provide services and resources for youth through collocation with other libraries and community agencies.
6. Preserve and improve the quality...through enhanced compensation and through opportunities for the professional development of the youth services staff.

Reprinted, with permission, from *Managing Change: Direction for Youth Services in Illinois Public Libraries*. Illinois Library Associations, 1993.

port. Patience is knowing that support is not going to come at today's meeting; persistence is preparing for the next meeting even knowing you might "lose" again. Most directors have everyone else in the organization doing the same thing you are doing—pushing their agenda. Your key is to use those YA skills of persistence and patience to outlast others. This is also a matter of "choosing your battles," because not everything is worth spilling blood. Constantly and forcefully pushing your agenda gets real old, real quick. Pick your skirmishes carefully.

Be a promoter: You want your director to take action, but before she can do that, marketing 101 tells us, she must first have her awareness increased. No one is going to do this for you, either—so bone up on humble-yet-effective self-promotion. Promote inside and outside the library. Promote YA services writing, in person, and over the telephone. See that the words *young adult* show up on library documents, annual reports, and see that YAs become visible as an important user group.

Find the locus of power within the organization: Maybe in your own library, you need to substitute *board president* or *development officer* for *director*, because that is where the real, not paper, power lies.

Speak admintype-speak: Directors won't ask "What does this cost?" Instead, they'll ask you to "consider the financial implications of the proposed program of service." Like YAs, administration types have a slanguage all their own. Learn it and use it. Directors are CEOs and prone for management fads. If your director is talking about teams, volunteer to lead or organize a YA team. If your director is carrying around a book about TQM, demonstrate how YA services fit perfectly into that model.

Be politically adept: Learn not just how to get things done, but how *not* to get things done. Don't burn bridges, don't make institutional enemies, etc.—you know all the clichés. Read Dale Carnegie or the latest business best-seller, and learn to "make friends" in the organization. The best political move, of course, is to succeed by demonstrating how serving YAs works for the library.

Goals of the Young Adult Library Services Association

The goal of the Young Adult Library Services Association is to advocate, promote, and strengthen service to young adults as part of the continuum of total library service. The following concerns and activities are interdependent in fulfilling the goal of YALSA.

The Young Adult Library Services Association:

1. Advocates the young adult's right to free and equal access to materials and services, and assists librarians in handling problems of such access.
2. Evaluates and promotes materials of interest to adolescents through special services, programs, and publications, except for those materials designed specifically for curriculum use.
3. Identifies research needs related to young adult service and communicates those needs to the library academic community in order to activate research projects.
4. Stimulates and promotes the development of librarians and other staff working with young adults through formal and continuing education.
5. Stimulates and promotes the expansion of young adult service among professional associations and agencies at all levels.
6. Represents the interests of librarians and staff working with young adults to all relevant agencies, governmental or private, and to industries that serve young adults as clients or consumers.
7. Creates and maintains communication links with other units of the ALA whose developments affect service to young adults.

Reprinted, with permission, from *Young Adult Library Services Association Handbook,* available at gopher://ala1.ala.org:70/00/alagophxiii/alagophxiiiyalsa/yalsa.hb.

Find partners: Better than your voice advocating YA services is a chorus of voices: teachers, principals, youth workers, professors, patrons, Friends of the Library, and even YAs.

Pounce on opportunities: There is much amazing research being published about YAs, but it is not in the library professional literature. For example, when *Business Week* featured the cover article, "Teens: They're Back," [13] every person making a case for YAs should have disseminated that information through the library.

Stay positive: Remain forward-looking, no matter what. If you don't, you will get cast into the "bad actor/not a team player" pile. If you're viewed as a whining, strident, and aggressive dissident (a *clubhouse lawyer*, in baseball lingo), no one will listen—would *you* listen to someone like that? Too often when youth librarians don't get their way, they think the director "hates kids." Again, in some cases that may be true, but most likely it is not. Yet, if you cast the battle in these terms, you will find yourself part of the bad-attitude club, which will hurt your cause more than help it. Instead, resolve to be a player.

Player: If you follow some of these strategies and investigate your own organization, you have a chance to become a player. The players are on the ground floor when it comes time to make decisions and set priorities. Although an adversarial relationship with administration might be natural, it is those "on the team" who get the support.

These elements represent strategies to follow, skills to learn, or attitudes to adopt. You might not have all of them and you might not need the whole nine yards, so pick and choose the ones that fit your needs. Develop your vision of serving YAs and work to get those setting priorities to see it, understand it, share it, or perhaps even push it.

3.4 FULFILLING THE ROLES

As mentioned, YA services need to fit snugly into the overall structure of the library. One structure many public library directors are very comfortable with is PLA's planning process/roles. If your library is now, or is about to become, involved in a strategic planning process, get involved. All eight public library roles have a YA component, with formal educational support and popular materials center foremost. Recent surveys of community leaders and the general public rank these as two of the most important roles a library should play in the community. If you are building support, you need to determine what the overall structure is and how you fit. This section examines (briefly here, but in more detail for most roles through the book) all eight public library roles and explores how YA services fit in these roles.

Public Library Roles

1. Community Activities Center:
"The library is a central focus point for community activity, meetings and services."

2. Community Information Center
"The library is a clearinghouse for current information on community organizations, issues, and services."

3. Formal Education Support Services
"The library assists students of all ages in meeting educational objectives established during their formal course of study."

4. Independent Learning Center
"The library supports individuals of all ages pursuing a sustained program of learning independent of any educational provider."

5. Popular Materials Center
"The library features current, high-demand, high-interest materials in a variety of formats for persons of all ages."

6. Preschoolers' Door to Learning
"The library encourages young children to develop an interest in reading and learning through services for children, and for parents and children together."

7. Reference Center
"The library actively provides timely, accurate, and useful information for community residents."

8. Research Center
"The library assists scholars and researchers to conduct in-depth studies, investigate specific areas of knowledge, and create new knowledge."

Adapted from *Planning and Role Setting for Public Libraries.* American Library Association, 1987.

COMMUNITY ACTIVITY CENTER

Two prime YA elements are at work in the library's role of community activity center. The first is the programming option. There is a long history and a great deal of literature about programming for YAs. Plenty of successful programs for duplicating and many reasons to do programming are available. [14] The second element is that many staff may not like the library being used as the community activity center for YAs. Many YAs do nothing in libraries but hang out. Yes, it is nerve-racking; because kids come in groups and they have energy, they can be somewhat scary even to those who like YAs. If they are disruptive because there is nothing else for them to do after school, your community has a problem which the library cannot solve on its own.

COMMUNITY INFORMATION CENTER

Maybe the best thing the library can do as a community information center for YAs is just support other efforts in the community. Become

Role of the Public Library:
Results of a Gallup Poll of Community Leaders

Formal Education Support Center	88.0%
Preschoolers' Door to Learning	81.3%
Independent Learning Center	78.0%
Community Information Center	65.0%
Research Center	55.7%
Popular Materials Center	52.7%
Reference Library - Business	47.0%
Community Activity Center	46.0%
Public Work Place	38.3%
Reference Library - Personal	38.0%

% = number ranking this role as "very important."

Adapted from George D'Elia and Eleanor Jo Rodger, "The Roles of the Public Library in the Community," *Public Libraries* (March/April 1995): 93–101.

involved in community-wide youth networks—most cities of any size have them—and if the library isn't going to be the clearinghouse of information, then it needs to be in the loop. The library also needs to plug into the YA community—it needs to know with whom and where to network. Another related issue emerges here: often rather than seeking out community resources, YAs will come to libraries for information about "problems" because they don't know where else in the community to turn. This means staff training, not just on information and referral transactions, but on reference work with YAs that does not invade a person's privacy. Simple seemingly harmless questions like "Is this for a report?" or even the less threatening "When is this report due?" cross the line and might cause embarrassment (or worse) on everyone's part. There is no reason to ask young adults "why" they need information—it doesn't answer their questions and invades their privacy. How much information, what type, what format, and when it is needed (not assuming that it is for school) will get the same results without unnecessary prying.

> 66 There is no reason to ask young adults 'why' they need information—it doesn't answer their questions and invades their privacy. 99

FORMAL EDUCATION SUPPORT

The "formal education support" role is a big one. Mary K. Chelton and Jim Rosinia's *Bare Bones: Young Adult Services Tips for Public Library Generalists*[15] deals extensively with how (and why) libraries can meet this role for YAs. This being the most visible, most staff-intensive, and the most troublesome, it is the role that demands attention and quality in order to gather support. If YAs cannot get proper assistance finding something they need, chances are that they won't come back for something they want. If YAs leave frustrated or unsatisfied, it is doubtful they will return to a place associated with failure. Similarly, if the reference staff is continually frustrated regarding school assignments, they won't supply support.

INDEPENDENT LEARNING CENTER

The most important element of the role of the library as an independent learning center deals with the perception of it as the role which helps "people become better people" or "helps them improve at their jobs." For YAs, this translates into the formal educational support role—going to school is a YA job. The 1995 NCES survey found that

Role of the Public Library: Results of a Gallup Poll

Role	%
Formal Education Support Center	88.1%
Independent Learning Center	84.6%
Preschoolers' Door to Learning	83.2%
Research Center	68.2%
Community Information Center	65.6%
Reference Library - Business	55.1%
Public Work Place	52.4%
Popular Materials Center	51.4%
Reference Library - Personal	48.4%
Community Activity Center	41.3%

% = number ranking this role as "very important."

Note: The survey population for both of these surveys consisted only those above the age of 18. This might in part explain the low ranking of popular materials.

Adapted from George D'Elia and Eleanor Jo Rodger, "Public Opinion about the Roles of the Public Library in the Community," *Public Libraries* (January/February 1994): 23–28.

a majority of libraries reported "heavy to moderate use" of services to assist YAs with homework assignments.[16] Around term-paper time, there are few more popular items than those materials that help students do their jobs and complete their school reports. Yet learning for many YAs goes beyond what is mandated by school. YAs are in the process of developing new interests and hobbies. In addition, they are curious about the changing world around them and their relationship to it. This non-curriculum-related learning is "independent learning." The primary characteristics of this role involve

[S]upport for a program of learning which is independent of any education process, determining needed resources and obtaining them from the library's collection or via ILL, a collection with a wide range of circulating materials relevant to the interest of independent learners of all ages. Staff needs knowledge about learning theory and skills in learners advisory service.[17]

This quote reads like a YA librarian's job description. Libraries can use a variety of methods to meet the needs of YA independent learners (see page 82). Serving YA independent learners helps them make the decision to become library users and lifelong learners. If a YA is curious, wanting to learn more, and can't do that at the public library, then we have failed not just in one of our roles, but in our entire mission. If anything, independent learning is a win-win proposition. In independent learning, the best elements of adolescents—enthusiasm, boundless energy, curiosity, and a willingness to learn—encounter our best elements: resources, services, and a helpful staff trained to help YAs.

POPULAR MATERIALS CENTER

The role of popular materials center means much more than YA literature; it means having all sorts of personal interest materials, not only a collection of hardback juvenile titles. The guts of any quality YA popular materials collection is its paperback area and its magazine section. Quality is measured by quantity; that is, a quality YA collection is one that produces a quantity of circulation. If you are going to build support, you need to prove the value of YA. Wouldn't

**Meeting the Needs of Independent YA Learners:
An Alphabet of Ideas and Questions**

Access: Does your library restrict YA access to any materials or services?

Borrowing: Can YAs borrow all materials, including using inter-library loan?

Cards: Does every YA in the community have a library card?

Development Tasks: Do you know the seven tasks of adolescent development?

Educate Staff: Has your library ever had an in-service training on serving YAs?

Formats: Are there resources available in formats other than print?

Groups and Clubs: Do you have a list from local schools of student groups and clubs?

"How do I...?": Do you have the tools to answer the basic question many independent learners ask; namely, "How do I do something?"

Information Literacy: Does your library have a library instruction or orientation program?

Jobs: Independent learning is often about helping people do their jobs, and the main "job" of most YAs is to complete a formal education. Are not these two roles really one and the same?

Know a YA: If independent learning is characterized by staff interaction, do you or other staff really know the names and interests of your YA independent learners?

Learners' Advisory: Can you adapt your readers' advisory skills to helping YAs find information sources that meet their needs?

Modems: Is your library wired and do YAs have access to the outside, not just the Internet, but the ability to use college and university library online catalogs via modem?

Networking: What is your relationship with other agencies and groups that serve YAs?

Outreach: How can YAs become independent learners in the library if they don't even use the library?

Programs: Can you work cooperatively with other youth-serving agencies to present programs of interest to independent learners?

Questions: How do you know what YAs want and need unless you ask them?

Readiness: Does YA service really have the ability to play its traditional role of moving youth from using the children's collection to materials in the adult collection?

Sex: What is the number one nonformal education learning interest of YAs?

Technology: Where can a YA get access to and use information technology to do research and write reports and resumes?

User-Friendly: Is your library an easy place for YAs to use?

Visits: If you can't get to the schools, can they get to you?

Work Together: Is your library's act together—do the various departments or agencies who serve YAs understand the needs of independent YA learners?

eXcitement: Are you prepared to deal with the excitement—both the good and the bad points—that YAs develop for independent learning pursuits?

Young Adult Librarian: Who can best help YAs meet their independent learning needs: a generalist without special training or a YA librarian?

Zeal: The excitement that independent learning can generate among YAs matched with the knowledge and advocacy of a YA librarian can lead to a true zeal for independent learning.

Adapted from Patrick Jones, "Role-Playing: YAs as Independent Learners," *Voice of Youth Advocates* (August 1993): 136–140.

it be better to say "I can document a 33 percent increase in circulation," rather than "I bought every book with a starred review in *Booklist*"? I'd rather make the numbers go up; if you build a collection with a core of stuff that kids want, the circulation will boom. Do this not just by giving them what they want but by giving them lots of what they want. There are no collection development police that will arrest you for buying multiple copies. Multiple copies means 10 copies, not two. They won't arrest you for passing on a new hardback novel with a starred review in *Booklist* (you'll get the paperback version in a year and no one will have missed it) and putting that $16.95 into a magazine subscription, a cheap CD-ROM, or a Smashing Pumpkins compact disc.

REFERENCE LIBRARY

For many YAs, the library's role as reference library translates into the educational support role, but let's examine two key words—*timely* and *useful*. Timely means online, yet most libraries do not offer the same level of timely online service to YAs that they do to adults. The issue in this role is really about policy and procedures: is reference service fairly delivered? Are all questions really treated equally? Are there limitations on "homework" questions? Become involved in your library's technology planning: most youth librarians blew it big time when Dialog hit because we left it to the adult reference librarians and they became the keepers of the keys. Do YAs get access to the Internet, CD-ROMs, and search tools like First Search? Would most librarians even consider asking a well-dressed man to "stop playing" with an electronic encyclopedia and yet think nothing of saying that to a teenage boy? A second issue is training, as in how many, if any, librarians working in your library have even had training in YA reference work. Part of the YA fit here is to see that YAs, in libraries with more than one service desk, are not shuttled back and forth between desks. YAs want what all patrons want—to be treated courteously.

RESEARCH CENTER

Two points about the library's role as research center—first, the fairness issue. Could YAs get one-on-one consultations for their research, like an adult would if this was your library's role? Lots of libraries set up business specialists to handhold adults through research, yet wouldn't consider doing the same for YAs. Can they get inter-library loans, extended loan periods, or other "perks"? This role assumes libraries should place a high priority on the few (and vocal) rather than on the many. To deal with the issue of serving scholars as opposed to YAs, you might want to ask (innocently) if there is a national survey of independent scholars, and if so, would it indicate that one out of

What YAs Need and Want from Libraries

Needs:
Hang out
Socialize/meet friends
Go to the bathroom/use phone/get a drink of water
Do homework/study
Find information for school
Find information for themselves
Get helpful service
Find a book for a book report
Learn how to use computers/ Internet

Wants:
Find all types of fiction to read for fun
Find nonfiction about their interests
Find music to listen to/videos to watch
Find magazines and comic books to read
Find computers to play/use
Find a friendly environment
Find programs of interest

every four library patrons is an independent scholar? So how is it, you would ask, that the library can justify serving these few researchers and not all these YAs?

PRESCHOOLERS' DOOR TO LEARNING

Serving YAs is merely a continuation of the role of the library to provide preschoolers with access to learning. It seems a tremendous contradiction for libraries to dedicate resources to younger children only to neglect them when they turn 12. This is not only a contradiction, but in this era of "financial implications," it is bad investment. If you don't continue to nurture YAs, then all your investment in preschool storytimes, summer reading clubs, and puppet shows was wasted. Expand this role to "youth's door to learning," where the library encourages all young people to develop an interest in reading and learning.

3.5 SERVICE PLANS

As you can see, serving young adults is an integral part of every public library role. Yet, libraries don't emphasize all eight roles; instead they prioritize. The question becomes, given limited resources, at which level the library can respond. Looking at the various levels available, you can determine where your library is now. You can assess this by evaluating yourself and by surveying your audience. Ask basic questions about the wants and needs of young adults in your area. If you are unsure of those needs, then ask the user group. You can use the evaluation form shown in Figure 3–2 to find the answers you need. Once you know what your audience needs and wants, do a self-assessment to determine the level of your current service. You need to know where you are to visualize where you want to be. Either develop your own instrument or use the one prepared for the NCES survey (see Figure 3–3). With your self-assessment, you determine the strong and weak points of your service. By developing a YA service plan, you can focus your resources on specific areas you want to improve. The service plan gets down on paper actually *what* and *when* and *how much* you want to accomplish.

Connecting YAs and libraries is a task full of contradictions. The last contradiction occurs in that even when you improve service, you cannot really know or measure whether you have improved the lives of the YAs you are serving. You can develop library instruction and measure its effectiveness based on evaluations, but you cannot really know if it actually saved YAs time and helped them write better pa-

---

Figure 3–2 YA User Survey

---

1. Which of these describes your use of the library?

   _____ 3 times/more a week   _____ Twice a week

   _____ Once a week   _____ Twice a month

   _____ Once a month   _____ Less than once a month

2. Do you have a library card?

   _____ Yes   _____ No   _____ Lost it

3. Enter a number to describe how often you visit the library to do each of these tasks (1 = Frequently, 2 = Sometimes, 3 = Seldom, 4 = Never):

   _____ Complete homework assignments

   _____ Check out materials to use for homework

   _____ Check out materials to read for fun

   _____ Check out materials to read for information

   _____ Check out tapes or CDs

   _____ Check out software/CD-ROMs

   _____ Access the Internet

   _____ Check out videotapes

   _____ Meet and talk with friends

   _____ Attend a library program

   _____ Study

   _____ Use equipment (copies, computer, typewriter)

   _____ Other:

4. Enter a number to rate the following features of this library (1 = Excellent, 2 = Good, 3 = Okay, 4 = Not so good, 5 = Poor):

   _____ Choice of books

   _____ Choice of reference books and indexes

   _____ Choice of magazines and newspapers

   _____ Choice of tapes and CDs

   _____ Choice of videotapes

   _____ Choice of software/CD-ROMs

   _____ Access to the Internet

   _____ Staff helpful finding materials for homework

_____ Staff helpful finding book to read for fun
_____ Library programs
_____ Computers and other equipment
_____ YA area

5. If you don't often use the library, why not?
    _____ Unable to get to the library
    _____ Not enough time/ too much else to do
    _____ Nothing at the library interests me
    _____ Don't need it
    _____ Bad experiences in the past with library staff
    _____ Do research/find reading material elsewhere
    _____ Not sure what the library has to offer me

6. Please tell us the following information about you:
    Male/female: _____   Age: _____   Grade: _____

pers. Although collections seem easier to measure, circulation counts only the number of books checked out, not the number read. Therefore, although you plan for YAs and measure services for YAs, it is only through talking with individual YAs that you really learn whether your plan had any real impact in the lives of young adults.

3.6 CHANGING THE QUESTION/ DEVELOPING A VISION

Isn't it time the question changed from "Why YA?" to "Why *not* YA?" Even though there are more YAs than ever before[18] and the benefits of offering YA services have been made clear, libraries give a number of reasons for not promoting YA services:

"WE DON'T HAVE ENOUGH MONEY."

The materials kids want for popular reading are paperbacks, the magazines they like are cheap, and although the reference books and products they use are costly, they are nothing compared to what an average

---

Figure 3–3 A Self-Evaluation Survey

Self-Evaluation Survey (Based on 1995 NCES Survey)

1. How does your library define *young adult*? _____

2. What percent of users are young adults? _____

3. Has ethnic diversity increased over past five years? _____

4. Does your library have a young adult librarian? _____

5. Does your library have a separate young adult collection? _____

6. Does your library provide ongoing training in serving young adults? _____

7. Does your young adult collection contain:
   Fiction_____   Nonfiction_____   Magazines_____   Music_____
   Videos_____   Computers_____   CD-ROMs _____   Internet____

8. Of the following, which does your library offer and how often is it used? (3 = Heavy)

	Service	Availability	Usage
a.	Reference	1 2 3	1 2 3
b.	Bibliographic instruction	1 2 3	1 2 3
c.	Summer reading program	1 2 3	1 2 3
d.	After-school programs	1 2 3	1 2 3
e.	YA advisory boards	1 2 3	1 2 3
f.	Non-English materials	1 2 3	1 2 3

9. During the past year, describe your library's interaction with the following (1 = Heavy)

a.	Schools	1	2	3
b.	Cultural institutions	1	2	3
c.	Youth organizations	1	2	3
d.	Recreational facilities	1	2	3
e.	At-risk programs	1	2	3

10. What is your number one external barrier?
    Competition_____   Safety_____   Lack of transportation _____
    Disinterest _____   No need _____

11. What is your number one internal barrier?
    Lack of materials _____   Lack of staff_____   Untrained staff_____
    Hours _____

> " Almost all library patrons have other resources available to solve their "problems," but because they choose us, their problems are now ours. "

public library might spend on business resources. If libraries cannot be all things to all people, we should serve those who do not have other options for information. Although it *is* the job of school libraries to support the curriculum, consider the resources, hours, and staffing of those facilities. They cannot bear the brunt alone. If a businessperson came in asking for research, would we brush him aside with "Did you check with your corporate library first?" When a patron wants a best-seller do we say "You could buy that book, you know?" Almost all library patrons have other resources available to solve their "problems," but because they choose us, their problems are now ours. That is our real business—not books, not reference, not the Internet—libraries are in the problem-solving business.

"WE DON'T HAVE ENOUGH STAFF."

Assumption: it is not just a matter of staffing, but rather the efficient and effective use of staff which presents a barrier. Is it a more efficient use of staff to have one person conducting library instruction for 30 kids at a time as part of a planned program than having the same 30 kids come up to the reference desk at different times asking the same question? Is it more efficient to have one person who knows the materials developing collections that will be used than someone who does not know the users purchasing books that won't get used and just be weeded in a few years? Is it more effective to have one person making contacts with schools than a staff of people trying to do it and getting nowhere? Finally, is it not more efficient to have one person responsible for proactively planning services than a group of people reacting daily? Generalists can serve YAs and will continue to do so—as well they should. Yet libraries also need staff with the expertise to help them do their work more effectively and efficiently.

Service Plan
Goal:

I. Assessment
   A. Evaluate current services and resources
   B. Identify needs of YA population
      1. Survey of staff
      2. Survey of YAs

II. Collection development
   A. Fiction
      1. Increase purchase of paperbacks by _____%
      2. Decrease purchase of hardbacks by _____%
   B. Nonfiction
      1. Increase purchase of CD-ROMs by _____%
      2. Decrease purchase of reference books by _____%
   C. Other:
      1. Increase purchase of magazines by _____%
      2. Decrease purchase of pamphlets by _____%
   D. Merchandising
      1. Weed collection by _____
      2. Reorganize to increase display space by _____

III. Services
   A. School contacts
      1. Meet with school librarians by _____
      2. Meet with principals/dept. heads by _____
   B. School services
      1. Increase # of tours by _____%
      2. Increase library card registrations by _____%
   C. Programs
      1. Increase booktalking visits by _____%
      2. Develop at least _____ cooperative program

IV. Evaluate
   A. Formal
      1. Conduct Outputs Measures by _____
      2. Increase of circulation, attendance, and library cards
   B. Informal
      1. Staff perceptions/comments
      2. User perceptions/comments

YA Space-Planning Questionnaire

1. Is the YA area easy to spot upon entering the library?
2. Is the YA area physically separate from any other collection?
3. Is the YA area secluded, allowing for privacy yet still easy to monitor and supervise?
4. Does the YA area include other formats in addition to books?
5. Is there a space to post announcements and flyers of local interest?
6. Are there plenty of comfortable places to sit?
7. Are the majority of books in paperback?
8. Is there something, such as magazines, to "pull" YAs into the area?
9. Are bookstore style furniture, fixtures, or display techniques used?
10. Are the shelves uncrowded, allowing for end-of-shelf displays?
11. Are the books in the area attractive?
12. Is the fiction collection shelved by genre?
13. Are booklists attractive and easy to find and use?
14. Are the displays filled with circulating materials and restocked regularly?
15. Do displays contain something other than books?
16. Is there a place to display and distribute documents, like program flyers?
17. Is the collection continually weeded?

Adapted from Cathy Carey and Sylvia Mitchell, "It's Not Totally Dreamland Quiz,"
Voice of Youth Advocates (August 1995): 150–151.

"WE DON'T HAVE ENOUGH SPACE."

YA service does not require a lot of room: it does require some planning[19] and a little "dreaming." Again, the building blocks of the book collection are paperbacks and 200–page nonfiction tomes. The reference materials are moving more and more toward CD-ROM. The magazines take up space, but serve a secondary purpose of promotion. Putting together a YA collection is easy. Not enough room? If you start the collection by pulling all the books from children's and adult areas that have YA appeal and put them together, then don't you still have the same number of books in the library? If you weeded from one area, doesn't that by definition free up space somewhere else? Shifting priorities might require only shifting books on the shelf at the beginning. It seems that any library that can find room on its shelf for every volume of *Contemporary Authors,* the *Thomas Register*, and other multi-volume shelf suckers should be able to squeeze in some room someplace for books that will actually circulate more than "sometime." What about the space gained from discarding print sources and replacing them with CD-ROMs? There is space if you want to find it.

It is a difficult time (as always) to be a librarian, especially a library manager. Everybody wants something and they want it now. Needs and demands go up, while resources stagnate. In a time of great change, you need to hold onto some constants. The first thing I did in library school was the "community analysis" project based on the idea that a library should serve its community. In a time when there are more teenagers than ever, when there are more sources of information than ever, and when libraries need to do things smarter than ever, the community needs a YA librarian. Although YA departments are not "springing up" across the country, the PUBYAC listserv[20] has had plenty of requests from people who are either setting up or expanding YA departments. Even though there are local demographic factors at work, could it be that libraries are responding to the fact that kids need libraries and that libraries need kids? Why YA? Because it works.

The Young Adult Library Services Association Vision Statement

In every library in the nation, quality library services to young adults is provided by a staff that understands and respects the unique informational, educational, and recreational needs of teenagers. Equal access to information, services and materials is recognized as a right not a privilege. Young adults are actively involved in the library decision-making process. The library staff collaborates and cooperates with other youth-serving agencies to provide a holistic community-wide network of activities and services that supports healthy youth development.

To ensure that this vision becomes a reality, the Young Adult Library Services Association:

- Advocates extensive and developmentally appropriate library and information services for young adults, age 12 to 18;
- Promotes reading and supports the literacy movement;
- Advocates the use of information and communication technology to provide effective library service;
- Supports equality of access to the full range of library materials and services, including existing and emerging information and communication technologies, for young adults;
- Provides education and professional development to enable its members to serve as effective advocates for young people;
- Fosters collaboration and partnerships among its individual members, with the library community and other groups involved in providing library and information services to young adults;
- Influences public policy by demonstrating the importance of providing library and information services that meet the unique needs of young adults;
- Encourages research and is in the vanguard of new thinking concerning the provision of library and information services for youth.

Reprinted with permission from the Young Adult Library Services Association.

DEVELOPING A VISION

"Kids need libraries" was a first crack at a vision statement. Vision statements are all the rage and for good reason: they provide not just a goal, but a motivation. In 1995, YALSA developed a vision statement to guide the organization and the profession. Although the vision is not a goal set in concrete, it is also not a mirage. Looking over the history of YA services and the recent horde of publications, the vision seems on target as it talks about access, participation, equality, and advocacy. These four ideals are the cornerstone of the YA profession and define what sets it apart. Even though YA services take many forms, from highly developed programs of service in systems like New York Public Library to successes in small rural libraries, every successful library interaction relates back to these cornerstones. If YAs don't have access and are not treated equally, and if those who care about them don't advocate for them and invite their participation, then the vision for public libraries will be dimmed.

With YAs and all patrons having more options for obtaining information for education and recreation, libraries must remain vital, even indispensable. The vision of the indispensable public library requires that the library:

> [I]dentify and choose for itself that array of services that will best meet the needs of its citizens and ensure ongoing support for the library operation.[21]

And what is one of those indispensable services? You guessed it, service to youth:

> [I]f people in the United States were asked to identify a single distinguishing public library service, the one most often mentioned would likely be service to…young people.[22]

Thus, the vision of YA services is an integral part of an overall vision for the indispensable public library.

ENDNOTES

1. *Beyond Ephebiphobia: A Tool Chest for Customer Service to Young Adults.* Young Adult Library Services Association, 1994.
2. *Services and Resources for Children and Young Adults in Public Libraries.* U.S. Dept. of Education, Office of Educational Research and Improvement, National Center for Education Statistics, 1995.
3. Mary K. Chelton, "Youth's Right to Know: Societal Necessity or National Oxymoron?" in *Your Right to Know.* American Library Association, 1993.
4. George D'Elia, and Eleanor Jo Rodger, "The Roles of the Public Library in the Community," *Public Libraries* (March/April 1995): 94–103.
5. George D'Elia, and Eleanor Jo Rodger, "Public Opinion about the Roles of the Public Library in the Community," *Public Libraries* (January/February 1994): 23–28.
6. Carnegie Council on Adolescent Development. *Great Transitions: Preparing Adolescents for a New Century.* Carnegie Corporation, 1995: 24–25.
7. *Youth Indicators 1996: Trends in the Well-Being of American Youth.* National Center for Education Statistics, 1996.
8. "Today's Teens: Dissed, Mythed and Totally Pissed," *Utne Reader* (July/August 1994): 50–69.
9. Joe Jackson, "You Can't Get What You Want Until You Know What You Want," on *Body and Soul.* A & M Records, 1984.
10. Virginia Walter, *Output Measures and More.* American Library Association, 1995.
11. Otto Kroeger and Janet Thuesen, *Type Talk at Work.* New York: Delacorte, 1992.
12. Mary K. Chelton, "Developmentally Based Performance Measures for Young Adult Services," *Top of the News* (Fall 1984): 39.
13. Laura Zinn, "Teens: They're Back," *Business Week* (April 1994): 1+.
14. L. Amey, "Special Case for YA Programming," *Emergency Librarian:* (January/February 1985): 25–26.
15. Mary K. Chelton and James M. Rosinia, *Bare Bones: Young Adult Services Tips For Public Library Generalists.* Young Adult Library Services Association and Public Library Association, 1993.
16. *Services and Resources for Young Adults in Public Libraries.* U.S. Dept. of Education, National Center for Education Statistics, 1988.
17. *Planning and Role Setting for Public Libraries.* American Library Association, 1987.

18. *Population Projects of the United States by Age, Sex, Race, and Hispanic origin, 1993–2050.* U.S. Bureau of the Census, Current Population Reports, 1993.
19. Laurie B. Reese, "Space Planning for Young Adults." *Voice of Youth Advocates* (October 1991): 213–216.
20. Shannon VanHemert, "PUBYAC: Yacking It up on the Internet," *Journal of Youth Services in Libraries.* (Fall 1995): 79– 85.
21. F. William Summers, "The Concept of the Indispensable Public Library," *Public Libraries* (July/August 1993): 217.
22. Summers, p. 213.

NOVEMBER

Goal: To investigate Internet resources for YAs and YA librarians.

1. **PUBYAC/LM-NET/STUMPERS:** Subscribe to one (or more) of these listservs to stay current about trends and issues in YA service. Better, find lots of practical advice: listservs are filled with solutions to common problems. Better still, use this as a door to network.

2. **Visit the YA Librarians' Help/Home Page:** Don't reinvent the wheel; instead visit this professional Web page designed to assist librarians serving young adults. Updated at least monthly, this page contains links to Internet information resources on a variety of topics of interest to anyone serving teenagers (see 9.5).

3. **Find new Web sites:** Look to the professional literature as well for information about Web sites of interest, in articles such as "BlenderWeb? Nerd World" from *School Library Journal* (July 1997) and YA Clicks from *Voice of Youth Advocates* (October 1997). Consider a subscription to magazines like *Technology Connection, Internet World,* or *NetGuide.*

4. **Create a YA area on the Web environment of your library:** In addition to using the sites located in items two and three, visit the sites of other public libraries with YA pages (see 9.4).

5. **Seek automation opportunities:** Look for training, committee assignments, or conferences concerning Internet utilization. Through training, you will learn how to better use the Internet for searching or for creating resources. Through committee assignments, you can see that youth issues are always on the agenda. Finally, through conferences and networking, learn how libraries are using the Internet: it can be a passive tool like any other reference source or you can learn methods to make it a proactive part of your YA service program.

PART IV: WHAT YA?

4 YA COLLECTIONS

Collections are one of the major ways libraries deliver to YAs. To create raving fans, however, we need to deliver what we promise, plus one percent more. That one percent could translate into many things: involving youth in the selection process, carrying a wide variety of media, collecting graphic novels, linking e-zines to the library's home page, or developing a magazine collection. That one percent could be just about anything that demonstrates to YAs that not only have you identified them, they have influenced you. Delivering that extra one percent means redefining quality and decision making. To help with that decision making, this chapter includes "top ten" lists that identify some of the best resources available in paperback for a variety of different genres and subjects. Although it is by no means complete or a core collection, these titles represent some of the best (good, accessible, timely) choices for jump-starting your collection development efforts.

The decision to build a YA paperback collection isn't an impulsive one. It comes about due to a series of choices that librarians make on both macro and micro levels, based on the library's priorities and the reading interests of YAs. YAs like to read a variety of books, as many types as there are genres of fiction. Nonfiction is in many ways even more popular: YAs read nonfiction not just for school reports, but also for recreational and informational reading. Periodicals—both magazines and newspapers—are the most popular recreational reading format of most YAs for a variety of reasons, one of which is that they provide a great deal of information in a graphics-heavy, easy, and quick-to-read fashion. That also sums up much of the library technology YAs like as well.

So although one part of collection development involves putting those *Sweet Valley High*s on standing order, many other collection decisions must be made. The selection tools to support those decisions are numerous and varied, providing librarians with solid information about what is available of interest to YAs.

4.1 YA LITERATURE

People make a common mistake when they talk about YA collections: they correlate YA collections with YA literature. Although this chapter cannot *not* mention YA literature, it provides considerable information on other materials used by YAs. One reason I give YA literature a light brush is that there have been so many good books and articles published in this field of late.

Young Adult Literature: Bib Squib

Aronson, Marc. "The YA Novel Is Dead," and other fairly stupid tales. *School Library Journal* v. 41 (January 95): 36–37.

Bushman, John H. *Using Young Adult Literature in the English Classroom.* New York: Maxwell Macmillan International, 1993.

Bushman, Kay Parks. *A Thematic Guide to Young Adult Literature: Annotation, Critiques and Sources.* The Writing Conference, 1993.

Cart, Michael. "Of Risk and Revelation: The Current State of Young Adult Literature," *Journal of Youth Services in Libraries* v. 8 (Winter 1995): 151–164.

——. *From Romance to Realism: 50 Years of Growth and Change in Young Adult Literature.* New York: HarperCollins, 1996.

Carter, Betty. *Best Books for Young Adults: The Selections, the History, the Romance.* Published in association with Young Adult Library Services Association. American Lib. Assn., 1994.

Donelson, Kenneth L. and Alleen Pace Nilsen. *Literature for Today's Young Adults*, 5th Edition. New York: HarperCollins College Publishers, 1996.

Gallagher, Mary Elizabeth. *Young Adult Literature: Issues and Perspectives*, Revised Edition. Haverford, PA: Catholic Library Association, 1990.

Herz, Sarah K. *From Hinton to Hamlet: Building Bridges between Young Adult Literature and the Classics.* Westport, CT: Greenwood Press, 1996.

Kaywell, Joan F. *Adolescent Literature as a Complement to the Classics.* Norwood, MA: Christopher Gordon Publishers, 1995.

Lenz, Millicent. *Young Adult Literature and Nonprint Materials: Resources for Selection.* Metuchen, NJ: Scarecrow Press, 1994.

Literature for Teenagers: New Books, New Approaches. Don Gallo, ed. Connecticut Council of Teachers of English, 1993.

Lukens, Rebecca J. *A Critical Handbook of Literature for Young Adults.* New York: HarperCollins College Pubs, 1995.

Lynch, Chris. "Today's YA Writers - Pulling No Punches," *School Library Journal* (January 1994): 37–38.

Peck, Richard. "The Silver Anniversary of Young Adult Books," *Journal of Youth Services in Libraries* (Fall 1993): 19–23.

Poe, Elizabeth Ann.; Samuels, Barbara G.; Carter, Betty, "Twenty-Five Years of Research in Young Adult Literature: Past Perspectives and Future Directions," *Journal of Youth Services in Libraries*, v. 7 (Fall 1993): 65–73.

Reed, Aretha. *Reaching Adolescents: the Young Adult Book and the School.* New York: Maxwell Macmillan, 1994.

Small, Robert. "The Literary Value of the YA Novel," *Journal of Youth Services in Libraries* (Spring 1992): 227–285.

> **"** The majority of collection use by YAs has very little to do with YA literature. **"**

Most books on YA literature cover the history of the literature, discuss major trends, and list significant titles. Donelson and Nilsen's *Literature for Today's Young Adults* and Michael Cart's *From Romance to Realism* probably are the two best books of this type. Donelson and Nilsen's tome is a standard text in library schools and in education courses, and Cart's should and will be. Donelson and Nilsen have sections that discuss use of YA literature which librarians might find practical, but their focus is more academic. Cart's book is "young adult literature—history and criticism" to a tee: dissecting books, authors, trends, and themes throughout the history of YA literature and making some predictions on its future.

The few library school courses with the term "young adult" in the title often focus primarily on YA literature. There might be a session on booktalking and discussion of popular fiction, maybe even some magazines, but most of the time goes to discussing classic YA literature. The majority of collection use by YAs has very little to do with YA literature. During a given day, the percent of a YA librarian's time dealing with YA literature is minimal: more time will be spent fielding questions for research papers, answering inquiries for homework, and enforcing discipline.

Writing in her last "YA Perplex" column for *Wilson Library Bulletin,* Patty Campbell noted that:

> Young adult literature is alive and well in the bookstores, but it is a different young adult literature . . . Nowadays every Borders, B. Dalton and Waldens have sections labeled "Young Adult" but the books that are found there are of far lower quality and aimed at much younger readers than those that are found on the similarly labeled shelves in public libraries. With the exception of Judy Blume, their Big Names are not our Big Names. The whole field has become strangely bifurcated and we seem to be moving in the direction of two separate literatures. [1]

Rather than two literatures, there are really four areas—literature, popular materials, information sources, and products. Of these subsets of books for young adults, perhaps YA literature is the smallest, defining it as the quality, hardback novels which show up in our reviewing sources. Library school students study that literature and librarians put it on the Best Books for Young Adult list, but it primarily is not what YAs read. YA popular materials are that glut of mass-market paperbacks found in bookstores and libraries.

Some YA products, we (and YAs) recognize instantly: series romances, thrillers and the like that sell primarily because they bear a certain brand name, such as *Sweet Valley High.* Zollo's research repeatedly points out the importance of branding in the YA market.

The printed materials most often used by YAs are information sources (books, articles, etc.) often for recreational reasons, but also read as a means to an end. Further, perhaps the most popular YA items in libraries are often not even books. Many more YAs want the new Boyz II Men CD, information off the Internet, a gaming CD-ROM, or a basketball videotape rather than Cynthia Voigt's new "best" book.

Some materials YAs use might not even be part of a YA collection. In addition to reference books, best-sellers and other popular adult authors are the grist of YA reading. John Grisham did not become the second most popular author of the 1990s (lagging behind R.L. Stine) because he sold books to adults; lots of YAs know and read his work. The core audience for Stephen King always has been teenagers. Danielle Steel, Mary Higgins Clark, and the rest of the best-seller list are of great interest to YAs. For many YAs, all that matters is the latest offering of science fiction and fantasy writers like Robert Jordan and David Eddings. It is a stereotype, however, to plug every YA reader as a fantasy buff just as much as it is to think they all read Richard Peck: YAs have a variety of reading interests.

Review of Reading Interest Surveys

1. Girls are the primary YA readers.
2. Periodicals are the most popular format.
3. YAs' interest in periodicals increases with age.
4. Although surveys vary, romance is the popular genre, followed by mysteries.
5. Science fiction has a consistent following of around 10 percent.
6. Paperbacks are the preferred format for books.
7. Subject of the book is what kids "like best" about a book.
8. Newspapers interest about 20 percent of YAs.

4.2 READING RESEARCH

Research about reading interests is essential. Without research, we can rely only on intuition. Intuition still is driving the engine, but research gives us the information we need to be customer focused. We can give YAs what they want because we know—not think we know—what they want.

A tremendous amount of research is done on reading interests, habits, attitudes and choices that speaks directly to libraries and young adults, but rarely rates a mention in our professional literature. The answers to many of our questions (such as "Should we have comic books?") are out there in the data.

Research answers the basic questions of who, what, how, and why. From research, we learn *what* structural elements YAs like in books, but also that YAs like books they can react to affectively. *How* a person reacts to book has many factors, but two certainly are gender and grade. *Who* reads, of course, directly impacts what is read. *When* data are available that allow us to looks at popular authors and genres and relate that to gender and age.

The Power of Reading

1. Access to a school library results in more reading.
2. Having a school librarian makes a difference in the amount of reading a YA does.
3. Larger school library collections and longer hours increase circulation.
4. Larger school library collections mean better results in high-reading scores.
5. Access to public libraries positively affects reading.
6. Libraries are a consistent and major source of books for free reading.
7. Magazine reading promotes more reading.
8. Young people's reading choices are influenced by their peers.
9. Young people prefer paperbacks to hardback books.
10. Comic book reading is not responsible for anti-social behavior.
11. General library use increases when comic books are available.
12. Comic books lead to other reading.
13. Reading teen romances generally promotes reading.
14. Television is not the culprit in the "literary crisis"; rather, the absence of good books is to blame

Adapted from Stephen Krashen, *The Power of Reading: Insights from the Research.* Englewood, CO: Libraries Unlimited, 1993.

What Do YAs Like?

AUTHORS: Betty Carter, Hollis Lowery-Moore, and Barbara Samuels
SOURCE: *ALAN Review* (Spring 1993): 52–55.
AUDIENCE: 2,367 participants in Young Adult Choices project
FINDINGS: Answers to the question "What did you like about this book?"

Category	% of Total 1987	% of Total 1988
Affective	28	34
Character	8	8
Content	.07	1
Genre	10	11
Illustrations	4	–
Plot	17	14
Setting	.03	1
Style	17	18
Subject	11	8
Thomo	0	4

Who Is Reading?

AUTHOR: Mary Moffer and Ellen Wartella
SOURCE: *Reading Research and Instruction* (Winter 1992): 1–17
AUDIENCE: Five high schools in central Illinois
FINDINGS:

Readers vs. Nonreaders by Grade Level

Grade	Readers	Nonreaders
9th	76%	24%
10th	73%	27%
11th	78%	22%
12th	86%	14%
TOTAL	78%	22%

Readers vs. Nonreaders by Gender

Gender	Readers	Nonreaders
Boys	65%	35%
Girls	85%	15%

Readers by Grade Point Average

GPA	Readers	Nonreaders
A	83%	17%
B	82%	18%
C	63%	37%
D	60%	40%

What Are YAs Reading? (By Category)
AUTHOR: Rick Traw
SOURCE: *Nothing in the Middle: What Middle Schoolers Are Reading.* ERIC Document #384864 (1993).
AUDIENCE: 55 8th graders from the Midwest reporting on books (627 total) they read.
FINDINGS:

Category	# Books Read
Teen issues	79
Romance	72
Mystery/suspense	61
Supernatural/horror	54
Fantasy	42
Science fiction	31
Historical fiction	17
Biography/autobiography	12
Adventure	9
Nonfiction	7
Humor	6

What Are YAs Reading? (Genres and Authors)
AUTHOR: Kathleen Isaacs
SOURCE: *New Advocate* (Spring 1992): 129–143.
AUDIENCE: Independent school in suburban Baltimore, survey of grades 6–8
FINDINGS:

Age of the Books
"Perhaps the most astonishing results . . . was the age of the books these students read most often. Over half their top twenty . . . were books published before 1980."

Favorite Topics
"Most of theses students liked suspense and horror stories."
"A small number of very prolific readers, almost all boys, concentrated on science fiction and high fantasy."
"Stories of family, school and camp life are always popular."

Favorite Authors
Piers Anthony—"most popular"
Lois Duncan—"appealed to both boys and girls across three grades"
Stephen King—"chosen by 7th and 8th graders, both boys and girls"
Judy Blume—"they have been reading her books for years"
Paula Danziger—"it is mostly girls—in all three grades—who read her"
J.R.R. Tolkion "boys are more likely to read . . . very loyal readers"
S.E. Hinton—"only . . . eighth graders"
V.C. Andrews—"described as 'addictive to read' by one student"
Cynthia Voigt—"readers are 6th and 7th grade girls who enjoy identifying"
Robert Cormier—"almost exclusively read by boys"
Agatha Christie—"readers have been mostly eighth grade boys"

What Are YAs Reading? (By Grade, Gender, and Category)
AUTHOR: Sandra K. Fronius
SOURCE: *Reading Interest of Middle Schoolers in Medina County, Ohio* (1993)
                ERIC Document #367337
AUDIENCE: 538 students from Midwestern suburban public library
FINDINGS:

Participation in Reading Program, by Grade Level

Grade	% Participation
6th	3%
7th	40%
8th	34%
9th	14%
10th	6%
11th	3%

Reading by Genre and Grade Level

Genre	6th	7th	8th	9th	10th	11th
Realistic	54%	42%	37%	37%	22%	20%
Mystery	20%	13%	21%	19%	31%	26%
Horror	-	9%	14%	18%	3%	7%
Humor	-	9%	3%	-	6%	7%
Nonfiction	13%	9%	9%	6%	-	7%
Fantasy	13%	5%	3%	6%	-	13%
Romance	-	5%	9%	4%	19%	7%
Historical	-	4%	1%	1%	6%	-
Sci fi	-	3%	2%	7%	13%	13%

Breakdown by Gender and Most Popular

Genre	Girls	Boys
Realistic	44%	10%
Mystery	18%	23%
Horror	12%	8%
Romance	8%	—
Nonfiction	7%	15%

Humor	3%	12%
Fantasy	3%	11%
Historical	3%	1%
Sci fi	1%	19%

Librarians and YAs choose books differently, which is no big surprise. That may be one reason why YAs do not turn to librarians for advice in finding new reading materials. The other reasons vary: part of it is image; part of it is just a YA thing. Young children (and their parents) rely on librarians much more than YAs—in part because younger children are not as set in either their reading attitudes or behaviors as high school students. Taken together, this research demonstrates that YAs are a diverse group in terms of reading—what they like, what they read, how they find out about reading material, and how they feel about it.

How YAs Choose Books
AUTHOR: Jeanne Gerlack
SOURCE: *Reading Horizons* (April 1992): 289–298.
AUDIENCE: 31 7th and 8th graders from a large, middle-class suburban public
                school
FINDINGS:

Criteria for Selecting Books

Criterion	% Responses
Summary inside flap	49%
Cover illustration	22%
Title	18%
Interest in topic	9%
Size of print	1%
Vocabulary level	1%

How Do YAs Find out about New Books?
AUTHOR: Don Gallo
SOURCE: *American Libraries* (November 1985) : 736+.
AUDIENCE: Students grades 4–12 in Connecticut
FINDINGS:

Method of Discovery	Grades 7–9	Grades 10–12
Friends' suggestions	42%	38%
Browsing in store	28%	31%
Browsing in library	27%	18%
Store display	7%	8%
Library display	5%	5%
Librarians	4%	2%

What Are YA Attitudes about Reading?
AUTHOR: Terry Ley and Terry Mitchell
SOURCE: *Reading Psychology* (Vol. 17, 1996): 65–92.
AUDIENCE: Students grades 9–12 in a southern industrial community
FINDINGS:

1. "Females reported significantly more positive attitudes toward reading . . . than did males."
2. "High school students in this study valued reading principally for achieving success in school."
3. "As grade level increased, students increasingly perceive reading not only as a means of attaining success in school but also as a tool that provides insight into self and others."
4. "Even those high school students who most value reading for enjoyment valued reading even more for its contribution to success in school or to personal development."
5. "Students reported low levels of recent voluntary reading activity at all levels."

4.3 READING INTERESTS

Maybe your community is different from those reported on in this chapter. You may see a marked interest in science fiction or have decidedly more male readers. The best way to document the interest in your library is to gather the data yourself, using a reading interest survey like the one shown in Figure 4–1. Doing this will consist of six steps:

1. Stating the objectives of the survey. (What do you want to learn?)
2. Designing the survey. (How will you learn it?)
3. Distributing the survey. (Who will complete the survey?)
4. Tabulating the survey. (What kind of results did you get?)
5. Analyzing the survey. (What does the data tell you?)
6. Taking action. (What will you do with the information?)

Figure 4–1 The Reading Interest Survey

Reading Interest Survey

AGE: SCHOOL: GRADE: MALE   FEMALE

We are interested in providing you with the very best reading materials, but we need your help. Please take a moment and fill out this survey and tell us what *you* want.

1. Which of these is your favorite to read?
    - (   )   Magazines (list your favorites on the back of this sheet!)
    - (   )   Newspapers
    - (   )   Books
    - (   )   Comic books

2. With books do you prefer:
    - (   )   Fiction
    - (   )   Nonfiction (true stories/biographies, etc.)

3. Which types of fiction do you like best?
    - (   )   Adventure
    - (   )   Historical
    - (   )   Fantasy
    - (   )   Horror
    - (   )   Humor
    - (   )   Mystery
    - (   )   Romance
    - (   )   Science Fiction
    - (   )   Sports
    - (   )   Teen problems
    - (   )   Other:

4. Which types of nonfiction do you like best?
    - (   )   Health
    - (   )   History
    - (   )   Music, TV, movies
    - (   )   Biographies
    - (   )   Poetry
    - (   )   "Coping" with teen problems
    - (   )   Other:

Please add any other comments about your library on the back of this sheet. Thank you.

The results of this survey will help you set collection development priorities. You can distribute the survey to every single YA in the community through the schools or hand it out randomly, if you choose. If your library has a teen Web page, publish the survey there. Regardless, this survey can provide you with some hard data to make hard choices necessary to develop a YA collection. This survey should not be a one-time thing, however; reading interests change, and those differences need noting.

4.4 COLLECTION QUESTIONS

What kind of YA collection do you want? A YA section is usually small enough that you can change it over a short period of time to meet someone's particular vision. What is your vision? That vision will be influenced by the following factors:

1. Your library's total collection development philosophy
2. The quality and quantity of school library collections
3. The budget, space, and staff available in your library
4. The reading interests of YAs in your community
5. Your own professional values
6. The needs that the YA collection should meet
7. Your goals for the collection
8. The roles the library has chosen for itself

Despite, or maybe because of, your "vision" for the collection, you need to set priorities because doing it all is not possible. Most people think a "balanced collection" is a desirable thing; however, if you really want to set priorities and concentrate your efforts, funds, and space on certain areas, the collection will be out of balance. The whole battle about collection balance (popularity vs. quality; breadth vs. depth) involves some basic philosophical issues.[2] Let's first look at some collection development choices, emphasizing the YA aspects. The following issues will help you focus on what you feel is important for your YA collections.

COLLECTION CHOICES

In creating, enhancing, or revising your YA collections, you must consider the answers to a number of questions about collection priorities. The issues in this section help you explore your vision for YA collections.

Demand vs. Quality: The oldest debate needs to be settled first. Here are the questions to consider:

- Do you buy series paperbacks?
- Do you buy multiple copies?
- If you have money to buy only one book and you must choose between a popular book and a quality one, which one would you choose?

Circulation vs. Standards: Does the library have a "responsibility" to provide YAs with materials of only high literary quality? These questions further target this issue:

- Is it to quantify an increase in circulation or the literary standards being upheld?
- How do you measure a book's "value" to the collection?
- Is "Will it move?" the only selection criteria?
- Will a book's appearance on a "best books" list merit its purchase and/or its place on the shelf?

Permanency vs. Immediacy: What should the turnover rate be in a YA collection? Should you stock it with hardbacks that will last decades and create a permanent YA collection, or should you fill it with books that meet immediate reading interests but, due to paperback format, will survive only two years? Both types are needed, but given the fact that most YA areas—and budgets—are small, my guess is that even if teens do not prefer the paperback format, librarians will.

Recreational vs. Educational vs. Information vs. Cultural: This choice ties into the roles libraries choose. This decision also hinges on the strength of the school library collections. Does the adult reference department buy sufficient copies of materials needed by YAs? What type of YA nonfiction is in the YA area?

Professional vs. Careful: This choice is the old debate about professional values, personal opinions, and community standards. The bottom line is this: should you buy YA materials that you and most adults object to, but YAs love? Here are more questions to ask along this line:

- Do you respond to your customers (YAs) or to "supporters in the community"?
- Do you buy rap music?
- Would you buy a professional wrestling magazine, a skateboarding magazine, or a tattoo magazine?
- Do you buy Stephen King for the YA collection?
- Do you collect books for gay and lesbian teens?

Librarian vs. Book Buyer: If your focus is popular reading, have you forsaken your "professionalism" to become a glorified Waldenbooks book buyer? A group of YAs could probably select a more responsive collection than many librarians (myself included) charged with developing YA collections. These are the questions you must wrestle with:

- Which parts of YA book selection take some degree of professional judgment?
- Is the best selector the person who selects the most titles that end up on a "best books" list or the one who selects all the YA best-sellers?

Customers vs. Collections (and Other Customers): A customer service centered process puts the customer first, and yet quality is an important issue. As librarians, we may have a different definition of quality than our customers. How is one way to measure satisfaction in customers? Circulation of materials. Part of a quality collection, admittedly, is diversity. An all *Fear Street* collection might be popular, but you would be missing out on serving many other customers if that is all you carry.

> " Obviously, limited resources should go toward materials of the highest quality. The question, is, however, "What is quality?" "

The ideas covered in this section should help you uncover your attitudes about collections. You can see what you think is important and how you would spend resources in your YA department. Obviously, limited resources should go toward materials of the highest quality. The question, is, however, "What is quality?" The next section takes a look at quality in terms of YA collections.

COLLECTION QUALITY

Here's the scenario: It is near the end of your fiscal year and you have dollars, literally just a few dollars, available to spend on books for young adults. On your desk, you have Bookmen's *Monthly Paperback News* and the latest issue of *Booklist*. You have $14.95 to spend—you can buy one of these hardback offerings, or several of the paperbacks. Some of the paperbacks are not only reprints of hardbacks, but originals, and most are part of a series. Where is that money going to go?

This is not really a choice about $14.95; it is instead the battle between quality and popularity. Deciding to buy the paperback series is really the result of a series of choices you have already made, in answer to the question "How does our library fulfill its role as a popular materials center?"

Let's change the debate from quality-vs.-popularity to quality-vs.-quality. One way to define quality is to measure success. One way to measure success is to measure library use. We can measure library use by tracking circulation—and one factor in circulation is the popularity of materials available; that is, providing materials that have a brand name popularity. Again, we are back to series paperbacks.

Libraries can only do so much. There is only so much money, so each choice on how to spend that money is a value decision. What do libraries value? YA services have a core set of values, one of which is "responsiveness." Although the most recent vision statement by the Young Adult Library Services Association does not use this word *per se*, it is a theme throughout the vision. Responsiveness means many things, but one thing it surely means is "giving them what they want."

Directions for Library Service to Young Adults also makes the case for responsive services, manifested by the purchase of materials in paperback series, in this passage:

> Collections for teenagers must appeal to their popular, current and ephemeral interests. Paperback series . . . will find avid teen audiences. Paperback books are typically more appealing to teenagers than hardcover books.[3]

Although it doesn't say so implicitly, *Bare Bones: Young Adult Services Tips for Public Library Generalists* discusses the need for popular materials in a public library and this includes series books. Silk Makowski's article, "Serious about Series: Selection Criteria for a Neglected Genre," presents a case for series fiction. In this article, Makowski describes the characteristics of this series genre, and then offers a multi-part answer to the question of "Why buy them?" Makowski prepared this article by reading "three installments of every teen paperback series I could get my hands on." [4] Cosette Kies in "Eeek; They Just Keep Coming! YA Horror Series" offered an overview (with a buying list) for horror/thriller series. The article is by no means a defense of series. In fact, Kies writes:

> There is slightly more acceptance . . . by adults because the kids are reading them, even if they may read little else through choice. Alas, a pessimistic thought to use for the ending of this piece.[5]

Kies' comment seems indicative of proponents of the reading escalator theory. Series books (or any popular fiction) are only good as a means to an end—to move the reader from the "substandard" to something of higher quality. Just reading them as an end, not a means, gets labeled "pessimistic." There are many examples of this schism in action, perhaps the most obvious being the wide difference between the books that YAs think are "best" and those YA librarians identify as best.[6] The difference in lists and attitudes stems from differences in values and definitions of quality.

Again, that word *quality* rears its ugly head. Perhaps reading of any kind by any teenager in a world so chock full of other options is quality. Perhaps series fiction provides teenagers with the type of reading experience they want at a particular time of their lives, and once

Criteria for Evaluating Series Fiction

1. Kids like them.
2. They fill a collection need.
3. They provide for collection development with the least output of time and money.
4. It is the duty of the professional to know YA needs.
5. They improve circulation.

Adapted from Silk Makowski's, "Serious About Series: Selection Criteria of a Neglected Genre," *Voice of Youth Advocates* (February 1994): 349–351.

How Does Series Fiction Meet the Needs of YAs?

1. Reassures them they are normal physically, mentally, emotionally, and socially
2. Presents opportunities for emotional independence from adults
3. Shows them how to resolve problems
4. Allows them to experience success
5. Helps them picture satisfying relationships
6. Provides help in establishing roles
7. Supports development of socially responsible behaviors
8. Helps them work out their personal philosophies
9. Furnishes opportunities for emotional engagement, pleasure, and relaxation

Adapted from "Meeting Kids' Emotional Needs Through Books," by Pat Scales (handout, Reading Connections Conference): Indiana Dept. of Education, 1993.

that time in their life has passed, they will move on to something else. Not because they want to move to "quality" literature, but because series reading no longer meets their emotional or recreational needs. And that is, in the final analysis, why series are popular and why series belong in libraries: they meet the needs of kids.

What are the emotional needs of YA readers? Take a look at the list of what younger adolescents (the primary series audience) are looking for in series fiction and you will see an almost perfect match with what happens in most of the *Fear Street* titles. You could run the same list with a *Sweet Valley High*, the various V.C. Andrews books, or almost any other series and find the same result: series books are responsive to kids' emotional needs.

The choices YA librarians are making about series are therefore similar to those that adult librarians make as well—not "Do we buy Danielle Steel?" but rather, "How many copies?" This involves a lot of hand-wringing about "soiling" our shelves with such "trash." Libraries and librarians often feel they have a higher mission to save people from their own bad reading choices, but sometimes that line of thinking hides in the argument "Well, at least they are reading something." The problem with that attitude is it tells the readers of that "something" that it really lacks value and thus the subtle message is that the readers themselves lack value. It sets up a caste system of reading, which is insulting, absurd, and counterproductive.

The only bad reading choice is the choice not to read, which is a choice many YAs make. The best thing libraries can do to influence that choice is provide materials that YAs want to read. The best type of material for YAs to read are materials that meet their needs, have proven popular, have peer approval, and lead them to reading something else, even if it is only another book exactly like the one they have finished.

4.5 SETTING PRIORITIES

You are probably getting a clear idea about what a library could and should mean in terms of its collections. Part of your vision is tied to having unlimited funds, which is never the reality of YA departments. The first step in creating a quality YA collection is to set some priorities. After defining what is important to you, you need to see how that fits your budget. The smaller the budget, the more important this priority setting becomes. For example, if you are given $5,000 to spend on YA materials (an insult to some, a dream to others), what would you do with it? Use Figure 4–2 to work through your answer to this question in light of your YA collection priorities.

Figure 4–2 Setting Your YA Collection Priorities

BUDGET: $5,000

Show how you would spend your YA budget on the various categories listed here.

PRINT: _____

NONPRINT _____

I. PRINT _____

BOOKS _____

MAGAZINES _____

A. BOOKS _____

FICTION _____

NONFICTION _____

1. FICTION _____

HARDBACKS _____

PAPERBACKS _____

STANDING ORDERS _____

MONTHLY PURCHASES _____

2. NONFICTION _____

RECREATION _____

INFORMATION _____

EDUCATION _____

STANDING ORDERS _____

MONTHLY PURCHASES _____

B. MAGAZINES _____

II. NONPRINT _____

A. LISTENING _____

TAPES _____

COMPACT DISCS _____

B. VIEWING _____

C. SOFTWARE _____

The results of this exercise might surprise you. Some categories you may have skipped altogether. You buy only what is a priority. There are practical trade-offs: For example, taking $75 from the book budget and spending it on magazines probably means buying five fewer hardbacks in exchange for at least five magazine subscriptions. With a small collection, a change in focus can really have impact.

One of the great potential benefits of the Internet is how it might free up more funds for print materials. Will libraries really need to spend money buying, for example, lots of college handbooks and directories when so many are available gratis via the Web? The Internet might, by becoming the leading source of "information," give librarians a chance to spend more time, effort, and resources developing print collections. Seen in this light, the information superhighway won't destroy the "fair garden" our libraries represent; it just might improve them.

4.6 FICTION

The lifeblood of any YA department is normally the fiction collection. YAs use nonfiction books from other parts of the library, but most looking for recreational and assigned fiction reading end up in the YA area. Knowing YA fiction becomes more difficult as publishers change, series start and stop, and one year's trend is killed off by the next year. This section spotlights some of the issues you need to consider as you put together YA fiction collections.

HARDBACKS

Bookstores don't stock them, reading interest surveys and casual observation show most YAs don't read them, yet libraries buy hardbacks. Some libraries have greatly reduced purchases in this area and reallocated more money toward paperbacks, periodicals, and nonprint items. Some libraries have stopped buying hardbacks altogether, but not everyone is willing or able to do that. What should you look for in the hardbacks you do buy?

Author: If it is Cooney, Crutcher, Cormier, Woodson, or any of the other top authors, buy it. If the author is always showing up on lists and has a mass appeal, take the plunge. If it is an adult author with YA appeal like King or Koontz, YAs will know about it and you will need to have it.

Controversy: If the book is getting wildly mixed reviews (e.g., *Tenderness* by Robert Cormier), it is worth a look and maybe a purchase.

**Top 30 YA Authors
(A Personal Opinion)**

1. Avi
2. Bennett, James
3. Block, Francesca Lia
4. Brooks, Bruce
5. Cooney, Caroline
6. Cormier, Robert
7. Crutcher, Chris
8. Cushman, Karen
9. Grant, Cynthia
10. Hobbs, Will
11. Hoh, Diane
12. Kerr, M.E.
13. Lasky, Katherine
14. Lynch, Chris
15. Marsden, John
16. Meyer, Carolyn
17. Myers, Walter Dean
18. Paulsen, Gary
19. Peck, Richard
20. Pfeffer, Susan Beth
21. Pike, Christopher
22. Pullman, Philip
23. Sleator, William
24. Stine, R.L.
25. Thomas, Rob
26. Vail, Rachel
27. Voigt, Cynthia
28. Williams-Garcia, Rita
29. Woodson, Jacqueline
30. Zindel, Paul

On a list: If the book is on a YALSA list, it should at least be considered.

Built-in audience: Despite the format, some hardbacks have built-in audiences because of the subject.

Great cover: If you can actually examine the book—or if the reviewer has—the cover might be a selling point. "You can't judge a book by its cover," but for YAs, you can use it to estimate the popularity.

Too good: Of course, then a book like *The Silver Kiss* by Annette Curtis Klause, *Deliver Us from Evie* by M.E. Kerr, or *Rule of the Bone* by Russell Banks comes out and blows all these reasons away.

The smaller the budget, the harder you look at each purchase. If you spend $16, how can you justify it? If every book has to earn its place on the shelf, the question is "What can this hardback bring to your collection, your YA population, and your circulation that several paperbacks or a magazine subscription cannot?"

PAPERBACKS

The advantages to a primarily paperback YA fiction collection are numerous, including:

Preferred format: For reading in the library, for checking out, for hiding in textbooks, for stealing, for everything.

Multiple copy option: The low cost means more copies of a hot title.

Meet fluctuating demand: All those Hammer or Vanilla Ice paperbacks you bought a few years ago no one wants to touch now. But because publishers use paperback to latch onto fads, libraries follow.

Cost: Is it more costly to buy and replace five copies of a title in paperback or keep a reserve list for the hardback copy? Is using Econoclad or Permabound most cost-effective?

Shelving: Paperbacks are the hubs of merchandising (see page 116). Because of their size, you can cram more of them attractively into a small area.

Covers and blurbs: Hardback covers interest readers, and the paperback cover excites them. The blurbs on the back are shorter, more like ad copy than the longer annotations on hardback covers.

Series: Series fiction is highly popular and normally available only in paperback format.

Every month about 50 mass market YA paperbacks are published: some are originals, some reprints, and the rest part of a series. In addition, mass market adult, humor, science fiction/fantasy, and movie tie-in titles are published which have YA appeal. Also demanding your dollars are copies in need of replacing due to theft or damage, books on reading lists, and older titles of popular authors.

A Merchandising Plan

I.   Collection development

    A. Weeding
1.   Make room for new purchases
2.   Have more space for display
3.   Does book "earn" its place on shelf?
4.   Sales per square foot: is space being used for maximum sales and circulation?
5.   Weed books that are tattered, without covers, etc. Replace with paperback versions.

    B. Selection
1.   Paperbacks, paperbacks, paperbacks
2.   Magazines
3.   Hot nonfiction
4.   Browsing items

II. Shelving

    A. Current
1.   Each shelf needs end space to display
2.   Rearrange to create more shelving

    B. New
1.   Zig zag
2.   Bookstore style slanted shelves
3.   Bookdumps: cardboard and permanent
4.   Shelf end display racks

III. Displays

    A. Current
1.   Table or shelf top
2.   Put in high traffic area
3.   Use floor, book trucks, etc.

    B. New
1.   Cubes or display units
2.   Book easels
3.   Container to hold/display lists

    C. Responsibilities
1.   Scheduling/planning/creating
2.   Shelving/maintaining

    D. Creating
1.   Use props
2.   Use signs
3.   Covers face out
4.   Multiple copies
5.   Eye level and in sight line
6.   Active, keep filled
7.   Change regularly
8.   Sign saying materials *can* be checked out
9.   Gimmicks
10. Interactive

Let's look at some of the more popular series and genres currently available. Although the market changes and changes fast, the categories outlined in the table Current YA Series seem to remain consistent in their popularity.

Table 4–1 Current YA Series
SOURCE: Bookmen's *Monthly Paperback News* (1/96 - 12/96)

Series	Author	Publisher	Genre
Baywatch Sprinters	Alicia Baldwin	Bullseye	Romance/Adventure
Code Blue	Lisa Rojany	Harper	Adventure
Dear Diary	Cheryl Zach	Berkley	Realistic
Distress Call	D.L. Carey	Pocket	Adventure
Fear Street	R.L. Stine	Pocket	Thriller
Hardy Boys Casefiles	Franklin Dixon	Pocket	Mystery
Hear No Evil	Kate Chester	Scholastic	Thriller
Last Vampire	Christopher Pike	Pocket	Horror
Love Stories	Alexis Page	Bantam	Romance
Med Center	Diane Hoh	Scholastic	Adventure
Nancy Drew Files	Carolyn Keene	Pocket	Mystery
Nancy Drew on Campus	Carolyn Keene	Pocket	Mystery
Night World	L.J. Smith	Pocket	Horror
Rebel Angels	Jahnna Malcolm	Harper	Romance/Adventure
Star War: Young Jedi	Kevin Anderson	Boulevard	Science Fiction
Summer	Kathleen Applegate	Pocket	Romance
Sweet Valley High	Francine Pascal	Bantam	Romance
Sweet Valley University	Francine Pascal	Bantam	Romance
Teen Angels	Cherie Bennett	Avon	Romance/Adventure
X-Files	Lee Martin	Harper	Science Fiction/Horror

TYPES OF SERIES

Girls' romances: The boom is certainly over because many of the old standbys (*Cheerleaders, Sweet Dreams,* etc.) have ceased publication, and even those hanging on don't seem to dominate the market as they once did.

Boys' series: Lots of publishers have tried, but except for *Hardy Boys' Casefiles,* none of the series have lasted.

Thriller series: After a decade of dominance, the YA thriller is just about dead, to which many—librarians, teachers, and even some teens—are happy to exclaim "Rest in peace." Whatever your opinion of YA thrillers, they were the dominant genre of the past decade. Like most teen fads, its success and overexposure led to its eventual downfall. When Stine and Pike started writing middle school thrillers, YA thrillers got the kiss of death.

Zollo, in writing about the rise and fall of MC Hammer, noted how his YA star "fell" as he became involved in product endorsements and Saturday morning cartoon shows. The same happened here. Suddenly a 14–year-old who read R.L. Stine caught on to the fact that his little brothers and sisters were reading the same author, and worse than that, toys and board games and fast-food kids' meal prizes were based on Stine characters.

BUYING SERIES

Getting information: You cannot count on the review media to publish data on series, even when a new series comes out. The monthly jobber catalogs, like Bookmen's *Monthly Paperback News,* will keep you current and most will enable you to place series on standing order. You need to investigate how they handle new series or spin-offs of old series.

Replacements: Series paperbacks have a short shelf life. Not just because of the poor quality of the binding, but also because they get passed around a lot. It is important to keep a full run of the most popular series. Just because *SVH* is up to number 80 does not mean that there isn't someone just starting the series that wants to read the first 10.

SHELVING SERIES

Although most YA paperbacks are showcased best in some sort of face-front unit, *SVH* and series like it do not need that kind of exposure. Normal library shelving adjusted to paperback height and depth serves the purpose just fine. There is no need for any signage or poster because a row of *SVH* with numbers 1 to 130 lined up will attract attention and meet the series patron's need.

GENRES

A subject of a book and/or its genre is one of the biggest selling points for a YA title. Many libraries shelve all paperbacks by genre rather than by author, or they provide extensive finding aids such as booklists to help students locate certain types of fiction books. YALSA got into the genre act by working with Baker & Taylor to produce genre book dumps based on the suggestions of YALSA genre committees. Committees produced several different lists [7-10] during this project. The genre committees were replaced by "popular reading" committees covering books more by format (graphic novels/picture books) or subject (homosexuality). Like series, genres change in popularity and sometimes some types of books will be more in demand than others, but here are the basic groups with suggested top 10 buying list:

Horror

YAs love scary movies and scary books, but unfortunately there are few good YA horror writers. Pike and Stine primarily write thrillers with some elements of horror, but they are normally not true horror. There are exceptions, like Pike's *Last Vampire* series and most of Stine's *Fear Street* trilogies and superchillers, but most are thrillers: a slick interweaving of mystery, suspense, and horror. Series like *Horror High* again are really more thrillers, but works by L.J. Smith and a few other YA authors give no pretense to realism, dwelling in the land of vampires and the supernatural that perhaps more characterizes horror fiction. Still, the most popular writers are adult authors like Stephen King, which has its share of problems. If YAs have read all of King, finding other adult authors for YAs is not an easy task. Once you start looking at the use of language, sex, and violence in these other works, King becomes mild. Anne Rice is hugely popular, although one suspects for very different reasons; it may be as much for her eroticism as horror.

Realistic Fiction—the Problem Novel

Sometimes it seems as though there is more suicide, incest, and divorce in YA novels than in YA life. The trend continues to be to combine problems. So now instead of a book about a teen alcoholic, the book might have a teen alcoholic with an anorexic sister who is having suicidal thoughts because their parents have just divorced. Also writers like Chris Crutcher and Chris Lynch [11] are using the sports novel as a jumping off point for hard hitting realistic fiction about young men. Most problem novels follow a model whereby a character has a problem or comes to that realization and then seeks to solve it. The one constant in almost all YA fiction is that the problem resolves, the protagonist grows, and life is good. One of the better problem novels over the past few years was *Crosses* by Shelley Stoehr[12] where this formula ending was a problem in itself. After 150 pages of tough stuff, the main character finds herself at the end quickly whisked away on the road to recovery. This kind of ending is found all too often in YA fiction, mainly because of the audience. YAs say they want realistic stories, but they also want successful conclusions: Hollywood endings. Thus, writers, publishers, and reviewers all try to figure out, like a chemistry experiment, the proper formula of problem and solution. This section lists the issues taken on in realistic YA fiction:

Sex: If Judy Blume's *Forever* is not the most read, then it contains the most read pages (p. 57 for example) of any YA novel in history. This book might not have the most circulation, but chances are it is the one that is most stolen, most beaten up, most often found anyplace but where it is supposed to be shelved, and most in need of replacement. Consequently, it is still one of the most challenged books. One of the major criticisms of *Forever* is its negative portrayal of a gay character, but the past years have seen an increase in novels about positive gay and lesbian characters, with two story collections about coming out stories showing up on the BBYA list. Another major trend is novels about sexual abuse. In many cases, it is not the YA who is abused but rather a friend or sibling. Some feature "repressed memories" and often involve a confrontation scene, which often explode into violence. Finally, novels featuring pregnant teenagers, many from the small press Morning Glory, remain popular.

Books about Sex and Sexuality (Mostly Fiction): Bib Squib

Am I Blue?: Coming Out from the Silence. Marion Dane Bauer (Editor). New York: Trophy Press. (ISBN 0064405877) $5.95

Davis, Jenny. *Sex Education : A Novel.* New York: Bantam (ISBN 0440204836) $3.99

Fenwick, Elizabeth. *How Sex Works : A Clear, Comprehensive Guide for Teenagers to Emotional, Physical, and Sexual Maturity.* New York: Dorling-Kindersley. (ISBN 0789406349) $9.95.

Garden, Nancy. *Annie on My Mind.* New York: Farrar Straus & Giroux (ISBN 0374404143) $3.95.

Kerr, M.E. *Deliver Us from Evie.* New York: Harper (ISBN 0064471284) $3.95

Rodowsky, Colby. *Lucy Peale.* New York: Farrar Straus & Giroux (ISBN 0374446598) $3.95

Solin, Sabrina. *The Seventeen Guide to Sex and Your Body.* New York: Aladdin (ISBN 0689807953) $8.99.

Stoehr, Shelley. *Weird on the Outside.* New York: Dell (ISBN 0440220106) $3.99

Woodson, Jacqueline. *I Hadn't Meant to Tell You This.* New York: Laurel-Leaf Books (ISBN 0440219604) $3.99

Wurmfeld, Hope. *Baby Blues.* New York: Puffin (ISBN 0140348700) $3.99

Substance abuse: The "Just say no" message is being buried inside many books these days, as opposed to the direct approach of a book like Shep Greene's *The Boy Who Drank Too Much*. Almost every book featuring YAs doing drugs or drinking contains severe, tragic consequences. Few books include casual drug use, with characters that use drugs or alcohol and do not have it screw up their lives.

Books about Substance Abuse (Mostly Fiction): Bib Squib

Cadnum, Michael. *Calling Home*. New York: Puffin (ISBN 0140345698) $3.99

Covington, Dennis . *Lasso the Moon*. New York: Dell (ISBN 0440220130) $4.50

Engel, Joel. *Addicted : In Their Own Words : Kids Talking About Drugs*. New York: Tor Books. (ISBN 0812594460) $3.95

Ferry, Charles. *Binge*. Daisyhill Press (ISBN 0963279904) $8.95

Heuer, Marti. *Teen Addiction*. New York: Ballantine. (ISBN 0345362829) $4.99

Lynch, Chris. *Blood Relations* (Blue Eyed Son, #2). New York: Harper Trophy. (ISBN 0064471225)

Reynolds, Marilyn. *But What About Me?* Buena Park, CA: Morning Glory (ISBN 1885356102)$8.95

Roos, Stephen. *You'll Miss Me When I'm Gone*. New York: Dell (ISBN 9992191554) $5.00

Ryan, Elizabeth A. *Straight Talk About Drugs and Alcohol*. New York: Facts on File (ISBN 0816035490) $9.95

Zindel, Paul. *David & Della*. Bantam (ISBN 0553567276) $4.50

Headline books: When some topics get "hot," you can count on a YA novel to follow. 90s issues like steroids, sexual harassment, guns in schools, and date rape spawned YA fiction.

Physically challenged: [13] A central theme in YA fiction is the overcoming of adversity. Books with physically challenged YAs always have high appeal.

The secret: [14] Christopher Pike's thrillers struck such a nerve not just because of the suspense but because his early books concerned characters with a "dark secret past." This works in the thrillers, but also figures into realistic novels like John Marsden's *Letters from the Inside*.

Violence: One of the other main appeals of the Pike-style thrillers is the violence. A violence-saturated media coincides with teens who are finding their own environment—schools, homes, and relationships—increasingly more violent. One of the arguments against thrillers is that they glorify or exploit violence in a time when teens need to have fewer images of violence in their lives. In fact, reducing violence in media is one of the central recommendations of the Carnegie Council final report.

Books about Violence (Mostly Fiction): Bib Squib

Canada, Geoffrey. *Fist Stick Knife Gun : A Personal History of Violence in America.* Boston: Beacon Press (ISBN 0807004235) $12.00

Cormier, Robert. *We All Fall Down.* New York: Dell (ISBN 0440215560) $4.50

Krisher, Trudy. *Spite Fences.* New York: Dell. (ISBN 0440220165) $3.99

Levy, Barrie. *In Love and in Danger : A Teen's Guide to Breaking Free of Abusive Relationships.* Seattle, WA: Seal Press (ISBN 1878067265) $8.95

Lynch, Chris. *Shadow Boxer.* New York: Harper (ISBN 0064471128) $3.95

Mazer, Norma Fox. *Out of Control.* New York: Avon (ISBN 0380713470) $4.50

Oates, Joyce Carol. *Foxfire: Confessions of a Girl Gang.* New York: Plume (ISBN 0452272319) $11.95

Rapp, Adam. *Missing the Piano.* New York: Puffin (ISBN 0140368337) $4.99

Tamer, Erika. *Fair Game.* Orlando, FL: Harcourt (ISBN 015227065) $3.99

Voigt, Cynthia. *When She Hollers.* Forestville, CA: Point (ISBN 0590467158) $3.99

Social issues: These books are different from headline books in that they have a little bit more meat on their bones. Issues like the environment, homelessness, sexism, and racism are showing up in more novels.

Social Issues Fiction: Bib Squib

Conly, Jane Leslie. *Crazy Lady.* New York: Harper (ISBN 0064405710) $4.50

Karas, Phyllis. *The Hate Crime.* New York: Avon. (ISBN 0380782146) $3.99

Klass, David. *California Blue.* Forestville, CA: Point (ISBN 0590466895) $3.99

Lasky, Kathryn. Memoirs of a Bookbat. Orlando, FL: Harcourt (ISBN 0152012591) $5.00

Neufeld, John. *A Small Civil War.* New York: Aladdin (ISBN 0689807716) $3.99

Peck, Richard. *Last Safe Place on Earth.* New York: Dell (ISBN 0440220076) $3.99

Ruby, Lois. *Skin Deep.* Forestville, CA: Point (ISBN 0590477005) $4.99

Temple, Frances. *A Taste of Salt.* New York: HarperCollins (ISBN 0064471365) $3.95

Uchida, Yoshinka. *The Invisable Thread.* New York: Morrow (ISBN 0688137032) $4.95

Wartski, Maureen. *Candle in the Wind.* New York: Fawcett (ISBN 0449704424) $4.50

Parent-teen relationship: The basic core conflict of adolescence is this relationship. What emerges in literature less than before is the "parents are evil" message; today, there is more of an attempt to show YAs the pressures and histories which parents and families have.

Death: These books might cover the death of a family member, a friend, a stranger, or the main character. With YAs so full of life, the preoccupation with death is easy to explain and hard to ignore when choosing books. The continued success of Lurlene McDaniel's tear-jerkers demonstrates this phenomenon.

Books about Death and Dying (Mostly Fiction): Bib Squib

Bode, Janet. *Death Is Hard to Live With*. New York: Dell (ISBN 0440219299) $3.99
Donovan, Stacey. *Dive*. New York: Puffin (ISBN 0140379622) $4.99
Draper, Sharon. *Tears of a Tiger*. New York: Aladdin (ISBN 0689806981) $3.99
Fox, Paula. *The Eagle Kite*. New York: Dell. (ISBN 0440219728) $3.99
Hosie-Bounar, Jane. *Life Belts*. New York: Dell. (ISBN 0440219310) $3.99
Lemieux, A. C. *Do Angels Sing the Blues?*. New York: Avon (ISBN 0380723999) $4.50
McDaniel, Lurlene. *Angels Watching Over Me*. New York: Bantam (ISBN 0553567241) $4.99
Nelson, Theresa. *Earthshine*. New York: Dell (ISBN 0440219892) $4.50
Ruby, Lois. *Miriam's Well*. New York: Scholastic (ISBN 0590449389) $3.99
Schwandt, Stephen. *Holding Steady*. Minneapolis, MN: Free Spirit (ISBN 0916793946) $5.95

Life or death fiction: This is the hot area in series fiction going into 1997. Like thrillers, these books still involve death, danger and suspense, but now the emphasis is on saving lives, not stalking them.

Like the disaster movies of the 1970s, these books featuring natural disasters or tragic accidents present YAs transformed by the experience. You get the thrill of thrillers without bad guys. The genesis seems to be the mega success of the TV show *E.R.* In almost all of these books, "normal" white middle class suburban teens find themselves thrust into the middle of some tragic event where they have a chance to shine and be transformed.

Books about Life and Death: Bib Squib

Carey, Diane. *Twist of Fate*. New York: Pocket (ISBN 0671553062) $3.99
Cooney, Caroline. *Flash Fire*. New York: Scholastic (ISBN 0590484966) $4.50
Hobbs, Will. *Downriver*. New York: Bantam. (ISBN 0440219817) $4.50
Hoh, Diane. *Virus*. New York: Scholastic (ISBN 0590543229) $3.99
Marsden, John. *Tomorrow, When the War Began*. New York: Dell. (ISBN 044021985X) $3.99
Myers, Walter Dean. *Fallen Angels*. New York: Scholastic. (ISBN 0590409433) $4.50
Paulsen, Gary. *Sentries*. New York: Simon & Schuster (ISBN 0689804113) $3.95
Rojany, Lisa. *In the Emergency Room*. New York: Morrow (ISBN 0688134025) $4.95
Shusterman, Neal. *Scorpion Shards*. New York: Tor (ISBN 0812524659) $4.99
Stevermer, Caroline. *River Rats*. Orlando, FL: Harcourt (ISBN 015201411X) $6.00

Body image: Zollo reported that teens' primary concern was "looking good" so it is no surprise that YA literature reflects this preoccupation. It takes many forms, but normally these books concern young women with eating disorders.

Books about Body Image (Mostly Fiction): Bib Squib

Bauer, Joan. *Squashed*. New York: Dell. (ISBN 0440219124) $3.99
Covington, Dennis. *Lizard*. New York: Dell (ISBN 0440214904) $3.50
Crutcher, Chris. *Staying Fat for Sarah Byrnes*. New York: Dell. (ISBN 044021906) $3.99
Frank, Lucy. *I Am an Artichoke*. New York: Dell (ISBN 0440219906) $3.99
Klass, Sheila Solomon. *Rhino*. Forestville, CA: Point (ISBN 0590442511) $3.99
Koertge, Ron. *Arizona Kid*. New York: Avon. (ISBN 0380707764) $3.99
Kolodny, Nancy. *When Food's a Foe*. Boston: Little Brown (ISBN 0316501816) $8.95
Newman, Leslea. *Fat Chance*. New York: Putnam (ISBN 069811406X) $4.95
Philbrick, Rodman. *Freak the Mighty*. Forestville, CA: Point (ISBN 0590474138) $3.99
Woodson, Jacqueline. *Between Madison & Palmetto*. New York: Dell (ISBN 0440410622) $3.99

Mystery, Suspense, and Thrillers

You could look at these as the BIG metaphor for YAs: looking for clues to the mystery of their own identity. Or, on the flip side, these books provide great escapism from all those issues.

Mysteries and Thrillers: Bib Squib

Cusick, Richie. *Summer of Secrets*. New York: Pocket (ISBN 0671549278) $3.99
Davidson, Nicole. *Dying to Dance*. New York: Avon (ISBN 0380781522)$3.99
Hawks, Robert. *The Substitute*. New York: Avon. (ISBN O380776227) $3.99
Hoh, Diane. *Prom Date*. New York: Scholastic. (ISBN 0590544292) $3.99
Nixon, Joan Lowry. *The Name of the Game Was Murder*. New York: Dell (ISBN 0440219167) $3.99
Pike, Christopher. *Execution of Innocence*. New York: Pocket (ISBN 0671550551) $3.99
Rice, Bebe. *Class Trip*. New York: HarperCollins (ISBN 0061061956) $3.50
Smith, Sinclair. *The Boy Next Door*. New York: Scholastic (ISBN 0590486772) $3.50
Springer, Nancy. *Toughing It*. Orlando, FL: Harcourt (ISBN 0152000119) $4.95
Stine, R.L. *The New Fear*. New York: Pocket (ISBN 0671529528) $3.99

Romance

Plenty of good romances come along which are higher quality than those in a series. The main factor in a romance is the author's gender. Although some authors, such as the late Norma Klein, wrote convincing first person male voice books, normally the gender of the author is the gender of the lead character.

Romances: Bib Squib

Applegate, Katherine. *Summer.* New York: Pocket (ISBN 0671510428) $3.99
Bennett, Cherie. *Girls in Love.* New York: Scholastic (ISBN 0590880306) $4.99
Brooks, Martha. *Two Moons in August.* New York: Scholastic (ISBN 0590459236) $3.25
Casely, Judith. *Kisses.* New York: Random House (ISBN 0679826726) $3.99
Chambers, Aiden. *Dance on My Grave.* New York: HarperCollins (ISBN 0064405796) $5.95
Cooney, Caroline. *Forbidden.* New York: Scholastic (ISBN 05904657540) $3.25
Hayes, Daniel. *No Effect.* New York: Avon. (ISBN 0380723921) $3.99
Klause, Annette Curtis. *The Silver Kiss.* New York: Dell (ISBN 0440213460) $3.99
Lee, Marie. *Finding My Voice.* New York: Dell. (ISBN 0440218969) $3.99
Powell, Randy. *Is Kissing a Girl Like Licking an Ash Tray?* New York: Farrar, Straus & Giroux (ISBN 0374432674) $3.95

Historical Fiction

If teachers didn't assign it, surveys show few YAs would ever read historical fiction, especially for pleasure. It's out there and it continues to be popular with writers, publishers, and reviewers, but historical fiction has a very limited YA audience. Ironically, it remains, among reviewers and list makers, the most popular type of book.

Historical Fiction: Bib Squib

Bunting, Eve. *SOS Titanic.* Orlando, FL: Harcourt (ISBN 0152013059) $5.00
Cushman, Karen. *Catherine Called Birdy.* New York: Harper (ISBN 0064405842) $3.95
Ferris, Jean. *Into the Wind.* New York: Avon (ISBN 0380781980) $3.99
Kawashima, Yoko. *My Brother, My Sister and I.* New York: Aladdin. (ISBN 0689806566) $4.50
Lasky, Katherine. *Beyond the Burning Time.* New York: Scholastic (ISBN 0590473328) $4.50
Lyons, Mary. *Letters from a Slave Girl.* New York: Simon & Schuster (ISBN 0689800150) $4.95
Myers, Walter Dean. *The Glory Field.* New York: Scholastic (ISBN 0590458981) $4.50
Ray, Karen. *To Cross a Line.* New York: Puffin (ISBN 0140375872) $3.99
Rinaldi, Ann. *The Secret of Sarah Revere.* Orlando, FL: Harcourt (ISBN 0152003924) $3.95
Temple, Frances. *Ramsey Scallop.* New York: HarperCollins (ISBN 0064406016) $4.95

Humor

Comics compilations: The latest compilation of Calvin and Hobbes will circulate more than just about any other item if it stays in one piece. In addition to these there are compilations for younger (Peanuts, Mad, etc.) and older (Gary Larson, Doonesbury, etc.) YAs. The most current ones are listed in the monthly jobber catalogs.

Comic novels: Teens love a good laugh and there are still YA authors that can provide them.

Comic Novels: Bib Squib

Bauer, Joan. *Thwonk* . New York: Dell (ISBN 0440219809) $3.99
Conford, Ellen. *I Love You, I Hate You, Get Lost.* Forestville, CA: Point (ISBN 0590455591) $3.50
Fine, Anne. *Flour Babies.* New York: Scholastic (ISBN 0440219418) $3.99
Hite, Sid. *Dither Farm.* New York: Dell (ISBN 0440219442) $4.50
Korman, Gordon. *Losing Joe's Place.* Forestville, CA: Point (ISBN 0590427695) $3.99
Lynch, Chris. *Slot Machine.* New York: HarperCollins (ISBN 0064471403) $4.50
Manes, Stephen . *Comedy High.* Forestville, CA: Point (ISBN 0590444379) $3.50
Okimoto, Jean Davies. *Take a Chance, Gramps!* New York: Tor (ISBN 0812543238) $3.99
Peck, Richard. *Bel-Air Bambi and the Mall Rats.* New York: Dell (ISBN 0440219256) $3.99
Vail, Rachel. *Ever After.* New York: Avon (ISBN 0380724650) $3.99

Science Fiction and Fantasy

Many librarians who publish in the YA field are science fiction and/or fantasy buffs. That means there is an inordinate amount of literature out there on science fiction topics[15-16] with *VOYA's* annual "Best" list appearing in the April issue.[17] Another reason this is such a big field is that like horror, there is very little of this material written specifically for the YA market. Much of the YA science fiction reaches older children because the YAs are already into the latest 600–page-plus trilogy by Brooks, Weis, or Eddings. To keep up on this field of interest, subscribe to *VOYA*.

Tie-Ins

One benefit of the entertainment industry conglomerates is that every big movie comes as part of a package deal. The package also includes soundtracks, posters, T-shirts, countless other merchandise, and a movie tie-in book. These books are gobbled up by the handful by YAs who either want to "relive" the experience of the movie or who want to read the book because the movie was rated R and they couldn't get in to see it. TV tie-ins are also popular, such as the books produced to accompany *The X-files, Late Night with David Letterman,* and almost every MTV show. Stocking these items at the front of the YA area will attract attention.

OTHER GENRES

In addition to the categories listed thus far in this chapter, you can also find a limited amount of original and reprint paperbacks on these subjects:

Sports: Two kinds of sport literature are popular. The grown-up Matt Christopher types with lots of action, in which the game is the most important thing. The second are books like those of Chris Lynch, Will Weaver, and Chris Crutcher, where sports is the subject, but not really the most important thing in the book. Like the life and death books, these novels give YAs a chance to view peers under pressure and, most often, see them excel.

Adventure: YAs who like *Hatchet* or *My Side of the Mountain* will want YA outdoor yarns. Although there are not many currently being published, this genre (unlike a problem novel) is rather timeless, so *Deathwatch* from the 1970s can meet this need. The "emergency room" series are working in the same territory, just moving the struggle from the wilderness to the city.

Short story collections: Donald Gallo has edited several excellent collections of stories by YA authors. These collections can meet two YA needs—first, often a student needs to read a story as an assignment so rather than suggesting Poe or de Maupassant, the stories in these collections present contemporary choices. Secondly, some YAs are completists and pride themselves on reading everything by a certain author. Collections of adult horror stories and annual best science fiction/fantasy collections are also available in paperback.

Multicultural literature: You will find lots of YA professional literature about this subject, most notably Hazel Rochman's *Against Borders*.[18] Although all the statistics demonstrate how YAs are more ethnically diverse and Zollo notes how African American cultural influences are predominant, YA literature is still predominately about white middle class suburban teenagers. Amazingly there are few authors writing about Hispanics and even fewer writing about Asian teenagers. Writers who work in this area run the risk of either being told their characters are not "ethnic" enough or that they are too "politically correct."[19]

Classics

The term *classic* means different things to different people. One definition is a book that is "never hot but never cold." Any book for which there is and will always be a demand is a classic. For titles that fit this definition, you will need to check periodically because they have a way of disappearing. Another definition of a classic might be any book a YA would reasonably expect to find in any library—again that covers a lot of ground.

The Classics: This time with a capital C—such as Dickens, Bronte, etc. Books primarily written before any YAs' grandparents were born, taught in school, and often read by YAs out of necessity rather than choice. YALSA's *Outstanding Books for the College Bound*[20] and Arco's *Reading Lists for College Bound Students*[21] are excellent sources to find a good list. Get these in Permabound editions so you don't have to rebuy them constantly. The primary audience for classics are those people who know exactly what they want to read. Don't waste valuable display space—put them on a bottom shelf somewhere near the back of the YA area.

Best Books: In addition to the yearly lists, YALSA held a "best of the best" conference to celebrate 25 years of the Best Books list (see page 129).

Best Authors: Another quick list is simply to choose titles from authors who have received the Margaret Edwards Lifetime achievement award. Awarded annually, this honor recognizes living YA authors for their body of work.

Summer reading lists: Most schools have summer reading lists filled with these books. Because many schools rarely change their lists, there will always be a demand for certain titles.

Underground classics: They don't always make our lists, but underground classics make several trips around a group of YAs. Some of these are on the "Best of the Best" list (like *Carrie* or *Go Ask Alice*), while others escaped attention. From Anne Rice's erotica to the dementia of *The Anarchist Cookbook*, these titles represent books for which YAs will be looking, but rarely asking, in a library collection. All will be popular; almost all present selection vs. censorship questions.

Cliff notes: These are the classics that YAs love to read. For every copy of *Moby Dick*, you should probably have a Cliff Note as well. Some libraries refused to stock Cliff Notes, but then there are always Monarch's notes and other similar sources.

OTHER TYPES OF YA PAPERBACKS

Comic books: Not Garfield, as discussed before, but Batman. The arguments for and against comic books in both libraries and classrooms are old ones. Cline and McBride provide an analysis in their text *A Guide to Literature for Young Adults*, including a section called "Comics as a Bridge to Further Reading,"[22] and Krashen's *Power of Reading* documents the research. These are discussed further in the magazine section.

Best of the Best of the Best: Margaret Edwards Award Winners

Gary Paulsen
Judy Blume
Cynthia Voigt
Walter Dean Myers
M.E. Kerr
Lois Duncan
Robert Cormier
Richard Peck
S.E. Hinton

100 Best Books

Angelou, Maya. *I Know Why The Caged Bird Sings*
Anonymous. *Go Ask Alice*
Anthony, Piers. *On A Pale Horse*
Avi. *Nothing But The Truth*
Baldwin, James. *If Beale Street Could Talk*
Blume, Judy. *Forever*
Bridgers, Sue Ellen. *Permanent Connections*
Brooks, Bruce. *The Moves Make The Man*
Cannon, A. E. *Amazing Gracie*
Card, Orson Scott. *Ender's Game*
Childress, Alice. *Rainbow Jordan*
Cole, Brock. *The Goats*
Cormier, Roberts. *We All Fall Down*
Crew, Linda. *Children Of The River*
Crutcher, Chris. *Athletic Shorts: Six Short Stories*
Crutcher, Chris. *Stotan*
Dahl, Roald. *Boy: Tales Of Childhood*
Davis, Terry. *Vision Quest*
Deuker, Carl. *On The Devil's Court*
Dickinson, Peter. *Eva*
Duncan, Lois. *Killing Mr. Griffin*
Fox, Paula. *One-Eyed Cat*
Gaines, Ernest J. *Autobiography Of Miss Jane Pittman*
Gallo, Donald R., ed. *Sixteen*
Garden, Nancy. *Annie On My Mind*
Gies, Miep & Alison Leslie Gold. *Anne Frank Remembered*
Grant, Cynthia D. *Phoenix Rising: Or How To Survive Your Life*
Guest, Judith. *Ordinary People*
Guy, Rosa. *The Friends*
Hayden, Torey L. *Ghost Girl: The True Story Of A Child Who Refused To Talk*
Hinton, S.E. *The Outsiders*
Hobbs, Will. *Downriver*
Holman, Felice. *Slake's Limbo*
Houston, James. *Ghost Fox*
Jacques, Brian. *Redwall*
Kerr, M. E. *Gentlehands*
King, Stephen. *Carrie*

Klass, David. *Wrestling With Honor*
Klause, Annette Curtis. *Silver Kiss*
Levoy, Myron. *Alan And Naomi*
Lipsyte, Robert. *The Contender*
Madaras, Lynda and Dane Saavedra. *The What's Happening To My Body? Book For Boys: A Growing Up Guide For Parents And Sons*
Madaras, Lynda and Area Madaras. *The What's Happening To My Body? Book for Girls: A Growing Up Guide for Parents And Daughters*
Mahy, Margaret. *Changeover: A Supernatural Romance*
Mazer, Norma Fox. *Silver*
McCaffrey, Anne. *Dragonsinger*
McKinley, Robin. *Beauty: A Retelling Of The Story Of Beauty And The Beast*
Miller, Frances A. *The Truth Trap*
Myers, Walter Dean. *Scorpions*
O'Brien, Robert C. *Z For Zachariah*
Paterson, Katherine. *Jacob Have I Loved*
Paulsen, Gary. *Hatchet*
Peck, Richard. *Are You In The House Alone?*
Pfeffer, Susan Beth. *Year Without Michael*
Plath, Sylvia. *The Bell Jar*
Pullman, Philip. *Ruby In The Smoke*
Rinaldi, Ann. *Wolf By the Ears*
Shilts, Randy. *And The Band Played On: Politics, People, And The Aids Epidemic*
Sleator, William. *Interstellar Pig*
Spiegelman, Art. *MAUS: A Survivor's Tale*
Swarthout, Glendon. *Bless The Beasts & Children*
Tan, Amy. *The Joy Luck Club*
Walker, Alice. *The Color Purple*
Westall, Robert. *Blitzcat*
White, Robb. *Deathwatch*
Wrede, Patricia C. *Dealing With Dragons*
Wyss, Thelma Hatch. *Here At The Scenic-Vu Hotel*
Yolen, Jane & Martin H. Greenberg, eds. *Vampires*
Zindel, Paul. *The Pigman*

Underground Classics: Bib Squib

Arnothy, Christine. *I Am Fifteen—And I Don't Want to Die*. Forestville,CA: Point (ISBN 0590403222) $3.50

Beat Voices: An Anthology of Beat Poetry by David Kherdian (Editor). 1st Beech Edition. New York: Beech Tree Books (ISBN 0688149162) $4.95

Bess, Clayton. *The Mayday Rampage : A Novel*. Lookout Press (ISBN 1882405013) $7.95

Block, Francesca Lia. *Weetzie Bat*. New York: HarperCollins (ISBN 0064470687) $3.95

Cooney, Caroline B. *Face on the Milk Carton*. New York: Dell (ISBN 0440220653) $4.99

Crutcher, Chris. *Chinese Handcuffs*. New York: Dell (ISBN 0440208378) $3.99

Duncan, Lois. *Who Killed My Daughter*. New York: Dell (ISBN 0440213428) $5.99

Filipovic, Zlata. *Zlata's Diary : A Child's Life in Sarajevo*. New York: Penguin (ISBN 0140242058) $7.95

Grealy, Lucy. *Autobiography of a Face*. New York: HarperPerennial Library (ISBN 006097673X) $12.50

Johnson, Angela. *Humming Whispers*. Forestville, CA: Point (ISBN 0590674528) $3.99

Koertge, Ron. *Where the Kissing Never Stops*. Flare (ISBN 0380717964) $3.99

Marsden, John. *Letters from the Inside*. New York: Bantam (ISBN 0440219515) $3.99

Pop, Snap C. *Yo' Mama! : Bust-O-Pedia*. New York: Berkley (ISBN 0425148610) $8.00

Powell, William. *The Anarchist Cookbook*. Fort Lee, NJ: Barricade Books (ISBN 0962303208) $22.50

Rampling, Anne (aka Anne Rice). *Belinda*. New York: Jove (ISBN 0515093556) $6.99

Sebestyen, Ouida. *The Girl in the Box*. New York: New York: Starfire (ISBN 0553282611) $4.50

Thompson, Julian R. *A Band of Angels*. Forestville, CA: Point (ISBN 0590431242) $3.99

Townsend, Sue. *Secret Diary of Adrian Mole, Aged 13 3/4*. New York: Avon (ISBN 0380868768) $4.99

Vail, Rachel. *Wonder*. New York: Puffin (ISBN 0140361677) $3.99

Woodson, Jacqueline. *Autobiography of a Family Photo : A Novel*. New York: Plume (ISBN 0452270987) $9.95

Graphic novels: These books show the blending of comics and the novel. This was a recent phenomenon in the underground but now is much more mainstream. A graphic novel is a more sophisticated book aimed at the older YA who is willing to sit through the 200–plus pages of ink and text. These are normally compilations of previously published individual comic books, and more seem to be coming to market. The best and only place in the library literature to keep updated on graphic novels is *Voice of Youth Advocates* with periodic updates from Katherine "Kat" Kan.

Trade paperbacks: Most YA areas are designed for the popular mass market format, thus even novels with YA appeal in this format just don't fit anywhere but with the hardbacks. Second, the trade size looks juvenile, because children's publishers use it for not only series but most other releases as well. Interestingly, this is the size of choice for YA books in most other English-speaking countries. Some publishers are testing this water with mixed success.

The genre of style: There are those authors who don't neatly fit into any category, either because they write in all genres or because they resist categorization. The best example is Francesca Lia Block whose main "selling point" is her style. Bruce Brooks is another example—his first book was a sports novel, his second was about music, and he has mixed titles in nonfiction. Other books have covered subjects as diverse as nightmare futuristic fiction to a sweet "coming of age" story collection. The other authors here represent the best of quality YA writing—they are experimental, challenging, and unique.

Genre of Style: Bib Squib

Avi. *Nothing But the Truth*. New York: Avon (ISBN 038071907X) $4.50

Block, Francesca Lia. *Missing Angel Juan*. New York: HarperCollins (ISBN 0064471209) $3.95

Brooks, Bruce. *What Hearts*. New York: HarperCollins (ISBN 0064471276) $4.50

Cadnum, Michael. *Breaking the Fall*. New York: Puffin (ISBN 0140360042) $3.99

Dickinson, Peter. *Eva*. New York: Dell (ISBN 0440207665) $4.50

Paulsen, Gary. *The Car*. New York: Dell (ISBN 0440219183) $4.50

Soto, Gary. *Local News*. Forestville, CA: Point (ISBN 059048446X) $3.99

Thompson. Julian. *Gypsyworld*. New York: Puffin (ISBN 0140365311) $3.99

Wolff, Virginia Euwer. *Make Lemonade*. Forestville, CA: Point (ISBN 059048141X) $3.95

Yolen, Jane. *Briar Rose*. New York: Tor (ISBN 0812558626) $5.99

Growing up: This is not so much a genre as an overriding concern with almost all YA fiction, from Bruce Brooks' highly sophisticated works to the dumber-than-dumb thriller series—all good YA books concern the problem that is adolescence. Looking at the winners of the Delacorte Press Prize for Best First YA Novel, most of these titles have no greater theme than this search for identity, independence, excitement, and acceptance.

This section on paperbacks gave you a very broad overview of the various types of genres popular with YAs. Although books vary in popularity from library to library, the paperback format is the most popular.

Winners of the Delacorte Best First YA Novel Contest

1983: WINNER: Sweeney, Joyce. *Center Line.*
  HONOR: Hughey, Roberta. *The Question Box.*
1984: WINNER: Forshay-Lunsford, Cin. *Walk Through Cold Fire.*
  HONOR: Malmgren, Dallin. *The Whole Nine Yards.*
  HONOR: Shannon, Jacqueline. *Too Much T.J.*
1985: WINNER: Maloney, Ray. *The Impact Zone.*
  HONOR: Plummer, Louise. *The Romantic Obsessions and Humiliations of Annie
  Sehlmeier.*
1986: WINNER: -NONE-
1987: WINNER: Cannon, A.E. *Cal Cameron by Day, Spiderman by Night.*
  HONOR: Crew, Linda. *Children of the River.*
  HONOR: Dines, Carol. *Best Friends Tell the Best Lies.*
1988: WINNER: Allen, R.E. *Ozzy on the Outside.*
1989: WINNER: Sauer, James. *Hank.*
  HONOR: Shriver, Jean Adair. *Mayflower Man.*
  HONOR: King, Buzz, *Silicon Songs.*
  HONOR: Reaver, Chap. *Mote.*
1990: WINNER: Covington, Dennis. *Lizard.*
  HONOR: Karl, Herb. *Toom County Mud Race.*
  HONOR: Stoehr, Shelley. *Crosses.*
1991: WINNER: Bauer, Joan. *Squashed.*
  HONOR: Obstfeld, Ray. *The Joker and The Thief.*
1992: WINNER: Hosie-Bounar, Jane. *Life Belts.*
  HONOR: Goldman, E.M. *Getting Lincoln's Goat.*
1993: WINNER: -NONE-
1994: WINNER: Moore, Martha. *Under the Mermaid Angel.*

4.7 NONFICTION

Some libraries with a YA area ignore nonfiction, purchasing and shelving it elsewhere. There are primarily four types of YA nonfiction:

1. Recreational
2. Informational
3. Educational
4. Reference

Recreational and informational nonfiction is normally housed in the YA area, but the others belong in the "regular" collection. This can result in titles getting lost in the shuffle between adult and children's selections. All four types of nonfiction are important. The recreational titles help YAs enjoy their lives, the educational and reference help them do their jobs, and the informational titles might just save their lives.

How does your library handle YA nonfiction? First consider the priority of YA nonfiction in your YA services. Use these ideas to help you discover your YA nonfiction priorities:

1. *Leave the building:* Begin investigating the strength of the school library collections. Look at the following:
   - The age of the books on the shelf (can you even find a non-fiction title published after 1990?)
   - The reference collection (age of encyclopedias)
   - Any big ticket items (SIRS, Contemporary Authors, etc.)
   - The budget (if they will tell you: Is it going up or down? Do they even have one?)
   - The mission and goals of the school library
   - The available technology (do they have Internet access? What types of CD-ROMs are available?)

2. *Explore the curriculum:* See whether you can get a copy of the curriculum of the school. Although not always followed to the letter, it might give you some idea on areas YAs might be studying.

3. *Explore your building:* What duplication is there in current selection practices in your own library? Do the adult and children's selectors get together about YA titles or do they both buy and / or ignore them? When Gale publishes an expensive but essential reference tool, who pays the bill?

TYPES OF NONFICTION

Recreational: Fiction is certainly not the only type of material that YAs read for fun. Part of being an adolescent is developing an intellectual curiosity and asking the question "Why?" YAs also develop special interests and for fun will read whatever they can lay their hands on about their own particular passions.

Informational: YAs have many questions about their changing bodies and changing lives. The need for such books was covered in section 2.3.

Educational: Currency is the watchword here. New topics become "hot" (Who was writing about the rain forest five years ago? Who is writing papers on solar energy now?), while others become almost classic in their constant popularity. Collecting materials for term papers involves a choice about should you spend it—on 10 different titles on the subject or 10 copies of the same? Each approach has problems: because of the number of YAs doing research, if there are 10 titles on a subject available, one YA can wipe out everything. If you buy 10 copies of the same title, 10 YAs get a book, but only one.

Informational Nonfiction: 15 Top Titles: Bib Squib

1. Abner, Allison. *Finding Our Way: The Teen Girls' Survival Guide.* New York: Harperperennial Library (ISBN 0060951141) $13.00
2. Baer, Judy. *Dear Judy, Did You Ever Like a Boy (Who Didn't Like You?)* Minneapolis, MN: Bethany House (ISBN 1556613415) $7.99
3. Bode, Janet. *Heartbreak and Roses: Real Life Stories of Troubled Love.* New York: Dell (ISBN 0440219663) $4.99
4. Carlip, Hillary. *Girl Power: Young Women Speak Out.* New York: Warner (ISBN 0446670219) $12.99
5. Goldman, Jane. *Streetsmarts : A Teenager's Safety Guide.* Hauppauge, NY: Barron's (ISBN 0812097629) $4.95
6. Hipp, Earl. *Fighting Invisible Tigers.* Minneapolis, MN: Free Spirit. (ISBN 0915793040) $10.95
7. Jukes, Marvis. *It's a Girl Thing : How to Stay Healthy, Safe, and in Charge.* New York: Knopf (ISBN 0679873929) $12.00
8. Kuklin, Susan. *Speaking Out : Teenagers Take on Race, Sex, and Identity.* New York: Putnam (ISBN 0399225323) $8.95
9. Llewellyn, Grace. *The Teenage Liberation Handbook : How to Quit School and Get a Real Life and Education.* Minneapolis, MN: Free Spirit (ISBN 0962959103) $14.95
10. Madaras, Lynda. *Lynda Madaras Talks to Teens About AIDS : Updated Edition.* New York: Newmarket Press (ISBN 1557041806) $14.95
11. McCoy, Kathy. *Life Happens : A Teenager's Guide to Friends, Failure, Sexuality, Love, Rejection, Addiction, Peer Pressure, Families, Loss, Depression, Change, and other tough stuff.* New York: Perigee (ISBN 0399519874) $11.00
12. Packet, Alex J. *Bringing Up Parents : The Teenager's Handbook.* Minneapolis, MN: Free Spirit (ISBN 0915793482) $14.95
13. Parsley, Bonnie. *The Choice Is Yours : A Teenager's Guide to Self-Discovery, Relationship, Values, and Spiritual Growth.* New York: Fireside (ISBN 0671750461) $10.00
14. Rosenberg, Ellen. *Growing Up Feeling Good.* New York: Puffin (ISBN 0140377182) $13.99
15. Warren, Jeanne. *Teenage Couples—Caring , Commitment & Change.* Buena Park, CA: Morning Glory (ISBN 0930934938) $9.95

In libraries without YA librarians, determining which might be the "best" one to buy, however, is not so easy. Coupled with shrinking materials budgets and staffing shortages, librarians are finding it difficult to do collection development to buy books kids need. More now than ever, publishers are turning to series nonfiction, flooding the market with series after series. Series nonfiction presents librarians with brand names they can trust to provide good information in easy-to-use formats.

Earlier, we noted an article that outlined the popularity of paperback fiction series. Interestingly, these are also reasons to buy nonfiction series:

1. Kids like nonfiction books because they are easy to use, well organized, timely, about "exactly" the topic they are researching, and thin—less than 200 pages.
2. They fill a collection need. Every collection needs books on "hot topics." Just as paperback series support the need for recreational reading, paperback nonfiction supports the need for educational materials.
3. If you find a series you like, you can save time by putting it on standing order. If you find a really good series, buy multiple copies—that saves time and money.
4. Nonfiction series books fulfill the needs of YA patrons and we should know about them—what series are available, what makes a series good, and which are the best series.

No series book ever makes the BBYA list, or gets 5Q 5P reviews in *VOYA,* and increasingly they are not even getting reviewed. *Booklist* lists mostly new titles, *School Library Journal* hits and misses, and even *VOYA* is reviewing fewer because, it is "overwhelmed by series books and could not possibly review them all."[23]

These journals really have no other choice: a great number of series are available and more are emerging every day. Almost every publisher of YA nonfiction produces series; some publish hardly anything else. Some series have subsets, as well. For example, a biography series might have subsets related to race, gender, or nationality. Science series have subsets related to different branches of science, science experiments, and issues. The focus here is evaluating "hot topics" series, books that focus on contemporary social, ethical, political, or economic issues.

Many argue that it is impossible to evaluate an entire series because some books are better than others. Yet, that approach misses the point, and in doing so, doesn't fill in missing information for librarians doing selection. Here are five reasons for evaluating a series:

1. *Supply demands it:* There is just no other way to sort through all the series. If there are 100 series, some will be better than others. If journals are not going to review new titles, there won't be any reviews and librarians must buy blind from catalogs.
2. *Publisher pressure:* Publishers are the main advertisers in most review journals and might "dislike" it if a whole series of books was reviewed poorly. Look in their catalogs and you will see how they will take a quotation about one book in a series to stand for the whole thing.
3. *Reviewer subjectivity:* Everyone has read poor reviews of books they loved or that have won awards. If you find two reviews of the same book, many times they are different. If you know, for example, that Greenhaven's *Opposing Viewpoints* series is wonderful, would you really not buy a title in the series just because of one bad review?
4. *Synthesis:* Librarians are great organizers of information, so it is odd there is no organization of information about series. Although the review journals do series "round-ups," they are listings, not reviews. There are no "best series" or even "best homework books" committees in YALSA, AASL, ALSC, PLA or RASD. Finally, *VOYA* filled the vacuum creating its own committee to bestow honors.[24]
5. *Uniform quality*: At every McDonald's just so much ketchup goes on each burger; much the same, each series has its rules and "quality control." Although the books in the series are not all of the same quality, they are supposed to be.

It is odd that we devote the most pages in review journals and give honors to the books which youths probably check out the least. Lots of titles on those lists are "should" reads—books librarians think are high quality and that YAs should read. Others are "gonna" books: a David Eddings fan doesn't need to see his latest book on a list to want to read it. Yet, most books on those lists are "wanna" books—books that kids look for when they want to read a good book. Nonfiction series represent the "hafta"; the books kids need when they have to do homework.

The criteria for evaluating nonfiction series are similar to that of looking at any nonfiction books. One of the best series publishers is Greenhaven Press. One of the reasons for Greenhaven's success is the books are exactly the type of information that young adults need for homework and term papers. Not only is the information solid, but the presentation "thinks" how students write—presenting an argument for/against a particular subject. Greenhaven has launched spinoffs (*Opposing Viewpoints Juniors*) and a separate imprint (Lucent), all of which are of the highest quality.

Like *Sweet Valley High*, Greenhaven's *Opposing Viewpoint* represents "quality" in series books by finding the right formula and delivering on it repeatedly. Greenhaven also produces series for each market, each niche, each audience. Although each series targets student's doing homework/writing reports, there are several different audiences within this group of series. Some series seem aimed at middle grade/junior high, while others at high school level; some at reluctant readers and others at more advanced students.

YA Nonfiction Series: Evaluation Criteria

1. **Readability:** Are the books easy to read? Is the author's style clear, concise, and understandable?
2. **Facts/opinions:** Are the books unbiased? Does the author present both sides, labeling facts and opinions? Are the facts accurate?
3. **Organization:** Are the books easy to use? Do they contain a detailed table of contents, indexes, and glossaries? If there's no index, how will a reader access the information?
4. **Format:** Are the books approachable? Is the format appropriate for young adults? Are charts, graphs and/or photos used? What about margins?
5. **Photographs:** Do the books have photos? Do they add to the text? Are they captioned? Are they of good quality? Are they color or black and white?
6. **Documentation:** Are the books well documented? Are all statements, statistics, etc. tied to sources?
7. **Timely:** Are the books current? Do books in the series get updated? How often and to what extent?
8. **Short:** Are the books under 200 pages? Are the chapters short and easy to photocopy?
9. **Reluctant Readers:** Could a nonreader use them? Is the vocabulary simple?
10. **The Back Pages:** Do the books have addresses for more information? Up-to-date bibliographies?

With the proliferation of Internet access and full-text magazine services on the Internet and CD-ROM, seemingly fewer students are requiring these types of books. A majority of students who have Internet access will use that first to do research on any topic, even if the net is not the "best" place to find information. The problem, of course, is that a student using the Alta Vista search engine looking for "abortion" is not going to find the same quality or organized quantity of information as a book would provide. Further, the time spent looking for such information would probably be less than it would take students to read a series book on their topic. Some teachers will resist technology and require only book sources, so there is still a need for printed information of this type.

Students do not do research primarily by reading books, but by gathering information from a variety of sources. The genius of most of the YA nonfiction book series is how they organize that information, how they gather material from other sources and how they present that information in an easy-to-read text, complemented by graphics. Often when students are looking for material for argumentative papers or speeches, I'll show them *Opposing Viewpoints*, noting the one essay which covers their topic, and say, jokingly, "Here's the report." But it is not a joke, because like *Sweet Valley High* and *Fear Street*, *Opposing Viewpoints* and other YA nonfiction series succeed because they give students not just what they want, but also what they need.

Reference: Reference books are a whole different area. Many professional publications concern books that never leave the library. These books, due in part to the proliferation of technology, are used less and less. Each year all the major journals list the best of the year: careful selection becomes extremely important as more and more titles, always expensive, come out. More information on reference is given in the section on technology, which seems to be where many reference books (and rightly so) are headed.

NONFICTION COLLECTION ISSUES

These issues will be part of your choices as you put together a YA nonfiction collection:

Currency: No YA wants to be doing a report on the space program and find books on the shelf about how "one day man will go to the moon" or of the perfect safety record of the Shuttle program. Nonfiction collections need to be continually weeded as information is outdated. This is true especially in the hard sciences where it is hard to find good material in the first place.

Organization: The more straightforward, the better. Books that provide lists, charts, graphs, etc., are liked by students because the information they need is presented to them in an easy-to-use way.

Format: Does it look like a children's book? Is it too big to fit on the shelf? Does the text have white space? Are illustrations and text mixed well? What a book looks like is important. If the format looks like a picture book and the text is dotted with illustrations of children, many YAs will pass on it even for a book report because it seems beneath them.

If the primary focus of your YA collection is popular materials (paperback fiction), these choices become even harder as less money is allocated. As more reference books and services become available through CD-ROM and online sources, libraries might begin to think differently about nonfiction collections.

4.8 PERIODICALS

Periodical collection also fall into the same four general categories of nonfiction: recreational, informational, educational, and reference.

Periodicals for nonrecreational use are in a state of flux as new technology is making full text available online and on CD-ROM. Given that change and how periodical collections affect the entire library, this section focuses only on recreational magazines. Not all of these magazines specifically target the YA market, as looking at content and advertisements will prove.

WHY DO TEENS LIKE MAGAZINES?

Teens are drawn to magazines for a number of reasons:

Fads: *Bop, Sixteen,* and other fanzines were on top of the Beverly Hills 90210 and Hanson craze before book publishers could rush out titles. Just the same, magazines drop fads as quickly as they pick them up. Old news is no news to many YAs, so the very nature of magazines makes them perfect YA reading.

Timing: One reason why many YAs, especially boys, don't read books is simply physical: it means sitting still for too long. Magazines can be read quickly in between classes or under a teacher's glance.

Perfect fit: Because magazines are so visual, they are appealing to the stereotypical members of the MTV generation. Magazines appeal to the short attention spans and busy schedules of many YAs.

Reading level: Many reluctant readers are not reluctant to read magazines. Readers who find books challenging will find in most YA magazines simple vocabulary, lots of pictures, and short articles.

Social aspect: Articles and pictures lead to discussions, sometimes heated and sometimes funny.

Peer points: A teenage boy who gets caught with a book by his friends in certain circles may be nerded out. The same kid seen with a magazine is asked to share it. Magazines don't have the same negative reading stigma as books.

Special interests: A YA interested in professional wrestling might be lucky to find one book in the library about this interest. But a library could meet this interest monthly with a magazine subscription. As YAs grow older, they begin to develop special interests which magazines can better respond to than books. The whole notion of magazines is to find a special interest group and provide a product for them to buy.

More than recreation: Although titles like *Seventeen* and *YM* are recreational, they are a great source of health and self-help information. The most current and often most readable information available for teens on sex does not come in books, but in the pages of these magazines.

WHY SHOULD LIBRARIES BUY MORE YA MAGAZINES?

In addition to what your reader survey probably told you (magazines are more popular than books), here are some other reasons your library should buy more YA magazines:

Reach nonbook readers: Magazines provide reluctant readers—always a difficult group to serve—with materials they can and will read. Although there are many reasons why YAs are reluctant readers, two primary reasons are that they cannot find materials that interest them and they find reading difficult because they lack skills. Magazines, by definition, aim to be of high interest and many are also low vocabulary/highly pictorial. If you group comics as magazines, you have even more materials for reluctant readers. Two caveats—first, just because a YA likes comic books doesn't make that person a reluctant reader: many "good" book readers also get a kick out of comics and/or graphic novels. Second, it seems foolhardy as well to classify magazines as less than books: reading is reading is reading. Often when librarians say that YAs don't like to read they must mean books, because YAs do like to read magazines.

Circulation: If you allow magazines to be checked out, they will be checked out repeatedly until they get ripped up or ripped off. A subscription to *Slam* will garner more circulation than purchase of similarly priced hardback fiction title.

Visibility: Magazine covers are bright, attractive, and attention-getting. Putting them within sight of your YA area draws teens in for a look. Face-out shelving is essential.

Crowd control: For the YAs who often do nothing but hang out and eventually cause disruption, more magazines can be one crowd-control method. The YAs are not simply disruptive; they are bored. Magazines conquer boredom and keep YAs occupied, at least for a few minutes once a week or month when the new issues come.

Excitement: YAs rarely run in and ask "Are the new hardback fiction titles here?" but they will ask when you expect the next issue of their favorite magazines.

Public relations: If you push your magazine collection, your message is not only more positive but taps a whole new audience who avoids reading. If you are trying to improve your library's image with YAs, adding titles like *Spin* or *Slam* will create more positive PR for you in the YA community than programs that would cost twice as much and wouldn't guarantee success.

Free posters: Most of the fanzines contain large and small posters. Rather than letting the YAs rip them out, which is a sure thing, you do it. Now you have a poster collection that you can use to either decorate the area or use as prizes.

Developmental tasks: Magazines help YAs do all the things they need to do to grow up healthy. They provide them with an outlet to show their excitement, they assist in developing an identity, they offer articles of the self-help variety to assist with acceptance, and finally, they are a mark of independence.

THE CASE FOR COMICS

Comic books come from the same subscription agent as magazines. They are monthly and processed like other periodicals, so obtaining them is quite painless. Yet many public libraries do not carry comic books. Reasons for this often include the violent nature of comic books and a desire not to waste tax dollars purchasing, processing, or circulating comics. Bluntly stated: libraries don't carry them because librarians don't like them. The sad thing about this decision not to carry comic books is that it flies directly in the face of overwhelming evidence about the value of comics. Since the big scare in the 1950s about comics causing juvenile delinquency, research about comics has actually been quite favorable.[25] Myths that comics retard reading skills, cause violent or anti-social behavior, and act as a general menace to society are falling away. Comics are an answer to a 12– year-old boy's question "What's here for me?" Comics provide libraries with a format that is hugely popular, inexpensive, easy to shelve, and offers high circulation. The real question shouldn't be whether you should carry comics; instead, it should be "Which ones should we carry?" (Hint: Buy *X-Men* and all its mutations.) Comics are, in many ways, another litmus test that separates libraries that buy materials for YAs as opposed to those who seek to create raving fans for its collections.

WHAT ARE THE DISADVANTAGES OF MAGAZINES?

Dealing with periodicals is a headache, from checking them in to claiming them to retrieving them. If at all possible, don't use subscription agents (and lose your discount); instead work out something with your local newsagent. This will allow for more flexibility in terms of titles and even the number of copies of each title.

Because magazines are so popular, they get stolen. This is almost unavoidable. If they are not stolen, then by the time they are read, passed around, thrown across the room, and clipped for photos, there is often nothing left. Accept magazines as disposable materials designed to meet an immediate interest and not part of a permanent collection. If you can get five circulations out of one issue of *Bop*, you have really achieved something. For many, this is a real philosophical leap because we think of libraries as storehouses, but that is not the purpose of this type of collection. If the magazines are in good condition a year from now, they probably are not the right magazines. You need to communicate to YAs that it is their responsibility to monitor these magazines among their peers: the magazines belong to them, not you.

If a high loss rate continues on certain titles, you might need to control the current issues by keeping them at a desk or choosing some other method of control. Certainly, if the same title is repeatedly being stolen and/or mutilated immediately after arrival and if none of your preventive measures work, keeping that title is doing a real disservice not just to the library, but to the teens themselves. Libraries have a responsibility to spend tax money wisely and not passively to allow magazines to be stolen and defaced, yet at the same time they

> " Accept magazines as disposable materials designed to meet an immediate interest and not part of a permanent collection. If you can get five circulations out of one issue of *Bop,* you have really achieved something. "

must face the realities of the nature of the audience coupled with the high interest rate of the material. *Value Line*, Sunday newspaper want ads, and *Sports Illustrated* swimsuit issues also disappear from libraries, but not because of 15–year-olds.

Sassy has undergone intellectual freedom challenges as has *Rolling Stone*. *Spin* magazine once put a condom in each issue and many music/rap magazines reprint all the words to all the songs including the ones you do not hear on the radio. In addition to articles, the ad content of magazines, in particular ones like *Thrasher,* boasts lots of questionable products. The "new" *Spy* magazine seems almost entirely financed by ads for the sex industry. Thus, make sure the collection policy covers magazines, and that under this policy, the titles you choose you could also defend.

One of the advantages of working in a larger library is having larger budgets to do things with—such as buy magazines. One disadvantage is the inability to monitor that actual acquisition of such titles. A few years back many librarians ordered (or tried to order) three new YA titles: *Quake, Tell,* and *Mouth2Mouth*.[26] Despite hype, big media pushes and riding on the wave of articles about the swelling YA population's spending habits, none of the titles survived. Undaunted, three new publishers are launching teen magazines in 1998. Weider Publications will launch a teen fitness magazine called *Jump,* while Bauer Publications pop *Snap* into the market. Time Warner gets into the teen market with its as yet untitled teen version of *People* magazine. There are, however, no titles aimed just for boys. *Sassy* magazine had been for years attempting to launch a boys' version called *Dirt*. Despite great amounts of marketing, test issues, and cross promoting (some came via shrink-wrap with selected Marvel comics), *Dirt* failed to take root. Although magazines are popular, there does seem to be a limit to how many the market can handle due to the number of advertisers willing to use print for promoting products, in particular to boys.

If you surveyed YA boys asking them for magazines to add to the library's collection, chances are good that more than a fair percentage of those surveyed would request *Hustler.* Magazines on tattooing, body art, dope smoking, and piercing have great appeal, yet often do not end in public libraries. Many newsstands house these magazines with the pornography or require a buyer to be 18 to purchase. Magazines repeatedly spin librarians around the "Is it censorship or is it selection?" issue.

WHERE DO YOU FIND MAGAZINES?

You find magazines anywhere but in our professional literature. The library review media is not that strong with magazines and almost nonexistent for YA titles. With few exceptions, it would be difficult to find reviews of the magazines listed in this chapter. To locate magazines, you need to go to the source. Observe, ask, and survey YAs about the magazines they want. Most YAs do not subscribe to magazines; instead, they pick them up at the newsstand or drugstore, which is probably the best place for you to find out about magazines. If you find them at the newsstand, your local distributor can get them for you, too.

The Internet is a new major source of magazines for teenagers. Chapter 9 discusses "best sites," but there is a great opportunity for YA interest as librarians begin to think about developing Web pages. After all, kids will find stuff for their special interests (music, actors, Sailormoon, etc.) on their own with simple searches, but probably would not think to seek out (and might have trouble locating anyway) e-zines (electronic equivalent of self-produced zines and newsletters) and cybermagazines (online versions of newsstand magazines). For more information on teen e-zines, search Yahoo in either the category Entertainment: Magazines: Children or Society and Culture: Age or read Jana Fine's "Teen 'Zines." [27]

WHICH ARE THE BEST MAGAZINES FOR TEENAGERS?

Not surprisingly, the most popular magazines differ by gender: boys like—because there is no alternative—adult magazines with YA appeal, while girls tend to favor those aimed directly at their age group (see Figure 4–3). Many of the same magazines were also most popular in public and school libraries. A recent survey of YAs shows many of the same titles at the top of the list (see Figure 4–4). What is "best" depends on where and when you are reading this. Community standards, likes and dislikes, and special interest will determine which magazines you want to purchase. The magazine publishing industry's flexibility combined with the faddish world of teen culture means some of the titles listed might no longer be available and/or will have been replaced with better titles by the time you set out to improve your YA department.

Most of the titles annotated in the remainder of this section target only YAs, although as mentioned there are plenty of adult titles with YA appeal. For a variety of reasons, these magazines get shelved in the YA area (although duplicates of *Sports Illustrated* and *Entertainment Weekly* seem sound if affordable) but they should be in a public library collection. Addresses for all these magazines are given in this book's appendix.

Beckett Baseball Card Monthly. Dr. James Beckett is the editor and publisher of this guide to sports card collecting. The bulk of each issue is the price guide section, page after page of card numbers and prices. There is also a calendar of shows, plus collecting tips.

Figure 4–3 Favorite Magazines by Gender

If you want to reach a dual audience of teen boys and girls,
magazines distributed in high schools can be especially effective.

(percent of teens who read a typical issue of each magazine, by gender, 1994)

Boys	percent	Girls	percent
Sports Illustrated	37%	Seventeen	46%
TV Guide	30	YM	38
Cable Guide	22	Teen	36
Scholastic Network		TV Guide	36
(gross measurement)*	21	Scholastic Network	
Game Pro	19	(gross measurement)*	28
Marvel Comics	19	Cable Guide	24
Sport	14	People	21
Electronic Gaming Monthly	13	Reader's Digest	20
Reader's Digest	13	Star and National Enquirer	
Inside Sports	12	(gross measurement)	19
DC Comics	12	Sassy	18
Rolling Stone	12	Glamour	16
Time	11	Cosmopolitan	14
Newsweek	11	Mademoiselle	13
People	11	Soap Opera Digest	13
		Sports Illustrated	12

*includes *Science World, Scope, Update, Choices, Jr. Scholastic*

Source: TRU *Teenage Marketing & Lifestyle Study*

Reprinted, with permission, from Peter Zollo, *Wise Up to Teens.* New Strategist Publications, 1995.

Top-Selling Magazines to School and Public Libraries
SOURCE: Ebsco (1993)

Boy's Life
Discover
Glamour
Mademoiselle
People Weekly
Sixteen
Sports Illustrated
Teen
YM

From Patrick Jones, "A to Z and in Between." *Voice of Youth Advocates* (February 1994) 352–357.

Best-Selling YA Magazines to Middle and High School Libraries
SOURCE: Dawson Subscription Service (1993)

Boy's Life
National Geographic World
Oasis
Pack-O-Fun
Plays
Rolling Stone
Sassy
Seventeen
Sixteen
Sports Illustrated For Kids
Teen
Zillions

From Patrick Jones, "A to Z and in Between," *Voice of Youth Advocates* (February 1994) 352–357.

Bop. The prototypical fanzine—a magazine that serves more as a conduit for posters than an information source. Loaded with photos, addresses, and mild gossip, *Bop* like the others in this genre see their fortunes fall and rise with that of the teen heartthrobs. Many of the others in this genre, such as *Teen Beat, Tiger Beat, 16* and *SuperTeen* are all published by the same company (McFadden), thanks to an early 90s merger with former owner Sterling Publications

Brio/Breakaway/Youthwalk. Brio looks a lot like a cleaned-up version of the other teen girl magazines. There are articles on fashion, dating, hygiene, "guy talk," and fiction. *Breakaway*, for boys, is thinner and relies slightly more on graphics than text. Lacking regular features, *Breakaway* addresses interests and concerns and includes fiction. *Youthwalk* is a Christian magazine first and a teen magazine second. There is an introductory page telling how to use the magazine; then a selected topic followed by devotional pages with Bible passages quoted to help the teen.

Circus, Hit Parader, Metal Edge, and *Rip.* The rust seems to have settled on heavy metal, but these four are still kicking and raising hell. More fanzines like *Bop* than a semi-serious book like *Rolling Stone,* these magazines help readers find their fill of interviews, reviews, and news about guitar heroes.

Comics Scene. This magazine consists primarily of profiles of the creators of comic strips, comic books, and other animated art forms. Plenty of artwork is included, most of it in color. Of course, this magazine should only supplement your comics collection.

Discover. Although might be thought of as a school-related source, *Discover* has browsing value because of the catchy layouts and heavy use of illustration.

Dragon. Published by TSR, this is the official Dungeons & Dragons magazine. The text is mostly playing hints, but there is also great artwork. Libraries already serving the D & D crowd should know about this, if not subscribe to it.

Electronic Gaming Monthly. Like *Nintendo Power*, this magazine is filled with tips for scoring high on various video games. A visit to any software store will show both how crowded this field is and how similar the magazines really are but *EGM* seems the best and most popular of the lot.

Entertainment Weekly. EW is one of the best magazines on the market and one that every public and high school library should own. The YA appeal is obvious: lots of articles about movies, TV, music, and media stars. If many YA and music magazines want to be the print MTV, then *EW* certainly succeeds in being the print version of TV's *Entertainment Tonight.*

Figure 4–4 Most Popular Magazines According to Librarians

Two hundred and thirty 13- to 18-year-olds in 10 states voted for their favorite and least favorite magazines. Here are the titles, by category, that received five or more votes. The survey shows that YAs are hardly a homogenous bunch: the same titles show up as both winners and losers.

Winners		Losers	
Seventeen	65	37	Time
YM	54	35	Sassy
Sports Illustrated	41	31	Teen
Teen	39	27	Seventeen
People	30	22	YM
Mad	15	21	National Geographic
Time	15	14	People
Rolling Stone	12	14	Reader's Digest
National Geographic	11	12	Newsweek
Vogue	9	11	Bop
Gamepro	8	10	Playboy
Sassy	8	10	National Inquirer
Vibe	8	10	Sports Illustrated
Source	7	9	Cosmopolitan
Car & Driver	6	9	Sixteen
Cosmopolitan	6	8	Better Homes and Gardens
Cracked	6	6	Good Housekeeping
Entertainment Weekly	6		
Playboy	6		
Reader's Digest	6		
Transworld Skateboarding	6		
Bop	5		
Ebony	5		
Glamour	5		

Adapted from Jana Fine, "Teen 'Zines: Magazines and Webzines for the Way Cool Set," *School Library Journal* (November 1996): 34. Reprinted with permission, from *School Library Journal* © Cahners Publishing, a division of Reed-Elesvier, Inc.

**Magazines Aimed at Adults,
Popular with YAs**

Car and Driver
Cosmopolitan
Ebony
Elle
Essence
Glamour
Hot Rod
Mademoiselle
People
Premiere
Rolling Stone
Spin
Sports Illustrated
TV Guide
USA Today
Vogue
Weekly World News (tabloid)
Wired

Fangoria. This magazine is what the quality vs. popularity *and* the selection vs. censorship debates are all about. No false advertising here for this 15–year-old magazine, which proclaims itself to be "the magazine of movie terror featuring the bloody best photos, makeup secrets and chilling interviews with the horror all-stars of movies, books, and video!" How could you defend a material that is nothing more than the gory photos taken from R-rated movies? Yet if you are trying to build a "response-popular collection," this probably fits. It is not, like *Playboy* or even some of the tattoo magazines, normally restricted access/sales on newsstands, yet is it library appropriate (for any age?). A tough case.

Hero Illustrated. Aimed at the serious comic book fan, this title comes from same folks who do *Electronic Gaming Monthly.* Readers would have to be real serious to get through the 150–pages plus each issue. There is a lot here, including interviews with artists, reviews, and sneak previews, plus "trade" news about comics and comics collecting. Done in full color unlike some other comics' magazines, *Hero* will appeal to the browser who will surely find in the massive text something to look at and comics to look forward to reading.

InsideOUT. This title, according to Jana Fine,

> [C]overs gay and lesbian youth issues from politics and organizing to coming out. Articles on contemporary figures and resources pages for support organizations are included.[28]

Mad/Cracked. The magazine for the pre-teen mind retains its readership sometimes all through high school. Wacky comic parodies, biting satire, and a poke-in-the-eye attitude have helped *Mad* survive for almost 50 years. *Cracked* is a 10–point match for *Mad*—same level of humor, same type of illustrations.

Merlyn's Pen. Although it has been around for a while, this magazine recently underwent a significant change by splitting into two magazines: the "original" edition for grades 7 to 10 and the new senior edition for grades 9 to 12. Both magazines will cover 9th and 10th grade work, on occasion exceptional pieces will be in both. The magazine features all types of writing, but poetry and short stories remain the staples. Unlike most of the other titles, YAs might have access to it through teachers. Libraries that produce literary magazines of their own might find this of particular interest for their young writers.

Nickelodeon. A magazine that isn't just fun for younger teens, it is funny. It has a *Mad*-like irreverence, including slam-bang, poke-authority-in-the-eye articles like "A Field Guide to North American Teachers." Although the magazine certainly pushes programs on the cable network, that is not its only purpose. There are plenty of puzzles, games, and contests (that's a problem for library subs) mixed in with the almost bad taste humor, characterized by the too gross/too funny duo of Ren and Stimpy. The layout is excellent, the writing aspiring to be sophomoric, and the attitude just right.

Nintendo Power. One of the best of its type in a very crowded group catering to the video game devotee. Published by Nintendo of America, it carries that stamp of approval that the other magazines do not. Essentially, *Nintendo Power* is a magazine of game playing hints, although there are some other features, such as new releases, reviews, and a player profile.

Rap Pages and *Nerve.* These titles try to capture the rebellious spirit of music, but without the fancy graphics. *Rap Pages* (from Larry Flynt Publications) claims to be "the magazine with an attitude," while *Nerve* boasts it is "the renegade rock-n-roll magazine." Consisting primarily of interviews with top rap acts, *Rap Pages* also covers other issues among the rap community. In addition to rap, *Nerve* also covers alternative music. Both magazines speak "to the street"; for example, *Nerve's* record reviews use the word *sucks* as a review classification. The interviews, lyrics, and even band names reflect the reality of hiphop and rock-n-roll culture; so be forewarned.

Rolling Stone. *Rolling Stone* is what magazines like *Nerve* are rebelling against—a very establishment conservative magazine that on occasion shocks. Nothing much to add—it is hugely popular with teens, yet obviously the ads aim for an older market. Although challenged in school and public libraries, it is a necessity for library collections serving high school kids.

Scholastic Update. Well known and often distributed in the classroom, *Update* is the only YA general interest magazine. Using a "theme" issue approach, *Scholastic* fulfills the education function but also provides plenty of solid information for teenagers.

Seventeen. The oldest of the magazines (it began in 1944), *Seventeen* has been the leader in the field for years. The challenges from first *Sassy,* then *YM,* however, led to several changes in the magazine that gave it not only a graphic makeover, but also seemed to have upped the interest level of the articles.

Slam. Although other sports are certainly popular among teens, basketball seems to have wide appeal among all ages, races, and geographic region. *Slam* is an exciting magazine laced with lots and lots of photos, plus well-written articles.

The Source. Subtitled "the magazine of hip hop music, culture, and politics," *The Source* is certainly not a fanzine. Much more serious in subject matter and tone, it is a magazine for those who care about rap music, not just those who listen to it casually. There are no posters or contests, but rather news, profiles, issues, and reviews. Since its debut, it has become the bible of the industry and its various devotees.

Spin. A looser version of *Rolling Stone* published by Penthouse (one issue contained a condom) with all the same disclaimers. *Spin* is less establishment—rap and alternative articles grace its cover more than "hot" pop culture figures. Interestingly, neither Zollo nor Fine listed it as a popular YA magazine, but my experience shows that it is in great demand.

Sports Illustrated for Kids. Aimed at the middle-grade reader, this is a highly graphic approach to sports reporting. There is less concentration on games and more emphasis of personalities and role models.

Spy! A totally irreverent humor magazine aimed at adults but of interest to "hip and well read" older teens. Although the magazine is at times too smug and smutty, it is usually down-right funny. *Spy!* was out of business for a while and it is back with some bark, but perhaps not as much bite as when Kurt Anderson ran the ship.

Starlog. From the same publisher as *Comics Scene* and *Fangoria*, this is a science fiction fanzine. The magazine attempts to do for the science fiction field what *Fangoria* does for horror, but with a lot less blood. Interest has boomed with success of the *X-files* and other shows of that ilk.

Teen. Although it is a little more lightweight than the others and normally chock full of first-person accounts and quizzes, *Teen* is essential for every library serving teen girls. The owners of *Teen* bought *Sassy* and it appears that they are trying to position *Teen* as the choice of younger teens.

Thrasher. A few years back, *Thrasher* ran a cover announcing the "death" of skateboarding. Around the same time, librarians began mentioning concern about the content of the magazine, in particular its ads. In the beginning, it seemed more focused on skateboarding how-to, equipment, acting as your basic enthusiast magazine. Then it slowly metamorphosed into a culture magazine that reported, reflected, and perhaps created a very raw, edgy, and often vulgar skate culture. Many librarians began deselecting it, not because of fear of challenges (and there have been some) but because the magazine no longer fulfilled its purpose of being about skateboarding. A better choice for that is the following:

Transworld Skateboarding. This company also produces other thrill sport titles, all of which seem more focused on achieving altitude than copping an attitude.

Vibe. After a brief hiatus since its first issue in fall 1992, *Vibe* is back. This magazine has major backing with impresario Quincy Jones listed as its founder and Time Warner as the publisher. *Vibe* is trying to be the *Rolling Stone* (it is the same size/shape) of hiphop culture and it might succeed; the layouts are sharp, the graphics impressive, and the whole package is very professional looking. There are a lot of articles covering not just music, but also fashion and film as well. The question for *Vibe* will be whether a slick corporate magazine can really cover hiphop, underground, and urban culture with any credibility.

WWF Magazine, Pro Wrestling Illustrated, and *WCW Magazine.* Professional wrestling remains popular TV programming, with shows like WWF's Monday Night Raw and WCW's Monday Nitro finishing regularly as top cable programs each week. *PWI* carries information on all wrestling federations and is a little less slick than the *WWF* that still sets the standard.

Warp. This title calls itself "the board-sports lifestyle magazine of the 90s." Covering not just skateboarding, but also surfing and snowboarding, *Warp* will reach teens on both coasts and some in-between. The graphics, lots of full color spreads of boards and riders in action, are abundant and exciting. In addition to board coverage, *Warp* also covers music, with an emphasis on rap and alternative music. In addition to being available at newsstands, *Warp* is distributed in record stores and action sports stores. *Warp*, like many other YA magazines, claims it will be the "print version of MTV."

Word Up!, Fresh, Right On/Black Beat. Word Up! is the leader in a crowded field—similar to magazines like *Rip,* except focusing on rap music. It has elements of *Bop*-like fanzines with lots of reader involvement and lots of contests and posters.

Writes of Passage. This new title is a magazine like *Merlyn's Pen,* but also an e-zine with a strong Web page. With fantastic covers and an overall "hip" look, *Writes* is fast becoming the best literary magazine for teens.

YM. From its original as "Young Miss" to its "Young and Modern" concept, *YM* has been trying to push *Seventeen* off the hill as queen of teen magazine mountain. With a little more focus on teen heartthrobs as hunks, *YM* is both popular and informative.

YSB. YSB stands for "Young Sisters and Brothers" and is the only general-interest magazine for African American teens. *YSB* reads a lot like *Teen* or *Seventeen*, mixing advice and fashion articles, but there are also profiles of celebrities. In addition, *YSB* includes articles on politics, history, and famous black Americans. The content and ads, however, reflect "young adult" in the more traditional sense as *YSB* seems now geared toward the 18 to 25 year market.

Zillions. Consumer Reports produced one of the first "spin off" magazines with this kids' version of their title. Young readers will find the same types of articles, ratings, and features found in *CR*. The main differences between the two are the choice of products (all youth market stuff such as in-line skates, earrings, and video game CD players) and the graphics—there are lots more and all of the photos feature kids. The information is solid and much of it YA interest; however, the use of 10–year-olds in photos and features like "Top Toys" makes it a hard sell in a YA area.

Establishing a collection of recreational reading magazines will attract both users and nonusers. You will see an increase in circulation and traffic in the YA area. On some level, your YA magazine collection will create good public relations, foster a different image of the library in the YA community, and even get YAs excited to come see what you've got on the shelves. Granted, magazines are expensive to purchase and maintain, but the number of YAs who can have a positive library experience as a result of this investment make allocating funds for this purpose worth it.

4.9 MUSIC

Your music collection impacts the library and your YA audience for the very same reasons magazines matter. But the high loss rate, coupled with the diverse range of YA musical interests, and the inability to get enough copies of the "hot stuff" pose significant challenges. Yet, music is essential to YA culture and therefore a perfect place for libraries to make connections. The essentialness of music to YA culture relates back to developmental tasks: the belief "You are what you listen to" is alive and well. The YAs who listen to punk and hard-core rock define themselves with that music and the accompanying fashion.

CHOOSING MEDIA

There is no *VOYA* equivalent for music reviews. *Rolling Stone* and some magazines review new releases, but those reviews don't work for the library audience. *Billboard* is a handy trade publication, but its reviews are always positive and not revealing. Given this vacuum, you need to use other methods to find out what types of music will appeal to your YA audience. Here are a few ideas:

Ask YAs: Set up a review committee to meet monthly and choose materials. You could provide *Billboard* or similar publications, give teens order slips, and stay out of their way. YAs are more than happy to share their opinions about music.

Visit music stores: You really can't buy music sitting behind your desk. You need to get out and visit record stores, not only to see what is new, but also to see what is being pushed or hyped. In addition, if you purchase music at a local record store, the manager can help you choose music and give you various promotional goodies to use.

Use the charts: If you have access to *Billboard*, you know the various charts can be very helpful. There are charts with the top pop, modern rock, rap, and R&B releases. *Entertainment Weekly* is another good choice because in addition to listing the top music releases, each week features what is on top in specific categories (for example, college rock). *Rolling Stone* and *Spin* also feature charts—pay attention to not only what is selling, but what videos are in heavy rotation on MTV.

In the first edition of *Connecting,* I included a large section on popular music. That is absent here for several reasons. First, when I was writing the first edition I was working as YA librarian and doing the music selection, with lots of YA input, so I was up-to-date on trends, groups, etc. When I took a job as branch manager, I delegated this task to a college-aged staff member who was also a musician. She and our YAs made the music selections and we soon had a reputation for having one of the best, most diverse music collections with a particular emphasis on alternative (for example, no one else had any tapes or CDs by the Butthole Surfers or lots of gangsta rap). Occasionally I made recommendations, but mostly I provided only a general direction, a budget, and some suggestions. The lesson learned was that although at one time I may have been the "best" person to do this job, I wasn't anymore. Delegating this task to another staff member is no crime, no shirking of responsibility: it might be the best way you can see the job done well. If you can't delegate this task to a staff member, hand it over to YAs—this really matters to them. Again, set general guidelines, establish a budget, and make suggestions. If you feel your library can't buy "parental advisory" labeled materials, tell them that. They won't like it but it should stir lively debate. Teens know more about this format, care more about it, and in many ways, have even more of an interest in seeing it done right. Finally, somewhere in-between the first edition and this one I switched from MTV to VH-1; started listening to audio books rather than music tapes; and found myself listening more to news radio than the alternative rock station. Chances are, many librarians working with youth could say the same. The bottom line? Be a good "library DJ" and have an all request show.

4.10 NONPRINT COLLECTIONS

YAs are tuned into media. The overriding image of teenagers is not one with their heads buried in books, but rather with their heads in headphones while watching something on a screen. Every time a new media emerges—home video games, cable TV, CD players, and now the Internet—it presents the YA with access to this technology with one more recreational option to choose instead of reading. Libraries have attempted to join 'em (since we can't beat 'em) by purchasing heavy in nonprint areas. The first big breakthrough was in buying lots of educational nonprint that helped transform school libraries into media centers. Now public libraries have joined the fray by purchasing recreational media, including videotapes, to almost a staff breaking point. Most public libraries have never met a technology or format they did not like—YAs are the same.

The YA nonprint collection, like the books and magazines, presents several important questions at the outset. Priority setting must take place to buy the best possible materials.

CHOICES AND PRIORITIES FOR NONPRINT

These issues are the ones you will need to examine as you make decisions about nonprint collections:

Demand vs. quality: This is also known as the Snoop Doggy Dog question. You cannot deny there is a demand for gangsta rap tapes, but many would have a difficult time defending these materials by any standard. Librarians who would defend *Forever* to the end become strangely silent when there is discussion of music that just happens to seemingly glorify violence, racism, and the degradation of women.

Circulation vs. standards: This is related, but with an important difference. Without the review media we have for books, how can anyone compare music releases using standards if the standards don't exist?

Recreational vs. educational vs. informational: You have $40.00 to spend on a videotape. Do you purchase a Michael Jordan human highlight video, Wrestlemania XII, an SAT review, or an AIDS awareness tape? You have money for software—do you buy a game or a learning experience?

Professional vs. careful: Anyone who wants to be careful selecting popular music for YAs in the 1990s had better hope for a Barry Manilow comeback. As rap and alternative music continue to solidify their positions, new lines are emerging as they were in the 1980s.

Librarian vs. deejay: Do you really need an MLS to know you need to buy a new Boys II Men tape?

Demand vs. reality: Suppose you want to give YAs what they want. But you cannot afford it across the board—nobody can. Even the hottest YA book will not have as many potential readers as a hot new tape or CD release. YAs are not hearing excerpts from YA novels on the radio or seeing videos to promote them. It is the same dilemma libraries face with best-sellers: there is never enough to meet the demand.

Scope vs. charts: Selecting music probably used to be a lot easier. In the old days, there were not groups like the PMRC, intellectual freedom issues were not tested in the same ways, and music sounded safer. Today, the scope of available music is very wide and getting wider. Because YAs are more likely to buy their own music as opposed to their own books, it is possible to have an eclectic music collection even if your book collection is demand-driven.

Listening vs. watching: Nonprint is expensive and it does not usually last long. In the exercise earlier in this chapter, you may have purchased a lot of nonprint. Perhaps you skipped over some media because you couldn't afford it. To have a strong video collection, you may have to leave out computer software. As new technologies develop (DAT, video discs) and libraries start circulating other technology (CD-ROMs), libraries will face other choices: whether to get on the bandwagon at all, and if they do, which media to abandon?

NONMUSIC LISTENING COLLECTIONS

Another potential collection development area is books on tape. Although it is not as large as the market for children's or adult tapes, some YA fiction, including books by Stine and Pike, are available in cassette format. Further, classics that are sure to be on school reading lists are available on tape. In addition, audio books serve other educational purposes such as study guides, learning languages, or other topics. A good turnout at a YALSA program at the 1996 ALA annual conference about teens and audio books certainly demonstrates an interest by librarians in this area.

VIEWING COLLECTIONS

Videotapes have revolutionized how Americans spend their leisure time and how public libraries spend their money. Videos have given everyone another recreational option to choose and provided libraries with another format collection to purchase, maintain, and circulate. Videos have not only allowed libraries to bring information to people in a totally new format, but boosted circulation levels. YAs have benefited greatly from the video revolution as the days of watching filmstrips in class are slowly fading away. Libraries can certainly improve services to YAs by creating or improving video collections for this audience. Developing a good YA video collection means considering the answers to these questions:

How old? Many libraries that have adopted the *Library Bill of Rights* forget it concerning videos. The past few years have seen flare-ups as library boards have debated and voted on restricting access to R-rated videos to those under the age of 18.

What types? Some libraries refuse to be small video stores and carry many entertainment tapes, while others seem more like a branch of Blockbuster than a public library. Three types of videos line the shelves:

- *Recreational.* Just about every area you can imagine offers a recreational video. Sports (especially basketball) and music are the most popular. Again, there are few review sources available.
- *Information.* Informational videos get reviewed the most in the literature but probably garner the lowest circulation. Unlike their paperback counterparts, a teen cannot slip into a corner and watch a video about AIDS prevention and might be unwilling to check out such a tape.
- *Educational.* Heavily reviewed in our media, video companies are churning out tapes to help libraries and schools replace their 16mm, slide, and filmstrip collections. Study tapes for SAT, ACT, GED, etc. are a good bet.

Purchasing nonprint for YA collections is a challenge as patron expectations of what we should have smack up against both what we can afford and what we can keep up with technologically. The basic questions about the library's role once again emerges: if your library chooses the role of "popular materials center" that implies you will buy multiple copies of Madonna tapes rather than having a more eclectic music collection or purchasing YA fiction on tape. The real difference in AV collections is this: libraries are not the only source. Yes, there are bookstores and other outlets for YA fiction, but school and public libraries are more likely places to find YAs looking for this material. On the other hand, go to any mall record store or video shop or software center and see the place teeming with teens. Nonprint makes the circulation numbers look good. Even with the loss rate, "hot" tapes, discs, and videos will fly off the shelf quicker than almost any YA book.

Nonprint is good PR, as well. You will win more friends at booktalks announcing you just purchased a bevy of popular CDs for the library than you would trumpeting the latest Isabelle Holland opus in hardback. And you will certainly have more YAs looking for Sega or the like as opposed to educational programs. But is that what we do here? If we are content to adopt a more bookstore attitude with print collections, can we do the same with our nonprint collections? With only $1,000 dollars and plenty of choices, that might be hard to do.

4.11 TECHNOLOGY

All those hard choices have grown even harder in the high-tech world in which most libraries dwell. Harder because there is often less money for "software" because so much goes into hardware. Harder because there has never been anything attacking the foundations of public libraries like the recent *Communications Decency Act*. Harder because the excitement of the new drives everyone faster. Harder because that $1,000 now has another choice—technology. Harder because technology creates so many opportunities, creates so much access, creates so many problems that it often seems as though the machines are the masters and we are the slaves. Finally, choices are harder because unlike choosing books, some difficult and expensive hardware choices are required to run the CD-ROMs.[29]

Those expecting a long section here will be disappointed. What I have tried to do throughout the book is weave the implications and applications of technology into the other sections. One reason, it seems to me, that librarians become paralyzed by technology is they treat it as something different, something foreign. Instead, we should look at it as a whole. Why do we still review CD-ROMs containing reference information separate from books containing similar information? Why are we reinventing wheels developing policies for selecting software or Internet use when so much of it is similar to the rest of our collections? This integration is not new—most libraries have successfully integrated online catalogs into their reference functions, integrated cataloging/acquisition utilities into their technical services routines, and integrated personal computers into their daily work. The issue here is not technology in the library but collection development *and* what makes collecting technology for YAs unique.

As mentioned previously, collections in general—and technology products in particular—serve four primary functions: recreational, educational, informational, and reference. The formats are CD-ROM, game cartridges, online services, and Internet. All of these involve collection development decisions; for example, the online service First Search. Available now to libraries as a catalog add-on, there are different packages available depending upon how much a library has to spend. Again, the new boss is same as old boss—the amount of information and access available through a library directly relates to its financial position. Yes, a small rural library can get onto Internet, but can it provide more than one terminal? Can it provide an Internet collection development—that is, design an interface for the library that selects and directs patrons to the "best" sources on the Internet, just as our collection development policy for books selected and directed patrons to the "best" in that area. The PUBLIB, PUBLIB-NET, and

LM-NET archives contain messages about these very issues. Let's look here at ten of the top issues related to technology collection development and teens:

Formats: The first choice is deciding what type of collection you are going to build and with which format. Some libraries are beginning to question buying quotation sources on CD-ROMs when such tools are available via the Internet or even forsaking print sources on colleges for the vast amount of tools, like Collegenet, on the Internet. These collection decisions come down to affordability vs. accessibility. Certainly an in-house CD-ROM is more accessible than a site on the Internet, but at what cost?

Selection tools: Almost all the youth selection tools provide information on CD-ROMs, although none suggest Internet sites. The reviews are similar to those for reference books: what type of information is available, how well is it arranged, and how easy is the information to access? Nonlibrary selection tools like *Computer Life* or *Internet World* do a good job of reviewing CD-ROMs and Internet sites.

Essential encyclopedia: The first step into CD-ROM technology most libraries made was an electronic encyclopedia. Much has been written comparing the products and even their usefulness,[30-31] but it is hard to imagine a library without a multimedia encyclopedia. The *Microsoft Encarta* seems to be the best for information, but also for access and extras (videos, audio, and Internet links). *Bookshelf* by Microsoft is probably just as indispensable with its seven-reference-books-in-one approach.

Essential periodical indices: Boy, have we come a long way from the *Reader's Guide*! There are so many periodical indices—some comprehensive ones like the Infotrac products, others concerning only one index (*Public Affairs Information Service*). Young adults (like most patrons) are going to want an index that provides full text, not just a citation or abstract. Those machines and their print buttons are addictive. *SIRS* has always been a big favorite of YAs, more so in its CD-ROM format.

Key types of sources: For serving teens, a few other types of reference CD-ROMs are useful:

- Poetry index, full text
- College information
- SAT study guides
- History/geographical
- Science encyclopedia
- Literacy criticism

In each of these areas, a variety of choices is possible. Because I am personally familiar only with one or two titles for each category, I would recommend looking at *Library Journal,* which does the best job of reviewing CD-ROMs for the general audience and various CD-ROM roundup articles.[32–33] The selection is going to depend upon lots of factors, including platforms, networking options, and compatibility. In this case, technology veers away from our current book selection decision-making strategies.

Internet collection development: So you have Internet access in your library? Patrons come up, click on Netscape, and what is the first thing they see? Probably your library's home page—but what does that have on it? Although lots of information is available about writing library home pages,[34–35] not every library is able to do so. In that case, certainly make the Internet Public Library your library home page. Patrons logging onto the Internet need to see something other than the Netscape ad, and they need something to guide them in their search of the Internet.

If a library is going to offer Internet access, it needs to really offer just that—access. We don't just throw our book collections on the shelf and expect patrons to find them; instead we choose, we catalog, we classify, and we create access. Why should the Internet be different? We should look at the needs of our particular patrons and identify those resources on the Internet of most use, and then make those easily accessible. Designing a Web page is not so much about technical HTML skills as it is about collection development choices—what to include and exclude.

Evaluating sites: Chapter 9 discusses at length the issue of selecting sites. For collection development purposes, it is important to realize we need to transfer our selection criteria. There is nothing new to invent; we just merely need to adapt and expand existing systems.

Game cartridges: Almost everything covered so far has been for reference or educational use, but the big draw in lots of libraries are Nintendo and Sega cartridges. The obvious advantages to pursing this type of collection are similar to why we buy magazines—the bang for the buck and great PR. The problem primarily is deciding which systems to support, keeping up, and setting a ceiling on how much money to put into this area because staying current with the popularity is difficult.

Circulation vs. reference: Patrons also want games on CD-ROM to take home. Again, there are many questions here (this pops up almost weekly on PUBLIB) about how to do such a thing. At the beginning, with a small collection, many libraries limit either the checkout period or the number of items. Decisions include what platforms to buy as well as the practical considerations of packaging, shelving, protecting, and replacing. For teens, we come back to selection vs. censorship collections. Lots of CD-ROM games are violent and are also quite popular among teenagers. Can and would the collection development policy of your library support purchasing *Doom* and its various bloody spin-offs?

Policies: As stated throughout, technology is just another format in many ways. Because of that, libraries need to make sure their collection development choices in this area can fit within their existing policies. Further, they might need to expand policies or update them. Does your library allow you to buy materials with "parents' advisory label" on them? The bottom line for YA librarians is unchanged, whether discussing books or bytes: equal access for everyone regardless of age. That credo is part of our operating system—it is what makes the YA machine run.

YAs like technology. First, because they are growing increasingly comfortable with it, to them it is nothing special. Second, technology speeds everything up, which given the hectic nature of YA life seems to fit nicely. Finally, technology provides YAs with more independence in their library use and, frankly, more excitement. YA librarians, thus, need to be not just advocates for access to technology, but require necessary skills and knowledge to turn advocacy into reality.

4.12 SELECTION TOOLS

The review media for each format has been mentioned in passing. Considering the small size of the YA field, the amount of literature is impressive.

BOOK REVIEW MEDIA

Jobber catalogs: Most YA paperbacks do not get reviewed and most do not really need it. Jobbers like Baker & Taylor, Ingram, and Bookmen all have monthly publications announcing new releases that include YA sections.

Publisher's catalogs: One method of developing retrospective collections is publisher's catalogs. For example, if you know you need more "hot topic" books and you also know that Greenhaven books are popular, catalog ordering seems on track. The appendix of this book lists the major YA fiction and nonfiction publishers complete with addresses and URLs.

4–43
YA Review Sources

YA only
Voice of Youth Advocates
Kliatt Young Adult Paperback
Book Guide
ALAN Review

YA and children (school focus)
Appraisal: Science Books for Young People
Bulletin of the Center for Children's Books
Emergency Librarian
Horn Book
School Library Journal
The Book Report

General media
Booklist
Publishers Weekly

Keeping up with trends
Most of the above and articles in:
English Journal
Journal of Youth Services
School Library Media Quarterly

Specialized sources
Bookseller's Journal
Science Books and Films

Professional periodicals: If you have been keeping track of the endnotes and sources of information included in this book, especially in this section, you will notice *VOYA* mentioned repeatedly. It is not just a good magazine; it is essential. Addresses for *VOYA* and all these publications are available in the appendix.

Annual lists: A variety of organizations produce "best" lists which can be used for retrospective buying. These lists are compiled and published in periodicals and/or pamphlet format (see page 161).

Other lists: The best source of booklists is *Booklist,* which runs a wide range of subject lists and special features (see page 162). Others journals publish lists less frequently but still of great use (see page 163).

Reference/retroactive collection development: Although keeping up with new offerings is important, often YA collections need beefing up with "older" materials. The amount of reference sources on YA books/ literature is ample. Many of these same titles act also as readers' advisory tools (see page 164).

4.13 COLLECTION CONCERNS

As though building an active YA collection is not challenging enough, librarians also face a series of special concerns. Some of these are large societal problems, while others are specific to libraries. Chapter 8 addresses many of these concerns (censorship, for example), but let's examine two key issues and audiences for collection development.

Weeding: It is safe to say that even libraries with separate YA collections do not have the luxury of space. Constant weeding is necessary, but not only for space considerations. First, if a YA is browsing the nonfiction area in the 780s and happens upon a Boy George biography or a book about Flock of Seagulls, that sends a clear message about your collection. Second, weeding is one of the best ways to increase circulation. For example, by doing a big weeding in your hardback area, you have freed up space for displaying at the end of the shelf range. So, show them the covers. Third, if possible, consider temporary weeding. That is, prune down to a couple copies of *Fear Streets* and store the rest until you need them in the summer. If not, then you are either forced to have an area overflowing or overstuffed with titles (which is not attractive) or weed them: these are not books you don't want, they are simply ones you don't have room for. Sure, storage is a problem, but find a box or two and an area in the basement or on top of a cabinet. These books have a value, but at times, supply far outweighs demand.

Annual Lists

LIST: Best Books
SOURCE: *School Library Journal* editors
OBTAIN: Appears in December issue of *School Library Journal*

LIST: Best Books for Young Adults
SOURCE: Best Books Committee/YALSA
OBTAIN: Reprinted in *Booklist* or from ALA

LIST: Best Science Fiction/Fantasy/Horror
SOURCE: Voice of Youth Advocate reviewers
OBTAIN: April issue of *Voice of Youth Advocates*

LIST: Books in the Middle
SOURCE: Ray Barber and Suzanne Manczuk
OBTAIN: June issue of *Voice of Youth Advocates*

LIST: Books for the Teenage
SOURCE: New York Public Library
OBTAIN: New York Public Library ($2.50)

LIST: Editor's Choice
SOURCE: *Booklist* editors
OBTAIN: January issue of *Booklist*

LIST: Popular Reading
SOURCE: Popular Reading committees/YALSA
OBTAIN: ALA

LIST: Outstanding Books for the College Bound
SOURCE: Outstanding Books for the College Bound committees
OBTAIN: ALA

LIST: Quick Picks for Great Reading
SOURCE: Recommended Books for the Reluctant YA Reader committee/YALSA
OBTAIN: Reprinted in *Booklist*/ALA

LIST: Special lists and features (index to lists)
SOURCE: *Booklist* Books for Youth Editors
OBTAIN: August 15 issue of *Booklist*

LIST: Young Adult Book List
SOURCE: Los Angeles Public Library
OBTAIN: Los Angeles Public Library ($5.00)

LIST: Fanfare (best books)
SOURCE: Editor, Horn Book Magazines
OBTAIN: March/April issue of *Horn Book Magazine*

LIST: Notable Children's Trade Books in Social Science
SOURCE: Children's Book Council
OBTAIN: April/May issue of *Social Education*

LIST: Bulletin Blue Ribbons (best books)
SOURCE: Editors, Bulletin of the Center for Children's Books
OBTAIN: January issue of *Bulletin of the Center for Children's Books*

LIST: "Teacher's Choices"
SOURCE: International Reading Association
OBTAIN: via the Children's Literature Web (http://www.ucalgary.ca/%7Edkbrown/)

LIST: "Young Adult Choices"
SOURCE: Young adults, via the International Reading Association
OBTAIN: via the Children's Literature Web (http://www.ucalgary.ca/%7Edkbrown/)

LIST: "Nonfiction Honor Roll"
SOURCE: *Voice of Youth Advocates*
OBTAIN: January issue

Lists from *BOOKLIST* (1990 - 1996)

After Macaulay: Technology Books of Interest to Junior and Senior High School [Ap 15 91]

After Sweet Valley Twins [N 1 90]

Art Works [Mr 15 94]

The Asian American Experience: Fiction [D 1 92]

The Asian American Experience: Nonfiction [N 1 92]

Back to School [S 1 93]

Before Oliver Twist [Ap 15 95]

Before Stephen King [Ja 1 95]

Being Gay: Gay/Lesbian Characters and Concerns in Young Adult Books [S 1 90]

Bilingual Books in Spanish and English for Children [O 1 90]

Biographical Sources for High School Science and Math [Ap 1 91]

Books to Read When You Hate to Read: Recommended by Reluctant YA Readers in Grades 7–12 [F 15 92]

Building a Home Library: Recent Middle-Grade Books [My 1 92]

Building a Home Library: Recent Young Adult Books [Je 1 92]

Cultural Awareness: Books for All Children [O 1 90]

Don't Forget to Booktalk Those Nonfiction Titles! [Ap 15 92]

An Endangered Planet [S 15 90]

Fiction for the Gifted [S 1 91]

Groundbreakers: 25 Books That Span the Decades [Je 1 & 15 95]

Growing Up Funny [Je 15 91]

Growing Up in the South [Je 1 & 15 93]

Growing Up Jock [N 1 93]

Growing Up Male: Boys in Love [Ja 15 92]

Growing Up Male: Fathers and Sons [F 15 91]

Growing Up Male: Friends [O 1 93]

Growing Up Religious [Je 94]

Homelessness in America [O 1 92]

I've Never Been in Love Before: Romantic Comedies [O 15 90]

Just Good Reads [N 15 91]

A Moving Experience [F 1 94]

Other Voices: Fiction by Chinese Women [Ja 1 91]

Picture Books for Young Adults [N 1 91]

The Political Climate [S 15 92]

Putting Religion in Your Library [S 1 95]

Real Terror: Violence in YA Fiction and Nonfiction [N 15 95]

Science Fiction: Highlights of the '80s, Part 2 [D 15 90]

Short Takes [Mr 1 91]

Telling It My Way: Diaries for Young Adults [F 1 91]

Through the Looking Glass: The Fictional Worlds of Virtual Reality [My 15 96]

Too Fat, Too Thin, Too Tall, Too Short [My 1 95]

Youth, Drugs, and Sports [Jl 92]

Other Lists

Beall, Carol. "Beyond Christy: New Demands for YA Christian Fiction," *School Library Journal* (September 1995): 130–131.

Bishop, Rudine Sims. "Books from Parallel Cultures: Growing Up Is Hard to Do," *The Horn Book* (September/October 1995): 578–583.

Blosveren, Barbara.; Quatrella, Laura. "Teen Scene: a Booklist of Young Adult Issues," *Journal of Youth Services in Libraries* (Spring 1994): 307–311.

Bradburn, Frances Bryant. "Informing Youth about AIDS: Responsible Resources," *Wilson Library Bulletin* (January 1993): 43–46

Caywood, Caroline "Computers in Fiction," *Voice of Youth Advocates* (December 1993): 275–277.

Chance, Rosemary. "Books for Young Adults; Hard Choices: Getting Where You Want to Go," *Emergency Librarian* (March/April 1996): 57–58.

———. "Books for Young Adults; Families: Novel Entertainment," *Emergency Librarian* (November/December 1995): 57–58.

———. "Books for Young Adults: Stories of Young Adult Relationships," *Emergency Librarian* (Sept./October 1995): 57–58.

———. "Books for Young Adults: Novels of Terror!" *Emergency Librarian* v. 22 (May/June 1995): 57–58.

Cockett, Lynn S. "Entering the Mainstream: Fiction about Gay and Lesbian Teens," *School Library Journal* (February 1995): 32–33.

Evans, Dari. "How About A Date? Best Historical Fiction for Young Adults 1990–1992," *Voice of Youth Advocates* (June 1993): 80–81.

Freebury, Dorie. "Young Adult Fiction about AIDS: An Annotated Bibliography," *Voice of Youth Advocates* (October 1995): 209–210.

Hunt, Samantha. "Undeathly Literature," (recommended titles about vampires) *Voice of Youth Advocates* (August 1995): 147.

Jenkins, Christine. "Being Gay, Gay/Lesbian Characters and Concerns in Young Adult Books," *Booklist* (September 1 1990): 39–41.

Kies, Cosette. "The Humor in Horror," *Voice of Youth Advocates* (August 1995): 143–144.

Kunzel, Bonnie Lendermon. "The Call of the Wild: YAs Running with the Wolves," *School Library Journal* (August 1995): 37–38.

——— and Suzanne Manczuk. "Here There Be Dragons," *Voice of Youth Advocates* (April 1995): 13–14.

Manczuk, Suzanne; Barber, Ray. "Books in the Middle: Outstanding Books of 1994 for the Middle School Reader," *Voice of Youth Advocates* (June 1994): 71–72.

——— . "Books in the Middle," *Voice of Youth Advocates* (June 1995): 88–90.

——— . "Books in the Middle," *Voice of Youth Advocates* (June 1996): 85–87.

Margolis, Sally. "Breathing Life into the Middle Ages for YAs," *School Library Journal.* (January 1996): 36–37.

Mills, Barry P. "Plays for YAs," *Voice of Youth Advocates* (December 1993): 284–285.

Nadeau, Frances A. "The Mother/Daughter Relationship in Young Adult Fiction," *ALAN Review* (Winter 1995): 14–17.

Schon, Isabel. "Recent Noteworthy Books about Latinos for Children and Young Adults," *Journal of Youth Services in Libraries* (Summer 1996): 414–418.

Schultz, Lois Beebe. "Youth Services Recommended Reference Sources Compiled by the Youth Services Reference Evaluation Committee of the Suburban Library System, Burr Ridge, Illinois," *Journal of Youth Services in Libraries* (Spring 1996): 280–288.

Vaneck, Evelyn. "Nonfiction for Reluctant Readers," *Journal of Youth Services in Libraries* (Summer 1997): 426–429.

Webunder, Dave; Woodard, Sarah, "Homosexuality in Young Adult Fiction and Nonfiction: An Annotated Bibliography," *ALAN Review* (Winter 1996): 40–43.

"Young Adults' Choices / Compiled by Readers in Middle Schools and Junior and Senior High Schools," *Emergency Librarian* (March/April 1996): 19.

Selection Tools: Reference Books

see also
"YA Literature Resources" in Chapter 4
"Readers' Advisory Tools" in Chapter 5
and Lenz, Millicent. *Young Adult Literature and Nonprint Materials: Resources for Selection.* Scarecrow Press, 1994.

Adamson, Lynda G. *Recreating the Past: A Guide to American and World Historical Fiction for Children and Young Adults.* Westport, CT: Greenwood Press, 1994.

Anderson, Vicki. *Fiction Index for Readers 10 to 16: Subject Access to Over 8200 Books* (1960–1990): McFarland & Company, 1992

Austin, Mary C. and Esther C. Jenkins. *Literature for Children and Young Adults about Oceania: Analysis and Annotated Bibliography.* Westport, CT: Greenwood, 1996

Beacham's Guide to Literature for Young Adults. 8v. Ed. by Kirk Beetz. Washington, DC: Beacham, 1989.

Clyde, Laurel and Marjorie Lobban. *Out of the Closet and Into the Classroom: Homosexuality in Books for Young People.* New Providence, NJ: R.R. Bowker, 1992.

De Long, Janice; Schwedt, Rachel E. *Core Collection for Small Libraries : An Annotated Bibliography of Books for Children and Young Adults.* Metuchen, NJ: Scarecrow Press, 1996.

Galant, Jennifer J. *Best Videos for Children and Young Adults: A Core Collection for Librarians.* Santa Barbara, CA: ABC-Clio, 1990.

Gordon, Lee; Tanaka, Cheryl. *World Historical Fiction Guide for Young Adults.* Fort Atkinson, WI: Highsmith Press, 1995.

Kaleidoscope: A Multicultural Booklist for Grades K-8. NCTE Bibliography Series. National Council of Teachers of English, 1994.

Kaywell, Joan F. *Adolescents at Risk : A Guide to Fiction and Nonfiction for Young Adults, Parents, and Professionals.* Westport, CT: Greenwood Press, 1993.

Khorana, Meena. *The Indian Subcontinent in Literature for Children and Young Adults: An Annotated Bibliography of English-Language Books.* Westport, CT: Greenwood, 1996.

Kies, Cosette. *Supernatural Fiction for Teens: More Than 1300 Good Paperbacks to Read for Wonderment, Fear and Fun,* 2nd Edition. Englewood, CO: Libraries Unlimited, 1992.

Kuipers, Barbara. *American Indian Reference/Resource Books for Children and Young Adults.* 2d ed. Englewood, CO: Libraries Unlimited, 1995.

Kutenplon, Deborah. *Young Adult Fiction by African American Writers, 1968–1993: A Critical and Annotated Guide.* New York: Garland, 1996

Lynn, Ruth Nadelman. *Fantasy Literature for Children and Young Adults: An Annotated Bibliography,* 4th Edition. New Providence, NJ: R.R. Bowker, 1995.

Malinowsky, H. Robert. *Best Science and Technology Reference Books for Young People.* Phoenix, AZ: Oryx, 1991.

Middle and Junior High School Library Catalog, 7th Edition. Juliette Yaadov, ed. New York: H.W. Wilson, 1995.

Miles, Susan G. *Adoption Literature for Children and Young Adults.* Westport, CT: Greenwood, 1991.

Osa, Osaymiwenee. *African Children's and Youth Literature.* New York: Twayne, 1993.

Palmer, Jean. *Kliatt Audiobook Guide.* Englewood, CO: Libraries Unlimited, 1994.

Rosenberg, Judith K. *Young Peoples' Books in Series: Fiction and Nonfiction, 1975–1991.* Englewood, CO: Libraries Unlimited, 1992.

Rothchild, D. Aviva . *Graphic Novels: A Bibliographic Guide to Book Length Comics.* Englewood, CO: Libraries Unlimited, 1995.

Sapp, Gregg. *Building a Popular Science Library Collection for High School to Adult Learners.* Westport, CT: Greenwood, 1995.

Schon, Isabel. *Recommended Books in Spanish for Children and Young Adults, 1991–1995.* Metuchen, NJ: Scarecrow Press, 1997.

Senior High School Library Catalog, 14th Edition. New York: H.W. Wilson, 1992.

Shapiro, Lillian and Barbara Stein. *Fiction for Youth: A Guide to Recommended Books,* 3rd Edition. New York: Neal-Schuman, 1992

Taylor, Desmond. *The Juvenile Novels of World War II: An Annotated Bibliography.* Westport, CT: Greenwood, 1994.

Weltson, Ann. *Explorers and Exploration: The Best Resources for Grades 5 through 9.* Phoenix, AZ: Oryx, 1993.

Attitudes: Looking at comments on PUBYAC or even listening to people talk at conferences about series fiction, in particular R.L. Stine's books, normally brings up the comment "Well, at least they are reading something." I touched on this briefly when we explored the question "What is quality?" but it is an important point worth restating and reinforcing. This, to me, is akin to walking up to a married couple and saying to the woman, "Well, at least you married someone." It is insulting. It devalues the reader as reader and as a person. It devalues the reading experience; it is elitist; and it is counterproductive. There are many attributes for this attitude, but most stem from the belief that kids not only should not be reading "junk," but that it will stunt their reading growth. It is a nice theory; but it is also quite wrong.

An award-winning research project by Dr. Catherine Sheldrick Ross found that series reading, far from being harmful, might be for some readers an essential stage in their development as powerful readers. After tracing the history of series books and looking at the text themselves (although not Stine), Ross concludes:

> In making the 'doorway to literacy' one of the central goals of public libraries, librarians have recognized their crucial role in the making of readers. My contention is that in their culture battles they have identified the wrong enemy. Rhetoric to the contrary, series books do NOT enfeeble readers or render them unfit for reading anything else. It is not helpful to establish a hierarchy in reading which a reader's passionate engagement with a pleasure book somehow does not count as 'real reading.' . . . Series books can be as allies in the goal of making readers. [36]

Ross further advances that the best way to create readers is to have lots of books available, and then to let readers choose. This is nothing new—the value of voluntary free reading has been well documented through readers' diaries, case studies, as well as anecdotal evidence. [37-39] What is new, and important, is that Ross has found that the theory of series hindering reading doesn't hold water. Even for people who endorsed series, this was always a point of some hedging. The research tells what kids knew—series readers are serious *real* readers, devoted readers, and on the path to becoming lifelong readers.

Such research was necessary and long overdue. Ross writes:

> [C]urrent critics who denounce series books as enemies of good reading are likely to be influenced by the interpretive activity of prior readers and certainly have the support of at least a hundred years of received opinion against series book reading. It appears that hostility to series books is part of a large configuration of attitudes involving the place of fiction in public libraries, attitudes that de-

veloped along side the revolution in reading and cheap book publishing that took place in the nineteenth century North America. Discourse on popular fiction has changed very little over the past one hundred years, as becomes evident when we compare what was said about 'trashy' fiction and dime novels in the 1880s with what is being said now about the horror series for young readers. [40]

Just as interesting is Ross's report on a 1994 conference of reading experts discussing children's series. Rather than talking about the usual suspects—mysteries and romances—the meeting turned into a Stine bash. Around the same time, Ross followed a discussion on the *rec.arts.books.children* newsgroup concerning the relative merits of Stine. Ross reports back some of the better comments, noting that rather than discussing the texts or merits of Stine's books, "the main argument turned on beliefs about what people thought was happening when children read." [41] What Ross did was fill in the blanks, substituting research for assumptions. Further, rather than assuming what children should and should not read, Ross writes "one of the most important reading lessons of all is developing confidence in one's ability to put a book down without finishing it. The librarians quoted from the library literature of the past 100 years seem, in hindsight, to have been overconfident in their ability to know better than the reader what choices are best. Readers reject this presumption." [42]

Balance, of course, would be best: some light series reading, some harder more challenging books. Yet, the first step in that "escalator" is learning that reading is indeed recreational.

Reaching rampant readers: Some YAs take the escalator on their own, which presents some special problems. The 7th graders who devoured and then bored of *SVH* might be coming to you by 8th grade for more serious romances. Eventually by 10th or 11th grade (if not sooner), the materials in the YA section will no longer be of interest to them. Finding materials for this group is often difficult because although their reading tastes, interests, and abilities have matured, many of the adult books might also be inappropriate. Some of these readers will be making a transition from popular YA fiction to popular adult fiction; from *SVH* to Danielle Steel or adult series romances. Others, however, will be looking for more serious works. *School Library Journal* contains a section on adult books for YA readers, and *Booklist* also notes adult titles with YA interest. There are many authors to consider when attempting to reach this rampant reader audience.

75 Adult Authors for Rampant Readers

1. Adams, Douglas
2. Anderson, Kevin (Star Wars/X-Files)
3. Andrews, V.C.
4. Angelou, Maya
5. Anthony, Piers
6. Asimov, Isaac
7. Atwood, Margaret
8. Auel, Jean
9. Baldwin, James
10. Bradbury, Ray
11. Bradley, Marion Zimmer
12. Braun, Lillian Jackson
13. Brooks, Terry
14. Card, Orson Scott
15. Christie, Agatha
16. Clancy, Tom
17. Clark, Mary Higgins
18. Clarke, Arthur C.
19. Cook, Robin
20. Donaldson, Stephen
21. Edrich, Louise
22. Ellis, Bret Easton
23. Finney, Jack
24. Gardner, John (Bond)
25. Godden, Rumer
26. Grafton, Sue
27. Grisham, John
28. Guest, Judith
29. Harris, Thomas
30. Hayden, Torey
31. Herbert, Frank
32. Hesse, Hermann
33. Hillerman, Tony
34. Holt, Victoria
35. Irving, John
36. Jackson, Shirley
37. Jordan, Robert
38. Kesey, Ken
39. King, Stephen
40. Knowles, John
41. Koontz, Dean
42. Kozinski, Jerzy
43. LeGuin, Ursula
44. Ludlum, Robert
45. McCaffery, Anne
46. McCammon, Robert
47. Michaels, Barbara
48. Michener, James
49. Morrison, Toni
50. Norton, Andre
51. Oke, Janette
52. Patterson, James
53. Plath, Sylvia
54. Potok, Chaim
55. Pynchon, Thomas
56. Rand, Ayn
57. Rice, Anne
58. Robbins, Tom
59. Salinger, J.D.
60. Salvatore, R.A.
61. Saul, Jon
62. Shatner, William
63. Sheldon, Sidney
64. Steel, Danielle
65. Steinbeck, John
66. Stewart, Mary
67. Tan, Amy
68. Terkel, Studs
69. Tolkien, J.R.R.
70. Tyler, Anne
71. Vonnegut, Kurt
72. Walker, Alice
73. Weis, Margaret
74. Wiesel, Elie
75. Wright, Richard

What Makes Readers Reluctant?

1. They associate reading with failure.
2. They are not interested in ideas.
3. They are not capable of sitting still long enough to read.
4. Their egocentric nature doesn't coincide with many of the books which are required reading.
5. Reading doesn't provide level of entertainment they desire.
6. They find it counterproductive to read or to read only certain types of materials.
7. They have grown up in a nonreading environment.
8. Reading is a solitary task and therefore considered anti-social.
9. Reading is an "adult thing" or "school thing" and therefore is rejected.
10. Reading is difficult for them because they lack reading skills.

Adapted from Lance Gentile and Merna McMillan, "Why Won't Teenagers Read?" *Journal of Reading* (1977): 649–654.

4.14 REACHING RELUCTANT READERS

Reluctant readers do normally want a thin book, but they want more books as well. The reasons for reluctant and aliterate readers vary.[43-44] Some are psychological, some physical, and others emotional. Reluctant readers are not stupid: they are kids who do not choose to read. Treating them like dummies is just as counterproductive as pushing Jane Austen down their throats. Because they are reluctant to read, in addition to materials which encourage them, they will also need encouragement from adults. I'm not talking about pushing, but real encouragement, matched with materials that will make reading a positive experience.

Reluctant reader titles take many shapes and sizes. Books like Walter Dean Myers' 300–plus-page *Fallen Angels* have appeared on the Quick Picks list, but so have wordless picture books. In general, fiction books for reluctant readers will

- Have a hook to get the reader's attention immediately
- Move at a fast pace with only a few characters
- Have a single point of view and few flashbacks or subplots
- Deal with real-life situations and high interest topics
- Have emotional impact; they are gripping and memorable
- Use short sentences and paragraphs and nonchallenging vocabulary
- Have attractive covers, wide margins, and easy-to-read typefaces
- Weigh in at less than 200 pages

Nonfiction will meet many of this criteria, but also will

- Contain lots of illustrations to complement the text
- Adopt a magazine-style layout approach
- Contain first-person narrative and real-life experience

One powerful tool has been YALSA's Quick Picks committee. The evolution of the committee has been interesting. It started as the "Hi Lo" committee, meaning high-interest, low-vocabulary group who found the Fry reading level for each book and listed titles for librarians to use with nonreaders. In the 1980s, the committee changed names to the Recommended Books for the Reluctant YA Reader committee and further evolved with more emphasis on the high-interest aspect and less on low vocabulary. In the 1990s, the committee changed names once again to the "Quick Picks" committee, reflecting its change in audience. The annotated list targeted YAs, YAs got involved in the selection process, and the committee moved away from looking at the number of words in a paragraph to looking at titles that would hook readers.

Librarians, of course, are not on the real front lines in this area—reading and English teachers deal daily with such students. The professional literature in education overflows with articles about methods of instruction, motivation, and encouragement. For librarians, reaching the reluctant reader takes rethinking some attitudes (the escalator theory; the only real reading is book reading; any thin book is okay for a reluctant reader) and developing methods to reach this audience. Let's examine the ABCs of promoting materials for the reluctant YA reader:

Advertise: Take out an advertisement in the school newspaper promoting one or more books. Or take out an ad in the PTA or PTO newsletter telling parents with nonreaders to contact the library for suggested books.

Booktalk: Make the books come alive to nonreaders. Booktalking is covered in detail in Chapter 6.

Contests: Run trivia contests about authors or subjects that connect YAs with your collection.

Dramatize: With a teacher's cooperation, lift dialogue sections out of YA novels and have the teens act them out. This makes the "action" in the book seem more real.

Educate teachers to library resources: Just as we are often lacking knowledge about what teachers are doing, they probably are not aware of our tools. Make sure that they get a copy of Quick Picks. Chances are that they have never heard about it, let alone seen the list. That is just one of several resources available to provide libraries with suggested titles.

Find out more: As mentioned, much of the best literature about reaching reluctant readers is not in our literature, but in the research on reading. Find out what teachers are doing and see how libraries can complement it.

Genres: Assume that reluctant readers are not looking for a certain book by a certain author, thus having books in order by author on the shelf for easy access does not really help. But, by organizing by genre, you are arranging books how YAs think rather than how we think.

High visibility: Pull out the Quick Picks and others with high appeal and get them in people's faces. Reluctant readers are often not reluctant library users so you can find them and help them find you.

Incentives: Offer prizes if the library is running a reading program or work with school to give extra credit.

Picture Books for YAs: Top 10 Titles Bib Squib

1. Base, Graeme. *Eleventh Hour.* Abrams (ISBN: 0810932652) $10.75
2. Bunting, Eve. *Smoky Night.* Harcourt (ISBN: 0152699546) $15.00
3. Drescher, Henrik. *The Boy Who Ate Around.* Hyperion (ISBN: 0786811285) $4.95
4. Goldberg, Whoopi. *Alice.* Dell (ISBN: 0553089900) $15.00
5. Gurney, James. *Dinotopia.* Turner (ISBN: 1878685236) $35.00
6. Macaulay, David *Motel of the Mysteries.* Houghton Mifflin (ISBN: 0395284252) $11.95
7. Manuki, Toshi. *Hiroshima No Pika.* Morrow (ISBN: 0688012973) $16.00
8. Szieszka, Jon. *The Stinky Cheeseman.* Viking (ISBN: 067084487X) $16.99
9. Sendak, Maurice and Arthur Yorinks *The Miami Giants.* HarperCollins (ISBN: 0062050680) $15.95
10. Van Allsburg, Chris. *Jumanji.* Scholastic (ISBN: 0590545507) $2.99

Adapted from "Sophisticated Picture Books for the Middle Grades" in *Teaching K-8* (May 1994): 54–57.

Joint ventures: Increase cooperation. Schools and public libraries can work together harder to reach this market than any other.

Knowledge: Many librarians working with YAs only know the name Christopher Pike as the first captain of the Enterprise on *Star Trek*. Pike was publishing great reluctant reader books like *Slumber Party* which YAs knew about, but most librarians were clueless.

Lists: Take a piece of legal-size paper and cut it in thirds. Now you have a skinny piece of paper. Fill it with the author, title, and one-word description of books under 150 pages. Now you have a list of skinny books on skinny paper.

Magazines: Remember that reluctant readers need items other than books.

Nonfiction: Most classroom reading is fiction, thus nonfiction is a welcome change and also mixes text and illustration.

Out loud: Not only small children like to be read to.

Picture books: An interesting trend that impacts reluctant (and rampant) readers is ageless picture books like the *Stinky Cheese Man*.

Quantity: Use bookdumps. If you have multiple copies, more people can read them. The more people reading them, the more people know about a title, then the more "cool" it is to read that book.

Reach out: Some students are talking loudly about a subject. They seem quite interested in the subject but you also know they are Quick Picks. Slip away and find something—a magazine article, an entry in a reference book, anything about this subject. Bring it back and mention it casually. Demonstrate in small ways the value of reading to obtaining information.

Samples: Take a toothpick, a photocopy of an interesting page or photo from a book, attach a tag on the page with full information about the book, and leave these free samples out.

Tie-ins: Take a rubber band, a book, and the movie based on the book and combine them together for a package deal. Or a rubber band, a fiction title, and a personal narrative. Or a rubber band, a photo of a celebrity, and a biography.

Urgent: If students are reluctant readers yet they are facing a reading assignment, chances are they will be reluctant about choosing their books. Thus, lots of that last-minute "I want a thin one" reference transaction is going to take place. Make sure that other staff have access to all the materials you have prepared. If a nonreader is willing to come in and get something out of an urgent need and we cannot supply it, then there is virtually no chance that a YA will leave the building with a positive attitude.

Video reviews: If you offered a YA a chance to be a video star by telling about a book or magazine article he has read, would he do it?

Writers: If a YA can see a real writer in person sometimes this makes reading a little more interesting.

X marks the spot: Using posters and other decorations, make the YA area a comfortable inviting place to be.

Yes: Find a way to say Yes to most any request.

Zippy and Ziggy: Comic books, graphic novels, and the like appeal to reluctant readers.

Reaching YA reluctant readers is not an easy task. A good deal of literature and a YALSA committee is out there to help, however. The market certainly is there, as every YA librarian knows. Meeting this market means adopting strategies, changing assumptions, and thinking creatively about ways to promote library materials. If we fail, then the reluctant readers are not the "dummies"; librarians are.

ENDNOTES

1. Patty Campbell. "Perplexing Young Adult Books: A Retrospective," *Wilson Library Bulletin* (April 1988): 20+.

2. Barbara A. Genco, et al. "Juggling Popularity and Quality: Literary Excellence vs. Popular Culture," *School Library Journal* (March 1991): 115–119.

3. *Directions for Library Service to Young Adults*, 2nd Edition. American Library Association, 1993: 13.

4. Silk Makowski, "Getting Serious about Series," *Voice of Youth Advocates.* (February 1994): 351.

5. Cosette Kies, "Eeeck. They just keep coming! YA Horror Series," *Voice of Youth Advocates* (April 1994): 19.

6. Lynn Cockett, "Best Books for Young Adults, Real Young Adult Opinions of the List, the Process and the 1995 Selections," *Voice of Youth Advocates* (December 1995): 284–287.

7. "YALSA Fantasy Genre List," *Journal of Youth Services in Libraries* (Spring 1996): 323–324.

8. "YALSA Humor Genre List," *Journal of Youth Services in Libraries* (Summer 1995): 418–419.

9. "YALSA Romance Genre List," *Journal of Youth Services in Libraries* (Winter 1996): 216–217.

10. "YALSA Sports Genre List," *Journal of Youth Services in Libraries* (Fall 1995): 112–113.

11. Chris Lynch, "Today's YA Writers - Pulling No Punches," *School Library Journal* (January 1994): 37–38.

12. Patrick Jones, "Crossing the Line in YA Fiction," *Michigan Media Spectrum* (Summer 1993): 39–40.

13. Joan Best Friedberg, et al., *Portraying Persons with Disabilities: An Annotated Bibliography of Nonfiction for Children and Teenagers.* New Providence, NJ: R.R. Bowker, 1992.

14. Patrick Jones, "Listen, Do You Want to Know a Secret?" *The New Booktalker, Vol 1.* Joni Bodart, ed. Englewood, CO: Libraries Unlimited, 1992.

15. Fred Lerner, "Keeping Classics in Print," (science fiction novels) *Voice of Youth Advocates* (December 1993): 279–280.

16. Fred Lerner. "Concerning Purely Personal Choices," Voice of Youth Advocates (October 1994): 200– 202.

17. "Best Science Fiction, Fantasy and Horror," *Voice of Youth Advocates* (April 1996): 17–18.

18. Hazel Rochman, *Against Borders.* American Library Association, 1993.

19. Jean Davies Okimoto, "Letters to the Editors," *Voice of Youth Advocates* (December 1995): 282.

20. *Outstanding Books for the College Bound: Choices for a Generation.* Marjorie Lewis, ed. American Library Association, 1996.
21. Doug Estell, *Reading Lists for College-Bound Students,* 2nd Edition. Arco, 1993.
22. Ruth Cline and William McBride, *A Guide to Literature for Young Adults: Background, Selection, and Use.* Glenview, IL: Scott, Foresman and Company, 1983: 151.
23. Dorothy Broderick and Mary K. Chelton, "Reviewing Philosophy and Policy," *Voice of Youth Advocates* (February 1994): 362.
24. Alice Yucht, et al., "VOYA's Nonfiction Honor List," *Voice of Youth Advocates* (August 1996) : 148+.
25. Stephen Krashen. *The Power of Reading.* Englewood, CO: Libraries Unlimited, 1993: 46–60.
26. Deirde Carmody, "Competition for Young Readers Has Magazines Totally Psyched." *New York Times* (January 18, 1983).
27. Jana Fine, "Teen 'Zines: Magazines and Webzines for the Way Cool Set," *School Library Journal* (November 1996): 34–37.
28. Fine, p. 36.
29. Peter Jacso, "The Hardware Helper: Taking the Guesswork out of Multimedia Systems," *School Library Journal* (November 1996): 30–33.
30. Peter Jacso, "State-of-the-Art Multimedia in 1996: The "Big Four" General Encyclopedias on CD-ROM," *Computers in Libraries* (April 1996): 26–32.
31. Barbara Hoffert, "The Encyclopedia Wars; CD-ROM or Online? Illustration or Information? Search or Browse? Don't Expect Easy Answers from Publishers," *Library Journal* (September 1, 1994): 142–145.
32. "Best CD-ROMs," *Library Journal* (April 15, 1997): 41.
33. Patrick Dewey, *303 CD-ROMs to Use in Your Library: Descriptions, Evaluations, and Practical Advice.* American Library Association, 1996.
34. Ray Metz and Gail Junion-Metz, *Using the World Wide Web and Creating Home Pages: A How-to-Do-It Manual.* New York: Neal-Schuman, 1996.
35. Sandra Matsco and Sharon Campbell, "Writing a Library Home Page," *Public Libraries* (September/October 1996): 284–287.
36. Catherine Sheldrick Ross, "If They Read Nancy Drew, So What? Series Book Readers Talk Back," *Library & Information Science Research* (Summer 1995): 234.
37. G. Robert Carlsen and Anne Sherrill, *Voice of Readers: How We Come to Love Books.* Urbana IL: National Council for Teachers of English, 1988.
38. G. Robert Carlsen, *Books and the Teenage Reader: A Guide to Teachers, Librarians, and Parents.* 2nd Revised Edition. New York: Bantam, 1967.

39. Mary Leonhardt, *Parents Who Love Reading, Kids Who Don't.*
New York: Crown, 1993.
40. Ross, p. 205.
41. Ross, p. 206.
42. Ross, p. 223.
43. Kylene G Beers, "No Time, No Interest, No Way! The 3 Voices
of Aliteracy," *School Library Journal* (February 1996): 30–33.
44. Kylene G. Beers, "No Time, No Interest, No Way! The Three
Voices of Aliteracy: Part 2," *School Library Journal* (March 1996):
110–113.

DECEMBER

Goal: To improve collections used by YAs.

1. **Weed:** A YA collection needs to be active. Perhaps the most valuable commodity of any service to YAs is space, so use it wisely. Every book needs to earn its place on the shelf because it "does" circulate, not because it "should." Either it moves, or it moves off the shelf.

2. **Reorganize:** Now that you have made room, use it. Look at the literature on merchandising and recognize that most YAs seek out books, rather than *a* book. Admit that most YAs find books because of covers, not reviews, or because of recommendations from friends, not from you. If you weed your hardbacks, you now have room to display the ones remaining, and their circulation will increase.

3. **Create impact:** Just about everything you learned in library school about collection development was wrong—wrong if you want to create impact, which will lead to increased support. Yes, it would be nice to have lots of titles, but a collection will have more impact with fewer titles and more copies. YAs want to read what their friends are reading: one hardback has no impact.

4. **Input:** Here is another chance to involve youth. Too many things to do? Then delegate selection to YAs. Each month put out the Bookmen's *Monthly Paperback News* (or similar jobber paperback monthly catalog) and tell the YAs how much they have to spend. Give them order slips and your selection becomes complete.

5. **Budget battles:** All those stats you gathered in September, you need to have ready. If you are working for a rational person in a rational organization, the assumption is that agencies/departments/services that achieve success (measured by increase in circulation) are rewarded with increased budget. This is critical to know going in: you need to know, first, whether circulation even matters to administrators, and secondly, whether there is any precedent of achieving departments that achieve more of a budget. Because the goal of any library is to serve its community, the resources of the library should be distributed towards those things that best serve the community. If you can demonstrate that serving YAs has "best" served your community (the circulation increases are the measures of success), then resources should follow. Thus, the key to creating support first is creating success.

YEAR-END REVIEW: YA BESTS

(VERY PERSONAL OPINIONS)

THE BEST BOOKS FOR YOUNG ADULTS
Books which appear on both YALSA's Best Books for Young Adults and YALSA's Quick Picks list. Currently such a list is not published.

THE BEST YA NOVELIST
Chris Crutcher, Caroline Cooney (tie)

THE BEST NEW YA NOVELIST
Rob Thomas

THE BEST YA FICTION PUBLISHER
HarperCollins

THE BEST YA NONFICTION AUTHOR
Janet Bode

THE BEST YA NONFICTION PUBLISHER (EDUCATIONAL)
Greenhaven Press

THE BEST YA NONFICTION PUBLISHER (INFORMATIONAL)
Free Spirit Press

THE BEST YA PAPERBACK WRITER
Diane Hoh

BEST YA PAPERBACK FICTION SERIES:
Fear Street by R.L. Stine

BEST YA PAPERBACK PUBLISHER
Bantam Doubleday Dell

THE BEST YA MAGAZINE (GIRLS)
YM

THE BEST YA MAGAZINE (BOYS)
SLAM

THE BEST YA AUDIO TAPE PUBLISHER
Recorded Books

THE BEST ELECTRONIC ENCYCLOPEDIA
Microsoft *Encarta*

THE BEST REFERENCE COMPACT DISK
Social Issues Resource Series

THE BEST YOUNG ADULT LITERATURE WEB SITE
Kay Vandergrift's YA Literature Web Site
http://www.sclis.rutgers.edu/special/kay/yalit.html

THE BEST YOUNG ADULT SERVICES WEB SITE
Internet Public Library - Teen Division
http://aristotle.sils.umich.edu/teen

BEST PUBLIC LIBRARY YOUNG ADULT WEB SITE
Berkeley (CA) Public Library
http://ci.berkeley.ca.us:80/bpl/teen

BEST INTERNET SEARCH ENGINE
Hotbot
http://www.hotbot.com

BEST YA PROFESSIONAL PUBLICATION
Voice of Youth Advocates

BEST BOOK ABOUT YOUNG ADULT LITERATURE
Cart, Michael. *From Romance to Realism: 50 Years of Growth and Change* (HarperCollins, 1996)

5 REFERENCE, READERS' ADVISORY, AND INSTRUCTION

Reference, readers' advisory, and instruction services are the primary interpersonal connecting points between YAs and librarians. Yet, more than just "professional" services, they are also customer services, something librarians seem to neglect on occasion. Reference service for teenagers is not radically different from that with other patrons: what works and does not work with others is similar with YAs. Because of YA developmental needs, however, there are some special considerations. Similar, readers' advisory service with YAs requires unique approaches. Library instruction and orientation for YAs is an essential area that can improve reference services, if libraries allot time to do it and do it right. Finally, because so much reference work relates directly to school work, developing lines of communication between libraries and schools can go a long way to improve reference service. All libraries provide reference service to teenagers, so that is not the issue. The issue arises when you try to answer the question "What is quality reference service?" And because reference is the primary interaction point between teens and librarians, that question becomes part of the bigger question "What is quality YA service?"

5.1 QUALITIES FOR QUALITY SERVICE

A YA's one-on-one interaction with the library, whether that interaction involves choosing materials or getting reference assistance, determines the teen's level of satisfaction. Recent research shows, at least for one large urban public library, what customers (not just YAs) consider to be excellent service (see "What Is Excellence in Library Service?" in this section). What is noteworthy here is that staff helpfulness was rated as one of the most important qualities—and that is one-on-one interaction. One of the main differences between the library with YA services and one without is staff helpfulness. Although computers might be making patrons less dependent on staff, it still seems that "satisfaction" relates to human, not computer, interaction.

What then makes for excellent service for YAs? Two resources propose lists—both YALSA's *Young Adults Deserve the Best* (see page 181) and Chelton and Rosinia's *Bare Bones* describe the most desirable qualities for a YA librarian. Not surprisingly, the lists overlap in many areas. In researching the top "rules for advertisers" for attracting YAs, Zollo found interesting information that relates to the desired qualities for YA librarians (see Figure 5–1). Even though all these findings are not applicable (librarians rarely need to use great music to serve patrons), many of the advertising techniques are also personality traits that librarians can use to provide quality YA service (such as using humor, being clear, and not preaching).

Like most tasks, providing service is a combination of skills, knowledge, and attitudes. The contention here is that YA work perhaps is different from other library work in that without the "right" attitude as a base, the other two traits do not matter as much. In training, I often use an exercise called "qualities for quality service" in which the participants choose the top 10 qualities a librarian working with teens should possess and then rank them. Repeatedly, the 10 items you see in the "Top Traits" sidebar on page 184 show up in the results.

"Approachable" comes in first because no matter how many other skills you have, if a YA does not feel you want to help, if your body language or maybe even the layout of the reference desk configuration says "Stay out," then the other skills won't be used. "Respectful" comes next and usually links with "nonjudgmental." Just as Zollo reported, most YAs feel that adults assume they are going to cause trouble and don't treat them with the same amount of respect, dignity, and patience as they treat others. "Knowledge of YA" is usually next; most librarians feel they need to know their user group. Finally, in the top five is the "patience/persistent" combination, although sometimes those qualities are required as much in dealing with other staff as they are with YAs. Instinctually, most librarians realize that Zollo is on target as a sense of humor is probably most important. Important because not only will most YAs appreciate it, but it also dispels many negatives stereotypes about librarians.

If these are the qualities YA librarians should possess, then how would that translate to an overall program of quality service? Drawing on YALSA's vision, the measurement of a quality YA service relates to how well it does the following things:

Young Adults Deserve the Best

Area 1: Leadership and Professionalism
1. Develop and demonstrate leadership skills in articulating a program of excellence for YAs
2. Exhibit planning and evaluating skills in the development of a comprehensive program for YAs
3. Develop and demonstrate a commitment to professionalism
4. Plan for personal and professional growth
5. Develop and demonstrate a strong commitment to the right of young adults to have access to information
6. Demonstrate an understanding of and respect for diversity
7. Encourage young adults to become lifelong library users

Area 2: Knowledge of Client Group
1. Apply factual and interpretative information on adolescent psychology in planning for materials and services
2. Apply knowledge of reading process and types of reading problems
3. Identify the special needs of discrete groups of young adults

Area 3: Communication
1. Demonstrate effective interpersonal relations
2. Apply principles of effective communication which reinforce positive behavior in young adults

Areas 4: Administration
1. Planning
    a. Formulate goals and objectives and methods of evaluation
    b. Design, implement, and evaluate ongoing public relations programs
    c. Identify and cooperate with other information agencies
    d. Develop, justify, administer, and evaluate a budget for YA programs
    e. Develop physical facilities
2. Managing
    a. Supervise and evaluate other staff
    b. Design, implement, and evaluate ongoing program of staff development

    c. Develop policies and procedures for efficient operations
    d. Identify external sources of funding
    e. Monitor legislation and judicial decisions pertinent to YAs

Area 5: Knowledge of Materials
1. Formulate a selection policy
2. Develop and maintain collection with all appropriate formats
3. Demonstrate a knowledge and appreciation of YA literature
4. Identify current reading, viewing, and listening interests of YAs
5. Design and locally produce materials to expand the collection
6. Incorporate technical advances in the library program

Area 6: Access to Information
1. Organize collection to guarantee easy access to information
2. Use current standard methods of cataloging and classification
3. Create an environment which attracts and invites YAs to use the collection
4. Develop special tools with which to process information not readily available
5. Devise and publicize pathfinders, booklists, displays, etc.

Area 7: Services
1. Utilize a variety of techniques to encourage use of materials
2. Provide a variety of information services
3. Instruct YAs in basic information gathering and research skills
4. Encourage young adults in use of all types of materials
5. Design, implement, and evaluate special programs and activities
6. Involve YAs in the planning and implementation of services

Figure 5–1 What Attracts Teens to Advertisements?

Rules for Advertisers

Nothing attracts teens to advertising more than humor.

(percent of teens selecting statement as one of top five rules for advertisers, by gender, 1994)

	total	boys	girls
Use humor/be funny	60%	62%	57%
Be honest	55	54	57
Be clear with message	45	44	47
Be original	38	36	41
Don't try too hard to be "cool"	37	38	36
Use great music that fits	34	35	33
Don't use sex to sell	33	25	41
Make ads teens can relate to	33	29	37
Grab attention right away	30	31	28
Show/demonstrate product	29	27	30
Don't preach	29	27	30
Show things/people realistically	29	25	33
Don't talk down to teens	27	26	28
Make ads to teens, not parents	23	24	22
Don't butcher a good song	21	24	18
Be politically correct	20	19	21
Don't try to be "teen"	19	19	19
Show sexy girls	19	34	3
Use current teen slang	14	14	15
Use new, different celebrities	13	13	14
Show teens or those slightly older	13	13	13
Use celebs who fit the product	12	12	11
Don't be obvious you're selling something	12	12	12
Show sexy guys	9	5	13
Use fantasy	8	10	6
Tell who the advertiser is right away	7	8	6

Source: TRU *Teenage Marketing & Lifestyle Study*

Reprinted, with permission, from Peter Zollo, *Wise Up to Teens*. Ithaca, NY: New Strategist Press, 1995.

Traits of an Effective YA Librarian

1. Respects patrons
2. Commits to meeting YA needs
3. Understands YAs
4. Responds to YAs by providing relevant resources
5. Uses knowledge of YAs in direct service interactions
6. Appears approachable
7. Possesses strong communication skills
8. Displays patience and persistence
9. Demonstrates a good memory
10. Empathizes with YAs
11. Shows ability to set and enforce limits
12. Maintains a sense of perspective
13. Demonstrates a sense of humor
14. Is everything a good librarian is, plus energy, enthusiasm, and intensity

Adapted from Mary K. Chelton and James Rosinia, *Bare Bones.* American Library Association, 1992.

1. Responds to YAs
2. Respects YAs as individuals
3. Readies YAs as they move from being children to adults
4. Reaches out to the community
5. Reaches in to involve everyone on the staff
6. Reacts to changes
7. Involves youth in the library
8. Resists efforts to restrict access
9. Advocates for youth, in particular for equal treatment
10. Creates raving fans

The key to all of this is simple. We must recognize that young adults have unique information needs and understand that they are important customers for libraries.

RAVING FANS

Reference service consists of two parts: reference and service. *Reference* means knowledge and skills—a librarian knows the best source for information or will use interview skills to determine it. A reference librarian, thus, is a reference librarian before anyone asks a question. But merely knowing is not enough: a librarian serving YAs needs the ability to apply these skills with a customer service based attitude. Not many publications explore customer service in libraries, in particular as part of the reference interview. Studying reference seems too often to concentrate on short-term solutions ("Did you find the answer?") rather than the long-term effect of patron satisfaction.

Michael LeBoeuf's book *How to Win Customers and Keep Them for Life* [1] is a "textbook" filled with ideas, slogans, and suggestions for improving customer service. Although LeBoeuf is aiming at the business reader, much of what he says is applicable to libraries—in particular,

Qualities for Quality Service

Energetic	Problem-solver
Articulate	Complaint handler
Evaluative	Knowledge of computers
Planning minded	Intellectual freedom fighter
Ethical	Interior designer
Respectful	Reviewer
Disciplinarian	Merchandiser
Encouraging	Booktalker
Knows YA psychology	Discussion leader
Knows YA literature	Instructor
Knows YA pop culture	Organizer
Communicator	Reference librarian
Research minded	Politically skilled
Creative	Youth involver
Promoter	Empathetic
Budget minded	Rule breaker/risk taker
Sense of humor	Statistician
Fund raiser	Enthusiastic
Nonjudgmental	Patient/persistent
Cooperative	Approachable

Top Traits

1. Approachable
2. Respectful
3. Nonjudgmental
4. Knowledge of YA
5. Patient/persistent
6. Sense of humor
7. Enthusiastic
8. Communicator
9. Energetic
10. Youth involver

Why YAs Are Important Customers

Note: This list relates to YAs as retail customers, but it also is applicable to YAs as library patrons.

1. They have discretionary spending power.
2. They spend the family's money.
3. They influence parents' spending.
4. They are trendsetters.
5. They will be customers in the future.
6. There will be more of them than ever in the years ahead.

Adapted from Peter Zollo, *Wise Up to Teens*. Ithaca, NY: New Strategist Press, 1995.

to libraries serving YAs: "The only two things people ever buy are good feelings and solutions to problems." [2]

That statement seems to sum up a YA reference transaction. Every reference transaction is about solving a problem: "I need three books on this," or "I need to find who did this," or "Where can I find this article?" The second part we all know—everyone wants to leave with good feelings. With YAs, this is vital because teenagers are emotional beings. They are stars in their own movies, and a reference transaction is just another scene. They can come out of the library feeling good about themselves they solved their problem and someone treated them with courtesy and respect, *or* they can exit the scene still with their problem and feeling bad, normally about themselves. Those are not customers we have won for life.

Another similar publication about customer service, one I've already referred to, is *Raving Fans* by Ken Blanchard.[3] Again, creating raving fans consists of three steps:

1. Developing a vision
2. Identifying the customer
3. Delivering, plus one percent (exceed expectations)

YA reference work begins, as Zollo wrote, with acknowledging the importance of YAs and recognizing their uniqueness. In order to deliver quality services, librarians need to practice their best skills and avoid their worst. For many librarians, this might take some retraining to learn the behaviors that contribute to correct answers. It is interesting to relate these skills and behaviors back to the list of "qualities for quality service" outlined earlier. They are almost identical.

You can use reference transactions to create raving YA fans by following these "Ten Commandments" of YA reference work:

1. Always let YA customers know what good service they are getting.
2. Always offer short-term follow-up ("Come back if this doesn't help") as well as long-term ("See me again when you have another paper due").
3. Always find a way to say yes, always find a way to agree, and whenever possible, demonstrate your competence.
4. Always show YAs you know your stuff—most act impressed rather than intimidated by your knowledge.
5. Always be sensitive to a YA's sense of space—in terms of eye contact, body language, and other nonverbal cues.
6. Always listen, learn, and then ask open-ended questions.
7. Always be prepared to do triage reference—working with several YAs at one time.

How to Win Customers and Keep Them for Life

A Customer is . . .
1. The most important person in our business
2. Not dependent upon us. We are dependent on them.
3. Not an interruption of our work. They are the purpose of it.
4. Doing us a favor when they call. We are doing them a favor by serving them.
5. Part of our business—not an outsider.
6. Not a number. They are human beings with feelings and emotions like your own.
7. Not someone to argue or match wits with.
8. People who bring us their wants. It is our job to fill those wants.
9. Deserving of the most courteous and attentive treatment we can give.
10. The lifeblood of this and every other business.

Five Basic Customer Service Facts
1. To win customers, you must reward them.
2. People buy only two things: good feelings and solutions to problems.
3. Whenever you contact a customer, you are the company to that customer.
4. Customers pay your wages; thus they are your real boss.
5. Always make customers aware of the great service they are getting.

The Five Best Ways to Keep Customers Coming Back
1. Be reliable.
2. Be credible.
3. Be attractive.
4. Be responsive.
5. Be empathetic.

Adapted from Michael LeBoeuf, *How to Win Customers and Keep Them for Life*. New York: Berkley Books, 1987.

8. Always be empathetic, relaxed, and maintain a sense of humor.
9. Always "reward" the YA customer through encouragement, positive re-enforcement, politeness, kindness, and by saying "yes."
10. Always think of every reference transaction as a moment of truth: the success or failure of it perhaps will determine whether your YA customer is coming back.

These commandments are built on a customer service base. Let's adapt Michael LeBoeuf's five best ways to keep customers coming back by incorporating the importance and uniqueness of YA interpersonal services: being reliable, credible, attractive, empathetic and responsive:

1. *Reliable means knowing and delivering.* Yes, it is difficult, but if students come for help and you don't have the knowledge to provide it, they can't depend on you. That is why gathering information about schools is important: if you understand the assignment, chances are that you can do a better job of providing reference.

2. *Credible means having authority.* When YAs need your help, you need to be able to answer completely, not speaking in half sentences or making assumptions, but knowing the information you have provided answers their questions. Credible for YAs means someone who speaks to them, not at them. Someone who lets them do the work, rather than ripping the mouse or keyboard out of their hands. Someone who has a working knowledge of the subject at hand and who approaches a problem working with students rather than around them.

3. *Attractive means many things, from nonverbal signals to the actual physical layout of the reference desk.* Attractive means attracting, but it seems most reference desks push people away with their architecture, constantly ringing telephones, untidiness, and sprawl. Look at the main reference area of your library, and then imagine going to a doctor or lawyer whose work area looked

Best Reference Transactions

1. Verifies specific question
2. Asks follow-up question
3. Uses open probes
4. Finds answer in first source
5. Paraphrases or clarifies
6. Gives full attention

Adapted from Lillie Seward Dyson, "Improving Reference Services," *Public Libraries.* (September/October 1992): 285

Worst Reference Transactions

1. Physical setting acts as barrier
2. Unwelcoming body language
3. Lack of follow-up questions
4. Failure to listen to questioner
5. Doesn't keep patron informed
6. Doesn't treat question as important
7. Gives up easily
8. Appears to want to "get rid" of patron
9. Doesn't volunteer explanations
10. No follow-up
11. Unfamiliarity with sources

Adapted from Catherine Sheldrick Ross and Patricia Dwedney, "Best Practices: An Analysis of the Best (and Worst) in Fifty-Two Public Library Reference Transactions," *Public Libraries* (September/October 1994): 261–266.

like that—would you be worried? Attractive means eye contact. One drawback of automation is the tendency to put our heads down and type away furiously at the start of a question, rather than listening, acknowledging nonverbally with good eye contact, and then using the computer. Interact with the YA first and the machine second.

4. *Empathetic means knowing the pressures and time constraints YAs feel.* Yes, it is their own doing, but that shouldn't leave us without empathy. Would it kill us to make a photocopy for a YA who doesn't have any money? What damage would it do to stay open an extra five minutes so students can finish printing their papers rather than turning off the computer at 9:00 on the dot? Empathetic means acknowledging how difficult an assignment might be, or sensing YAs' confusion. Empathetic simply means trying to remember what it is like to be 16 and being faced with those issues.

5. *Responsive means what we have outlined all around: knowing needs and making an effort to meet them.* If all students are researching a particular site on the Internet, bookmark it or put in on the library's Web page. Make the customer the focus.

LeBoeuf and Blanchard's theories on customer service are designed to increase profits, which is something libraries can't do. But the philosophy behind creating ravings fans, or customers for life, is exactly what libraries must do when serving YAs.

5.2 REFERENCE SERVICES

We've already established that most teenagers have a job and that job is going to school. In order to do that job well, they often need to visit libraries to obtain the resources they need. For reasons also discussed previously, barriers abound. Let's first examine what we want reference service to accomplish, consider the reference process by looking at common questions we hear from YAs over the desk, and then provide possible answers.

Goals of reference services for YAs:

1. Help YAs find needed information
2. Help YAs by being friendly and approachable with inviting body language
3. Provide instruction so YAs can work independently

Behaviors That Contribute to Successful Transactions

Approachability: smiles, makes eye contact, gives a friendly greeting
Comfort: speaks in related tone and is mobile
Interest: gives patron full attention; makes attentive comments and maintains eye contact
Listening: does not interrupt, but asks clarifying questions and rephrases/repeats
Inquiring: asks open-ended questions
Searching: searches in best source first and keeps patron informed
Informing: speaks clearly, verifies understanding, and cites source
Follow-up: asks "Does this completely answer your question?"

Adapted from Lillie Seward Dyson, "Improving Reference Services," *Public Libraries* (September/October 1992): 285

4. Follow up to see that YAs have found what they needed and that the experience has been a positive one
5. Reduce YAs' frustration by doing the first four

In many ways, these goals are not much different than all reference services, but look at them in the context of the uniqueness of doing YA reference work. This uniqueness begins with the nature and context of YA reference transaction.

STATEMENTS AND STRATEGIES

By looking at some common reference questions and situations the uniqueness of YA reference work becomes clear.

"My paper is due tomorrow!"

The hectic nature of YAhood often flies smack in the face of good planning. YAs (and librarians) put off unpleasant tasks until the last moment and, for some people, nothing can be as unpleasant as writing reports or term papers. When the student is feeling rushed, it is not the time to go into teacher mode and demonstrate how things work, but rather find something for them quickly. When adults come in looking for a car repair manual or information on a company, they have an immediate need which we meet. With students, you want to walk with them to the shelves and help them find one or two sources. Think about the retail experience—are you more likely to buy a product if someone points to where it is or if they walk you to it and put it in your hand? You need to meet that immediate need. And you need to help relax and reassure the student if possible. No, you won't be able to find everything that YAs need for their papers, but make sure they do not leave empty-handed even if it means handing a resource to them.

"I have to do a paper on . . . "

When most people come to the library looking for information not only do they know *what* they are looking for but also *why* they need it. YAs are different often in that regard—sure, they know why they need the information (to complete the assignment), but many times they don't know or don't understand the context of the question they are asking. Nor will they even know how to phrase the question, which results in the "garbled assignment" problem.

Sometimes you can have several students all working on the same assignment and not realize it because each one has garbled and interpreted it so differently. With all assignments, you want to attempt to obtain a copy of the assignment sheet if there is one. Some teachers actually put assignments in writing and amazingly some students actually hang on to them. Copy these assignment sheets and organize a space at the reference desk to store them. Note on the copy the grade/ class/teacher's name and the assignment's due date. On this sheet, you can also list possible reference books or search strategies.

"I want a book exactly on . . . "

The opposite is the YA who doesn't like anything you come up with. The question the teen asked you is probably the thesis statement of the report and the YA wants you to find a book that exactly answers that question. And it has to be an entire book and it needs pictures and . . . Here is the opportunity to explain in simple terms what the student really needs is not a book but rather certain information contained in several books or other sources. This is probably harder to communicate because although we "give 'em what they want," we normally don't try to "tell 'em what they want." Sometimes you have to make it clear that exactly what they want is not available, but your library does offer a number of ways to find the information they seek.

"I can't use an encyclopedia . . . "

Actually, this is more of a teacher issue than a student one. Even if you suggest another reference source, if the source has the word *encyclopedia* in the title, the student may think they cannot use it. Normally teachers mean they don't want the *World Book* used. If you're unsure about what the teacher wants, but you know, for example, that the *New Catholic Encyclopedia* is the best source, encourage the student to use that source. Give them a copy of your card to take to the teacher if there are problems, or try to contact the teacher yourself. This one issue can be a real mess because libraries spend thousands of dollars on reference books and CD-ROMs which many students believe are off-limits. Make sure to point out to student that it is certainly appropriate to use an encyclopedia to gather background information, to identify important people/places/events, and to find bibliographies.

"Do you have any books on religion?"

Beware of broad questions for underneath lurks the real one. Pointing to the 200s is, of course, not the answer. But the best strategy is not always to ask directly ("What is it you want?"). If they wanted to tell you that, they might have asked it that way. Provide the YA with options. Sure some YAs ask directly if you have *The Satanic Bible,* for example, but the "books on religion" question is the normal route. Don't invade a YA's privacy any more than you would that of an adult.

"Do you have any books on health?"

We certainly cannot always assume that YAs asking questions are working on papers; sometimes they are working out a problem. Be careful not to let embarrassing situations occur by asking the student who wants books on AIDS when the paper is due only to find out it is not for a paper. Not only are these situations quite embarrassing and even emotional, but they bring up questions about the types of responsibilities librarians serving youth have and how much (if any) they should intervene.

"My son has to do a paper on . . . "

If there is one type of patron perhaps universally loathed by many, it is the parent doing the research for their child.[4] This presents all sorts of potential problems, not the least of which are your own feelings about the situation. Some parents do this willingly, others out of desperation. Helping them is a challenge because you can't do a strong reference interview because more often than not they don't know about what they need. Because you can't present them with options to narrow the search, broaden the search giving them many materials to take home so their child can choose the best ones. Related, often the parent will come in with the child, but the parent will do all the talking. Focus your eyes on the student and ask them the follow-up questions because they are the ones who will help you complete the reference transaction. Whenever possible you want to separate the YA from the parent; if you don't you will never learn what the student really needs—instead you will learn only what the parent thinks he needs.

"Everyone has to do a paper on . . . "

The nightmare question. Again, the best course of action is to contact the teacher or at least the school librarian. This is when our skills as reference librarians get a workout. Rather than finding information directly on a subject (it's all gone by now), we have to think of the subject heuristically—what is the range, the field, and the wave. By adapting problem-solving techniques to reference, we can avoid problems and seek solutions.

"Why don't you have any books on . . . ?"

YAs are easily frustrated. Despite how easy we think it is to use the library and no matter how easy we say it is in library instruction, it isn't. Finding information is easy for us because we do it every day; but it is not easy for many YAs who don't like and don't want to research. Over the desk, you'll be dealing with frazzled students who looked in the card catalog under "CIVIL WAR" and found only one

> **The key to doing reference work with students is finding ways to reduce their frustration level.**

book. How would they know the correct subject heading or a better search strategy in an online environment? The key to doing reference work with students is finding ways to reduce their frustration level.

"Where's the card catalog?"

As libraries automate, this question comes from every patron. The special challenge with ego-driven YAs is that most will tell you they know how to use it even if they don't. If you don't have library instruction available, you need to do it on the fly with individual patrons. The technique matters: go slowly, keep it simple, and repeat everything. Always let the YA use the mouse or do the typing—don't just say "Click there," but explain briefly why that is the thing to do. Don't assume that students know how your online catalog works just because they are not afraid of computers. Don't assume every YA is computer literate and pay attention to the different ways in which girls and boys approach using computers.

"I couldn't find it on the shelf."

We tend to anchor at our desks, but walking to the shelf with the student is a valuable technique. Not only does it greatly increase the chance that the YA will find the requested material and have a positive library experience, but it offers side benefits as well. First, YAs see that you are a real person, with legs and everything. Second, you are reinforcing the fact that you really do care that they find what they need and you are reversing the idea that all librarians do is sit and point like a Cocker Spaniel. Third, you have the opportunity to use that time walking to the shelf to make a connection with a student—find out a name or a school, at least.

(While looking in the fiction section) "Why don't you have any books about Hemingway?"

Library organization might be clear to us, but it is not to too many YAs, even with some instruction. Shouldn't everything having to do with Hemingway be in the same place? To them, that makes perfect sense. If they are not finding what they need, communicate that it is not because they have made a mistake or are looking in the "wrong" place, but rather because things in the library are organized differently and that you will gladly show them the 813s.

(The same student doing Hemingway) "Why can't I find any articles on him on Infotrac?"

Again, here is another situation where the student has good intentions but just doesn't have the right tool. Without much detail, you want to explain the topics Infotrac (or whatever) are good for, and those that it doesn't work so well for, like literary criticism.

"How many books am I allowed to check out?"

Sometimes you get this question from a student who is holding a stack of books but is doing only a three-page paper. Although our instinct perhaps is to want the student to take them all out, we know better. You don't want to correct or discourage, but you do want to lend some experience and tell the student that having the most books does not always equate to having the best paper.

"How do you do an outline?"

You might find yourself helping with more than research. Often students will ask you to help them do certain parts of a project or interpret what their teachers have asked them to do. This is a tough call: the student wants help, not for you to hand them a copy of the *MLA Handbook*. The best bet is to help students by asking questions to help focus their thinking or by talking through the problem at hand.

"Why can't I ever find anything here?"

The YA may be telling the truth or exaggerating. But even one bad library experience can be enough for some. Reference service to YAs has to be positive—look for a way to say "Yes." There are times when there is no other answer ("Can I take this reference book home?"), but often there are options ("Let's see if we have a circulating one/let's make a photocopy/the same information is available in this other book /let's see if there is a related Web site," etc.)

"Where are the horror books?"

Wouldn't it be nice to be able to answer that easily? Normally the answer is not an easy one. "Well, the paperback horror is over there, collection of horror stories are there, and then you have to look in the fiction for individual authors like Stephen King." Because libraries don't (and probably can't) organize their entire collections by genre, they can at least divide paperbacks by genre and they can prepare and train staff to do effective readers' advisory service.

"Where can I find a bibliography on President Kennedy?"

Ah, a teachable moment. Chances are that the student wants a biography, not a bibliography. Maybe it is important to correct the word choice, but only after you have helped them get the correct book in their hands.

"How do I find poetry on the Internet?"

Again, a teachable moment. If a student needs a poem on a certain subject, chances are that the Internet is not the best choice, especially if your library has a poetry CD-ROM or even a nice poetry book collection. Helping students decide the best source for each inquiry (one tool doesn't fit all) is part of our job of teaching information literacy.

"Where can I get a term paper?"

This is more of an ethical question than a reference question, but consider it. You know where: *Rolling Stone* magazine runs ads for companies that offer "term paper" assistance and Internet sites like Schoolsucks make them readily available. It is a legitimate question to which you know the answer, but do you answer it?

"How do I do a bib card for a Web page?"

Have ready, either in print format or bookmarked, a style sheet which provides students with the proper style for citing electronic resources.

"How do I find a book?"

Well, there is a broad question. After burrowing, you'll probably get to the real inquiry. But the core issue is that of reference vs. instruction. Should you, if time is available, teach YAs how to fish or fish for them? It is a tough call. On one hand, you want to encourage YAs to be independent, to develop skills, and to succeed; yet, on the other hand, helping people find things is what we do. The "always" here is "always be flexible." Don't dominate the interview, but let it flow.

Get a sense of how interested the YAs are in learning how to search and research. They make the call—not you. Most, however, are eager to learn and catch on quickly if you provide appropriate and friendly instruction. Sometimes you might want to do one search first as a demonstration, show them a successful result, and then watch while they repeat and change the search. Instruction also includes teaching what to do after they find what they need on a computer. The transition from a successful search to actual location of the information or document can be difficult and frustrating for some library patrons.

Imagine how frustrating it must be for a student to walk into a library (I need help), ask a question (I don't know something), ask for instruction (I don't how to do something), and still not get their needs met (I can't find anything, I won't get this done, I'll fail this class). For us, that question the student asks is just one hash mark on a statistical sheet, but for them it might be the most important thing in life at that moment. And if we want those students to return, not only do we need to answer the questions, but do so in a way that gives them "good feelings." One method of doing this is delivering plus one. That does not mean going the extra mile, but sometimes just going an extra step away from the desk.

Homework Collection: Fact Sheet

What is a homework collection? A separate collection of materials gathered in one area to assist students in completing common school assignments.

What is *not* a homework collection? A regular reference collection, a temporary reserve shelf, or an encyclopedia set. Nor is it a homework center, which implies tutors and other intensive services.

What is the purpose of a homework collection? To make use of the library a less frustrating experience for students by gathering materials in one easy to locate area, providing multiple copies of materials, offering special materials designed to meet their needs, and making items available to be retrieved independently and quickly. Designed as a self-service reference center, the homework collection is designed for the student who needs only a few resources to start on a paper and not more detailed instruction.

Who uses a homework collection? The center is designed for students in grades 7 through 12.

How do you create a homework collection?

1. Identify materials of use.
2. Survey schools and library staff about most popular term paper topics (also called "pop tops")
3. Arrange signs and displays
4. Organize facility
5. Measure use

Note: An additional step might be acquiring outside funding.

Materials

Pop Tops: Pop tops are a series of folders with information often requested by students for term papers and reports. The reason for pop tops is to see that students looking for information on topics where all books may be checked out will not leave empty-handed. These folders may not be checked out, but materials may be photocopied. Each folder will contain an "opposing viewpoint" pamphlet on the topic, five overview or "pro and con" articles either photocopied, purchased, or downloaded from the Social Issues Resource Series, a 10–item bibliography, and a list of valuable Web sites. (The purpose of this 10–item bibliography is not to replace periodical indexes, but to meet the expected demand for information on these topics.)

Circulating Reference Books: The center will contain multiple copies of various standard reference works available in paperback. These can be used either in the homework collection or be taken home for overnight loan. Works might include the following:

- Dictionary
- One-volume encyclopedias
- Thesaurus
- Foreign language dictionary
- Almanacs
- Medical dictionary
- *Guinness Book of World Records*
- Mythology dictionary
- Science/technology dictionary
- Atlases
- Geographical dictionary
- One-volume biographical dictionary
- Quotation dictionary

Student Helpers: The center also will contain multiple copies of various handbooks instructing students on the following topics:

- How to write a term paper
- How to write a book report
- How to footnote correctly (MLA)
- How to do a science project
- How to use reference materials

Opposing Viewpoints: The center also will have multiple copies of paperback editions of books in the Greenhaven Press series. Books will cover those topics in the Pop Tops folders and others.

Internet Access

Necessary to any collection or program directed at homework assistance is access to the information resources available on the Internet. Similar to how the rest of the homework collection pulls from the larger collection those items of special interest, a homework page should be created or linked to provide students with fast links to the best homework related resources available.

What is the goal of a homework collection? To increase independent access for students to the rescues most often needed to complete homework assignments

A quote on homework collections: "To most patrons, the library is simply a means to an end. To the students, the "end" is a completed paper and a passing grade, and the amount of help given by the librarian should be adjusted to the reality." Mary K. Chelton from "Young Adult Reference Services in the Public Library," in *Reference Services for Children and Young Adults.* Binghamton, NY: Haworth Press, 1983

Homework Centers: Elements of Success

A homework center differs from a homework collection in that services are also available, including these:

1. One-on-one tutoring
2. Library skills instruction
3. Phone or e-mail homework help
4. Literacy training
5. Quiet study space
6. Dedicated computers with information producing, word processing, and CD-ROMs

The elements of success for a homework center are these:

1. Sound planning
2. Dedicated/outside funding
3. Youth input
4. Support from schools
5. Support from community
6. Involvement of volunteers
7. Public relations
8. Flexibility
9. Multiple locations and support for location managers
10. Dedicated space

Adapted from description of homework center programs in *Excellence in Library Services to Youth: The Nation's Top Programs*, Mary K. Chelton, ed. American Library Association, 1994. Rosellen Brewer, "Help Youth At Risk: A Case Study in Starting a Public Library Homework Center," *Public Libraries* (July/August 1992): 208–211.

PROACTIVE REFERENCE

Then there is the problem of YAs who will not take one step toward a reference desk. Some don't ask for help because they want to do it themselves, and others think they should do it themselves and won't seek assistance. Then there is plain old fear: they are unsure of what or whom to ask, so it is easier not to bother. Whatever the reason, it is safe to say that a large percentage of YAs use libraries without seeking assistance. Here are strategies to help YAs use the reference services at their disposal:

Proactive: If they won't come to you, you need to find them. They are easy to spot either wandering in the stacks like lost tourists or anchored at a computer terminal. Your approach must be careful. Rather than asking "Need help?" you could ask "Are you finding what you need?" It is a subtle but crucial difference—they can admit they need assistance without admitting they need help. Hang out at teen clothing stores and observe how the professional sales people approach their teen customers.

User friendly: We try to make libraries into self-service centers, but it just does not always work. A step in this direction is developing special homework collections that give students the information they need in the approach they want. The purpose of these collections and any other related services (tutors, peer assistance, homework hotlines, term paper workshops, etc.) is to meet the goals of YA reference service. *Excellence in Library Services* contained examples of successful homework center projects. Reading through the description of these projects, you can see common themes about the "elements of success" for public library homework centers and collections.

Pathfinders: It is often not possible to put together homework collections such as these. The next best thing is to put it together on paper. In other words, produce for distribution documents that will help students help themselves. Most pathfinders will do the following things:

- Define the topic
- List subject headings in catalogs and indices
- List special reference books
- List browsing call numbers
- List cross references, including names

The pathfinder is a shortcut for both the student who doesn't have time or choose to seek assistance and for the librarian to use with the most requested topics. Sometimes these are called *homework cards* and are kept in files accessible to students. Technology, however, has made pathfinders more available and accessible. Setting up pathfinders as Web pages in a networked environment can provide students with an easy step-by-step approach to finding information. For library staff, pathfinders ease the burden of dealing with repeat assignments on an *ad hoc* basis.

Research guide: Another kind of pathfinder is one that focuses more on the library's reference collection. More than just listing sources, these research guides take the students step-by-step through the research process. These work best on larger topics to help students narrow their search and use the right tools for their topic.

A ready reference collection: No matter how good a reference interview is, the idea of reference is to relate a question with an answer. The entire collection is available, but it is often the reference collection librarians turn to first. Most libraries have a ready reference collection for immediate staff use or one that is easily accessible to the public. An overlooked source of reference information, however, is the circulating collection. In particular are "question and answer" books which mirror the reference process. Although many of these books are lacking in documentation or source notes, the information presented is based on research and/or consultation with scholars and is presented in a nontechnical, easy-to-read style. In some ways, these sources resemble the hard question files kept in reference departments where new librarians can find the answer to inquiries handed down from generation to generation of librarians in the department. Similar to these files is the Stumpers listserv—in fact, more than a few stumpers have been solved through this ready reference.

Reference service to YAs requires all the same skills and techniques used with other patrons. In particular with YAs, the developmental tasks play a huge role. The self-consciousness of YAs is a major barrier—after all, a reference question is admission of not knowing. By utilizing the techniques of customer service, by adopting a proactive posture, and by integrating a customer centered/problem solving focus, reference services to YAs will create raving fans. But more than that, YA reference can create winning staffs. Just as good customer service solves problems and creates good feelings, it also is rewarding for the providers of that service.

5.3 READERS' ADVISORY SERVICES

As we learned earlier, librarians are often not where YAs turn to get advice on what to read. Because they don't ask us, we don't do it enough. Because we don't do it enough, we can't or don't keep up on

---

Fun Fast Facts: Bib Squib

Achenbach, Joel. *Why Things Are*. New York: Ballantine (ISBN 0345377982) $10.00
———. *The Big Picture: Why Things Are Vol. II*. New York: Ballantine (ISBN 0345362241) $9.00
Adams, Cecil. *The Straight Dope*. New York: Ballantine (ISBN 0345333152) $5.95
———. *More of the Straight Dope*. New York: Ballantine (ISBN 0345351452) $10.00
———. *Return of the Straight Dope*. New York: Ballantine (ISBN 0345381114) $10.00
Berliner, Barbara. *The Book of Answers*. New York: Prentice Hall (ISBN 0134065549) $9.95
Burnam, Tom. *Dictionary of Misinformation*. New York: Harper (ISBN 0069131350) $11.00
Feldman, David. *Do Penguins Have Knees?* New York: Harper (ISBN 006092327X) $10.00
———. *How Does Aspirin Find a Headache?* New York: Harper (ISBN 0060925582) $10.00
———. *Improbables*. New York: Morrow (ISBN 0688059147) $9.00
———. *When Did Wild Poodles Roam the Earth?* New York: Harper (ISBN 0060924322) $10.00
———. *When Do Fish Sleep?* New York: Harper (ISBN 0060920114) $10.00
———. *Why Do Clocks Run Clockwise?* New York: Harper (ISBN 0060915153) $10.00
———. *Why Do Dogs Have Wet Noses?* New York: Harper (ISBN 0060921110) $10.00
Poundstone, William. *Big Secrets*. New York: Morrow (ISBN 0688048307) $10.00
———. *Bigger Secrets*. Boston: Houghton Mifflin (ISBN 0395530083) $10.95
———. *Biggest Secrets*. New York: Morrow (ISBN 068813792X) $10.00
Zotti, Ed. *Know It All*. New York: Ballantine (ISBN 0345362322) $9.00

---

the literature. Because we don't know, we often give bad advice. Also because there are so few YA librarians most library staff are not reading YA books. Because we don't read it, we don't feel comfortable recommending titles. Finally, given lack of training and lack of information, too many fall back on prejudices about what YAs should read as opposed to what they want to read. That's a harsh statement, but it is reflective of the need to move toward a customer centered base service: their needs become our needs.

Goals of readers' advisory service:

1. Match YA reading interest with library collection
2. Provide access for readers to library collection
3. Learn the likes/dislikes of YA readers
4. Promote reading through use of documents
5. Find the right book for the right YA at the right time for the right reason

STRATEGIES FOR READERS' ADVISORY

Don't wait for them: Many YAs do want help but just won't ask for it. Bad experiences or maybe just plain shyness cause this hesitancy, so you need to go find them when they are browsing in the stacks.

Ask questions: All of the obvious ones. Not just what they read, but what they liked or didn't like about a book.

Then, ask more questions: Often "I don't know" is the response to your perfectly asked query "What is the last book you enjoyed reading?" Ask about movie or TV shows: anything that will give you an idea on what interests this YA.

Develop your own core collection: Either on paper or in your mind, set down with some of the tools and develop a core list of authors and/or titles. Learn the names of at least three mystery authors you can always recommend; three historical authors, etc.

Narrow: Ask do they care if it's a boy or girl? Younger or older? Scary or funny? Fat or thin? First person or third person? Hardback or paperback? Rural or urban? Even if you can't recommend certain books, at least help the person develop an idea of what they are looking for and then maybe together you will find something.

Eliminate: A lot of YAs are inarticulate telling you the books they like, but real quick to list all the things they don't like in books, with "fat" and "boring" being chart toppers.

Use the books: If you have discovered something they have read before, find it and examine it. Most paperback publishers included "if you liked this book, then try" ads right in the books. It is the cheap way out. Related, you can quickly scan book spines for books by the same publisher. It is not the best way, but you might stumble on something.

Be smart: If the person hasn't expressed a real interest in reading and has told you they have a book report due tomorrow, then set *Moby Dick* aside. There is nothing wrong with asking someone if they want a "thin one."

Use the return cart: Everyone knows the best books are the ones just returned. Bring over the items to be shelved and go through them together.

Be aware: You need to be very sensitive to how the person is reacting to you. If they are quiet, stay low key.

Things not to say include: "I loved (*gush gush gush*) this book!" or "I loved this book in school," or "My teenager son/daughter loved this book," or "They use this in many schools," or "Teachers often recommend this book," or "Everyone should read it!"

Find a fit: If possible you always want to avoid stereotyping, but often a YA's clothing, hair, and manner does say something about their identity and possibly their reading tastes. In other words, consider suggesting *Weetzie Bat* to anyone sporting a pierced nose. But at the same time be careful of stereotyping and handing a person of color any book by an African American author. I'd say let them "open the door" and then be ready with a fit.

Aim high rather than lower: You will immediately lose whatever minimal credibility you have by suggesting a book that is below the YA's reading level or tastes. As a rule, figure most YAs want to read about kids one to two years older. Thus, your high school juniors/seniors want recommendations out of the adult collection, not "YA kid stuff."

No advice can be best advice: If you cannot really peg the kid or nothing comes to mind, then just admit it. Remember a lot of YAs get turned off because they get bad advice rather than no advice at all. The worst thing you can do is recommend the wrong book. If you just can't get a good read, suggest several titles rather than just one.

Recommending without request: Sometimes a person browsing is doing just that, and they don't want or need help. This time. If you see they have tucked away a particular title (*The Outsiders* for example), then jot down some titles for next time.

Recommending by special request: Offer a personal bibliography service for your avid readers. Have people fill out a card and then mail them the results of your search. Hang on to their cards and as new books come in, notify them. Figure 5–2 gives you an example of a card you can use or adapt for your library.

Recommending by parent's request: Many times it is mom who has come in to pick up something for her non-reading son hoping (again) to find that one book that will hook him. Every YA area should have easily accessible for staff and patrons a copy of Quick Picks for just such an occasion. If the YA is there with the parent, as with the reference interview, you want to try to get the YA away from the parent long enough to gather information without commentary. You want to find what the YA wants to read, not what the parent thinks he should read.

Use tools: The professional literature is loaded with tools recommending books because they are "best," or "just the thing," or "like another book." Although it is impossible to purchase all of these tools, at least one needs to be bought for every library serving young adults.

Figure 5–2 Personal Bibliography Card

Personal Bibliography Card

Want to find more good books to read? Here is an easy way. Just fill out this card and one of the librarians will mail you a list of recommended books based on what you told us about what you like and don't like. It should take about two weeks to compile your first list

NAME:

ADDRESS:

EMAIL ADDRESS:

SCHOOL:　　　GRADE:　　　AGE:

1. Name three of your favorite authors or books:

2. Please circle the kinds of books you like best:

Humor　　Mystery　　　　　Romance　　　　　Nonfiction　　Horror

Fantasy　　Science Fiction　　Realistic　　　　　Thrillers

Other:

3. Which of these do you like the least?

4. Do you prefer books about

　　Characters Your Own Age　　　Older Teenagers　　Adults

5. Do your prefer books

　　Under 150 Pages　　　Under 200 Pages　　　Doesn't Matter

6. Is there anything else you can tell us which would help us find books for you?

YA Readers' Advisory Tools: Bib Squib

---

see also
> YA Literature Resources (page 98)
> YA Selection Tools (page 164)

Bodart, Joni. *One Hundred World Class Thin Books: Or What To Read When Your Report Is Due Tomorrow.* Englewood, CO: Libraries Unlimited, 1993.

Books for You: A Booklist for Senior High Students. 11th Edition. Shirley Wurth, ed. National Council of Teachers of English, 1992.

Estell, Doug. *Reading Lists for College-Bound Students,* 2nd Edition. New York: Prentice-Hall, 1993.

Estes, Sally. *Genre Favorites for Young Adults.* American Library Association, 1993.

——. *Growing Up Is Hard to Do.* American Library Association, 1994.

——. *Popular YA Reading.* American Library Association, 1996.

Gillespie, John Thomas. *Best Books for Senior High Readers.* New Providence, NJ: R. R. Bowker, 1991.

——. *Best Books for Junior High Readers.* New Providence, NJ: R. R. Bowker, 1991.

Helbig, Alethea K. & Agnes Regan Perkins. *This Land Is Our Land: A Guide to Multicultural Literature for Children and Young Adults.* Westport, CT: Greenwood, 1994.

Herald, Diana Tixier. *Genreflecting: A Guide to Reading Interests in Genre Fiction.* Englewood, CO: Libraries Unlimited, 1995.

——. *Teen Genreflecting.* Englewood, CO: Libraries Unlimited, 1997.

Hunt, Gladys. *Read for Your Life: Turning Teens into Readers.* Grand Rapids, MI: Zondervan, 1992.

Lynn, Ruth Nadelman. *Fantasy Literature for Children and Young Adults: An Annotated Bibliography,* 4th Edition. New Providence, NJ: R. R. Bowker, 1995.

Outstanding Books for the College Bound: Choices for a Generation. Marjorie Lewis, ed. American Library Association, 1996.

Reed, Arthea. *Comics to Classics: A Parent's Guide to Books for Teens & Pre-Teens.* International Reading Association, 1988.

Rochman, Hazel. *Against Borders: Promoting Books for a Multicultural World.* American Library Association, 1993.

Schon, Isabel. *Books in Spanish for Children and Young Adults,* 4th Edition. Metuchen, NJ: Scarecrow, 1993.

Sherman, Gail and Bette Ammon. *Rip Roaring Reads for Reluctant Teen Readers.* Englewood, CO: Libraries Unlimited, 1993.

Spencer, Pam. *What Do Young Adults Read Next?* Detroit, MI: Gale, 1993.

Totten, Herman and Risa Brown. *Culturally Diverse Library Collections for Youth.* New York: Neal-Schuman, 1994.

Your Reading: An Annotated Booklist for Middle School and Junior High, 1995–96 Edition. National Council of Teachers of English, 1996.

Zvirin, Stephanie. *The Best Years of Their Lives: A Resource Guide for Teenagers in Crisis.* American Library Association, 1992.

10 "Big Ones"

1. Cooney, Caroline. *Face on the Milk Carton.*
2. Crutcher, Chris. *Staying Fat for Sarah Byrnes.*
3. Duncan, Loïc. *I Know What You Did Last Summer.*
4. Hinton, S.E. *The Outsiders.*
5. Kerr, M.E. *Fell.*
6. Klause, Annette Curtis. *The Silver Kiss.*
7. Myers, Walter Dean. *Scorpions.*
8. Peck, Richard. *Remembering the Good Times.*
9. Pike, Christopher. *Slumber Party.*
10. Pullman, Philip. *Ruby in the Smoke.*

Use technology: Not surprisingly, readers' advisory is being automated. Maybe a machine can't ask the question, but it can provide the answer. Most of these CD-ROM programs allow users to find fiction (but not nonfiction) by searching by genre, historical period, other authors, just to mention a few. Products like these have long been available for children, but seem now well established for adult collections.[5]

Use conversation: Approach YAs who you know are avid readers and get input from them about what they liked and why they liked it. Listen in on conversation in the stacks, ask opinions, and gather information from readers.

Use statistics: Do periodic checks about which YA titles have holds and/or are circulating the most; then buy more copies, because those titles just might be examples of the "big ones."

The big ones: In addition to your personal core collection, you should choose a personal favorite—the book you would recommend to almost any YA. The big one actually might be six titles instead—one for boys and one for girls for each group—middle, junior, and senior high. This is necessary if all other 21 strategies fail.

STRATEGIES FOR LETTING YAS HELP THEMSELVES

Many things help readers and help you learn how best to serve them at the same time.

Card file: Because a friend's recommendation is one of the primary ways YAs learn about books, sanction that activity. With a card file, you can ask YAs to write what they liked about a book and then file the cards by author, title, or even by the "reviewer." This is a low-cost, low-maintenance activity that can prove to be very helpful, but make it clear on the form that the recommendations will be available to the public. Technology fits easily here; you can either keep a simple database file or use the local options in the electronic readers' advisory tools. Further, you can create a Web page allowing YAs to complete surveys about books they have read and would recommend.

Newsletters: You also could take the same information and edit the best reviews together in a newsletter. Better yet, try to recruit some YAs to do it for you. You could post this newsletter in the YA area, distribute it to schools or school libraries, and send it to your local newspaper for inclusion in their teen section. Or you could create a Web page, ask YAs to post reviews on bulletin boards, or add reviews as links to your library's Web pages.

If you like lists: Readers' advisory is matching a book YAs have liked with one they will like. A series of lists in the "If you liked this book . . . " variety prominently displayed can work to that effect. Choose a popular YA author and/or title and list those titles with either a similar plot, theme, tone, or hook.[6] You might even want to display these on the shelf where the popular author's books are located. Just the exercise of doing such a list should expose staff to many YA authors. Again, this list could be posted on a Web page.

Leave out jobber catalogs: Rip out or copy the YA pages from Bookmen or other monthly paperback catalogs. These will tell YAs about upcoming releases, complete with short descriptions.

Collect booklists: *VOYA*, *Booklist* and other journals continually publish booklists (refer back to lists in Chapter 4). Three hole punch 'em, put on a subject heading, and display them in a binder for people to use, noting which titles your library holds. Put any of your own lists or lists you have collected from colleagues or conferences in the binder, as well.

Collect reviews: In your peer review card file, you can also keep copies of reviews from the professional journals. The best source is the *ALAN Review* because those reviews come in ready-to-cut-out index cards, covering both paperback and hardback books.

Displays: Creating catchy displays that change monthly is an excellent method of helping YAs find materials. Every display should have a theme, a list, and a gimmick or prop to attract attention.

Do your own booklists: In addition to an "if you liked this book . . . " series, you might want to put together other lists. Some research indicates that lists are a tremendous waste of trees, while other studies seem to prove they can be an effective method of increasing patrons' awareness about titles. Before you begin putting together a list, there are a few things to consider. Doing a booklist is a simple task, but there are methods you can use to make the list more effective so that it doesn't become like the books you are trying to promote: shelf sitters.

BOOKLIST STRATEGIES

Choose a format: First, you might want to use a form like the one shown in Figure 5–3 to help organize your information. You will want to consider some format guidelines, such as

- In which tense will annotations be written
- How long will annotations be
- How old the books are
- In print status
- Number of pages
- Reading/grade levels

Figure 5–3 A Form for Preparing a Booklist

Preparing a Booklist

Title of List:

Audience: Children   Young Adults   Adults

For each title on the list, please complete the following information:

Author:

Title:

Call:

Publisher/Year:

Annotation:
 (Use no more than three sentences; use action verbs; model from back of cover blurbs.)

How should list be arranged? (Circle one.)

   Author   **Title**   **Call Number**   **Other:**

Where will list be distributed? (Circle all that apply.)

Library   **All Agencies**   **School Library**   **Teachers**

What will be done to promote the list? (Circle all that apply.)

Display   **Press Release**   **On Web Page**   **Other:**

Name: **Date Needed:**   **Date Submitted:**

Quick, not comprehensive: Maybe our dream is to find every book on a certain subject, but a short list is better. It is less intimidating and easier to use. If you list everything, you are not creating a readers' advisory tool (to recommend); instead you are creating a mini-catalog of your collection. Thanks to David Letterman, the "top ten" list seems to be the standard for just about any list.

Hooks, not books: Don't put any books on the front of the list. Instead, start the list with a question. For example, a booklist on teen stress might begin with the question "Feeling stressed out?" Then when the YA opens the list, the "answer" to the question is the list of books you have gathered. You want to hook them first on the idea of the list.

Active, not passive: For the same list, you could also add a stress test. Direct mail marketing tells us that if you give people something to do, it increases their interest in the piece. Much the same, make part of the booklist interactive.

Pbk all the way: Why create 500 copies of a list containing books for which there are only a limited amount of hardback copies? Granted, if every person who got the list wanted even one paperback copy, you would not be able to meet the demand, but you would meet it better than you would with one hardback copy. Also, if the list *does* generate interest, you can get paperback copies cheaper and get them into the patron's hands more quickly.

Create, don't mimic: You don't need to do a list on teen suicide; that is why you have a catalog. Lists should not duplicate access available through the catalog, but rather provide access to like items. Rather than subjects, broader themes could serve as the topic (teen problems). For fiction, look not so much for genres or subjects, but for emotions.

Mimic, don't create: Write publishers and get permission to use the cover art as part of your booklist. If you use the recognizable cover of a popular book as your graphic, the list is instantly recognizable. Why do you want to use clip art when you could use the works of professional artists whose job it is to create interest in a book?

Excite, don't annotate: An annotation tells readers only what a book is about; instead it should tell readers why they would want to read the book. The annotation should then be a tagline: a one-sentence catchy phrase that defines the book. Like a short booktalk, it should excite the reader about the prospect of reading the book.

Borrow, don't write: Take a look at the back of popular paperbacks; see how the people whose job is it to write for a living create an interest for a book in just a few sentences. Borrow heavily from their ideas, phrases, and words.

Display, don't let lay: Once it is completed, don't just leave your list on a table somewhere. Gather the books on the list and pull together related titles. Enlarge a copy of the list to poster size. Stuff each book with a list. Make the list and the books move.

Measure, don't treasure: Before you put out the list, log the status of the books on the list, and then monitor the circulation.

Share, not spare: Depending on your relationship with the school librarian, you might want to work on the list together. If that is not possible, ask the school librarian to look at the list and indicate those titles the library owns. You then can customize copies of the list sent to that school with a simple * next to those titles and a note at the bottom of the page. It is better to share the work and the info rather than just dumping your leftover lists on the school as an afterthought.

Redo/revise: Once you develop a core group of lists, you should also develop a revision schedule so the lists remain fresh and up-to-date.

Benefits, not boom: No list is going to quadruple YA circulation, but there are many other benefits. For the people compiling the lists, the time spent wading through catalogs and other tools has helped them learn more about the literature. If you have involved the school, completing a project together builds the relationship.

Mix n match: Don't just do a list with row after row of annotations—include a section of unannotated titles. Use a graphic such as a photo of the author, graphic design elements like borders, columns and/or shading.

Tech connect: Just because you primarily are interested in reading doesn't mean you can't add Internet sites or CD-ROMs to provide the reader with more information about an author or genre.

Supplement and succeed: Not every YA hates every book they have to read in school—lots of them enjoy these titles and would like similar books. Get copies of school lists and use them as a basis for developing your lists.

Formats, not formula: Another element to add to a list is nonfiction. Also related movies might be a popular addition.

Steal, don't re-invent the wheel: Lots of booklists already exist, so use them as ideas or jumping off points. Just because someone published a booklist on body image books doesn't preclude you from doing the same promoting materials in your collection.

Teachers talk: Especially in the school setting, involve teachers in putting together lists. Send them possible topics and/or a rough draft of your list, welcoming their feedback. Give them a chance to contribute their favorite titles and authors. By giving them some ownership, they might be much more willing to promote the list (and the library in general) in the classroom.

Like reference work, readers' advisory requires a mix of skills, knowledge, and attitudes. It also requires a proactive stance because it is an uphill battle. YAs don't turn to us for advice that often, so when they do that is a "critical customer service moment."

5.4 LIBRARY ORIENTATION AND INSTRUCTION

We know that 23 percent of public library patrons are YAs, but we don't know what percentage of YAs use libraries. Library instruction and orientation provide methods for increasing that percentage by designing a program which will over a certain amount of time bring in as many YAs as possible. Orientation means simply to orient YAs to physical surroundings. It is not being a teacher, but rather a tour guide. The questions answered here are "Where?" and "What?" You might show the students the catalog so they know where and what it is, but a tour is not the place to teach them how it works. Library instruction covers those details. Bibliographic instruction might answer the why question and be more detailed, covering not just tools but also concepts of search strategy. Which type of activity a library offers depends not so much on the library's needs, but on the services that the teachers and YAs are looking for.

A volume of literature is available about both library instruction and orientation; however, very little of it deals with public libraries and YAs. Instead, the information focuses on instruction either in school libraries or academic libraries. The rationale for instruction from these two institutions provides the purpose for these activities in the public library. Moreover, the public library can act as an agent to bridge the gap between those two learning experiences. The public library also can benefit from providing such instruction.

JUSTIFICATION FOR ORIENTATION AND INSTRUCTION

Efficiency: Instruction and orientation enable libraries to directly reach YAs. Rather than explaining the same source over and over again, an instruction session explains use of the source to all students at one time.

Fairness: Instruction provides the same information to a group of students at the same time. The philosophy of public librarianship is that all patrons are equal; the reality of busy reference desks often causes this not to happen. Sometimes students do not receive the help they need because their questions seem unimportant or because some staff don't do a good job helping teenagers. If one staff member can provide information through an instruction session, everyone gets a fair shot. The reality is that students who come in early on Saturday morning when the reference desk is slow might receive better instruction and assistance than the students who come in on a busy night.

Library literacy: Although schools provide the first instruction, public libraries need to augment this instruction. Because normally the public library is larger, sources which can help students can be found there rather than in the school library. Some school libraries have flexible hours, but most are not open enough hours or at the right times (the night before the paper is due) for students to use them as they should or could. In many communities, the public library is more automated than the school library, as well. Finally, all learning needs to be reinforced. If the public library can complement instruction already provided in the school library, the student has heard the information twice. All libraries should care about skills transfer: the skills learned in a school library adapt in a public library, and then again in the college library setting.

Future users: Not all students go to college, and for those who don't, the transfer of skills may not be as important. Nonetheless, the skills developed in researching papers adapts readily to finding other types of information that students might need later in life.

Positive experience: For some YAs, the trip to the public library during an orientation or an instruction session might be the only one they ever make. The instruction session shows the library in a positive light. If students choose to follow up on the instruction and actually visit the public library, they are more likely to have a positive experience because they have some context for the experience—they are not starting from scratch. Even if they don't remember how a particular source works, they at least know it exists and they can use it. Going through instruction and orientation up-front can help decrease frustration and failure for students later.

Community relations: But what does orientation and instruction do for the library? First, it looks good. Working with schools and bringing in busloads of YAs makes a very positive impression. Secondly, for the YA librarian, orientation and instruction help introduce them to YAs and the school community—it gets librarians' faces and names known. This recognition factor is important in all phases of YA work. Thirdly, it establishes a working relationship between the library and schools that can be helpful in so many ways. Finally, it increases use of services. If you are bringing YAs in by the busload, signing them up for library cards, showing them materials, and teaching them how to use various tools to find other materials, the use of the library by YAs will increase.

Professional responsibilities: By providing library instruction and orientation, we fulfill a professional obligation. The American Library Association lists instruction as a main priority area, with a goal of making "instruction in information use . . . available to all." [7]

Reduce staff frustration: People ask me how I started working with YAs. I was working as an entry-level reference librarian in Georgia. It seemed that after school and on weekends almost every question was from a student having to do a literary research paper. Answering the same question over and over was frustrating, exasperating, and led me to believe there had to be another way. Thus, with the help of another reference librarian and the cooperation of the schools, we developed a library instruction program which benefited the kids, but the genesis was totally selfish. [8]

Information overload: Instruction used to be essential because there were so few tools for finding information. Today, there are not only more tools, but much more information available, as well. Part of instruction has to be process: introducing the particular tools for a particular assignment, teaching how to use the tools, and then finally helping instruct students on evaluating the information they find.

It just makes sense: When you put all these arguments together, you can see that it just makes sense to provide library instruction. Instruction is efficient, fair, consistent and effective. But effectiveness needs qualification. It would be excessively optimistic to think that all YAs are going to recall each search strategy or tool from an instruction session; instead they might remember one or two things. Hopefully one thing they will remember is you—so they feel they have someone they "know" at the library they can turn to with their questions.

The advantages of library orientation and instruction are numerous for everyone involved. Although there has been revisionist thought about the effectiveness of instruction, including an article in *Library Journal* called "User Instruction Does Not Work," [9] there is a long history that suggests it does. If libraries are in the information business, the first step seems to be to provide information to our users on how we store information so that they may retrieve it.

LIBRARY ORIENTATION: STRATEGIES AND DOCUMENTS

Planning: Every library probably conducts some sort of tour. The first step is to organize your tours as a coordinated library program: something you can define, plan, implement, and then measure. Organizing

> "When you put all these arguments together, you can see that it just makes sense to provide library instruction. Instruction is efficient, fair, consistent and effective."

Library Orientation: Planning

1. Contact schools
2. Develop planning documents
   A. Fact sheet
   B. Set objectives
   C. Set policies
   D. Develop evaluations
3. Develop materials
   A. Teaching outlines
   B. Handouts
4. Recruit teachers
5. Schedule tours
   A. Fill out form
   B. Check for conflicts
   C. Confirm date with teacher
   D. Mail out library card applications and pre-test
6. Conducting tours
   A. Gather materials
   B. Alert other departments (especially circulation)
   C. Conduct tour
   D. Distribute library cards
   E. Distribute post-test
7. Evaluate tours
   A. Review student evaluations
   B. Review teacher evaluations
   C. Correct/evaluate pre- and post-tests
   D. Complete reporting form
8. Evaluate program
   A. Review objectives
   B. Compile statistics/ reporting forms

will help you collect more information to evaluate tours in order to improve them. Organizing the tour program also expands tours beyond the same teachers who contact the library each year.

Explaining: The fact sheet informs both internal and external users. The library staff needs to know what you are doing, what their involvement will be, and what you will accomplish.

Setting objectives and limits: The objectives will be flexible, based upon what the teacher needs, but the basic objectives should always stay the same. The policies will determine what you will and will not do and need to be established up front.

Testing: Tours may not be instruction, but they are still educational experiences. To learn how much students already know (as opposed to what they claim to know), a pre- and post-test can be effective. These tests should be short and easy to grade, and you can conduct them in the classroom or on the bus to and from the library. This is the only actual handout you will need for each group. Because the idea of a tour is to have students looking at the things you are showing them, it is not really necessary to prepare other materials.

Conducting the tour: Each library will have different things to cover on a tour, and each librarian certainly has his or her own style. Any tour, however, should consist of the following major sections:

The Hook: Let's assume that most students are not fired up about visiting the library. The first thing to be done is increase their level of interest. The tour should start with something that gets their attention: a section of YA movie tie-ins, videos, magazines, a site on the Internet, or some other like item. You want YAs excited right off the bat to get them interested in the tour, in the library, and in you. Demonstrating the catalog won't do this.

The Walk: The major part of the tour is being a guide—lots of walking and pointing. The tour route should be logical and follow the path the student is likely to follow in doing research. Be careful not to overload YAs with information. At each point, you stop (for example, at the catalog) explain what the item is, when you might use it, and where to find materials after you have used it. Use examples and analogies. Invite participation and allow interaction if possible. Again—say what is it, what it does, show an example, ask questions, reinforce, and move to the next stop.

Library Orientation: Fact Sheet

What is a library orientation tour? A library tour is an orientation to the physical structure and arrangement of the library and an introduction to some of the library's resources.

What is *not* a library orientation tour? A library tour is not library instruction, a set PR spiel, a talk about the history of the library, or gushing about how wonderful the library is. Also, library orientation does not have to be boring.

Who participates in library orientation? Tours are conducted by a staff member who is comfortable speaking both to groups and to YAs. The audience should be limited to no more than 40 students. All staff in the department that will be visited on the tour should be informed in advance (for example, tell the checkout desk staff about the tour so staff members aren't taking breaks when the tour group is ready to apply for cards or check out materials).

Where is the tour given? Tours may be given of the whole library or limited to one department.

When are tours given? Tours are most effective when they are related to a specific assignment or informational need. Tours also could be scheduled at the beginning of school year.

Why should you give library orientation tours? Tours are conducted to encourage students to use the library by making them more familiar with the building, the services, and the staff.

What is the goal of library orientation? The goal of any tour is to attempt to make students feel more comfortable in the library.

A quote about library orientation: "Tours make that all important first impression on potential users. Someone on the staff should see the impression is the one the library wants to make. Contrary to popular belief, it is not a simple matter to conduct an effective tour." *Educating the Public Library User.* John Lubans, ed. American Library Association, 1983. p 254.

The Grill:	You should ask YAs questions and allow them to ask you. You can sometimes use a question to begin a part of a tour or ask for examples of things to search for with each source.
The Card:	Have library cards ready before the visit and be prepared to distribute them. Only those students with problems need to interact with the desk staff, and others can be given their new cards. Showing YAs library materials without giving them access is useless.
The Search:	You want to reinforce what you have just shown. Leave time at the end of the tour for YAs to use the sources, visit the departments, and examine the machines. You need to circulate among students, answering questions. This can either be an organized activity (making up a list of things to find) or free time.

Contacting the schools: Although you can do tours for groups other than schools, they are your main contacts. At this point, you know what you want to do, why you are doing it, and how you will do it. Now you need an audience. Working with schools is the single most enjoyable and frustrating experience for most YA librarians.

Scheduling: Once you have contacted teachers and/or developed your program, you are ready to schedule visits. Check whatever master calendar there is for the building so you are not doing tours on the same days as other departments (unless it is a real big building) or even on days with less staffing. The tour needs arranging, not just to fit around your schedule, but to fit the whole library's plans for the day.

Doing the tour: Earlier I outlined the five major parts of most tours. Here are a few more strategies to consider:

- *Start young:* The youngest grade in your library's YA scheme is the grade to start. Not only are 7th graders still open to changing their impressions, but also by concentrating on the younger YAs for this activity, you have laid your groundwork. The 7th graders this year will be with you and your library for six years.
- *Keep your cool:* Because this is a group activity, the group has a peer leader who might challenge you. Refer back to the skills on dealing with YAs and take it with good humor. Even though that YA may not care about a good first impression, you still have to.
- *Amaze them:* So much technology is out there that it is getting harder to "wow" YAs, but you still have to try. Use the machines you have, microfilm printers for example, and make a copy of something to put in somebody's hands. Let at least one person (maybe the leader as mentioned previously) walk away with something tangible.
- *Reinforce:* After you have visited each stop on the tour, reinforce either through statement or question ("What is the name of the machine we use to find magazines?") what has just been covered. Do a quick review at the end.
- *Say yes:* During the tour, YAs will ask questions, reference or otherwise. If you can't answer then, make sure to get the YA's name and find the answer.
- *Keep it simple:* This is hard because most of us want to share the wonders of libraries, even with those who don't want to hear it. The goal is to make these YAs feel comfortable about finding information, not to give them so much information that it overwhelms them.
- *Be prepared:* Being ready counts, especially in all the small ways. If you are going to demonstrate a microfilm copier, do you have

the machine ready? Did you put an "out of order" sign on it about 10 minutes before the tour to make sure it is available? Do you have a dime to use in the machine? Is there toner in the machine? All of these tiny things make a world of difference. By making the tour go smoothly, you are showing your audience that you are credible.

- *Listen to yourself:* Every now and then tape yourself or ask another staff member to listen in on your presentation. Because tours are usually all the same, it is easy to fall into a rut doing them. If it seems boring to you, imagine how it will seem to your audience.
- *Know-it-alls:* For some YAs in your group, this is all going to be a rehash of things they've already heard. Consider acknowledging that up front, and then talk about the need to get everyone on the same page. Expect everyone to know some of what you tell them, but the purpose of the tour is also to be sure everyone has the same knowledge and that the information is in context.

Evaluations: After the tour, give students a post-test to measure the success of the learning experience. The post-test either can be the exact same test you handed out beforehand, or it can be identical in the types of questions it asks. In addition, both students and teachers need to fill out short evaluation forms. Figure 5–4 provides a form you can use for students; Figure 5–5 gives you an example of an evaluation form for teachers.

Evaluation: After receiving the evaluations, and "grading" tests, you need to analyze this information and report it. A reporting form, shown in Figure 5–6, organizes all the information in one place and will be handy when it comes time to do statistics for the whole program.

The library orientation program is an important first step in establishing YA services. It creates good will with schools, brings YAs into the library, puts your face in front of them, and exposes the rest of the staff to the YA beast. Utilize any of these documents to establish the program, although after time you might not find it necessary to use all of them. The purpose of these forms and all other documents in this book is to provide structure for services that you wish to initiate or improve in your library.

Make sure that the tour is good. For many YAs, the tour is the first time they have been in your library, or at least the first time they have been there without their parents. The tour is your chance to make a good impression and maybe wipe out bad impressions or negative stereotypes YAs might have about your library. Finally, the tour is the place to make the connection. On tours, you will meet YAs who will come visit you that very same day and ones who will see you on the

Figure 5–4 An Evaluation Form for Students

Library Orientation: Student Evaluation Form

SCHOOL: DATE:

TEACHER: GRADE: CLASS:

All day long students ask librarians questions; well, now it is our turn. Please tell us what you thought about the library tour because it is the only way we can improve our service. (Please complete the following statements by checking the most appropriate answer.)

1. This presentation was

_____ Organized   _____ Somewhat organized   _____ Disorganized

2. This presentation was

_____ Interesting   _____ Somewhat interesting   _____ Boring

3. I already knew

_____ Most of this   _____ Some   _____ Very little   _____ None

4. This information should be

_____ Very valuable   _____ Somewhat valuable _____ Of no value

5. I now have a better idea of what is available in the library

_____ Agree _____ Disagree

6. I use the public library

_____ All the time   _____ Often _____ Now and then   _____ Never

The most important thing I learned today was

_____

_____

_____

Comments (Use back of page):

_____

_____

_____

Figure 5–5 An Evaluation Form for Teachers

Library Orientation: Teacher Evaluation Form

DATE: TIME:

TEACHER: SCHOOL

Number of students: Grade: Class:

1. Did this presentation meet your objectives?

      _____ Yes   _____ No

2. This presentation was

      _____ Well organized   _____ Somewhat organized   _____ Disorganized

3. This presentation was

      _____ Interesting   _____ Somewhat interesting   _____ Boring

4. This information should be

      _____ Very valuable   _____ Somewhat valuable _____ Of no value

5. Would you recommend this service to colleagues?

      _____ Yes   _____ No

6. What did you like best about this presentation?

_____

_____

7. What did you like least about this presentation?

_____

_____

8. How could this presentation be improved?

_____

_____

Other comments:

Figure 5–6 A Sample Reporting Form

Library Orientation: Reporting Form

DATE: TIME:

TEACHER   SCHOOL:

Number of students: Grade: Class:

Librarian:

Student Evaluation Totals

1. _____ Well organized _____ Somewhat _____ Disorganized
2. _____ Interesting _____ Somewhat _____ Boring
3. _____ Most of this _____ Some _____ Very little _____ None
4. _____ Very valuable _____ Somewhat _____ Of no value
5. _____ Agree _____ Disagree
6. _____ All the time _____ Often _____ Now and then _____ Never

Test Results

pre-test   5/5 _____   post-test   5/5 _____
            4/5 _____   4/5 _____
            3/5 _____   3/5 _____
            2/5 _____   2/5 _____
            1/5 _____   1/5 _____
            0/5 _____   0/5 _____

Teacher Evaluation Totals

1. _____ Yes _____ No
2. _____ Well organized _____ Somewhat _____ Disorganized
3. _____ Interesting _____ Somewhat _____ Boring
4. _____ Very valuable _____ Some value _____ No value
5. _____ Yes _____ No

Comments (Use the back of this page)

street or in their school and remember you. The key to making the connection is making an impression, and that is what a good library orientation strives to accomplish. Remember those rules of customer service—be reliable, credible, attractive, empathic, and responsive.

LIBRARY INSTRUCTION

Library instruction is the next step. You might do instruction with the same group of YAs later in the year, provided they have an assignment. Most likely, however, you'll do instruction more with high school students who are deep in the term paper bog. There are primarily two kinds of instruction—the general "how to do any term paper" type and the more detailed focused instruction on certain types of sources. Both kinds of instruction operate on the same principle—not just teaching which tools to use, but also teaching how to use them and why.

Here are a number of library instruction strategies and documents you can use in setting up your program:

What is being done in the schools by teachers? The first step in developing a library instruction program is to find out what is being done in the schools. If nothing is being done at all, that could be because the school library is not strong or teachers in the school do not believe in the value of the program. It seems amazing that you would have to convince teachers that students need to know how to use libraries, but that is often the case. Instructing teachers on the importance of library instruction is the hardest instruction of all.

What is being done in the schools by librarians? Instruction requires cooperative planning with the school library. As stated in the section of tours, the school librarian can help you make contacts. A strong public library instruction program should not be seen as a threat by school librarians, but often it is. Often it is a turf issue rather than one of providing students with the information they need to be library literate. Settle the turf issue; in a good program, both libraries win by having students gain a better understanding of how all libraries work.

What is being done in your own library? A related turf issue might be in your own library. Maybe each department does its own instruction and thinks it should stay that way. To be most effective, instruction needs to be coordinated by one individual who can then involve other staff as needed. You also will need to convince your director that it is worth the effort. Given diminished resources it seems any program that organizes resources better, creates more knowledgeable and independent users, better utilizes the resources available, and eliminates duplication of staff effort would be a favorable feature—library instruction can do all of those things.

> "Given diminished resources it seems any program that organizes resources better, creates more knowledgeable and independent users, better utilizes the resources available, and eliminates duplication of staff effort would be a favorable feature—library instruction can do all of those things."

What will library instruction entail? Library instruction is more time-consuming than orientation tours. Although you can develop general materials, teachers might want each session tailored to their specific needs. Even though you can do the general term paper talk, you might have to add (or subtract) certain sources given the nature of the assignment. Teachers and your own staff need to know how the instruction program is different from what is already being done.

What will instruction accomplish? The objectives and policies of library instruction are similar to those already outlined for orientation. Two important differences exist, however. Even though orientation is educational, you want students leaving not with skills but rather with information and positive feelings about the library. Instruction, however, is educational, resulting in new skills. The second difference is that the objective changes from learning where things are to learning what they are and how they work. Modify the pre- and post-tests to reflect accurately the content of the instruction.

Library Instruction: Fact Sheet

What is library instruction? Library instruction is the process of teaching users and/or nonlibrary users how to access the library's resources to meet their information needs.

What is *not* library instruction? Library instruction is not a course in library science or bibliography or a repeat of instruction in the schools. Also, library instruction does not have to be boring.

Who does library instruction? Library instruction is provided by a staff member who is comfortable speaking in front of a group and YAs.

Where is library instruction done? Instruction occurs in the library.

When is library instruction given? Instruction is most effective when it is related to a specific assignment.

Why should your library give instruction? Library instruction is an efficient method of directly reaching students. Instruction will complement similar activities in the school by providing information regarding sources unique to the public library and by introducing students to the concepts of search strategy and information retrieval.

What is the goal of library instruction? The goal of library instruction is for the student to be able to identify, understand, and utilize the library's resources effectively to fulfill his or her educational or information needs.

A quote about library instruction: "The public library needs to augment school library instruction by helping students to focus their attention on the information uniquely available or differently arranged in the public library. Comparisons between the two types of libraries should be continually made. The distinctions in organization, subject strength, and service provide topics for presentations." *Educating the Public Library User*, John Lubans, ed. American Library Association, p. 36.

The Big Six

1. *Information Seeking Strategies*
   What is my task?
   What information do I need?

2. *Identification of Sources*
   What sources are available?
   What are the best sources for my task?

3. *Access and Location*
   Where is the information located?
   Do I know how to find the information?

4. *Recording Information*
   How will I record my information?
   How will I evaluate the information?

5. *Synthesis*
   How will I present the information?
   How will I credit my sources?

6. *Evaluation*
   What could I have done differently?
   Was I satisfied with my final product?

Adapted from "The big six" (http://edweb.sdsu.edu/edfirst/bigsix/bigsix.html), developed by Mike Eisenberg and Bob Berkowitz, Syracuse, NY.

How is instruction arranged? After your initial contacts with schools, you need to contact individual teachers regarding the scheduling of sessions. Because each teacher will want to focus on different sources, you need to gather more information from them than you did when scheduling a tour. Educating teachers about libraries often has to come first.

What needs to be instructed? The literature of school librarianship is filled with articles about methods of instruction. School librarians are really classroom teachers, with a great deal of emphasis in the school program on providing instruction for students. Some do it haphazardly, some have it well planned, focusing on different grades during different times of the year. Regardless, one method that seems to have taken hold is the "big six" system, which breaks research into a series of easy-to-follow steps and evaluations. By structuring instruction around a method like this, librarians are providing students with information on a process of research. The process is, for the most part, applicable to any research need.

One way to integrate the "big six" method into instruction, both active and passive, is by developing "big six" home pages for specific assignments (see Figure 5–7). Although such a task might be more easily and appropriately completed by a media specialist, it is also a project for public libraries to consider on their own or in cooperation with schools. Such pages take the process and provide hypertext links along the way.

For task definition, a link is provided to a copy of the assignment either stored on the school's server or, if provided, on the library's server. The next step is to identify sources of information, which could be as general as listing the name of the library's online catalog to providing specific search times to providing the call numbers and titles of reference books. The third step might provide instruction on physically locating and using various sources. The fourth step asks the information seeker to both record and evaluate the information—hotlinks to pages listing criteria for evaluating Web resources would be appropriate here. The next step is to synthesize or prepare the research, part of which is crediting sources so that a big six page would link to the school's style sheet or a general one on the Internet listing correct bibliographic formats. Finally, the sixth step uses a form to ask the information seeker to evaluate his or her own work and the library. Once one of these pages is constructed, it serves as a model for others to follow. Pages can be heavy with graphics or light, depending upon the subject matter. The purpose of these pages is threefold: first, like a pathfinder, these pages enable you to eliminate repetitive questions and therefore free librarians to assist with more in-depth information seeking. Second, these pages teach, through

Figure 5–7 Using the "Big Six" Method

The Big Six in Action
American Poets

In this project, students will apply the "Big Six" information gathering process to do research on an American poet.

The Big Six

1. Task Definition

    What am I supposed to do? (link to assignment)

    What information do I need?

2. Information Seeking Strategies

    What are the possible sources of information I can use?

    What are the best sources for this assignment? (internal link to bottom of page)

3. Location and Access

    Where will I find these sources?

    School Library

    Public Library (link to catalog)

    Do I know how to use them?

    Do I know how to use Internet Search Engines (link)?

    Search tips: Alta Vista (link)

4. Use of Information

    How will I record information?

    How will I evaluate the information? (link)

5. Synthesis

    How is the information best presented?

    How will I credit my sources? (link)

6. Evaluation (internal link to bottom of page)

Possible Sources of Information

Books

    Use the OPAC computer to find books in school library

    Consult reference books

The Oxford Companion to American Literature (REF 810.9 HAR)

The World's Best Poetry (REF 808.81 WOR)

American Writers (REF 810.9 AME)

Survey of American Poetry (REF 811.08 SUR)

Critical Survey of Poetry (REF 821.09 CRI)

Great Writers of the English Language: Poets (REF 820.9 GRE)

Magazines

    ProQuest cd-rom index

CD-ROMs

    DISCovering Authors

    Roth World of Poetry

    Britannica

Internet

Search Engines

    Alta Vista

    Yahoo

    Hot Bot

    Lycos

Bookmarks

    Electronic Texts

    Perspectives in American Literature:

    Yahoo's Poets page

    Poetry Links

    Literature Resources

    American Authors on the Web

Evaluation

Please enter your name:

Please enter your e-mail address:

Was the problem solved?

Yes No

Did I credit my sources used?

Yes No

Am I happy with the product I turned in?

Yes No

Did I select the best sources to complete the task?

Yes No

Did I use my time efficiently in locating and using the sources I selected?

Yes No

Did you like having this assignment on a Web page?

Yes No

Comments/suggestions:

THANK YOU FOR COMPLETING THIS EVALUATION

Big Six Information Solving Approach, copyright of Michael B. Eisenberg and Robert E. Berkowitz.

---

simple repetition, the big six process. Finally, these pages provide students with a starting point to the vast amount of resources—instead of merely typing *American poetry* into a search engine and landing a couple thousand hits, this type of project does what librarians should do and directs students to the best resources available. It does not preclude or limit students from searching beyond the sources listed, but it does ensure that they learn one important lesson: the Internet can be a valuable information tool for research as well as just for kicks.

Yet, within the Big Six method, examples are used relating to the assignment at hand. Although you have asked teachers to help tailor each session, you will find the need to have a couple of set teaching outlines. These outlines help you organize your thoughts and are valuable in case you want to involve others in this process. You need an outline for the general "any topic" term paper and probably want to develop a general one for American history, literature, and whatever subject specialty your library offers. Much like a tour, it is important not to jump to the catalog 10 seconds into the thing. You need to "win them over" and try as much as possible to get them to pay attention. Tell them, "If you give me your attention for the next 20 minutes, it will probably save you hours of frustration." Ask how many YAs want to spend hours doing research instead of doing the hundreds of things they would rather be doing. Library instruction saves them time, and it saves you time as well.

The inner workings of each source and machine would be nice to cover, but there is not enough time and the smaller the detail, the smaller the number of students who will remember it. Along the way, reinforce each point with questions and restatement. When teaching technology, always teach where the HELP and the PRINT buttons are—those seem to be the features students need most. You also need to say at every opportunity that if students have questions about how to find something or even how a machine works, they need to ask. You need to tell YAs what we all already know—the most valuable library resource is the staff.

> " You need to tell YAs what we all already know—the most valuable library resource is the staff. "

This teaching outline can be covered in under 30 minutes. With technology, if possible, you want to have students working on computers while you teach. Keep them on task by walking them through sample searches. Regardless of the technology, you will want to show them the following items for each computer program:

- How to start the program
- Where the search bar is located
- Rules for searching
- How to truncate and/or expand/limit searches
- How to print and preview printing
- Where to find help

Instruction sessions need hands-on work time. Unless students can immediately apply the skills and succeed, they will forget the skills quickly, no matter how well you taught them. To help YAs work after the instruction and best use their resources, you and the teacher should set objectives for each visit. Divide classes into groups, and have some working on books, others on magazines, etc. Not only will it create less confusion, but it might "force" students to use the time effectively.

You can develop various types of instruction aids. Pathfinders were discussed earlier in this chapter, as were booklists. You could also have handouts on specific tools (such as how to use Infotrac) left near the machine or the "point of user instruction."

How is instruction evaluated? The evaluation tools used for tours work as well for instruction. Staff needs to observe the following:

- Do students seem to work more independently?
- Are questions more sophisticated (asking about a particular magazine citation as opposed to asking how to find magazines)?
- Are the reference materials mentioned used more often and without as much difficulty?
- Does the staff feel time has been saved?

You will also want to follow up with teachers to get their comments about the term papers the students were researching. Among the questions you could ask might be these:

- Did students list more types of sources in bibliographies?
- Did students comment positively on the experience?

And, of course, you want to have the students complete an evaluation form that asks the following questions:

- Did you learn from the instruction?
- Did it help you save time?
- Did it teach you about resources you didn't know existed?
- Did it help you write a better paper?

By teaching, not only are you helping students achieve independence, but you are better using all your resources in terms of staff and materials. The staff handles more sophisticated questions, and the students become aware of more sources. In other words, students have more information to find information. You will create raving fans of both students and staff by providing quality library instruction.

5.5 SCHOOLS AND LIBRARY COOPERATION

One of the keys to providing quality YA services in the public library is to develop a quality working relationship with schools. For schools, the advantages to working with the public library are numerous:

- Complement their own educational resources
- Share resources in a time of diminishing budgets
- Develop innovative programs and activities
- Broaden students' access to information and materials

- Increase students' library literacy
- Network within the community

For libraries, there are even more advantages:

- Increase students' library literacy
- Provide better service to students by having more information about their needs
- Work with captive audiences
- Share resources in a time of diminishing budgets
- Develop innovative programs and activities
- More fully utilize the library's resources
- Fulfill many libraries' educational mission
- Network within the community
- Eliminate misunderstandings

The student, however, gains the most when schools and libraries work together. Students will find that cooperation might lead to

- Reduced frustration in using libraries
- Increased access to information
- Ability to obtain materials easily
- Library staff with better understanding of their needs
- Innovative programs to meet their needs
- Reduced stress in using libraries
- Clearer assignments
- Reduced time spent in the library after school
- Increased access to recreational reading
- Increased access to information technology
- Better instruction in use of libraries

So, if cooperation is such a wonderful thing where everybody wins, why do schools and libraries sometimes have problems cooperating? From the school's point of view, reasons might include these:

- Lack of time to establish contacts
- Lack of understanding of the library's role
- Past unsuccessful contacts
- Lack of administrative support
- Lack of classroom time to dedicate to outside activities
- Feelings of being self-sufficient
- Lack of perceived need
- Lack of information about library's resources
- Lack of planning
- Arrogance ("We don't need your help!")

Libraries are often unsuccessful in working with schools for a variety of reasons, such as the following:

- Failure to communicate to proper channels
- Past unsuccessful contacts
- Lack of time to establish contacts
- Arrogance ("They need us!")
- Lack of administrative support
- Inability to influence decision-makers
- Lack of time to plan or implement programs
- Lack of resources to meet school's needs
- Unwillingness to dedicate staff to this role
- Interdepartmental rivalries
- Lack of innovative programs to offer schools

Each library and school might have other barriers to cooperation as well—sometimes it is something as absurd as the person in charge (principal or director) just not caring. Many public library directors also engage in political pouting and posturing. Because schools get so much more money from the community, they argue, it is not the public library's role to provide any services to schools or even school-age children. That's the extreme case, but it runs through many directors' thinking on working with schools. One possible counter is to go back to the research on the roles that the public and community leaders expect libraries to fulfill: the formal education support role is at the top of the list. In order to achieve success in that role, cooperating with those providing the formal education is necessary to maintain support.

Looking at these common problems and barriers, apparently the relationship needs developing along these lines:

1. Initial communication at any level
2. Follow-up communication at decision-making level in each agency
3. Recognition of strengths and weaknesses
4. Discussion of shared needs and goals
5. Creation of shared agenda
6. Avenues and contacts for ongoing communication

When schools and libraries do not work together, students—clients for both—suffer. Reference questions like the following often lead to frustration for the students, as well the library staff. In each of these cases, if a school and library have not connected, students will find frustration. If they do connect, however, as shown here, many of these problems can be eliminated or reduced.

"Everyone in my class has to read . . . "

1. The school sends to the library a list of books required during the school year or the library surveys teachers for titles.

2. The school sends to the library individual titles before they are assigned so the library can purchase extra copies and/or gather all copies in the library system.
3. Together, the school and library can investigate grant or other outside agencies to fund a cooperative supplemental reading collection.
4. For a library serving many schools, libraries could explore developing special collections of the most requested titles used for "literature based" curriculums.

"I have to do a scrapbook on . . . "

1. You need to communicate directly with the teachers giving these assignments, explaining the problems these projects introduce when students think they are supposed to cut up library periodicals.
2. You could offer vouchers for free photocopies for students in these classes.
3. You can save magazine discards and route them to these teachers for their use.

"My whole class is researching . . . "

1. The teachers can be contacted or surveyed as to each term's research projects.
2. Schedule library instruction sessions.
3. Collection development can be focused in these areas.
4. "Temporary reference" collections can be established.
5. Librarians can develop pathfinders and mail them to teachers.
6. Because many teachers don't change assignments from year to year, libraries could better document which assignments can be expected.
7. The library can distribute postcards to teachers at beginning of each term that teachers then mail back (see Figure 5–8), or set up a Web page allowing for form submission by teachers for assignments. Distribute the URL widely among school faculty.
8. If assignments are on paper, the library can photocopy the assignment and post it at reference desk, listing possible sources and strategies.
9. Distribute assignment alert sheets to school libraries so they can notify the public library when assignments are coming their way (see Figure 5–9).
10. Identify "problem assignments." If possible, staff should ask students about the teacher and the school where the assignment was made and then contact the teacher for more information (see Figure 5–10).

Figure 5–8 Teacher Postcard

Teacher Postcard

TEACHER'S NAME:_____

SCHOOL:_____ GRADE:_____

CLASS: _____ NUMBER OF STUDENTS:_____

Help us help your students by alerting us to those assignments which might require your students to use our library. Thank you for your cooperation.

ASSIGNMENT: DATE:

1._____   _____

2._____   _____

3._____   _____

4._____   _____

5._____   _____

---

11. Schools and libraries can communicate about such issues, which should revolve around the needs of students, not each institution's agendas and excuses.
12. School librarians and public librarians need to work together on educating teachers. Together, they could host a workshop, sponsor a lunch, prepare publications and documents, reward teachers who do cooperate, and troubleshoot problem areas.
13. Libraries can communicate back to teachers through students about frustrations student encountered and why students could not complete the assignment (see Figure 5–11).

Figure 5–9 Assignment Alert Form

Assignment Alert Form

Dear Media Specialist,

As you know, often students will use the public library to find resources to complete assignments. Help us help them by alerting us as soon as possible to assignments which require library use. Together, we can help students use the wide variety of resources available in libraries, both school and public.

MEDIA SPECIALIST:_____ DATE:_____

SCHOOL:_____ TEACHER:_____

GRADE:_____ CLASS:_____ #STUDENTS:_____

ASSIGNMENT:_____

_____

DATE ASSIGNMENT IS DUE:_____

SPECIAL REQUIREMENTS (# OF SOURCES, LIMITS, ETC):

_____

_____

COMMENTS

"My teachers said you would have . . . here."

1. Teachers make assumptions about what libraries do and do not have. Better communication would lessen this likelihood.
2. Libraries can contact schools about being part of new teacher orientation programs.
3. Libraries can put together annual teacher appreciation days which serve both to recognize teachers who do cooperate and attempt to educate others.
4. Libraries can offer refresher courses to schools as part of their in-service program.

Figure 5–10 A Sample Teacher Letter

Letter to Teacher

Dear Teacher,

During the past week, I've been able to help several students from your _____ class work on their homework assignment/term paper. I'm delighted to see that you have encouraged them to use our library. Thank you.

There is one thing that you could do to help us help your students learn even more. Some students won't ask for assistance, and others simply won't come to the library. You could help us help your students by:

- Arranging for them to visit the library as a group to receive library instruction

- Notifying us (and your school librarian) at least a week in advance of assignments so we may gather materials for them

- Allowing us to prepare pathfinders or other handouts which would help them help them-selves

Again, I'm pleased to see so many of your students in our library. Please contact me so we can arrange the activities mentioned above to benefit your students. In this "information age," it is important that all students learn how to access the vast amount of information available to them; that is why we're here and we'd like the opportunity to work with your students at your convenience.

Sincerely,

"I need a fiction book on . . . "

1. The library can send teachers any prepared lists the library has created or has used from the ALA.
2. Libraries can work with the school librarian to develop lists containing materials in both collections.
3. YA librarians can share resources (*Fiction Catalog, Books for You*, etc.) with teachers.
4. Librarians can send along with students a copy of their business cards when recommending books for students.
5. The librarian can call teachers and offer to booktalk for their classes.
6. Libraries can set up special collections of books which meet assignment criteria.
7. YA librarians can share any teachers' guides sent to the library by publishers.

Figure 5–11 Materials Unavailable Card

Materials Unavailable Card

LIBRARY:_____ DATE:____

Dear Teacher,

Your student _____came to the library today to find materials on _____. We are sorry to report that we were unable to help your student because:

_____ All materials were checked out

_____ A reasonable search failed to find materials.

_____ Materials are for "in library" use only

_____ Clarification of request is needed

_____ Other:_____

 If you have any questions, please contact me. Often we can better help students and reduce their frustration in using libraries when we are notified in advance about school assignments like this one. Then, we can provide instruction and gather materials and other services to benefit all of your students.

LIBRARIAN:_____ PHONE#:_____ EMAIL_____

"I need a filmstrip on . . . "
1. Librarians can share with teachers any library produced AV catalogs, either through the department chair or school librarian.
2. The library can send each teacher a list of media available and *not* available, complete with rules and procedures for using and booking media.

"How do you do a bibliography card?"
1. Librarians can request from each school librarian the style sheet teachers use, and keep it posted at reference desk. Alternately, you can keep at the desk a copy of whatever source was used to create the style sheet.

2. With schools, libraries can put together a term-paper kit or research guide for students to use.

"I need to read . . . this summer."

1. Librarians can contact the school librarian in early spring about the school's summer reading list.
2. The library can lobby for inclusion of YA titles (most won't have them) in the school's summer reading list.
3. The library can buy extra copies of titles and *Cliff Notes*. Purchase audio books if money is available.
4. Librarians can offer to booktalk titles from the reading list.
5. YA librarians can post and file all lists where all staff can find them.
6. Libraries can buy titles on more than one list in Permabound editions.
7. Look through book donations for these titles—many students who did buy the book will sometimes donate it to the library.
8. Provide feedback to schools on number of copies in the system and in-print status.
9. Reach out to bookstores as an ally if there is a problem—they will have just as many YAs coming in looking for the title.

Most teachers feel they have too much work and too few resources. Libraries need to reach out to teachers and help them understand how the library can operate as a resource for them and their students. Some teachers are very good about working with libraries in both their schools and the public library, but others are hopeless. As with YAs, there is a vast "silent majority" of teachers who have some awareness, yet have not been moved to action. Let's also have some sympathy for the teachers here—their first responsibility is teaching their students in the classroom; and in addition, they have just a few other chores, such as giving make-up tests, working one-on-one with students, grading papers, making up lesson plans, reading papers, and preparing class notes. Then, just in case they find some extra time, they can always meet with parents, attend department meetings, attend faculty meetings, attend parent organization meetings, and attend union meetings. If they find an additional few hours in their day, they can always read professional literature, coach a team, sponsor a club, be a class sponsor, sit on faculty committees, monitor the lunchroom or hallways, or read books in their subject area. Then maybe, just maybe, after they have all of these things done, they might have a chance to learn about libraries. It is not a teacher's job to keep up-to-date with libraries; instead, it is our job to teach them.

METHODS FOR CONTACTING TEACHERS

Colleague: Start with the librarian in the school or the media coordinator for the school system. This seems easy enough, but even this first simple step contains some pitfalls.

Librarians in schools are no different from most teachers in that they feel they have too little time and resources. Work around their schedules and share resources with them—professional magazines, for instance. The message you want to send is "We can help each other," but sometimes that looks like a turf grab and thus is resisted.

They have their own problems, even if they are also yours. They know all about teachers not notifying them about assignments. They will be amazed that you expect a teacher to pick up the phone to call you or write you a letter when that same teacher will not even walk down the hall to tell them. Their problems are your problems, and hopefully both of you will be willing to help each other find solutions.

If you look good, they can look bad. If you work with a teacher and make visits to booktalk, that school librarian might look bad because he or she doesn't offer the service. If teachers begin to take you up on offers for library instruction or other services, then there becomes a question on why this is not being handled in the school. All activities need planning not only with the full knowledge of the school librarian, but also by involving him or her in the planning stages and inviting participation in all aspects.

School librarians also can feel under-appreciated. You should look for ways to provide them with recognition because it is a smart bet they are not getting much in their school. Every time they help you, write a thank-you note, and sending an occasional letter to the principal is a nice touch. Invite school librarians to join in professional activities or associations.

Because they feel so overwhelmed, even as much as they might agree on the principle of cooperation, the reality of making it work seems time-consuming. The best road to cooperation is to work cooperatively. Instead of your laundry list of cooperation opportunities, pick one small project the two of you can work on together. Maybe it could be a union list or reference book rotation plan, or maybe customizing some of the documents in this manual, but choose one project that needs both sides. After planting the seed, larger projects involving more cooperative planning become possible. The relationship might be stronger and as allies you can work toward ending some of your mutual frustration with teachers.

School librarians might not be willing to share. For some, they have absolutely nothing to gain by working with you—they know their teachers and what they need. If they "tell you" about those teachers, then maybe those teachers will take their business elsewhere. There is a subtle competition between libraries just as there is competition between branches in a library system. You have to find what you can "exchange" in order to get the school librarian to help you. It really needs to become a win-win situation. Sometimes you can figure it out, but sometimes you just have to put the question to them simply, as in "Now, what can I do to help you?"

Navigating the school maze: Every school has a different understanding of proper protocol and libraries are different as well. It seems often the first "official" contact comes at an administrative level with a library director contacting a school superintendent. Best case scenario is that your director writes the superintendent and explains ideas for working with the schools and asks for permission to make contacts. This next contact again might vary depending upon the school. You might have to work through another layer and work with a curriculum supervisor such as the English Department or maybe the coordinator for media services. Depending upon the size of the school, after talking with the school librarian, you can contact teachers directly or work though a department chairperson. If you can invite yourself or, better yet, get invited to a department meeting, you have finally reached teachers. After you have formally met them at these department meetings, you can begin making individual contacts.

Who you contact depends not only on the culture of the school and library, but also on what your objectives are at first. If you want to publish and distribute a newsletter for teachers, that will be an administrative decision. If you, however, want to begin booktalking, perhaps the reading teachers are your best contact. You will want to develop a log sheet so you can keep track of all your school contacts.

Documents: The school planning form can assist you in obtaining and organizing information about schools (see Figure 5–12). When completed, it serves as a planning tool, and at the end of year, it serves as a document to evaluate cooperative activities. The document takes you step by step through the kinds of information you will need to work through with schools. Once you obtain it, you can use the information (as well as that from other materials such as the teacher and club lists) to put together a mailing list. This list will be invaluable. To compile it, either stop in or call and ask to speak to the school secretary. Make sure to call during what would be slow periods for a school office so they will have time to talk with you. Once you have list of contacts, you want to tell teachers whom they can contact. Such a list should also tell teachers what services you have available. Instead of services, use the same document to highlight your collection. Distribute poster size copies of this document to school librarians and administrators. Another variation: shrink the services section onto a blank pre-addressed post card and print one out for each teacher. If you have put together a successful program with a teacher and school librarian,

---

Figure 5–12 A School Planning Form

School Planning Form

SCHOOL:_____

ADDRESS:_____

PHONE#:_____ FAX#:_____

PRINCIPAL:_____

LIBRARIAN:_____

SCHOOL SECRETARY:_____

ENGLISH DEPT CHAIR:_____

READING DEPT CHAIR:_____

SCIENCE DEPT CHAIR:_____

SOC SCI DEPT CHAIR:_____

GUIDANCE DEPT CHAIR:_____

PRIMARY CONTACT PERSON:_____

OTHER KEY PERSONNEL:_____

_____

1. Created mailing labels?   _____ Yes _____ No

2. Obtain school calendar?   _____ Yes _____ No

3. Obtain school handbook?   _____ Yes _____ No

4. Obtain list of teachers?   _____ Yes _____ No

5. Obtain bell schedule?   _____ Yes _____ No

6. Obtain list of clubs?   _____ Yes _____ No

7. Obtain info on PTA/PTO? _____ Yes _____ No

8. Obtain copy of school newsletter? _____ Yes _____ No

9. Obtain copy of PTA/PTO newsletter? _____ Yes _____ No

10. Obtain copy of school newspaper? _____ Yes _____ No

11. New teachers invited to orientation? _____ Yes _____ No

12. Library card applications prepared for new students? _____ Yes _____ No

13. "Welcome" letters sent in late October to all contacts? _____ Yes _____ No

14. Regular meetings scheduled with school librarian? _____ Yes _____ No

15. Tours arranged for ___ grade(s) _____ Yes _____ No

16. Library instruction for ___ grade? _____ Yes _____ No

17. Booktalks for ___ grade(s)? _____ Yes _____ No

18. Summer reading promotion for __ grades(s)? _____ Yes _____ No

19. Attend dept. meeting(s) ? _____ Yes _____ No

20. Contact for Banned Books Week? _____ Yes _____ No

21. Contact for National Library Week? _____ Yes _____ No

22. Obtain summer reading lists? _____ Yes _____ No

23. Obtain yearbook? _____ Yes _____ No

24. Obtain exam schedule? _____ Yes _____ No

25. Thank you notes to all contacts? _____ Yes _____ No

On the back of this page, list all contacts made during the year—include teacher's name, date, and reasons for contact.

you can write that up as a press release filled with quotations from the teachers and distribute it widely. Let teachers "put you over" with other teachers.

Like so much of YA service, school-library cooperation presents a contradiction. Nothing would help YAs more than for these two institutions, which both strive to meet YA needs, to really work together; yet for many reasons it seems nothing is sometimes easier to do. A personal aside: I did everything wrong in working with a school in one of my YA librarian jobs. I let someone else make the initial contact for me; it was one of those "my boss will call your boss" situations. So the first the school library media specialist heard of me was from her principal. I didn't make an informal contact first, so my going in seemed very awkward. When I did make contact, it didn't go well. She had her agenda, and I had mine. Her assistant had his agenda, and I had mine. I had a clear list of things to do: cooperative instruction, booktalking, serials list, journal routing, shared resources, etc., etc., etc. They had a clear list and it didn't involve me. They had been doing fine without me and would continue to do so. Besides they had enough to do and no stomach for anything else. They were not buying what I was selling, in part because they were selling the same products, or something similar. In effect, I was asking my competition to give me access to their markets with little profit for them.

Almost every librarian could tell a story about a teacher marveling at a CD-ROM product or the like, amazed at what is available. Unless they have gone back for retraining or the school has been proactive, most teachers' research notions stem from pre-high-tech times. They are still thinking books and magazines, instead of full-text articles and Internet documents. And it is not because they are Luddites, but because their experience is not with technology and like most of us, they would prefer to stay where they are comfortable. For the school library, there also are advantages to increasing cooperation with the public library.

Although school-public library cooperation is not addressed at all in *Information Power*, areas such as networking and resource sharing are highlighted. The first four of the "challenges" to the school library's mission beg the cooperation question, but it is the last challenge, to participate in networks, which speaks directly to the issue. *Information Power* states: "Library media specialists are concerned about creating partnerships that enhance access to resources located outside of the school." [10]

Libraries are sold on cooperation. Our history shows the advantages: from the development of library systems to the creation of automation networks to the daily proof-in-the-pudding known as *interlibrary loan*, libraries know it works. Convincing teachers to work with libraries, either school or public, is not quite as easy. Libraries often call themselves partners in the educational process, but some teachers see us more as step-children. We talk about cooperation, but the subtle undercurrent is competition.

Thus, let's take a marketing approach to the problem. We can take another look at the marketing mix—product, place, price, and promotion—and develop ideas for improving cooperation between schools and libraries. The first step, though, is to define the audience: we talk about cooperation between schools and libraries, but rarely do cooperative ventures reach the entire school. The market segments are definable subsets of the larger market, linked either by shared characteristics or shared interests. For each of these segments, there are different needs. Students in senior honors English have different needs than freshmen in Math 101. By thinking in market segments, libraries can focus their efforts, especially in the beginning, on small groups.

Determining Your Products

Of all the things libraries do or can do, what are the appropriate products for the school setting? Take a few moments and brainstorm: really think hard about the types of services, materials, and programs that school libraries and public libraries can offer schools. There is a gamut ranging from merely making the library available for students to do research to triangular planning of lessons and assignments.

Establishing Your Price

One of the barriers to cooperation is that it takes time. The time is normally up-front in the planning stages, but that certainly is a cost. Think through the cost of *not* doing it: what is the cost to the library in answering 250 student questions of "Where is *Contemporary Authors?*" when a library instruction session could reduce that number. Think not just in actual time, but also in related costs like staff frustration, morale, and burnout. Suddenly the cost of no cooperation is quite high. For the library, there are other costs. Time in the classroom or working with a school librarian is time away from the desk. There is also a fairness issue: can any library really afford to work cooperatively with every school, especially if home schools are included? Could cooperative instruction lead to so many students using both libraries that extra reference books, sources, CD-ROMs, and the like become necessary? There is also a cost even in cooperating in staff morale: all those kids coming in might be good for you and for them, but bad in the eyes of the circulation or magazine clerks.

Determining the Place

Determining the place seems easy enough: you've got one of three choices—in the classroom, in the school library, or in the public library. The classroom is the best case scenario for some activities (booktalking), while the library works best for instruction. The key to choosing the place is distribution; thus it becomes an access issue. The first two challenges in *Information Power* are access issues: how to provide students with access to all types of resources. This is all determined mostly by geography. A public library within walking distance to a school naturally will see more cooperation than one set apart, unless the school has a generous field trip policy. A media center and public library's hours are important aspects of place: are media centers open after hours, and are students allowed in public libraries during school hours?

Promotion

Promoting cooperation takes place in both passive and proactive ways. Passive methods might include posters, "back to school" kits, newsletters, or other print documents. The most proactive approach is the one which marketing cannot control: word of mouth. Companies spend millions advertising products or hyping new movies, but word of mouth makes or breaks the product. Teachers have grapevines and ways to disseminate information within the building. Normally, this is all very informal. The key is getting the library's success stories talked about, thus generating interest. Every program, class, or booktalk I do ends with me handing my card to teachers and asking them to tell their colleagues about the service and suggesting that they contact me. It works.

The Element of Success

Let's look at the "elements of success" for successful school and public library cooperation using a mnemonic called FASTING:

- Fitting in
- Asking
- Scheduling
- Teaching
- Intervening
- Networking
- Goal Setting

Fitting in: Curriculums dominate school planning: so much material needs to be covered in so little time. Teachers want to cover as much as possible and many "resent" any interruption to that schedule, whether it be assemblies or library activities. For best results, when booktalking, promote titles tied to the unit the teacher is doing.

Asking: It seems obvious, but the need to gather information is paramount. You need to know which schools are in your service area, who works there, and a myriad of other details. It won't fall in your lap; you need to go out and get it using the form provided.

Scheduling: Many public libraries spend time preparing extensive "back to school" flyers for teachers during the summer and then drop them off at the beginning of the school year. They are dismayed when the document produces no results, oblivious that the start of the school is the worst time to give teachers anything because they are doing daily triage to keep their heads above water. Learn from the school librarian the rhythms of a school and find out the best times to intercede.

Teaching: The process of cooperation is really one of teaching and educating. Teaching teachers about libraries; teaching administrators about YAs, and often teaching other staff about how to teach students is all part of the job.

Intervening: Look for "teachable moments"; that is, situations where you can educate a teacher about what libraries have to offer.

Networking: Make yourself available to attend department meetings, or better yet, try to attend and speak at PTA and PTO meetings to get your message out. It is much better to have teachers and parents promoting cooperation, rather than just you.

Goal setting: As mentioned, do one small thing with one teacher. When it succeeds, that teacher will sing your praises. My experience in working with teachers has been that once a teacher "buys in," they are willing to shill for you

Teachers are, however, merely a means to the end of reaching YAs. They are a distribution channel to young adults. Many YAs cannot go to public libraries, or are not allowed, but by working with teachers, public libraries can make connection through programs, services, and materials with teens who never even cross our threshold. You can't create raving fans or satisfied customers until that moment. Cooperation among public librarians, school librarians, and teachers has many rewards for the participants, but even more for the young adult, who is the real customer.

ENDNOTES

1. Michael LeBoeuf. *How to Win Customers and Keep Them for Life*. New York: Berkley, 1987.
2. LeBoeuf, pp. 74–78.
3. Kenneth Blanchard and Sheldon Bowles, *Raving Fans: A Revolutionary Approach to Customer Service*. New York: Morrow, 1993.
4. Nancy Loorie, "Whose Homework Is It, Anyway? Helping Parents at the Reference Desk," *New Jersey Libraries* (February 1993): 15–17.
5. Pauline Iacono, "Fabulous Fiction Finders," *Public Libraries* (November/December 1995): 342–345.
6. Evie Wilson-Lingbloom, *Hangin' out at Rocky Creek: A Melodrama in Basic Young Adult Services in Public Libraries*. Metuchen: Scarecrow Press, 1994: 256–260.
7. "ALA Policy ," in *ALA Handbook of Organization 1996–1997*. American Library Association, 1995: 29.
8. Patrick Jones and Candace B. Morse, "What to Do When the *World Book* Is Missing," *RQ* (Fall 1985): 31–34.
9. Tom Eadie, "User Education Does Not Work," *Library Journal* (October 15, 1990): 42–45.
10. *Information Power: Guidelines for School Library Media Programs*. American Library Association, 1988.

JANUARY

Goal: Pull together everything you've done so far and start the New Year off right.

1. **Annual report:** If your library does an annual report, contribute to it generously. If not, consider doing your own. Gather all those stats, information on professional development, and a report on how serving YAs helped the library achieve its goals and/or mission, and put this into one report. If possible, add some photos or documents. Something like this, once established, can become an important and powerful vehicle for increasing awareness. Jazz it up by creating charts with Excel, or instead of printing the report, present it in a slide show using PowerPoint or turn it into a hypertext Web document.

2. **Start a monthly report:** Similarly, if your library requires a monthly report, think of it not as some rote exercise, but rather a chance to get the "word out" about YA. If your library does not do a monthly report, then do your own. Use it as a planning tool for next month by writing the words "TO DO" at the bottom of the report. This also makes annual reports easier to do.

3. **Thank you notes:** Provide recognition to anyone who helped you last year. Any clerk, librarian, or board member who showed an interest in YAs, should get a thank-you for their support. Don't forget to mention that their assistance in the future will be greatly appreciated.

4. **Establish contacts with schools:** Although you might have meetings about collection information earlier, the fall is no time to connect with schools: teachers, librarians, administrators are just too busy. By January, the big push is behind them and they might be able to find some breathing room for serious conversation and connections, in particular for the spring spate for research papers.

5. **Sign or re-up to YALSA:** Okay, so your membership was due in December—this a reminder to make sure you have sent it in. In addition to a subscription to *The Journal of Youth Services in Libraries,* there are many other benefits in joining the division. This becomes clear in January when the various "best" lists are announced.

6 BOOKTALKING: DON'T TELL, SELL

Booktalking is perhaps the best example of the raving fans approach to YA librarianship. Although we deliver collections, booktalking provides that important "one percent more" by creating excitement about those collections. Booktalking allows librarians to go before YAs and show customer service in action. Booktalks are demonstrations of librarians being reliable, credible, attractive, empathic, and responsive. Booktalking works—the research, although limited, is quite clear about its effectiveness. You can create a lot of attention and interest by using booktalks; you simply need to follow a few simple rules and add "hooks" to transfer the inherent drama and emotion of a YA book to its presentation. Finally, by putting together a series of booktalks as a presentation, you can deliver more than information about books; you can generate excitement and enthusiasm about libraries in general. Booktalking is manipulation in the name of motivation.

Motivating teenagers to read is no easy task. The competition for teenagers' time is fierce, as books battle it out with much more appealing media. Although illiteracy is still a problem, perhaps *aliteracy*—the ability to read but choosing not to—is even more frustrating. It is not for lack of skill that most teenagers don't read, but because of a lack of caring and action. Thus, motivating students to read requires first that their awareness of books be increased, which should then lead them to action, and perhaps over time, cause a change in attitude.

6.1 RESEARCH

One time-tested and researched reading motivation technique is booktalking. In the 1950s, A.H. Munson's *An Ample Field*[1] discussed the craft, and Margaret Edwards popularized her techniques in the 1970s.[2] Since Edwards, Joni Bodart has been the leader in the field, publishing a variety of booktalking resources. Bodart wrote her dissertation on the effectiveness of booktalking, concluding that although booktalking dramatically affected behavior (titles booktalked circulated from the library), it did not affect overall attitudes toward reading.[3]

Bodart Booktalking Resources

Booktalk! New York: H.W. Wilson, 1980.

Booktalk 2. New York: H.W. Wilson, 1985.

Booktalk 3. New York: H.W. Wilson, 1988.

Booktalk 4. New York: H.W. Wilson, 1992.

Booktalk 5. New York: H.W. Wilson, 1993.

Booktalking with Joni Bodart (video). New York: H.W. Wilson, 1985.

Booktalking the Award Winners 1992 - 93. New York: H.W. Wilson, 1994.

Booktalking the Award Winners 1994 - 95. New York: H.W. Wilson, 1995.

Booktalking the Award Winners: Young Adult Retrospective Volume. New York: H.W. Wilson, 1996.

Booktalker's Companion 1 and 2. Bookhooks Publishing, 1995 - 1996

New Booktalker 1 and 2. Englewood, CO: Libraries Unlimited, 1992–93.

Bodart's study was one of the first to measure the success of booktalking. Those practicing the craft in schools and libraries could attest to its effectiveness, but data documenting booktalking success emerges sparingly. For example, a librarian at a high school wrote after me after a booking visit to her school that:

> [W]e compared our circulation for ten school days following his (booktalk) program to the same period last year. In 1987, we circulated 38 fiction books. After his visit, 153 books were signed out. Some of the books he highlighted are still on a waiting list and the others are actively circulating.

Published recently, however, is some hard data backing up the contention that, indeed, booktalking works. Terrence David Nollen's dissertation studied the effectiveness of booktalking on reading attitudes and behaviors. He found that:

1. Booktalking had no effect on reading attitudes.
2. Booktalking had significant effect on students' decisions to check out the booktalked titles.
3. Booktalking affected student choice, but only for a very short time.

In addition to these questions, Nollen also looked at reading interests, gender issues, and the long-term effect of booktalking. In conclusion, Nollen writes:

> The results of this study seem to indicate that booktalking can build students' knowledge of books and generate excitement for reading . . . the data from this study would seem to indicate that booktalking can be an important teaching resource to develop reading interests.[4]

In her dissertation, Gail Reeder conducted a similar type of research, reaching many of the same conclusions:

1. Booktalking significantly increased the circulation of booktalk titles.
2. Booktalking did not result in a change in reading attitudes.
3. Booktalking increased circulation of selected titles but didn't extend to other books.[5]

Perhaps the most interesting and alarming finding by Reeder was a huge gender gap. Although she could not attribute this finding directly to booktalking, she found that males were not as positive toward reading as females.

Pamela Dahl's thesis examined the same types of questions, getting similar results:

**Planning Process:
Booktalking**

1. Contact schools
2. Prepare documents
   A. Fact sheet
   B. Objectives/policies
3. Recruit teachers
4. Schedule booktalks
5. Prepare booktalks
   A. Prepare reading list
   B. Fill out booktalk cards
   C. Arrange presentation
   D. Order extra copies of
   books
   E. Gather books to take to
   school
6. Present booktalks
   A. Have copies on hand
   B. Distribute list of titles
7. Evaluate
   A. Review student
   evaluations
   B. Review teacher
   evaluations
   C. Complete reporting form
   D. Watch circulation
   measures
8. Evaluate program
   A. Review formal
   measures
   B. Review informal

1. Booktalks can have an effect on the number of pages that students report for independent reading.
2. Booktalks did not have any effect on students' reading attitudes.
3. Gender breakdown in terms of reading interests was pronounced: 61 percent of females read one book a week compared to 21 percent of males.[6]

Dahl also has similar ideas for areas for further research; the most important being the long-term effects of booktalking.

All three of these studies seem to validate what practitioners have long claimed: booktalking works, at least in terms of changing behaviors as documented by circulation of materials. Because this seems to be a short-term phenomenon, booktalking needs to become a regular part of a library or reading program. Perhaps then changes would occur not just in behavior but also in attitudes. Nothing will change, of course, unless librarians go out into the schools and demonstrate the effectiveness of this activity.

6.2 RULES

Like other activities, booktalking requires planning, involving more preparation time than instruction and orientation. You also need some special talents to be a good booktalker. Every booktalker, like every storyteller or reference librarian, has a different style. Style can be copied, but it can't be taught. Techniques for booktalking, on the other hand, like those of storytelling or reference, can be learned. Often people will see someone else booktalk and say, "I couldn't do that," which is exactly the case. No two people could, would, or should booktalk exactly alike.

Most libraries have trouble finding enough bodies to cover the desk. Bringing in tours is traditional, and at least no one has to leave the building all day. Booktalking is different: it is outreach. To do it, someone (perhaps the director or the supervisor) is going to have to make time for you to leave the building to plan with teachers and do the actual talks. When staff is short, how can they spare you leaving? You will have to bone up on your justifications for undertaking a booktalking program:

1. Booktalking increases circulation (see the research results, later in this chapter).
2. Booktalking promotes the library as a recreational place for YAs.
3. Booktalking allows the YA librarian to work with schools and students.

4. Booktalking is an efficient method to promote YA collections.
5. Booktalking provides YA librarians with the opportunity to use their creative talents for the good of the library.
6. You will reach more YAs in one day of booktalking than you will probably see in a week in the library.
7. Booktalking is one of the few library activities in which nonusers are the primary audience. You can increase circulation two ways: get current users to check out more books or create new users. Booktalking can accomplish both tasks.
8. Booktalking presents the library as an active force promoting reading in the community rather than a passive warehouse of books.
9. Booktalking increases the audience's awareness of the library. The first step to get people moving toward an action is increasing their awareness.
10. Booktalking is good PR—in the schools, in the community, and personally for the successful booktalker.

Fact Sheet: Booktalking

What is a booktalk? A *booktalk* is a presentation designed to persuade an audience to read a book or books.

What is a booktalk *not*? A booktalk is not a book review, literary criticism, or a public reading, and it does not have to be boring.

Who provides a booktalk? Booktalking is provided by a staff member who is comfortable performing in front of a group of YAs. The audience should be limited to no more than 30.

Where are booktalks given? Booktalks may be conducted in the library, the school library, or the classroom.

When are booktalks given? Booktalks can occur whenever teachers want to encourage students to read on their own. They can be most effective if the teacher has required students to choose a book for outside reading for a book report. They can also be used by the library to promote new books and promote reading programs

Why should librarians give booktalks? Booktalks expose students to books they might not hear about through other channels. Booktalks excite YAs about reading and provide the library with an opportunity to meet students on the student's turf.

What is the goal of booktalking? The goal of booktalking is to encourage YAs to read more.

A quote about booktalking: "A good booktalk reaches out to the listener and involves them so they become not merely listeners, but participants. It makes them care enough about the people in the book to want to read it and see what happens after the end of the talk." Joni Bodart from *Booktalk!*, H.W. Wilson, 1980.

If you can sell your boss on booktalking, then selling it to teachers should be no problem. First, you need to increase their awareness. Booktalking is a no-lose argument because what teacher wants to come out against promoting reading? In addition, many teachers are looking for supplemental titles to promote to their students. Booktalking provides a classic win-win situation.

The time for booktalking has never been better. Many teachers, especially English teachers who feel tied to text, are feeling very intimidated by the technology sweeping over their school and public libraries. Many feel the death of the book is at hand and that librarians are co-conspirators. Rather than feeding that paranoia, play to it. Present booktalking as a method to encourage reading of books, as a method to introduce students to literature, and as a something they can do to keep kids focused on texts, not on computer screens. Booktalking is very traditional—it is about connecting young adults and our collections in a simple, no-frills manner.

BOOKTALKING OBJECTIVES

Booktalking: Policies

Goal: To encourage young adult to read more

Objectives:
1. Increase YA awareness of YA collection
2. Increase circulation of YA collection
3. Provide a cooperative program between the library and schools

Policies:
1. All booktalks must be scheduled at least two weeks in advance
2. Booktalks will last one period
3. Teachers must stay in the room during booktalks
4. Classes should not be combined
5. Teachers will provide information about class reading interests and levels

The objectives of booktalking are the same as most libraries' PR department: increase awareness to increase use. The books you cover will change, but the objective always stays the same. You might also want to set policies, such as limiting how many talks you will do in a day. Some people don't mind doing all six or seven class periods in one day, while others won't do that many talks in a row. Combining classes might mean different grades and reading levels in the same room. The best setting is the classroom with the librarian "taking over" the class for that period.

SCHEDULING BOOKTALKS

Scheduling booktalks takes a lot more work. You need to do a really good interview with teachers who use your service for the first time. If you don't have any ideas going in about this class, you probably will not do well. Part of scheduling is also choosing the time of day. Because booktalking requires energy—both yours and and the class's—the end of the week is not a good time for a booktalk nor are classes first thing in the morning or late in the afternoon. Classes right after lunch are the most fun and challenging as the Twinkie rush kicks in during the middle of the presentation. Finally, booktalk for entire class periods only. Darting in and out of rooms every 10 minutes is too confusing for the teachers, provides too little interaction with YAs, and is too herky-jerky on you to get into a good pace.

BOOKTALKING ASSUMPTIONS

Once you have scheduled the session and the teacher is expecting you, you have only one simple job: develop a 50–minute presentation that will excite teenagers about reading. Let's look first at some of the assumptions about booktalking:

Students won't be thrilled to see you: I know, it is hard to believe that someone from the library coming to talk about books won't set off a celebration. Often you will find yourself scheduled in reading classes, which, more often than not, are classes filled with poor and/or non-readers.

Students may be cool at first: They may not be hostile, but don't expect an immediately warm reception. Your assumption then is that you have to win them over, and fast.

You are a performer: That is hard for some people, but look at the physical reality of the situation: you will be standing in front of a room, similar to being on-stage. The YAs will be at their desks, like an audience. The third element of performance is a certain set of expectations from the audience. That does not mean you need to be theatrical,[7] but rather that you need to consider the setting, the audience, and expectations.

You are a salesperson: Although the activity is called book*talking*; you are really selling reading as an activity. You are trying to persuade, convince, and even manipulate this audience to sell a product. If that is the case, remember what Zollo found to be some of the most effective characteristics used by advertisers trying to appeal to teens: a sense of humor, directness, and not preaching. You don't have to be a Nike commercial, but you should be aware of what YAs respond to in advertising because that is what you are doing.

Find models: Look at what other "performers" and "salespeople" do with their audiences. Some examples:

- *Movie previews:* Just like a booktalk, movies aim to create an interest in a product by telling just enough about it. Normally, previews show the lead characters, explore the conflict, and then cap the whole thing off with a tagline or lasting image.
- *Pop music:* Tune in your radio and listen to songs that capture your attention. Think about what makes that song inviting. Most great songs have what are known as *hooks* which generate interest. The hook could be anything: the beat, the chorus, a sing-along part: anything that makes the song "catchy." One example of this is Bob Dylan's classic "Like A Rolling Stone"—it is a great song, but a better booktalking model:
  1. The first thing you hear is a single drum beat—it gets your attention and makes an impression.
  2. The first line of the song is "Once upon a time"—right away you learn you are going to hear a story.

3. The first line of the chorus is "How does it feel?" He speaks directly to the audience and talks about feelings, appealing to the emotions.
4. The last line of the chorus "like a Rolling Stone," which is the punch line of the song. The whole song builds to it and—guess what? It is the title of the song.

A booktalk can be built around the same structure with great success.

- *Stand-up comics:* Not that you should tell jokes, but for some good booktalking ideas, look at the assumptions and the construction of a stand-up comedian's act. Jokes usually have a tried and true beginning ("A funny thing happened," or "A guy walks into a bar"). The jokes develop using limited detail and some characterization, and then end with a punch line. Structure booktalks in the same way.
- *Storytellers:* This example is much closer to home. Many children's librarians understand this performance aspect of their jobs. They sell the story through characterization, sound effects, use of props, or a variety of other ways. Many librarians know that two things need to happen: they need to go beyond the text by making the story come alive, and they must see what they are doing as a performance. Do librarians giving booktalks undergo a similar type of leap in role? Do they realize it is show time? There is a strong school of thought against "performance" storytelling; people think that the storyteller is merely a vehicle and the story is entertaining enough on its own. Although it is *not* a case of "if you can't beat 'em, join 'em," you must recognize that children and YAs are conditioned differently and have different expectations. Blame it on MTV for wearing down attention spans or Sesame Street for making children think all learning is fun and entertaining.

WRITING BOOKTALKS

After examining your assumptions about what booktalking is and what it can be, you are ready to write some talks. This becomes a matter of individual choice. Sometimes the teacher will give you a reading list and ask that you booktalk titles off only that list. Some people write booktalks as new titles cross their desk, while others take home stacks of paperbacks at a time. Some people never write them down at all—everything goes to memory. And some you can steal, if you need to. Sometimes after reading a book, you just can't figure out what to say about it. There are several sources of already published booktalks that you can either lift verbatim or use to give you an idea on which direction to head.

If you are just starting, you probably will want to write the booktalks down. A booktalk card helps you organize your thoughts and keep them so you can refer to the booktalk later (see Figure 6–1). Keep these cards handy when you are reading. Immediately write down all the important pieces of information like character names so you won't have to dig for them again. Do the same with the plot outline. From this working draft, you can begin to build a booktalk. Once you have completed these cards you can file them for ready access. Although the actual talk probably will differ from what you write, this card represents your approach to the material.

Figure 6–1 A Booktalk Card

Booktalk Card

Author:

Title:

_____ Fiction   _____ Nonfiction

Subjects:

Main Characters:

Summary of Plot:

Themes/Emotions:

"Hooks":

Possible Approaches:

_____ Plot based   _____ Character based/which one:

_____ Scene based/what page: _____ Mood based/what page:

Booktalk (write on back)

Do's and Don'ts of Booktalking

DON'T:
1. Booktalk books you have not read
2. Booktalk books you did not like or would not recommend
3. Gush
4. Give away the ending/the secret/the surprise
5. Give a book review
6. Label by gender/race/other
7. Oversell
8. Read unless you hafta
9. Talk about sex/drugs/violence without clearing it with the teacher
10. Booktalk books you don't have in multiple copy
11. Be boring to yourself
12. Start booktalks with booktalks

DO:
1. Bring books with you and check them out
2. Memorize talks and have cheat sheets
3. Vary the themes and the types of talks
4. Keep good records of visits
5. Be prepared to ad-lib and interact
6. Vary length of talks
7. Start strong and end strong
8. Have realistic expectations
9. Be organized, cool, and confident
10. Relax and enjoy
11. Measure success
12. Learn from your mistakes

TYPES OF TALKS:
1. Mood
2. Plot
3. Scene
4. Character

NEVER EVER:
Say "read this and find out"

Booktalk Styles

Four common approaches are used in writing booktalks:

Plot summary: Summarize the plot to a certain point, and then stop. This cliffhanger approach works well with suspense and mysteries, but also will work with almost any book. How much of a summary you need depends on how long the book goes on before something "big" happens—sometimes it is 100 pages in; sometimes it happens on page one. The plot summary booktalk is the easiest type to do because it is the one most people already do when talking about a book.

Character based: The attractive thing for YAs about YA literature is that the characters are their age. Because of this, the things that happen to a character relate to your audience. Sometimes, as well, the most interesting thing about a book is one character. You can describe that character as you booktalk or even speak as that character.

Mood based: The mood-based booktalk picks up on the author's use of language to create a certain mood. Convey mood by your tone of voice, choice of words, and emphasis. Scary stories work very well with this type of talk. This also works well with senior high students who might be more appreciative of an author's language. Why summarize Maya Angelou when you can let the power of her words do the work?

Scene based: If there is one gripping scene that really hits you when reading the book, you can pull that scene out for your booktalk. Rather than telling the whole plot or even a fraction of it, tell only the events in this scene that make it dramatic or funny or whatever it was that made you remember it.

You also can combine all of these booktalk styles. Sometimes a particular scene hits you because of the mood; you might want to read it. Or maybe the character sets the mood. The key is to write booktalks in each type or try books different ways. As you read, you probably will see into which one of these categories the talk "fits." There is no wrong one or best one, but there are a few do's and don'ts to remember. There are rules, and then there is the prime directive: *remember your audience.* When you are writing, attempt to visualize not just you doing it (that will help with the performance), but your audience. As you plan a 10–minute booktalk summarizing every key scene in the book, can you visualize your audience sitting in rapt attention?

The First Sentence

Your first sentence is the most important. It needs to get people's attention right away. Much like the four approaches, several different types of first lines work well in effective booktalks. Start off with one of these elements:

A character: Use a quotation or a description, but in the first sentence give the audience a good (or bad) first impression of the character. If you use a quotation, do it with a fake voice. This gets attention and announces that something is different about this book.

An emotion: If you are doing a book like *When the Phone Rang*, your first sentence might be one about loss or grief. You can do this through questions (how does it feel?) or by using declarative statements.

An action: You could start with something somebody does that is dramatic and attention-grabbing: an act of violence, daring, or even stupidity.

A shared experience: Your first line could involve something that was felt, done, or said. For example, if you are booktalking *The Pigman*, the first line of the talk could be, "Ever make a prank phone call?" Right away the audience focuses on something they have done or know someone who has done. Again, your first sentence might best be a question.

A shocker: A shocker is the cheap way to get heat, but it works. Many books have shocking incidents. Rather than building up to them, leap off from them.

Many booktalks end with the title of the book, which acts as the punch line. The idea is that the last line should be memorable, and what is the one thing you want all the YAs to remember? The title. The ending variations are similar to the first sentence. Personally, I think forcing the title with something like "and if you want to learn more, then read . . . " rings false, but maybe that's a personal style thing. But you shouldn't force a booktalk to an awkward conclusion just to work in the title, and doing it every time probably borders on compulsive and annoying.

The middle of your booktalk is the hardest part to create. Many people write the first and last sentence before anything else. In this middle section, you want to

- *Keep it simple:* Use mostly short declarative sentences.
- *Follow a narrative:* Go from point to point without detours.
- *Keep to a few characters:* The more characters you mention, the better your chances of getting confused and baffling your audience.
- *Repeat things:* In instruction you always repeat what you want people to remember. It's the same with booktalking. Work in several times the book's key phrases (the title perhaps) or whatever "tagline" you devise.
- *Watch words:* A booktalk is not the time for a vocabulary lesson. Make sure that the words, images, and allusions are appropriate for your audience and grade.

- *Read sparingly*: Your task is to sell the book, not recite it. Reading takes your eyes off your audience and your audience's eyes off you.
- *Watch time*: You don't want to cover three years' time in one talk. The book's time frame will determine this, but events you are telling about should not happen that far apart.
- *Watch the mood*: Unless you have something tricky in mind, you shouldn't alter the mood of the talk. It is really jolting—and not in a good way—to have YAs all hooked into a real somber talk, and then throw in some humor.
- *Watch your watch*: Movie trailers and pop songs (two booktalk models) last about two to four minutes. Anything over a four-minute booktalk should be pretty special.
- *If in doubt, leave it out.*

6.3 HOOKS

Paperback publishers are great with hooks and taglines—find them on the cover or in big letters on the back of the book. The hook is what keeps you interested in the book and the thing that answers the question "Why should I want to read this book?" Your best models are paperback backcover blurbs. They manage to introduce the character, describe the conflict, outline the emotions, and ask a question that reading the book will answer.

Booktalks can have hooks in the exact same way. The way a hook makes each book different and memorable, each booktalk can have a different spin. Sometimes the hook will come naturally out of the book and at other times it takes more creativity to develop. As a new booktalker, you just want to get all of the characters' names correct—you won't want to think about adding anything to the talk. After a while, especially after doing the same books, you will notice what types of things work with an audience.

A HOOK ALPHABET

What follows is an alphabet of hooks. Each one represents a different angle to a booktalk, something to make the talk, and thus the book, more memorable.

A **Accents/dialects:** Do the booktalk in first person. Change your voice and speech patterns. This is a good method for your first talk because it alerts listeners right away that they are in for a performance.

B **Blurbs:** Rather than racking your brain to come up with catchy quick booktalks, just read the copy to sell the book: after all, that is the purpose of backcover blurbs.

C **Conditional:** Build the entire booktalk around the "if, then" construction.

D **Diary:** Obviously many YA novels come in diary format and that authentic voice can be a real selling point. For example, use the diary entries in Cynthia Grant's *Phoenix Rising*.

E **Experience:** Relate a real personal experience that serves as a lead-in to a talk, or better yet, do a short booktalk pretending the events that happened to the character really happened to you. For example: Tell the title story in *Southern Fried Rat* by Daniel Cohen not as a booktalk, but as you would an urban legend.

F **False Finish:** Do a standard cliffhanger booktalk, and get to the stopping point. Pause, count one, two. Then start the booktalk again and go to another cliffhanger. In booktalking *Crazy Horse Electric Game* by Chris Crutcher, I build to the dramatic pitch, do a false finish, and then go on to the point of the accident.

G **Gimmicks, your own:** Maybe your gimmick is magic or riding a unicycle, whatever what works for you. Part of getting booktalks "over" is getting yourself over as someone interesting that your audience will want to listen to.

H **Heat:** Many books have good guys and bad guys. In your talk, tell all the terrible things the bad guys have done, especially to the sympathetic good guy. This will (as they say in professional wrestling circles) "draw heat" and make your audience want the good guy to get revenge. In *Running Loose* by Chris Crutcher, I try to stack the odds against Louie so the audience will be pulling for him and wanting him to pay back the bad guy.

I **Interview:** Do the booktalk as an interview. You could act as an interviewer talking to the main character in the book. Or you could write your interview questions for an audience member to ask you. Or you could merely tell a little bit about the character, something which should be mysterious, and let the audience ask the character questions.

J **Judge:** This works best with a mystery or thriller by laying out the facts of the "case" and asking the audience to decide the guilt or innocence of the character. Example: Use Pike's *Fall Into Darkness,* which centers on a trial.

K **Kiss and Tell:** Young adults are interested in sex. Talk with the teacher first to get an idea of how much, if any, freedom you have to discuss sexual content. Even then, you will more want to allude to the sexual aspects of a book rather than playing kiss and tell.

L **Lists:** This alphabet is an example of a hook. Rather than presenting the information in a "standard" format, I have used this hook, thinking it will be more entertaining and thus maybe memorable to you, the reader. Using lists like this could work in a booktalk as well.

M **Mix and match:** Instead of building a talk around one hook, use several. Mix and match different hooks to find the best combination.

N **News story:** Present the booktalk as a news story, either as the character to a broadcaster or in the same style. Use the who, what, where, when, and how approach, but leave the audience wondering why.

O **Omit a fact:** This is similar to the false finish. Build to the finish, and then stop and slip in a shocking fact. If booktalking *The Silver Kiss* by Annette Curtis Klause, tell your audience everything they need to know about Simon and Zoe. Get to the point of the first kiss, and then stop and say you forgot to say that Simon is a vampire.

P **Pantomime:** Don't go overboard, but adding just a little bit of movement and action every now and then will make talks more entertaining for the audience and for you.

Q **Quick and clean:** Use blurbs or one-sentence talks to tell your audience about a lot of books in little time. Or after doing a talk, say "if you liked this" and then mention similar titles.

R **Rashomon:** Use a multiple viewpoint approach, telling several characters' sides of the story. A great book to do this with is Avi's *Nothing But the Truth*. You could take this approach and mix it with doing an interview-based talk or one using accents.

S **Soap opera:** Present the book as a soap opera, complete with all the main characters, their relationships, and the tragedies that befall them.

T **Telephone:** Remember Bob Newhart's comedy routines? All of the best ones were him pretending to talk on the phone with someone. Certainly talking on the telephone is something teens have in common so this a good technique.

U **Unifying experience:** Get everyone thinking about the same thing by asking questions about something almost everyone will have in common. Examples: Talking on the phone as an introduction to *The Pigman* by Paul Zindel, getting mail as an introduction to *I Know What You Did Last Summer* by Lois Duncan, etc.

V **Vocabulary:** Begin a talk by asking the audience to define certain words. Repeat these words throughout the talk, and then come back to them at the end.

W **Why?** As an experiment, break the number one rule of booktalking and give the ending away, and then hook your audience not on what happened but why it happened.

The Original Alphabet of Hooks for Books

A Audience participation
B Boring, but
C Cliffhanger
D Definitions
E Empathy
F First sentence/one
   sentence
G Gross out
H Headlines
I Interactive
J Jump cut
K Know a secret
L Link
M Mystery
N Next line
O O. Henry
P Props
Q Questions
R Repetition
S Sound effects
T Themes
U Unexpected
V Victim/draw heat
X X-rated
Y You directed
Z Zonk

Adapted from Patrick Jones, "Don't Tell, Sell," in *Booktalk 4.* Joni Richard Bodart, ed. H.W. Wilson, 1992.

X **Xerox:** If you were booktalking *Scavenger Hunt* by Christopher Pike, photocopy and distribute the pages with the list of things on the hunt. Other books which have short easy-to-read documents (letters, comics, etc.) would work as well.

Y **Young Adult Literature:** Use booktalks as an opportunity to talk about YA literature. Rather than booktalking *The Outsiders* by S.E. Hinton, talk about how and why it was an important book.

Z **Zany:** A little humor goes a long way.

Adding these hooks or others to your booktalking takes you beyond caring just about telling the story and helps you enhance how you tell the story.

A SAMPLE BOOKTALK

Let's take a look at one booktalk, complete with "stage directions" to see how hooks are used to booktalk Lois Duncan's *I Know What You Did Last Summer:*

(STANDING)

How many of you like to get mail? It is best around your birthday because you know those envelopes come stuffed with cash. This is a story about a girl named Julie. Julie comes home from school one day and her mother tells her "you've got some mail." Julie opens one letter and it says, "Congratulations, you have been accepted to Smith College." Julie is a high school senior and this is the letter she's been waiting for—she's been accepted to Smith, which is a very good college. She's still thinking how happy she is when her mother hands her another letter. But when Julie (TAKE OUT LETTER, AND OPEN IT) opens this one—she is not so happy—she looks on the front of the envelope (DO SO), and there's no return address. There's no letter . . . There's just a note inside and it says . . . (PULL OUT LARGE SHEET OF PAPER WITH WORDS WRITTEN ON IT) *I know what you did last summer.* Julie throws down the letter (DO SO) and picks up the phone (PANTOMIME OR USE A PROP) and calls her best friend Helen. Helen calls up her boyfriend Ray, and Ray calls up Barry and the four of them talk about what they did last summer. (SIT) What happened last summer? The four of them were at a party; they were coming home. Barry who was the oldest was driving. They had the windows rolled all the way . . . down. They had the radio all the way . . . up. And Barry had his foot almost all the way to the . . . floor. They were driving, laughing and having a great time and (SLAP HAND HARD AGAINST BOOK)—Barry saw the little boy on the bicycle just a second before he slammed the car into him. The girls screamed and Barry knew what he had to do. He took his foot and he put it on the . . . gas pedal, and got out of there as fast as he could and left that little boy there to die. That's what they did last summer. (STAND) They stop at a phone. Ray calls the police. He says "I need to report an accident." The policeman says "Start by telling me your name" and Ray says, "My name is—" (SLAP HAND AGAINST BOOK HARD). Barry slams down the receiver. "What are you doing?" Ray asks. "You're not going to tell the police because I'm not going to jail because of some stupid kid. Look," Barry says, "the four of us have to make a pact never to tell anyone. In fact (SPEAK VERY SLOWLY, TRY TO MAKE MAXIMUM EYE CONTACT) this . . . never . . . even . . . happened. This is our—secret." But if they didn't tell anyone and if that little boy is dead and buried, then why do bad things start to happen? Why is Barry shot at? Why does Ray get a copy of the little boy's obituary in the mail? Why does Helen find a picture on her door of a little boy on a bicycle with the head ripped off? And why does Julie get this note that says (SHOW NOTE AGAIN) *I know what you did last summer*? You (POINT AT AUDIENCE) know what happened; the four of them know what happened. Someone else knows and that someone wants (SLAP HAND HARD) - revenge. Revenge because (SHOW BOOK COVER) I know what you did last summer, by Lois Duncan.

When I first started doing this talk, I did not write down these directions; they evolved over time, and so did the hooks. This booktalk has plenty of them—audience participation (if you time your pauses right, you can get audience to say some parts out loud), cliffhanger (somewhat, but a shorter version such as stopping when Julie gets the note would be a better example), know a secret (obvious), mystery (you know somebody did something), props (the note), repetition (the title is repeated), questions (the talk starts with one), sound effects (slapping the book), pantomime (not elaborate, just to add action), and unifying experience (everybody likes to get mail). This isn't new or groundbreaking. It is just a way of labeling something lots of booktalkers do and don't even realize it.

They are tools of the trade; this means librarians can use them to improve their booktalks. After accepting that booktalking, like storytelling, is a performance and admitting that you want to influence your audience, you begin to handle your booktalks differently. You learn to perform rather than recite your talks and you learn your own performance style. The style you choose is the one best suited for you to get your point across. Gushing over a book is not getting your point across, nor is it "getting you over." By that, I mean where you become accepted by your audience as someone who will entertain them, someone they will want to have visit them again, and someone they will want to visit in the library. By arousing the audience's curiosity, using sound and movement and repetition and other hooks, creating empathy for characters, and evoking emotions while entertaining, you will have a lively and successful presentation.

As you booktalk more, you will find that both your styles and your techniques will change. When I started booktalking, I would do just about anything to get a reaction out of my audience, including jumping on top of tables.[8] The more talks I did, the more confident I became and was less theatrical, letting the book, not me, take center stage. I still use hooks, and reuse them constantly. The hook of "next sentence" can work in any booktalk if you build correctly to it. Building isn't theatrical, but you do use elements of drama in these booktalks. Books are dramatic—they are about people in conflict and I think rather than ignoring that when booktalking, we should exploit it.

ELEMENTS OF BOOKTALK SUCCESS

This section lists some other elements of success—characteristics for booktalk building that will make booktalks more effective and crowd-pleasing.

1. **Know the crowd—don't be too proud or too loud:** The teacher needs to tell you as much as possible about the classes you will be visiting. You don't want to go into a class of low-level readers and do books they couldn't read, nor do you want to visit a group of students with high reading levels or sophisticated tastes and do Jay Bennett mysteries.

2. **Speak to feeling, not lofty ceilings:** Emotions are going to grab YAs more than anything else about a book. Being ego-oriented as YAs are, they will be looking for characters like themselves in your booktalks, not elements of style or literary devices. The group may have a variety of different reading levels and interests, but as stated before, as YAs, they will have certain emotional similarities. With senior high students, the language of the book might have as much appeal as the emotional impact.

3. **Don't just speak out, seek out:** As often as possible, involve the audience. In a performance setting, the audience gives energy back to the performer. Booktalks also are more interesting and YAs are more likely to listen if peers get into it.

4. **If you want a reaction, create an action:** The worst thing during a booktalk is total silence. You don't know whether you are getting through, and the students are not giving you any clues. If you want them to react, you need to create situations for them to react to. Let the books do the work—tell the one-liners in Danziger's books if you want to hear laughter, or read the graphic descriptions of horror in King to get a groan.

5. **Use your style, not cards from a file:** When you write the talk, you probably will not have a hook in it right away. Only through

practice and experience will you move from file cards to recreating the talk as something to be performed rather than read.

6. **Think stage, not printed page:** Again, write your booktalk, but think about adding movement. Think about adding sounds or props as you write. Challenge yourself by working one of the hooks into a talk already in your file.

7. **Be yourself, lose yourself:** You have to be yourself when you speak in front of a group. YAs in particular will pick up on a falseness in your presentation. Don't load down your talk with slang or attempts to be something you are not. But as a performer, you will notice a change. For some it is gradual, but for others it is a very dramatic change and part of developing performing style.

8. **No matter what you try, answer the question why:** Hooks are gimmicks and like most gimmicks, they only go so far. You can never get away from the central point of your booktalk, which is telling a group of YAs the reasons they should take their precious time and read a certain book.

9. **Find the hook, push the book:** As you are reading, you will find that hook. As you are writing, you will discover how to work that hook into the booktalk. As you perform it, you will learn which things work and are the most effective for pushing the book.

10. **Remember needs, not just deeds:** When deciding which books to booktalk, look not so much for plot and action as what is really happening in the book, which is normally the "journey" the teen protagonist is experiencing. Chances are that they are grappling with issues like independence, acceptance, identification, and excitement. Those are the real selling points.

11. **Separate, don't segregate:** In retrospect, one of the biggest mistakes I've made in booktalking is choosing titles which have a harder edge to them. In doing so, although it might have been appealing to some members of the audience (boys), I was probably equally turning off other members (girls). I am certainly not alone in failing at fairness,[9] but that's no excuse. Although you should never say "This is a girl's book," there are certain types of authors and themes which will appeal to only one gender; make sure to mix up your talks to include titles that do not speak only to one half of the audience. That's why thrillers are just about your best bet—not only to do they lend themselves to booktalking easily, but as we saw in the reading research, it is a gender neutral genre.

12. **Don't tell, sell:** Talking about a book is one thing; persuading someone to read it is quite different. Booktalking is the art of convincing.

6.4 SHOWS

After you have written your individual booktalks, you need to structure them into a presentation. If you have seen the group before, either for booktalks or for a tour, you don't need to go through the whole "introduction" section and can jump right into books. If it is your first time, however, then an introduction is necessary. You need to decide how many books you will do given the time you have. When a band puts together a concert, they break the total time up into sets. In each set, they structure the songs to a particular effect. Lots of bands begin with "old favorites" to get immediate recognition, and then play new material, and encore with more old favorites. That's a good model to keep in mind when putting together booktalking presentations. Here are some other ideas:

Don't start with books: As you learned in Chapter 5, this is not the format of choice. Introduce the library by connecting with something YAs already like: your magazine titles.

Go next to AV: Again, speak to your audience's interest in order to get it. Show them some of the recent AV acquisitions in your library, including videos. Give away movie posters if you have them on hand.

Movie tie-ins: A good first booktalk is to do a title students recognize, which probably will be one with a movie tie-in or one on which a movie was based. You can do something current, or because of video/cable, a classic like *The Outsiders* is a good beginning.

Use a known author: At this point, you are establishing credibility and making students listen to you. Doing an R.L. Stine or a Stephen King book establishes the common ground between their interests and your resources. You don't need to sell Stephen King, but you do need to sell the idea that your library has "good stuff."

Series: By the same token, you can also mention the various series books, especially to younger YAs. Mention a few titles, and then proceed.

Use questions: Asking questions is a good transition from booktalk to booktalk. A lot of the hooks involve this technique, and it is a good habit to develop.

Relate personal experiences: No, don't bore them with the story of your high school prom, but you probably can dig into your experience and relate it. That personal anecdote makes you more of a person to them and speaks to common YA emotions.

Relate inside information: If you can relate any personal information about the author, it makes the book more real.

Set the mood: You can change the mood not just by reading, but by altering the room. Shut drapes and dim lights if you do a scary story—it is not subtle, but it is effective.

Use themes: As you prepare booktalks, note the subjects or themes each book concerns. Relate your theme presentations to a unit a teacher is developing or instructing.

Booktalk in teams: Booktalking in teams means not only will people have to prepare less material, but it offers other advantages as well. Team booktalking allows both people to booktalk from their strengths and keeps a higher energy level. It also provides an opportunity to learn new techniques and even steal other people's material. Finally, team members can have a lot of fun playing off each other.

Take requests: Once you have been doing booktalking for a while, you can put together a list of books you can do easily. You then can pass out this list and ask the audience to tell you based on the title and maybe a one-sentence tagline which book they want to hear.

Make a list: No matter how hard you try to work in the title of a book, many kids just are not going to remember. Always have a copy of the books you plan to booktalk. You also might want to consider using this list as an "if you like . . . " list. List the titles you are going to talk about, and then also list similar titles. You also could hold up those books as part of the presentation. Make sure that you distribute a copy of the list to the school librarian and within your own library system so when YAs come looking for a title (and they forgot the list) someone can still help them.

Give something away: End the booktalk presentation by putting something in their hands. It could be another booklist, a flyer about a program, or even posters from magazines.

Use your captive audience: Give students a short survey of some kind. Use one from this book or design one of your own to solicit responses about whatever topic will help you plan better services. Ask them about their music or programming interests, or any other kind of information you would like to collect. If you are trying to do a YA advisory group, give people a place to write down their name, e-mail address, and phone number.

End with a bang: You should save your best talk for last. Be careful of the timing though; you don't want your best talk cut short by the bell.

Pace yourself: After the introduction, do a couple of short talks, and then build to a longer one. In a normal 50–minute period, you should be able to cover six to nine titles if you've started with the introductory material,. You could do probably 10 to 15 if you are booktalking to a class that knows you, and you got right into the booktalks.

Transitions: The transitions between your talks need to be smooth to give the impression that the "act" fits together instead of being a random selection of books. Try to make the last word of one booktalk the first word of the next. If you are doing horror stories, a basic transition is "you thought that one was scary, then . . . "

Talk with the teacher first: Not only do teachers need to introduce you, but they will also help (or hinder) you in setting the mood for the class. If you want the YAs excited and even talkative, tell the teacher this. If not, while you are trying to "get them up," the teacher is at cross-purposes trying to settle them down.

Always prepare more than you need: You don't want to run through all of your titles in 20 minutes and utter "Any questions?" Have long and short versions of titles so that you can stretch or shorten depending on the time factor but also based on your audience's reactions.

Keep notes handy: Some people bring a written booktalk with them, and others go entirely from memory. A good compromise is your booktalk card—stick it on the back cover of the book so that as you hold the book for the audience, you can look at it. Simply list the names of the major characters and one- or two-word reminders of the talk outline so that you can get from point A to B, even with sudden memory loss.

Consider AV: Some people use slide shows with the book jackets, and some school librarians do booktalks over the PA system. You could use AV to complement the booktalk or videotape it to replace your visit. Maybe background music or even sound effect tapes could be effective if not overdone and/or played too loudly.

Check out books: Best case scenario would be multiple copies of titles you could take with you on the visit and check out in the classroom. It will answer the immediate need the YA has for the book, which despite your booktalking experience might cool before they can get to the library. Sure, you will lose some of the titles, but the idea is to get the books into YAs' hands. You'll get a kid that's delinquent, but think of the YAs who got the book HOT and NOW. If you cannot bring books with you, take names and hold the books for YAs or place reserves.

Bring your calendar: If you've arranged to visit only one teacher, ask that teacher to invite others to your booktalk. Chances are that you'll land some more visits.

EVALUATING BOOKTALKS

After each booktalking session, you will want to evaluate how well you did. Ask both students and teachers; you'll do a self-evaluation as well.

Figure 6–2 provides a sample evaluation form for students; Figure 6–3 provides a similar form for teachers. Some people like to tape themselves on audio or video, and others find that once they become aware of their "tics," they feel inhibited by them. You cannot always judge the success of the talk by the reaction or nonreaction you are receiving from the audience. Often the teacher sets the tone and there is nothing you can do to break it. Anytime you try out new talks, you might be met with stony silence until you get down the hooks and the delivery. But after a while, each booktalk will become finely tuned. The responses on the evaluations can be surprising. The talk you thought just died might have been the most popular or vice versa. The most concrete measure of booktalk success is the circulation of the books.

Figure 6–2 A Booktalk Evaluation Form for Students

Booktalking: Student Evaluation

SCHOOL: GRADE:

TEACHER: CLASS:

Please answer these questions. Your answers will help us improve our services to you.

1.   This presentation was

_____ Very interesting   _____ Somewhat interesting   _____Boring

2. I already knew about

_____ All of these books   _____ Some _____ A few _____ None

3. The thing I liked best about this presentation was

4. The thing I liked least about it was

5. The best booktalk was

6. The worst booktalk was

COMMENTS:

Figure 6–3 A Booktalk Evaluation Form for Teachers

Booktalking: Teacher Evaluation

TEACHER GRADE(S):

SCHOOL CLASS(S):

DATE: TIME: #STUDENTS:

Please answer the following questions:

1. This presentation was

_____ Interesting   _____ Somewhat interesting   _____ Boring

2. Did this presentation meet your expectations?

_____ Yes   _____ Somewhat   _____ No

3. Would you recommend this service to your colleagues?

_____ Yes   _____ No

4. Did the librarian hold the students' interest?

_____ Yes   _____ No

5. Did the librarian adequately involve the students?

_____ Yes   _____ No

6. Were the books appropriate in terms of content?

_____ Yes   _____ No

7. Were the books appropriate for reading level?

_____ Yes   _____ No

8. What did you like most about this presentation?

9. What did you like least about this presentation?

10. This presentation could be improved by

You'll want record information using a reporting form similar to ones used for instruction/tours (see Figure 6–4). Because you will probably see the same students again next year, you want accurate records so you don't repeat yourself. The best way to do this is to do only certain books for certain grades. You can add books, but don't shift them between grades. If you are not careful, you will find yourself in the middle of a booktalk and someone telling the ending or moaning loudly "We heard this one before."

Figure 6–4 Reporting Form for Booktalking

Reporting Form

TEACHER:

SCHOOL:

#STUDENTS: GRADES: CLASSES:

DATE/TIMES:

LIBRARIAN STUDENT EVALUATION SUMMARIES:

1. _____ Interesting   _____ Somewhat interesting   _____ Boring

2. _____ All   _____ Some _____ Few _____ None

3. Liked best:

4. Liked least:

TEACHER EVALUATION FORM (ATTACH)

LIBRARIAN EVALUATION:

1. Problems:

2. Plusses:

3. Changes:

Increase in circulation of talked titles for month:

Overall increase in YA circulation for month

It seems simple enough: read a book and tell someone about it. Effective booktalking involves planning, preparing, and finally evaluating. Because booktalking is a performing art, the thing that makes you better is doing it often. You can practice, write talks down, and try them out on your friends, but eventually it is getting in front of that classroom of YAs that makes you better.

If your barrier to booktalking is stage fright or fear of public speaking, there are certainly books out there to help overcome those barriers. If your barrier is fear of YAs, then that is something you need to get over if you plan on serving this age group. If your barrier is your administration, refer back to the beginning part of this section about the advantages of booktalking. If your barrier is the fact that you haven't done a booktalk before, that is an easy one to get over because you only have to break through it once.

6.5 BOOKTALK EXAMPLES

This section gives you some examples of booktalks that demonstrate the various hooks:

WEETZIE BAT BY FRANCESCA LIA BLOCK

Listen: Once upon a time there was a girl named Weetzie Bat. She lived in ShrangiLA; LA as in Los Angeles, but mostly Venice where everything was possible.

Listen: Weetzie Bat was a skinny girl with a bleached blonde flat top. She wore pink Harlequin sunglasses, strawberry lipstick, earrings dangling charms, and sugar-frosted eye shadow.

Listen: Weetzie Bat hated high school because no one understood. She looked around at the clowns and the gowns and she knew they didn't even realize they were living. No one cared. Was she the only one even alive on this earth?

Listen: Weetzie Bat met Dirk and he cared and he understood. But Weetzie Bat wanted more, she wanted a Secret Agent Lover Man. But Dirk wanted more, he wanted a Duck. So, they got a house and moved in together: Weetzie Bat, Dirk, Duck, Secret Agent Lover Man, and a pet named Slinskter Dog.

Listen: Sure it is confusing, but isn't that what being 16 is all about—being confused. Seems like every time you come up with the answers, they change the questions. Well, Weetzie, Dirk, Duck, Secret Agent Lover Man, and a pet named Slinskter Dog are playing by a whole new set of rules in a world they are making on their own.

Listen: This ain't no party, this ain't no disco, this ain't no fairy tale, but real life LA style. If you want a little "oh isn't that nice" book, don't read this one. If you want a nice little book about football players and homecoming queens, don't read this book. If you want a nice little book where everybody is white bread and smiles, don't read this book.

Listen: Don't read this book unless you think you are ready for Weetzie's world.

BREAKING THE FALL BY MICHAEL CADNUM

You have to hold your breath.

"Stanley, that's all you have to remember—"

You have to hold your breath.

Jared tells Stanley that's the key to the game. And the game is one of thrills. The game makes Stanley feel alive.

You have to hold your breath.

Stanley felt like he was dead. His parents are breaking up, his grades are a mess, his life a walking death, but then came the game. Jared's game made Stanley feel alive.

You have to hold your breath

The game is simple. You find a house; it must be occupied. You go into the house at night. You go into a room and you steal something—anything—but prove you've been there. That's the game. But when you are in the house, you must be perfectly quiet. You must not make a sound. You—

You have to hold your breath.

Stanley waits to prove himself to Jared. Prove he's not a failure, prove he's alive. Prove he can play and win the game. Prove that he knows the rule—

You have to hold your breath.

Jared waits outside. Stanley goes inside. As he walks across the floor, the floor below him squeaks. The sound is deafening. He waits, he remembers—

You have to hold your breath.

He finds the stairs. He starts up them. With each step, the stair below him creaks. The noise is deafening. He waits, he remembers—

You have to hold your breath.

He gets to the top of the stairs. He sees the room at the end of hall. He goes to the door. He turns the knob and it squeaks. He waits, he remembers—

You have to hold your breath.

He sees a dresser. On top, a locket. He walks across the bedroom toward it. He reaches toward it, then he hears the—sound.

You have to hold your breath.

The man in the bed grunts. The man turns over. He grunts again, then he mumbles "Who's there?" Stanley waits, he remembers—

You have to hold your breath.

Stanley hears the—sound. A drawer being opened. Something is being removed. A noise—it is deafening. It is the sound, the sound of—a gun. A gun being loaded.

You have to hold your breath. You have to learn how to go about *Breaking the Fall* by Michael Cadnum.

CHILDREN OF THE RIVER BY LINDA CREW

Look around you—take a long look at your classmates, at your friends. Look outside—take a long look at this school. Go home tonight and take a long look at your family, your house. Look at everything, and then imagine someone took it all and you had nothing. Imagine you had left everything—every last thing—behind.

Sundara left everything behind. When she fled Cambodia, killing fields, she left her world behind—her friends, her family, her boyfriend, and her way of life. She moved to the U.S. to live with her aunt. It is not easy fitting in. Not just because she speaks and acts and looks differently—and she does. Sundara tries her hardest, but no matter how smart she is, she knows she always will be an outsider. Until she meets Jonathan. He's your basic All-American milk commercial high school poster boy. Sundara has a crush on him, and the feeling is returned. But she is not allowed to date Jonathan. Her aunt refuses to hear of it.

"But everyone else—" Sundara says.

"You are not like everyone else," her aunt says. "Our ways are different."

"But—"

"No, he is no good for you," her aunt says. "You will forget him; you will forget him." Imagine those words: being told about someone you care about, being told to forget him. Knowing that dating that person might at long last make you an insider, instead of the kid on the outside of the group who looks different, talks different, acts different. Everything was taken away from Sundara, including her dreams. Her future is in jeopardy because her past won't let her forget who she is and what she is: from Cambodia, one of the *Children of the River* by Linda Crew.

ZERO TO THE BONE BY MICHAEL CADNUM (PROP: TELEPHONE)

(*Hold the telephone receiver in your hand.*)

The telephone. Think about it for a second. How much time to spend it on every night? What do you talk about? Gossip—school—homework—boyfriends—girlfriends—you talk about everything.

Anita is your typical teenager in that way. She loves to talk on the telephone. Her parents and her brother Cray tease her about her being such a gossip. Tease her about talking on the phone. Cray wonders how a person could spend their entire life wrapped around a telephone cord.

One night, Anita went out with some friends. Like always, she said she'd call if she would be late. When she doesn't come home, her parents wait. And wait. And wait. They look at the telephone, but it doesn't ring.

You know this story. You've heard about it a hundred times. A missing child. The police are contacted; they run Anita's picture on TV. Everything has a phone number on it. Cray and his parents look at the telephone but it doesn't ring.

They make up posters. They put them everywhere. "Have you seen this girl? If so, then call." But no one calls. The phone doesn't ring. Then Cray realizes the joke is on them—that he and his parents are the ones whose lives are now wrapped around a telephone cord.

And if, if the phone should ring how would they feel? Their hearts would jump, their pulses would race. They'd go to the phone, pick it up, but—what would they hear? Cray imagines the voice on the other end—"It's Anita, I'm alive." But sometimes Cray imagines another voice on the other end, that of the police. "It's Anita, she's dead."

It has been months. They are sitting at home one night. The phone rings. Cray hesitates. He looks at his mom, his dad. Could this be it? He picks it up, and the voice on the other end says—*Zero to the Bone* by Michael Cadnum.

ATHLETIC SHORTS BY CHRIS CRUTCHER.

(*Write the words "revenge" and "mercy" on the blackboard and ask the audience to briefly define each word.*)

Lionel's father was a head-shaker. You know the type; you do something wrong and before he lets you have it, he shakes his head and sighs, expressing all the disappointment in the world. Lionel does stuff without thinking. He just does it and there's his father, shaking his head, then saying, sometimes yelling "THINK!" or "You just need to THINK!" Sure enough, one summer day, Lionel is out on the lake fishing with his father, mother, and brother from their boat. Lionel's done something wrong and his father is shaking his head back and forth. He hasn't said it but Lionel was ready, ready for his father to say "THINK!" Lionel's always wanted to tell his dad that sometimes, sometimes stuff just happens, you don't have time to think. Sometimes, it just happens.

It just happens. Neal—a guy Lionel has known most his life—and his buddies are out in the lake that day in a powerboat. They're drunk and they're headed straight at Lionel's boat. Lionel sees them coming.

But it happens, it happens too fast, there's no time to react, no time to THINK. And in a matter of seconds, the time it takes to blink an eye, Lionel's parents and his brother are killed. In an instant, Lionel's life has changed forever.

Now, it's four years later. Lionel has done his best to get on with his life, but he's never left it behind. He can't help but THINK about what happened—what he could have done different. THINK about why it happened. THINK about that day. THINK about Neal, who he has not seen since he saw him kill his parents. He keeps wondering why Neal did it; why didn't Neal stop and THINK.

There's a knock at Lionel's door. Lionel goes to the door and on the other side is Neal. On the other side of the door is the person who killed his parents. On the other side of the door is the person who ruined his life. On the other side of the door is a person he has never wanted to see again, yet Lionel wants and needs this moment.

(*point to the words on the board*). Revenge or mercy. Lionel sees Neal standing on the other side of the door and knows, now more than ever, he has to THINK. So why don't you THINK about reading "Goin' Fishin' by Chris Crutcher, just one of the stories in the collection *Athletic Shorts*

STAYING FAT FOR SARAH BYRNES BY CHRIS CRUTCHER.

(*Walk over to someone in audience, lean down, and in a stage whisper, ask—*)

Do you want to know a secret?

Is there a better question to have someone ask you? Who would say, "No, I'm not really interested in hearing a secret." And if hearing a secret is one of the best things, isn't keeping a secret just about the hardest? This is a book about secrets.

Eric was a fat kid. So fat that nobody called him Eric; instead they had a nickname. Moby. After Moby Dick because he was just a big fat whale. I guess it wouldn't have mattered because someone will always find a reason to make fun of you—you might be too fat, too thin, too short, too tall—doesn't matter. People will find a way to get to you and they will.

Because of this, Eric doesn't hang out with the popular kids at his school. He's friends with the other rejects, the other freaks. His best friend is named Sarah Byrnes. And isn't that ironic her name, Byrnes, because that is what makes her a freak. The whole side of her face was burned. She told people who dared ask about the accident when she was three, how she spilled boiling water on herself. Now what boils in Sarah is rage and anger and bitterness at those who make fun of her and at her father who wouldn't allow her to have plastic surgery to make her less of a freak. People try to find a way to get to Sarah Byrnes, but they can't. She's closed down—she's a human secret.

Things change. As Eric gets older, he thins out a little. He loves to swim; the more he swims, the more weight he loses. The more weight he loses, the faster he swims. Nobody calls him Moby anymore, instead those same people now want to call him friend. Nobody calls him Moby, that is, except Sarah Byrnes.

Sarah is still Eric's best friend. Even as he is changing, he tries to hold on to that, yet he can feel it slipping away. Then something happens. Sarah ends up in the hospital. Eric goes to see her, but she doesn't respond. Their talk goes something like this:

"How's it going?" Eric asks.

"Same," Sarah says.

Eric tries to break through, but he can't reach her. Finally, in anger, he says—

"Look, Sarah Byrnes, I'm your friend. I've been up here every day. You're still the person who knows me best and you scared me."

Sarah says, "Friends aren't the same for me as they are for you, no matter how scared you were or how fat you used to be."

"What do you mean?" Eric asks.

"Look at my face!" Sarah almost hisses the words.

"I've seen your face," Eric says.

Sarah stares him down. She is so angry, so hurt, so bitter; she is bursting inside.

"Do you want to talk about the accident?" Eric asks.

"Accident," Sarah says. She pauses; she ponders. She's closed down—she's a human secret.

"This—" Sarah says while pointing to her scarred face. "This— was no accident. Do you want to know how this happened to me?" (*Lean back down to person in audience.*) "Do you want to hear a secret?" *Staying Fat for Sarah Byrnes* by Chris Crutcher.

THE SILVER KISS BY ANNETTE CURTIS KLAUSE

This is a love story about a boy named Simon and a girl named Zoe. Kind of a weird name, huh? Well, Zoe is kind of a weird girl. She is preoccupied with dark thoughts. Thoughts of sadness, loneliness, guilt, and death. Zoe thinks this way because every time she sees her mother, she knows the truth. Her mother is sick; her mother is going to die. And Zoe is going to be sad and lonely.

Simon too knows something about loneliness, guilt, and death. When they first meet in the park, Zoe is attracted to him immediately. He's gorgeous, he's bright, and he makes her feel good. Sometimes Zoe didn't think she would ever be able to feel good.

One night, Zoe invites Simon into her house. They talk. He understands, he really understands how I feel, Zoe thinks. She didn't think anyone could understand about her feelings of sadness, loneliness, guilt, and death. They talk; she feels close to him. Very close. They are sitting next to each other, talking, then touching. He reaches over, they look into each other's eyes, his face is next to hers. His lips part slightly, then he—

Oh, one thing I forgot to tell you. You see the reason that Simon understands so much about death is really quite simple. Because he's already dead. What's it like to fall in love with a vampire and receive *The Silver Kiss* by Annette Curtis Klause.

THE GIVER BY LOIS LOWRY

I didn't wake up one morning and decide I wanted to be a librarian in (*insert city name*). Things just don't happen that way. Instead, you make small choices along the way that eventually lead you to a some job in a some city.

Imagine, though, a place where it wasn't that way. A place where you didn't get to decide what you were going to do with your life. Instead, someone decided that for you and they decided it when you were 12 years old. They line you and your friends up and say—"You'll be a doctor," and "you'll be a lawyer," and "you'll be a judge," and "you'll pick up the garbage." Would you want to live in a place like that?

Well that is the bad part; here is the good part. No hunger. No crime. No violence. No abuse. No disagreements. Bliss—everyone gets along with everyone. Maybe for all of that, having your job picked out for you at age 12 isn't that bad.

Jonas is 12. And he's getting nervous awaiting the "ceremony of the twelves." That's the ceremony they hold where everyone you know—your family and friends—watches as the Elder of the Community gives you your job. Jonas doesn't feel confident. He doesn't feel special and so he is worried that he won't get a good job and he'll be standing there in front of everyone and be embarrassed.

Here's how the ceremony of the twelves works. Each person is given a number. When your number is called, you proceed to the front, and the Elder gives you your job. Every one is watching you. Jonas is scared. He's number 19. When the Elder calls number one, Jonas feels tense. As they get closer—12, 13—he feels almost sick. Closer now—14, 15—Jonas is looking at everyone and thinks they are all looking at him as he gets ready to stand up. Almost there—16, 17. Jonas takes a deep breath—18—he lets the breath out, he waits and he hears———20. Jonas can't believe it. They missed him—they left him out. Everyone looking down at him knows it. Jonas sits scared, trying not to cry wondering why he has been singled out.

After the last number has been called, the Elder says he wishes to apologize and he asks 19 to stand up. Jonas stands. "Come forward," the Elder says, and Jonas starts to walk forward with every single person looking, staring right at him. "We have not passed you," the

Elder says as Jonas walks closer. "We instead have something special for you," the Elder says as Jonas reaches the front and turns to face everyone. Everyone is looking at him, right at him, when the Elder says, "Your job is special. Your job—" Jonas swallows hard, waits and hears: "Your job is to be . . . *The Giver*" by Lois Lowry.

ENDNOTES

1. Amelia Munson, *An Ample Field*. American Library Association, 1950.
2.. Margaret Edwards, *The Fair Garden and the Swarm of Beasts*. New York: Hawthorn Books, 1970.
3. Joni Bodart-Talbot, *The Effect of a Booktalk Presentation of Selected Titles on the Attitude toward Reading of Senior High School Students and on the Circulation of These Titles in the High School Library*. Thesis (Ph. D.) Texas Woman's University, 1985.
4. Terrence David Nollen, *The Effect of Booktalks on the Development of Reading Attitudes and the Promotion of Individual Reading Choices*. Thesis (Ph. D.) University of Nebraska—Lincoln, 1992.
5. Gail Reeder, *Effect of Booktalks on Adolescent Reading Attitudes*. Thesis (Ph. D.) University of Nebraska, 1991.
6. Pamela Kay Dahl, *The Effects of Booktalks on Self-Selected Reading*. Thesis (M.S.) Moorhead State University, 1988.
7. Kent W. Graham, "Dramatic Booktalks (for the Untheatrical)," *Voice of Youth Advocates* (December 1993): 282–283.
8. *Library Video Magazine*, Vol 3. no 1 (1988).
9. Myra and David Sadker, *Failing at Fairness: How America's Schools Cheat Girls*. New York: Scribners, 1994.

FEBRUARY

Goal: Plan a young adult summer reading program

1. **Get people involved:** If you plan your summer reading program in a vacuum, it will occur in a vacuum. Because you will not be around every minute of every day next summer, it will be necessary for other staff to not only "do" the program, but also to sell it. How can they sell it if they don't know about it? Involve other staff if not in planning meetings, then in informal ways such as T-shirt drawings, contests, or other methods. If you cannot generate excitement about reading programs among staff, how do you expect to do it for YAs? Most importantly, involve youth. The evidence is clear about using YAs to plan YA programs. This often takes the shape of a YAAC (young adult advisory council) or some such organization. The goal of youth participation is the worthiest of all, and the more time and energy they spend planning means less time and energy required of you.

2. **Remember developmental tasks:** Most YA summer reading programs involve youngish YAs. Knowing this, it is important to plan the program around the developmental tasks of young adolescents. (See 2.2.) These tasks are the elements of success for a summer reading program. For example, if YAs are trying to define themselves, they often do so by the books they choose. They also are attempting to become adults and hate being treated like children. Thus, a program that keeps the children's model of requiring participants to read either certain books or even certain kinds of books might not be as successful as one in which YAs choose what they want to read. Keep the best aspects of children's programs, but lose the greasy stuff and cheap-looking prizes and incentives.

3. **Have realistic expectations:** You can promote summer reading programs in high schools, but the middle grades are more likely to turn out more participants. Kids there are closer to the idea of summer reading, perhaps are not as busy, and still are not so "independent" that they might like a structure for their reading. Did the children's department keep the names and addresses of those who participated in their program? If so, pull out the 5th and 6th graders and invite them to help you plan a YA program. Then as you do the program, get names and addresses to create a mailing list for next year's programs and other activities.

4. **KISS it:** We've all heard this saying: "Keep it simple, stupid." Keeping summer reading programs for YAs simple is important because most libraries do not have a separate YA department, which means that a YA program must use less staff than, say, children's summer reading programs. Adopting a kind of a self-service approach can help.

5. **Return on investment:** YA reading programs do not have to cost a lot. You might be able to find donors in the community—many businesses might want to increase their YA market share as well, which is a win-win proposition. Your costs will be for materials and for a few nifty prizes: YAs do not want to read 60 books and "win" a pencil. Have YAs help you choose the prizes. If you need library money, then stress to administrators that a YA summer reading program helps to get a return on our investment from children's programs.

PART V: HOW YA?

7 SURVEYING THE FIELD

The field of YA services is, on the surface, stronger than ever as libraries prepare to enter the next century. Bolstered by new research providing hard numbers that document both use and needs, plus a slew of professional publications suggesting practical applications, librarians serving YAs have a shed full of new tools. A glimpse at the history of YA services shows how today's state-of-the-art emerged from an evolution of ideas and activities on both the national and local levels. A great deal of emphasis has been placed, correctly, on marketing, measurement, and evaluation. They are two sides of the same coin: a coin that recognizes that what we do must have a purpose, must reach an audience, and must be evaluated as to the effectiveness of the services we offer.

We'll talk more about evaluation later, but a key to coming up with a vision is realizing that you could do better. Many libraries think they are doing a fine job of serving YAs with that rack of *Sweet Valley Highs*, but how much longer is that going to work? You don't see the YAs *not* come in; their response to poor service is stealth, as they vote with their feet. In fact, YAs might be a

> [R]evolt waiting to happen. They're only satisfied because their expectations are so low and because no one else is doing any better... having satisfied customers isn't good enough any more. You don't own those customers. They're just parked on your doorstep and will be glad to move along when they find something better. [1]

7.1 A SHORT HISTORY

The history of YA services in libraries is an interesting one with similar waxing and waning tendencies that produce two common themes. First, there is a huge gap between what libraries know they should do and what they do. This gap comes from the normal factors which separate library dreams from library reality, but with YA there seems to be a deeper philosophical question underneath: should YAs be treated as a special group? Some libraries have a long history of recognizing YAs as special, while other systems—large public library systems—have been unwilling to do so. To classify YA as a special population is to admit that it needs a special service and that means special staff and collections. Special not meaning "extra," but rather identifying the group as having unique information needs which require staff with "specialized" training and materials that are unique to that group.

The other theme in YA services in libraries is that it mirrors what is happening with YAs in the nation. Just as each decade has seen different kinds of teens and teenage problems, every 10 years something big has happened in library services to YAs. A thumbnail chronology of important events related to the professional associations and publication of important YA documents shows this pattern (see page 301).

Examining each of these documents or events, it is easy to see where YA services have been. The early drive was just to establish and recognize YA as a specialized service. This specialization meant specialists serving YAs, a separate professional association/division, separate YA collections and budgets, and separate YA programs and services. By the late 1960s, social changes in the country were reflected in library service and literature for teenagers. With the publication of YA novels S.E. Hinton's *The Outsiders* and Paul Zindel's *The Pigman*, it became obvious that YA was a very specialized form of literature and not just children's books for older readers. Edwin Castagna's article, "YA Services on the Public Library Organization Chart,"[2] provides

Figure 7–1 YA Statistics

Number of Young Adults Is Growing

	1993	1995	2000	2005	2010	2015	2020
Total, all ages	257.8	263.4	276.2	288.3	300.4	313.1	325.9
0 to 24	92.8	94.5	97.7	101.4	103.8	106.3	108.2
Under 5	19.7	20.2	19.4	19.3	20.0	21.1	22.0
5 to 13	33.5	34.3	36.5	36.8	36.2	36.9	38.7
14 to 17	13.9	14.6	15.8	16.9	17.4	17.0	17.1

NOTE: Details may not add to totals because of rounding.

SOURCE: U.S. Department of Commerce, Bureau of the Census, Current Population Reports, *Population Projections of the United States, by Age, Sex, Race, and Hispanic Origin: 1993 to 2050* and *U.S. Population Estimates, by Age, Sex, Race, and Hispanic Origin: 1990 to 1994*, PPL-21.

Findings of the Carnegie Council

Populations at Risk

In 1993, 7.3 percent of the U.S. population was comprised of young adolescents, aged 10 to 14. Of these, approximately 20 percent were living below the poverty line.

Minority adolescents were disproportionately poor.

By the year 2000, more than one-third of young adolescents will be members of a racial or ethnic minority.

Health Risks

The firearms homicide rate for 10 to 14–year-olds more than doubled between 1985 and 1992.

In 1992, 12 to 15–year-olds were victims of assault more than any other age group.

Approximately 20 percent of child abuse/neglect cases in 1992 involved 10 to 13–year-olds.

Among 8th graders, marijuana use doubled between 1991 and 1994.

By the age of 14, girls are twice as likely as boys to suffer from depression.

From 1980 to 1992, the rate of suicide among young adolescents increased 120 percent.

Educational Risks

Only 28 percent of 8th graders scored at or above proficiency reading level in 1994.

By 1992, 12 percent of the class of 1988 had dropped out of school.

Adapted from "Young Adolescents Face Serious Risks," *Great Transitions: Preparing Adolescents for a New Century.* Carnegie Council on Adolescent Development, 1995.

an overview of YA services at the end of the 1960s.

By the late 1970s, things were a little bit different. That's when JoAnn Rogers edited a volume called *Libraries and Young Adults: Media, Services and Librarianship*. It is interesting to note the first word in the subtitle is "media," although there is only one article about nonprint media. The YA novel was continuing to gain in popularity and acceptance, as was the paperback. Ms. Rogers wrote an essay in this volume called "Trends and Issues in YA Services,"[3] which sums up where YA was and offered some predictions on its future.

Around the same time, Thomas Downen surveyed 254 public libraries,[4] asking the directors of these systems to express their opinions not about the current state of YA services, but about its future. They were asked to imagine both the desirability and the probability of various YA services in the year 1993.

Since 1993 there has been a flurry of publishing about YA services and YA literature. At the same time, however, other events cause doubt. For example, the decision by the ALA graphics department to drop the YALSA booklists from ALA graphics catalog[5] struck a raw nerve with many. The controversy around this has abated, but it was a reminder for everyone connected with YALSA that YA is often the first service booted come belt-tightening time. Two steps forward, one step back seems to be the overriding trend in YA services. Whether YALSA can survive under yet another round of the seemingly endless ALA reorganizations is anyone's guess.[6]

7.2 BY THE NUMBERS

Just the facts: by the year 2000 there will be more YAs in the United States than ever before because YAs are the fastest growing segment

Summary of: *Youth Indicators 1996*

Demographics and Families

By 1997, total elementary and secondary enrollments are projected to surpass the previous high set in 1971 and are expected to continue to rise into the next century.

The demographic composition of America's youth is also changing, with projected increases in the minority composition for preschool age children through young adults.

The proportion of children under 18 living in married couple families declined by 10 percent between 1970 and 1994, while the proportion living in single-parent families grew.

In 1994, 59 percent of black children lived in single-parent homes compared with 19 percent of white children and 29 percent of Hispanic children.

Schools

The composition of the student body has been gradually changing, with minority populations growing as a proportion of the total population. Between 1975 and 1994, the proportion of white students declined, while the proportion of black students grew 14.5 percent to 16 percent, and that of Hispanic students grew rapidly, rising from 6.5 percent to 13 percent.

A major influence on students' later educational and occupational opportunities is the type of high school program in which they enroll. In 1992, more 17–year-olds reported enrolling in college preparatory and academic programs than had reported enrolling in such programs in 1982.

High school completion rates improved during the 1970s and 1980s: black students are staying in school longer, with more completing high school and college. In contrast, there were relatively small increases for whites, and Hispanics completed less school than other groups.

A much higher proportion of students are completing high school today than in the 1950s. In 1950, barely half (53 percent) of 25 to 29–year-olds had completed high school, and only 8 percent had completed four years of college. In 1995, the figures had climbed to 87 percent completing high school and 25 percent completing four years of college.

The reading achievement between 1988 and 1992 fell among black 17–year-olds and remained stable among Hispanic 17–year-olds. Sizable gaps in test scores between whites and blacks and between whites and Hispanics remain.

NAEP science scores, which declined in the 1970s, recovered somewhat between 1977 and 1992. Science scores for 13–year-olds were about the same in 1992 as they were in 1970, but were lower for 17–year-olds.

NAEP results in mathematics are more positive, with 9 and 13–year-old students' average mathematics proficiencies significantly higher in 1992 than they had been in 1978 (#35). The 17–year-olds scored about the same in 1992 as in 1978.

In a 1991 international reading assessment, the United States performed in the top group for both 9 and 17–year-olds. However, in an international comparison of mathematics and science performance among 13–year-olds, students from the United States performed at or near the average in science, and below the average in math.

Health

Although people live longer than ever before, youths still suffer their share of life threatening problems. The number of deaths per 100,000 men 15 to 24–years-old fell from 168 in 1950 to 144 in 1993. For young women, the rate fell from 89 to 49.

In 1992, the leading causes of death among 15 to 24 -year-olds were motor vehicle accidents, homicide, and suicide.

White male suicide rates exceeded those for women or black males.

The homicide death rate for black males was particularly high. Between 1985 and 1992, the homicide death rate for black males rose from 66 to 154 per 100,000. This rate is many times the rates for white males or black or white females.

Motor vehicle accidents continue to be the leading cause of death among 15 to 27–year-olds, although the rate has been declining and is lower now than in 1960.

Homicide is now the second leading cause of death for young adults.

Citizenship and Values

The proportion who felt that religion was important in their lives dropped from 65 percent in 1980 to 58 percent in 1994.

Young people two years out of high school in 1994 placed more value on finding work and providing better opportunities for their children than young people 10 years earlier.

On the less positive side, crime among young people has been on the rise. In 1993, about 45 percent of those arrested for serious crimes were under 25 years old.

Adapted from *Youth Indicators 1996*. National Center for Education Statistics, 1996.

The Youth Market

Teen population will grow at close to twice the rate of the overall population.

By the time population peaks in 2010, it will top the baby boom teen population of 1960s.

The population of 30.8 million teens will be the highest ever.

One in three teens belongs to a minority, compared to one in four in the general population.

One of every four households is headed by a single parent, up from 8 percent in 1970.

Teenagers are more responsible for far more decisions than other generations.

These pragmatic, precocious kids could become the highly educated work force needed in the technology based global marketplace of the future.

Adapted from "Teens: They're Back" by Laura Zinn, *Business Week* (April 11, 1994).

of the population. In the fall of 1996, newspapers carried stories of school overcrowding, especially at the middle school level. [7] Businesses are taking note—articles, books, and conferences are springing up across the country to help corporate America reach this growing and lucrative market. [8-9] Businesses are poised, developing ad campaigns, new products, and services, thinking of new ways to reach the "youth market." Meanwhile, in libraries, we still hold conferences asking "Why YA?," debate whether we should buy popular YA paperback series, and do planning that seems oblivious to facts about the fastest growing part of most communities. In 89 percent of public libraries, there are people serving YAs, but no YA librarian providing the necessary leadership. *VOYA* editor Dorothy Broderick writes:

> What a YA librarian can bring to a public library in addition to being the 'point person' on YA issues, is an understanding of 'the market': who YAs are, why they behave the way they do and what services/resources can meet their needs. A generalist can help them once at the desk, but only a YA specialist can understand what brought YAs to the library in the first place and what will bring them back. [10]

What businesses are doing and libraries are not is developing a vision to serve the market and gathering information to create better products and services. They are creating customers for life, while libraries repeatedly let teens slip through the cracks.

Beyond the sheer numbers, like every generation, these YAs are different from previous YAs. They are, in summary, more demographically diverse, more independent, and more of them are at risk. The Carnegie Council on Adolescent Development collected information on the state of America's YAs in the 1990s (see page 281). A new edition of the government publication *Youth Indicators* echoed many of these findings (see page 282). Research from marketers and other organizations have provided a broad snapshot of the YA market at the end of the 1990s and its importance (see sidebar). Newspapers like *USA Today* on a regular basis provide factoids on YA life (see page 284). In short, there has never been more or better information available about YAs.

And have libraries responded? The numbers suggest the answer is— no. The 1988 NCES survey noted that only 11 percent of public libraries had a YA librarian on staff. The 1995 NCES survey found no change (see page 298). In this instance, the 1995 survey duplicated a question from the 1988 survey, but in general that wasn't the case. Regardless, the information provided in the 1995 survey, like that in 1988, is an excellent tool for comparing, studying, and case-making. As mentioned, the percentage of YAs using the library did decrease slightly, although it is not clear what caused this drop (see page 298).

USA Today Surveys

"Teens' Use of Drugs Rises 78%"
  USA Today, Final Edition (Tuesday Aug 20, 1996) Sec: A p: 1
"Push to Abstain Doesn't Lower Teen Sex Rates"
  USA Today, Final Edition (Wednesday Jul 10, 1996) Sec: D p: 1
"Young People Lacking on Facts of Life, Poll Finds"
  USA Today, Final Edition (Tuesday Jun 25, 1996) Sec: D p: 1
"Around World, Basketball Ranks No. 1 Among Teens"
  USA Today, Final Edition (Tuesday Jun 18, 1996) Sec: C p: 2
"Teen Smoking Rate Highest Since 1970s"
  USA Today, Final Edition (Friday May 24, 1996) Sec: A p: 1
" Malls Are Like, Totally Uncool, Say Hip Teens"
  USA Today, Final Edition (Wednesday May 1, 1996) Sec: A p: 1
"Teens Believe in Community Involvement"
  USA Today, Final Edition (Thursday Sep 7, 1995) Sec: D p: 1
"Middle-Class Students Most Likely to Work"
  USA Today, Final Edition (Monday Aug 21, 1995) Sec: D p: 1
"Teens' Growing Marijuana Use Is 'Dangerous'"
  USA Today, Final Edition (Wednesday Jul 19, 1995) Sec: A p: 1
"Teens Worry Most about Illegal Drugs"
  USA Today, Final Edition (Tuesday Jul 18, 1995) Sec: D p: 1
"Is Your Teen Addicted to Gambling?"
  USA Today, Final Edition (Wednesday Apr 5, 1995) Sec: A p: 1
"Teens Themselves Say TV Is a Bad Influence"
  USA Today, Final Edition (Monday Feb 27, 1995) Sec: D p: 1

When librarians described factors limiting services to YAs, they suggested that competition from other activities was the number one reason YAs did not use libraries (see Figures 7–4 and 7–5, pages 287ff). For an internal factor, the majority suggested the lack of participation was due to insufficient services, resources, and programs (see Figure 7–6, page 290). There is the rub—we do not have any research based on why YAs do not use libraries from YAs themselves.

One logical explanation for the lack of teen use is as suggested—YAs are too busy. YAs dedicate time to after-school projects: they also work, take care of younger children, and participate in various other activities. You also can't discount that YAs (or adults), given a choice of going to the library or the recreational options posed by having access to 500 cable channels and the myriad of other media available, might not choose the library. Yet, could not another logical explanation be that libraries are not doing a good job of serving YAs? If business at the local burger joint goes down it is normally not only because of competition, but often because of drops in the quality of product and/or service. Public libraries do not have staff with specialized knowledge about YAs and that staff is not getting training. Generalists do their best, but they cannot provide the same level of quality service a YA librarian could, nor can generalists know the products and materials as well. The NCES research indicates that heavier library use is more likely with the presence of a YA librarian. This begs the question: is the use heavy because the YA librarian can offer more services or because they offer better services?

When a business fails, is it the "fault" of the consumer or the business? If libraries delivered, customers would come in and come back. But if you don't deliver—you have kids begging for computers and few available; you have kids needing help with homework only to meet up with staff who just don't get it; you have YAs wanting something to read after school only to find a magazine section giving them a choice of *Boys Life* or *Teen,* and they won't come back. They won't come back as YAs, or as some research has suggested, they won't be returning as adults either.[11] That's not building customers for life—that's shooting yourself in the foot.

Figure 7–2 Results of Staffing Survey

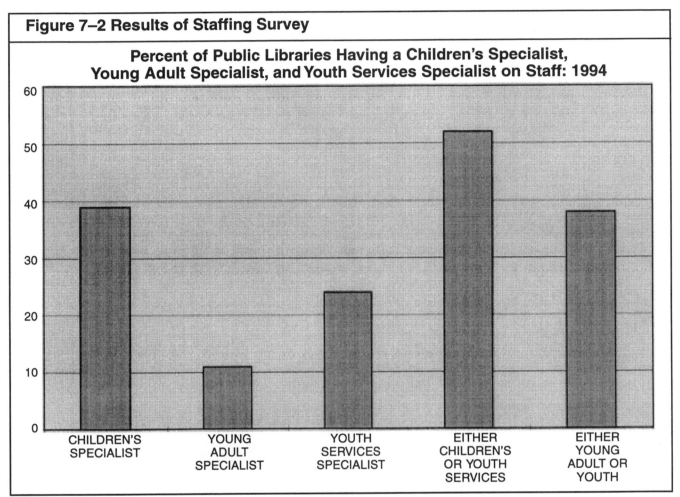

Percent of Public Libraries Having a Children's Specialist, Young Adult Specialist, and Youth Services Specialist on Staff: 1994

Reprinted from *Services & Resources for Children and Young Adults: Statistical Analysis Report.* U.S. Department of Education, National Center for Education Statistics, 1995.

The NCES survey contains other interesting data, yet without a wide distribution of the survey results as with the first survey, [12-13] its findings are not well known. To date, only Mary Kay Chelton's article in *Public Libraries* has detailed the overall findings of the survey and examined the implications of the findings. Chelton looked not only at the YA section, but also explored the statistics concerning children in public libraries. She noted,

In a typical week during the autumn of 1993, public librarians themselves reported that three out of every five public library users were youth—37 percent were children and 23 percent were young adults. This means, in essence, that public library services, regardless of how they are otherwise categorized, funded or staffed, are primary services to youth. Young people are major users of public libraries right now. [14]

Figure 7–3 Results of Youth Survey

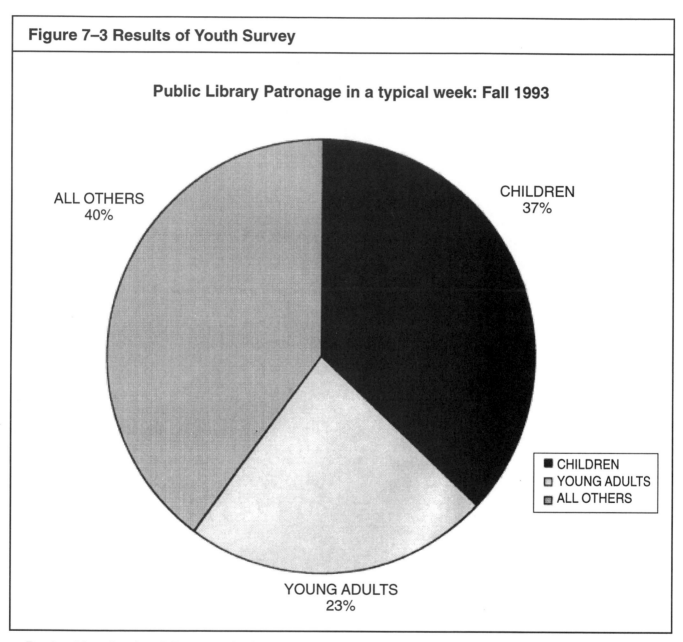

Public Library Patronage in a typical week: Fall 1993

ALL OTHERS
40%

CHILDREN
37%

YOUNG ADULTS
23%

■ CHILDREN
▢ YOUNG ADULTS
▣ ALL OTHERS

Reprinted from S*ervices & Resources for Children and Young Adults: Statistical Analysis Report.* U.S. Department of Education, National Center for Education Statistics, 1995.

Figure 7–4 Percent of public libraries indicating various factors are frequently a reason or the primary reason that some young adults in the community do not use the public library, by library characteristics: 1993–94

Library characteristic	Competition from other activities	Lack of interest In library services, resources, programs	Lack of knowledge about library services
All libraries	74	38	31
Geographic region			
Northeast	74	42	29
Southeast	72	36	32
Central	76	33	27
West	71	41	39
Metropolitan status			
Urban	73	53	40
Suburban	71	44	33
Rural	76	28	27
Patrons per week			
Less than 200	64	33	26
200–999	75	39	27
1,000 or more	82	40	40
Young adult/youth services specialist			
Have	76	37	33
Do not have	72	38	30

Figure 7–4 (cont.) Percent of public libraries indicating various factors are frequently a reason or the primary reason that some young adults in the community do not use the public library, by library characteristics: 1993–94

Library characteristic	Lack of transportation	Lack of school assignments requiring library services	Neighborhood safety
All libraries	13	8	3
Geographic region			
Northeast	17	9	5
Southeast	18	6	3
Central	9	7	2
West	12	9	4
Metropolitan status			
Urban	9	6	11
Suburban	15	8	5
Rural	13	8	0
Patrons per week			
Less than 200	11	10	*
200–999	13	8	5
1,000 or more	16	5	5
Young adult/youth services specialist			
Have	18	6	5
Do not have	10	8	2

*Less than 1 percent.

Source: U.S. Department of Education, National Center for Education Statistics, Fast Response Survey System, "Surveys of Library Services for Children and Young Adults in Public Libraries," FRSS 47, 1994.

Figure 7–5 Percent of public libraries indicating various factors are reasons that some young adults in the community do not use the public library, by frequency: 1994

Reason	Never a reason	Seldom a reason	Some-times a reason	Fre-quently a reason	Primary reason
Lack of transportation	23	27	37	10	3
Competition from other activities	4	18	45	29	
Neighborhood safety	66	22	9	3	1
Lack of school assignments requiring library services	36	33	24	7	1
Lack of interest in library's services, resources, programs	9	12	42	27	10
Lack of knowledge about library services	12	17	39	24	7

Source: U.S. Department of Education, National Center for Education Statistics, Fast Response Survey System, "Surveys of Library Services for Children and Young Adults in Public Libraries," FRSS 47, 1994.

With only this lone article, library directors are probably unaware of the recommendation section of the report that states:

Insufficient staff is a leading barrier to increased service for both children and YAs . . . staff size may be associated with library activities and programs conducted out the library, such as librarians visiting schools. The number of librarians is also likely to be associated with the provision of services requiring supervision of dedicated staff time including computer technologies and homework assistance programs. [15]

Figure 7–6 Percent of public libraries indicating various internal factors are moderate or major barriers to increasing services and resources for young adults, by library characteristics: 1994

Library characteristic	Insufficient services, resources, programs	Insufficient library staff	Insufficient hours of operation
All libraries	61	58	32
Geographic region			
Northeast	63	58	31
Southeast	60	62	25
Central	54	48	28
West	68	67	45
Metropolitan status			
Urban	65	67	29
Suburban	62	63	29
Rural	59	51	36
Patrons per week			
Less than 200	51	45	49
200–999	71	64	27
1,000 or more	61	64	19
Young adult/youth services specialist			
Have	59	58	19
Do not have	61	57	40

Source: U.S. Department of Education, National Center for Education Statistics, Fast Response Survey System, "Surveys of Library Services for Children and Young Adults in Public Libraries," FRSS 47, 1994.

Figure 7–7 Percent of public libraries indicating various ways they serve young adults as a distinct user group, by library characteristics: 1994

Library characteristic	Maintain budget line for young adult materials	Collect statistics on young adult circulation	Train library staff who deal with the public on serving young adults
All libraries	43	40	30
Geographic region			
Northeast	44	42	28
Southeast	41	40	38
Central	40	40	26
West	47	40	31
Metropolitan status			
Urban	45	46	34
Suburban	45	42	36
Rural	39	37	25
Patrons per week			
Less than 200	42	38	22
200–999	37	39	28
1,000 or more	49	44	41
Young adult/youth services specialist			
Have	51	49	43
Do not have	37	35	23

Source: U.S. Department of Education, National Center for Education Statistics, Fast Response Survey System, "Surveys of Library Services for Children and Young Adults in Public Libraries," FRSS 47, 1994

Figure 7–8 Percent of public libraries that maintain a distinct young adult collecton of books and materials, by library characteristics: 1994

Library characteristic	In a separate young adult room or area	Shelved with the adult collection	Shelved with the children's collection	No collection
All libraries	58	15	16	11
Geographic region				
Northeast	54	16	16	13
Southeast	54	13	20	13
Central	63	14	15	8
West	61	17	14	8
Metropolitan status				
Urban	67	16	7	10
Suburban	59	18	12	11
Rural	56	12	22	11
Patrons per week				
Less than 200	54	11	20	15
200–999	57	16	18	10
1,000 or more	65	18	10	7
Young adult/youth services specialist				
Have	68	15	12	5
Do not have	53	15	19	14

Note: Percents may not sum to 100 because of rounding.

Source: U.S. Department of Education, National Center for Education Statistics, Fast Response Survey System, "Surveys of Library Services for Children and Young Adults in Public Libraries," FRSS 47, 1994.

Figure 7–9 Percent of public libraries indicating they occasionally or frequently engaged in various cooperative activities with local schools specifically for young adults, by library characteristics: 1993–94

Library characteristic	Class visits from school	Resource sharing (inter-library loans)	Visits from public librarians to schools for book talks/library use, promotion
All libraries	60	58	40
Geographic region			
Northeast	47	63	34
Southeast	66	58	50
Central	61	61	40
West	68	47	40
Metropolitan status			
Urban	61	39	49
Suburban	59	57	43
Rural	60	62	36
Patrons per week			
Less than 200	40	60	23
200–999	68	59	45
1,000 or more	72	54	54
Young adult/youth services specialist			
Have	70	59	54
Do not have	54	57	32

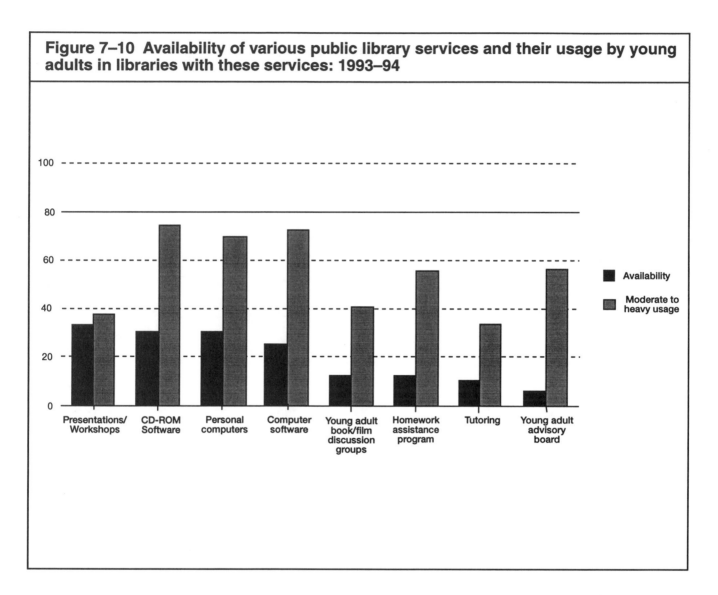

Figure 7–10 Availability of various public library services and their usage by young adults in libraries with these services: 1993–94

Source: U.S. Department of Education, National Center for Education Statistics, Fast Response Survey System, "Surveys of Library Services for Children and Young Adults in Public Libraries," FRSS 47, 1994.

Figure 7–11 Percent of public libraries reporting how the ethnic diversity of children and young adults has changed in the last 5 years, by library characteristics: 1994

| Library characteristic | Ethnic diversity | | | | | |
| | Increased | | Stayed the same | | Decreased | |
	Children	Young adults	Children	Young adults	Children	Young adults
All characteristics	44	41	53	56	3	4
Geographic region						
Northeast	42	40	54	59	3	1
Southeast	54	37	41	54	6	9
Central	34	38	63	56	3	6
West	52	48	47	52	*	0
Metropolitan status						
Urban	57	53	37	46	5	1
Suburban	52	48	47	51	1	*
Rural	35	31	61	61	4	8
Patrons per week						
Less than 200	28	24	65	67	7	9
200–999	44	43	55	56	1	1
1,000 or more	63	56	36	43	1	1

*Less than 1 percent.

Note: Percents may not sum to 100 because of rounding.

Source: U.S. Department of Education, National Center for Education Statistics, Fast Response Survey System, "Surveys of Library Services for Children and Young Adults in Public Libraries," FRSS 47, 1994.

Summary of 1988 National Center for Education Statistics Report

Libraries surveyed: 846 across the country

- One out of every four public library patrons was a YA patron (between the age of 12 and 18). Moderate and heavy use of public libraries by YAs is mostly after-school (76 percent).
- 65 percent of libraries reported "heavy or moderate use" of services to assist YAs with school assignments.
- 76 percent of libraries reported "heavy or moderate use" by YAs loaning books/other printed materials.
- Only 11 percent of public libraries have a young adult librarian.
- Over 40 percent of libraries do not have access to the assistance of a coordinator or consultant.
- Over 80 percent of libraries require no continuing YA training.
- 16 percent of libraries do not offer a section or collection of materials designed for YAs.
- YA collections are primarily in hardback (60 percent), fiction (73 percent) and made up for juvenile and young adult materials (85 percent).
- 55 percent of libraries indicate an increase in services to YAs.
- The major barrier to YA use of libraries was seen by 87 percent of libraries as competition from other activities.

The report concluded that "based on findings, statements about association between survey items and libraries with different character can be made; e.g., libraries with young adult librarians are more likely to report modern or heavy use by YA after school than libraries that do not have a YA librarian."

Adapted from *Services & Resources Young Adults in Public Libraries*, U.S. Department of Education, National Center for Education Statistics, 1988.

Yet looking at the results, in many libraries not even the most basic things are being done. Under half provide even the most "bare bones" administrative support for serving YAs in terms of budgeting, evaluating, and training (see page 291). Although it is true that 89 percent of libraries report having a YA collection, the "real" number is for those separate collections (see Figure 7–8, page 292). The reasons for separate YA collections are numerous, with benefits for both the user and the library. One wonders about those 16 percent of libraries with YA collections shelved in the juvenile area—does Judy Blume's *Forever* sit on the same shelf with Michael Bond's *Paddington*? Does a book like *How Sex Works* sit on the nonfiction shelf with *Where Did I Come From*? Does *Spin* magazine sit next to *Stone Soup* in the juvenile periodical section? Not only does that limit YA use of collections (they are not children and don't want to be in the children's room), it seems to be opening up the library for materials challenges. Thus, it is really to a library's advantage to have a separate YA area. Yet one could bet those YA collections shelved with the juvenile collection don't have *Forever, How Sex Works,* or *Spin* and are passing off middle-grade hardback fiction as their YA collection. YA collections with only those materials, and without titles like *How Sex Works*, are not really YA collections at all.

I recently visited a large public library without separate YA section. I spent lots of time walking back and forth between the children's room, the popular reading area, adult fiction, and nonfiction looking for YA titles. I can't imagine a teen wanting recreational reading taking the effort to traverse this maze. Forget the online catalog because technology is only as good as the data that goes in and this system did not think making information available about paperbacks like the *Fear Street* series worth doing. In the same library, when a problem arises with a school assignment, rather than having a YA librarian who can cultivate a relationship with local schools to problem solve such incidents, department managers call teachers directly, out of the blue, resulting in mutual frustration and suspicion. This library is indicative

Figure 7–12 Differences between Libraries with/without a YA Librarian

1995 NCES Survey: Differences between Libraries with/without a YA Librarian

Data Element	With YA Librarian	Without YA Librarian
Have separate YA room	68%	53%
Have no YA collection	5%	14%
Maintain budget line	51%	37%
Collect statistics	49%	35%
Train staff	43%	23%
Multicultural materials	94%	78%
Audio recordings	88%	68%
Materials not in English	76%	56%
CD-ROM software	45%	23%
Personal computers	40%	24%
Reading lists	89%	66%
Readers' advisory	90%	62%
Summer reading program	69%	50%
Computer information services	75%	40%
Programs/presentations	52%	21%
Homework assistance programs	16%	9%
YA advisory board	10%	4%
Cooperated with schools	86%	70%
Youth organizations	63%	49%
At-risk programs	36%	21%
Class visits from schools	70%	54%
Visits to schools	54%	32%
Information sharing meetings	41%	22%

From *Services & Resources for Children and Young Adults: Statistical Analysis Report.* U.S. Department of Education, National Center for Education Statistics, 1995.

Comparison of 1995 and 1988 NCES Surveys

Data Element	1995	1988
YA % of users	23%	25%
Libraries with YA librarians	11%	11%
Libraries with YA collection	89%	84%
Libraries providing YA training	30%	19%
Availability of reference	98%	87%
Of reader's advisory	73%	88%
Of reading lists	74%	78%
Of personal computers	30%	26%
Of college/career info	93%	92%
Of audio recordings	76%	68%
Of video recordings	75%	34%
Barrier to use: competition from other activities	74%	87%
Barrier: lack of interest	38%	81%
Barrier: lack of services/programs/ resources	61%	67%

From *Services & Resources Young Adults in Public Libraries*, U.S. Department of Education, National Center for Education Statistics, 1988 and *Services & Resources for Children and Young Adults: Statistical Analysis Report*. U.S. Department of Education, National Center for Education Statistics, 1995.

> “In almost every single data element in both the 1995 and 1988 survey, YAs were more likely to have available (and use) a wide variety of services, materials, and resources in a library with YA librarian than one without a YA librarian.”

of the research regarding cooperation with schools as making even the most basic contact with schools is not even close to standard practice in American public libraries.

It is no surprise to youth librarians that lack of staffing is the culprit. Given, however, that most librarians are not increasing youth services staffing, what else can this report do for us? The report does point out things we are doing where the availability outweighs the use and then where the converse is true. Despite the increase in multicultural materials and the ethnic mix/make up of YAs users, that connection does not seem to be working in the libraries reporting on the survey. This is *not* to say these things are not important and don't reach a critical YA audience; they do. Given limited resources perhaps redirecting energies where the usage far outweighs the availability might be a better use of resources. In the case of multicultural materials, the answer probably lies beyond the library's four walls. Materials are of no use if the intended audience doesn't or can't come get them, which again, is a lack of staffing issue.

And what a difference staffing makes. In almost every single data element in both the 1995 and 1988 survey, YAs were more likely to have available (and use) a wide variety of services, materials, and resources in a library with YA librarian than one without a YA librarian. This isn't a point of debate or contention; the evidence from the surveys is overwhelming. The chart on this page contrasting the 1995 and 1988 NCES surveys lists only some of the largest area of discrepancies or importance, but in almost every library of any size in any geographic area, there is a double digit difference in services between libraries with and those without a YA librarian. In particular, the differences in technology areas show the importance of a YA librarian.

Thus, this survey documented the state of the art, but in doing so pointed out some glaring omissions: namely, that there is a severe and seemingly growing discrepancy between who our patrons are and what resources are dedicated to serve those patrons. After looking at these numbers, Mary Kay Chelton concluded that:

If youth are 60 percent of the public library's clientele, as public

Why Hire a YA Specialist? Because YA librarians:

1. Have a positive impact upon YA user satisfaction
2. Have a positive impact upon YA participation in library services
3. Influence use of services, such as interlibrary loan
4. Provide programming and activities which YA will attend
5. Provide YAs with health-related information
6. Provide popular materials to a greater degree than generalists
7. Provide booklists
8. Provide space to meet YA recreational needs

Adapted from Susan H. Higgins, "Should Public Libraries Hire Young Adult Specialists?" *Journal of Youth Services in Libraries* (Summer 1994): 387.

Critical Needs Facing Young Adult Librarians

Acquire information about YA needs

Assist YAs in coping with social problems and life skill development

Funding

Human resources: attracting/retaining professionals to serve YAs

Intellectual freedom

Involve young people in promoting and organizing programs

Library school curricula, update to better prepare YA librarians

Literacy

Programs for small libraries

Promote YA services to library boards and administrators

Space available for YA services/activities

Support from professional community

Technology, making effective use in delivering YA services

Adapted from Kathy Howard Latrobe, "Report on the Young Adult Library Services Association's Membership Survey," *Journal of Youth Services in Libraries* (Spring 1994): 253.

librarians themselves have reported here, then some institutional changes are called for, starting with the allocation of resources. While much room remains for varied models of service, the social indicators for the youth population make it clear that no pubic policy agency can afford to ignore youth for long before the results of such neglect become blatantly apparent. For the public library, the long-term result will most likely be shrinking use and reduced public support by adults badly served there or neglected as youth.[16]

Despite the slogan, public libraries without trained and qualified youth librarians are indeed making kids wait, and sending them a message that they don't count. That is not creating raving fans; that is cutting your own throat.

The importance of a YA librarian was also documented in the 1988 NCES survey. Although not reprinting the charts and hard data in this chapter, the same huge gaps in providing services, resources, and materials were identified. Yet despite these findings, there was no increase in the number of libraries employing a YA librarian. In most areas, there was little change whatsoever between 1988 and 1995. One encouraging change is increase in training, although this might be illusionary due to the differences in the questioning—in 1988, libraries were asked about "requiring continuing training in YA services and materials" and in 1995, the question was whether libraries "train library staff who deal with public on serving YAs." One of the most striking differences was barriers to serving YAs. In the 1995 survey, the question was split into two parts, asking for both external and internal barriers, while the 1988 survey just inquired about barriers. Still, in 1988 a whopping 81 percent of libraries responded that YA lack of interest was a barrier, and only 38 percent responded the same in 1995. So although the results of 1988 were not radically different than those in 1995, the 1988 survey did quantify for the first time what was happening nationally.

In between these two national number-crunching efforts, two interesting surveys appeared in the professional literature. The first survey compared services between a library with specialized YA services (Mesa, AZ) and a library where generalists served YAs (Orlando, FL). The results of this sur-

Output Measures and More Data Elements

Library Use Measures
Visit to library by young adults
Building use
Furniture/equipment use
Homework Center visits

Materials Use
Circulation of YA materials
Circulation of materials by YAs
In-library use of YA materials
In-library use of materials by YAs
Turnover rate of YA materials

Materials Availability
YA fill rate
Homework fill rate

Information Services
YA information transactions
YA information transaction completion rate

Programming
YA program attendance
Program attendance per YA

Community Relations
YA school contact rate
Annual number of YA community contacts

Young Participation
Young Participation Rate
Annual number of YA volunteer hours

Adapted from Virginia Walter's, Output Measures and More. *American Library Association, 1995.*

vey are shown in the sidebar section "YA Services in 1968" on page 302. A questionnaire measured the satisfaction level among YA users at each location. The article, based on the writer's thesis,[17] asked, "Should Public Libraries Hire YA Specialists? (see sidebar on page 299)." The answer was yes. The researcher reached several conclusions leading to the recommendation that:

[L]ibrary systems should utilize the assistance of YA librarians since their presence encourages library usage by YAs. If the employment of a young adult specialist is not possible, such amenities of service as increased collection emphasis on material of popular appeal, provision of booklists on YA reading, and provision of local information and referral pamphlets for crisis intervention should be instituted as they have been shown to motivate library use.[18]

The second was a survey of the YALSA membership. In addition to providing information about the needs of YALSA members, a more general question was asked: "In your opinion, what are the most critical needs facing YA library services today? (see sidebar on page 299)." Although not compiled numerically, the researcher presented a range of concerns which seem to echo the NCES findings. (You can review these findings in the sidebar on page 302, "YA Services in 1979.") The two National Center for Education Statistics surveys (page 299) coupled with these two research articles provide a clear documentation on the state of the art of serving YAs libraries. These are tools to build a subjective vision of YA services based on objective facts.

Output Measures and More[19] is another such tool, aimed at providing libraries with a local picture of YAs by the numbers. Co-published by YALSA and PLA, this document like others in the series before it[20-21] provides users with formulas, worksheets, and other documents to gather, organize, and then analyze information about YA users. *Output Measures and More* contains instructions for collecting a variety of data. Yet unlike other publications in the PLA evaluation series, more than output measures is covered, as the title suggests. Information on conducting a needs assessment and developing a plan for services is also included. Throughout the document, the *how* and *what* are explained, but the *why* is also. In most planning documents, measurement and evaluation is listed as the last step, but it is really the first—you develop a vision with imagination, evaluation, and documentation.

Capsule History of YA Services

1929	Formation of Young Peoples Reading Round Table as part of ALA's Children's Library Association
1937	Publication of first YA professional book, *The Public Library and the Adolescent* by E. Leyland
1941	Round table becomes part of ALA's Division of Libraries for Children and Young People
1948–1950	ALA published Public Library Plans for the Teen Age. The Round Table becomes a section under title of Association of Young People's Librarians. Amelia Munson's *An Ample Field* published in 1950.
1958	Section becomes the Young Adult Services Division (YASD)
1960	ALA issues Young Adult Services in the Public Library from its Committee of Standards for Work with Young Adults
1968–1969	*Library Trends* publishes issue called "Young Adult Service in the Public Library," which provides an excellent overview of the status of YA services entering the 1970s. A year later, Margaret Edwards publishes *The Fair Garden and the Swarm of Beasts.*
1978–1979	YASD publishes *Directions for Library Services to Young Adults* to provide the profession with a document to help them plan services. One year later, Libraries Unlimited publishes *Libraries and Young Adults*, which provides an excellent overview of services entering the 1980s.
1988	*Library Trends* publishes another YA dedicated issue "Library Services to Youth: Preparing for the Future," which looks at various issues from the 1980s and looks into the next decade. The same year, the National Center for Education Statistics releases a report called *Services and Resources for Young Adults in Public Libraries.* It is the first comprehensive survey of the field.
1994	Under ALA President Hardy Franklin, a triple-play of publications coincide with the ALA President's Program and a customer service award through the Margaret Edwards foundation. Three publications, *Excellence in Library Services to Young Adults*, a reprint edition of *The Fair Garden and the Swarm of Beasts*, and YALSA's *Beyond Ephebiphobia* join ALA's *Best Books for Young Adults*, and Scarecrow's *Hangin' Out at Rocky Creek* for the most prolific year of YA professional publishing and YA visibility.

7.3 BY THE BOOKS

Output Measures is just one of several important publications on serving YAs to emerge in the past few years. Even though the 1990s may not have seen an increase in YA librarians or YA services, there has been a surge in professional materials about YA services. A large number of YA literature surveys and bibliographies have been published, but more important are these publications that put services first:

Bare Bones: Young Adult Services Tips for Public Library Generalists, by Mary K. Chelton and James M. Rosinia.[22] Much like *Output Measures and More, Bare Bones* is not just for reading but for using. Chock full of practical advice, *Bare Bones* covers the bulk of YA work: providing popular materials and homework support. Aimed at non-YA librarians, Rosinia and Chelton also explore issues affecting services and outline the qualities for an effective YA librarian.

Excellence in Library Services to YAs: The Nation's Top Programs, edited by Mary K. Chelton.[23] Funded by a grant for the Margaret Edwards Trust, this book presents information on the top 50 YA service programs. For each program, information on the sponsors, customers, setting, funding, and a contact person augments a description of the program. The top 10 programs, which received cash prizes, are first profiled. The other 40 programs are organized into subject categories. Chelton's introduction highlights the common themes of the programs, emphasizing the need for programs for at-risk YAs. A new edition is forthcoming.

Beyond Ephebiphobia: A Tool Chest for Customer Service to YAs, compiled by YALSA.[24] This document was distributed at the 1994

YA Services in 1968
Libraries surveyed: 32 libraries in 19 states

- 27 had YA coordinators or supervisors, indicating "an overwhelming consensus on the importance of work with young adults"
- About half of these people reported directly to either the library director or assistant director, indicating "the importance many administrators attach to young adult service"
- 17 libraries reported a separate YA materials budget
- 21 libraries had YA collections in the central library and 22 had collections in branches

The report concluded, "I believe if one went around to visit the libraries included in this study and many others . . . one would find . . . a high value attached to public library service to young adults. And this high value would be reflected in a respectable place well up in the organization chart, provision for adequate collection, space and staff, and a growing attention to the young people who are the most numerous and heaviest users of public libraries."

Adapted from Edward Castagna, "Young Adult Services on the Public Library Organization Chart," *Library Trends.* (October 1968): 137–139.

ALA Annual Conference's President Program where the awards were given for the top YA programs. Including the article "Beyond Ephebiphobia," [25] this document also contains lists of magazines, professional resources, and an extensive bibliography.

The Fair Garden and the Swarm of Beasts: The Library and the Teenager, reprint edition, by Margaret Edwards, with a foreword by Patty Campbell. [26] This book, also from 1994, is a reprint of Margaret Edwards' classic tome on the library and YAs. What is new is a foreword by Patty Campbell, who provides a biography of Edwards based in part by interviews with YA librarians who trained under Edwards. More interesting is what is *not* included here: Campbell's more critical look at how Edwards' ideas have fared over time that appeared instead in a non-ALA publication. In her article "Reconsidering Margaret Edwards," Campbell examines Edwards' stance on YA literature (Edwards wasn't so much for it), assisting students with homework (again, not so much for it) and other issues. Although a lot of what Edwards wrote held true, much has changed among both the Garden and the swarm of beasts. As Campbell writes:

YA Services in 1979
Libraries surveyed: None
The study's author wrote: "[I]n the absence of a much-needed national survey of public library services for young adults, identifying meaningful trends for this age group is a difficult task."
The study used reviews of the literature and news from state and national associations.

Findings
- Most libraries have a separate "space" assigned to attract YAs.
- Institutional support for YA services had not kept pace with making YA service a more dynamic part of the total library program.
- Expanded coverage of YA issues in library literature reflect both more recognition of the importance of YA work and more emphasis on YA services in public libraries.
- Libraries are accepting some responsibility for responding to the recreational needs of adolescents and are attempting to determine other needs to which the library might respond.
- Helping the young person to communicate needs to a library professional is a current focus of young adult work.

The study concluded, "perhaps now that YA services have become recognized as a legitimate and necessary facet of the library program package, evaluation of different types of programs and services . . . will reveal which of the many services are the most effective. If young adult specialists . . . can point to success with a large proportion of the young adults in a community, some of the traditional and newer types of services . . . will have a good chance of surviving and growing."
Adapted from JoAnn Rogers, "Trends and Issues in Young Adult Services," *Libraries and Young Adults: Media, Services, and Librarianship.* JoAnn Rogers, ed. (Englewood, CO: Libraries Unlimited) 1979: 67–74.

YA Services in 1993 (Predicted)
Libraries surveyed: 234 library directors of systems serving at least 100,000 people

Findings:

- 81 percent felt the continuation and expansion of YA service was desirable; however, only 41 percent felt it was probable this would occur in the future.
- 63 percent felt that YA service being nonexistent in 1993 was undesirable and 51 percent thought it was improbable.
- 79 percent expressed it was desirable to move away from programming and toward a "general education for lifetime use of libraries."
- 99 percent felt it was desirable and 80 percent probable there would be a re-emphasis on reading for enjoyment.
- Increased library instruction was desirable by 90 percent but probable by only 52 percent.
- Using paperbacks in YA collections was seen as desirable by only 62 percent and probable by just 58 percent.
- Continuing education related to YA was seen as desirable by 83 percent but only probable by 39 percent.
- Merging YA into children's departments was seen as both undesirable (94 percent) and improbable (81 percent).

The study concluded that "In these times of financial stringency, it is a fact that many programs . . . are being curtailed or eliminated. It is encouraging that an overwhelming majority (81 percent) of respondents felt that service to young adults should be continued and expanded. But YA librarians should take special note that 47 percent of respondents were uncertain whether or not this would be the case by the year 1993."

Adapted from Thomas William Downen, "YA Services: 1993," *Top of the News* (Summer 1979): 347–353.

[T]here are areas in young adult librarianship today for which Margaret Edwards can offer us no help, simply because they are products of our own times: the ethics of privacy from parents, new ideas about management methods, measurement skills, liaisons with community agencies, the expansion of information technology, and the broadening of the concept of library materials.[27]

Hangin' Out at Rocky Creek: A Melodrama in Basic YA Services in Public Libraries, by Evie Wilson Lingbloom.[28] Like *Bare Bones, Hangin' Out* is a primer for entry-level YA librarians and generalists. With years of experience as a YA librarian, Wilson-Lingbloom surveys basics such as references, collection development, and reading promotion. There is, however, a real focus in "hanging out"; that is, providing active library services and working in the community to serve at-risk YAs. The entire book is a case study, loaded with practical solutions to everyday YA-related problems.

Directions for Library Service to Young Adults, 2nd Edition, published by the Young Adult Library Services Association.[29] *Directions* provides a compact outline for setting up YA services. *Directions* sketches the philosophical basis, with practical examples of information services, collection development, programs, youth participation, cooperation and networking, and access to information. *Directions* lays out a YA vision and outlines how to enact it by advocating, justifying, and explaining the core of YA services.

In addition to these more general books, other books about YA literature, booktalking, programming, and youth participation have been published in the last few years. Coupled with the heavy use of listservs such as PUBYAC and LM-NET,[30] information about and interest in serving YAs seems to be at an all-time high.

7.4 MARKETING TO YOUNG ADULTS

Marketing in libraries continues to receive a great deal of attention. More importantly, marketing library services to youth has come to the forefront. Writing about marketing research, Barbara Dimick zeroes in on youth services, writing that youth are

> [S]een as a primary market—they have money of their own to spend; as an influence market—they directly and indirectly influence household purchases, and as future market—the market that has the greatest potential . . . Libraries rely on youth services to build future users and to maintain a loyal customer base into the future. [31]

The article describes marketing in the context of giving the customers what they need and want, which is often different from traditional library services:

> Collections and programs are driven by what is known about the needs of the target market and may or may not parallel traditional library service offerings. This can be, and has been, a difficult concept for many librarians, including those in youth services.[32]

Although Dimick writes of youth services, the focus of the article is on children. That libraries should be customer-centered should come as no surprise nor be a great change. For most YA librarians, building around users' wants and needs has always been vital.

Around the same time, Virginia Walter, author of *Output Measures and More*, penned an article noting the trends in marketing to children and the library implications:

> If public libraries understood that children are not only significant customers in their own right and influence participants family decisions about library use but are also the future adult of users of libraries they might put more effort into developing long term customer loyalty in their young patrons.[33]

Even though both Walter's and Dimick's work stem from writing specifically about marketing to children, the implications for marketing to YAs are obvious. A marketing approach moves a library along a continuum that starts with input (we have x numbers of books) to output (we checked out x numbers of books) to customer-centered (customers need x types of books). The formula is simple:

determine needs + match them with input = more output/success

Marketing is not public relations or even promotion: it is the prior step. Marketing is defined many ways, but a good definition is "getting your goods or services to your customers or patrons." And it is not a flip thing to refer to patrons as *customers*: customers "buy" a service, and libraries offers services. Putting up a display of horror titles is not marketing: marketing is deciding why you are doing this display, when and where you are doing it, figuring out whom the display attracts, determining what materials you will purchase and promote, and knowing what you hope to accomplish with the display.

MARKET SEGMENTS

The term *library market* refers to the audience for library services. The market is subdivided in many ways. One division is by age, which is where we get the YA market segment. User groups or market segments are to also be divided by

1. Geographic factors
2. Economic factors
3. Social factors
4. Amount of library use
5. Reasons for library use
6. Types of library use
7. Reading interests
8. Library knowledge
9. Awareness of library services
10. Time spent in the library
11. Methods used to find materials
12. Non-users

Within the YA market, look for segments like these:

1. Boy or girl
2. Age and/or grade
3. School
4. Academic achievement
5. Clique
6. Reader or nonreader
7. How free time is spent
8. Special interests
9. Working vs. nonworking
10. College bound vs. non-college bound
11. Library card holders vs. non-holders
12. Attitudes about the library

You need to know as much about your market as possible. You do not want to plan GED programs in a community with virtually no dropout rate. Your planning of services will hinge on what you know.

USING SURVEYS

Earlier in this book, you saw a sample user survey. This really was a "potential user" survey because you want it to reach those who are not already in your library. After tabulating the results of the survey, the following information about your market emerges:

1. Amount of library use
2. Percentage of card holders
3. Why YAs use the library (and what they don't use it for)
4. Why they don't use the library
5. Gender
6. Age and grade (and school)

With your survey results, can you answer the following questions:

1. Who is the "average" YA user?
2. Why do YAs use the library?
3. Why don't they?
4. What do YAs like most/least about the library?
5. What is the most surprising statistic?
6. What type of follow-up questions are needed?
7. Given this, what should the priorities of YA services be?
8. What programs and services could break down the barriers?

Once you have this information and the answers to these questions, you can begin to focus your efforts. You need to think about what you have learned about YA interests and your library's strengths and weaknesses. After determining within the YA market which specific user group you want to focus on, you begin looking for the meeting point between their interests and your services.

THE MARKETING PLAN

Libraries can better serve users and reach the non-users by employing the "marketing mix." The mix consists of four elements:

- **Products:** What you offer
- **Price:** What it costs you
- **Place:** Where you offer it
- **Promotion:** How you tell people about what you offer

To develop a marketing plan, you need to determine at the outset the answer to the following questions:

1. **Why** do you want to reach this market?
2. **What** is your objective?
3. **Who** is your audience?
4. **What** products will you offer?
5. **When, where,** and **how** will these products be offered?
6. **How** (on what sort of timeline) is this going to happen?

Let's further examine question 4. In your own self-evaluation, you thought about YA products. Let's re-examine those products quickly and consider the other elements of the mix:

Products

1. A building with chairs
2. Collections of print and non-print
3. Information services
4. Staff
5. Programs and activities

Price

1. Cost to buy, prepare, and house products
2. Staff cost
3. Cost of program and activities
4. Opportunity costs; that is, if you do YA services, what will you *not* be able to do?

Place

1. Where in the library (if in the library at all) will you offer the services?
2. How much space is available?
3. Where will you offer services outside of the library (outreach)?
4. Does it need to be a physical or virtual place?
5. Can YAs get to the place: is it convenient and safe?

Promotion

1. Inside the library
2. Outside the library
3. For programs and activities
4. Community relations
5. Intensity and timing of public relations

After stating the objectives, defining the mission, and targeting the segments, the various parts of the mix can come together in a marketing plan (see Figure 7–13). Obviously you can't do all of these things at the same time: the cost factor in terms of staff time would be too much. This is an example of choosing one small segment of the potential library audience and designing products to meet the documented or assumed interests of that audience.

Figure 7–13 YA Marketing Plan

YA Marketing Plan

OBJECTIVE: Increase YA circulation by _____%
TIMELINE: By the end of year

I. Identify YA market segments:

II. Choose segment: [reluctant readers]
   A. Characteristics of this user group
   B. Recreational interests [movies/videos?]
   C. Current awareness of group
      1. Of library services
      2. How can awareness be increased?
      3. What will move them to action?

III. Products:
   A. Collections
      1. Videotapes
      2. Movie soundtracks on CD/tape
      3. Magazines about movies
      4. Books about movies
      5. Movie tie-ins
      6. Movie posters
      7. Access to the Internet
         a. Set up bookmarks to movie studios
         b. Set up bookmarks to film review sources
         c. Set up bookmarks to movie star sites
   B. Services
      1. Circulation of above products
      2. Booktalking movie tie-ins
      3. Programming
         a. Film or video series
         b. Movie trivia contests
         c. Read the movie discussion group
         d. Make your own movie/video
         e. Reading contest movie tie-ins
         f. Favorite movie star polls
         g. Storyboard YA novels
         h. Scripts for YA novels

IV. Price:
   A. Cost of materials
   B. Staff cost
   C. Opportunity costs

V. Place:
   A. Within the library
      1. Decorate YA area with movie posters
      2. Create movie tie-in display
      3. Move some videos in YA area
      4. Meeting room to show videos
   B. Outside of library
      1. Promote/booktalk in schools
      2. Work with local theater/video store

VI. Promotion:
   A. Within the library
      1. Flyers/posters
      2. Book/movie list
      3. Movie posters
      4. Change screen saver marquee on computers
   B. Outside of library
      1. School visits
      2. Press releases
   C. Programs
      1. Kickoff film or similar big event
      2. Ongoing contests/activities
   D. Priority
      1. This will be the major YA fall project
      2. All materials have YA logo
      3. Try to get photo/article in school or local paper

VII. Measures:
   A. Formal
      1. Circulation
      2. Program attendance
      3. Restocking of displays
      4. Activity/contest participation
   B. Informal
      1. Comments from users
      2. Comments from parents/teachers/staff

VIII. Conclusion
By marketing to a specific group [reluctant reader] through the use of high-appeal items [movie/videos], the awareness of what the library offers to this user group should increase, which should result in an increase in library user/circulation by members of this group.

Developmentally Based Performance Measures

Goal: Young adult services are provided to promote the healthy development of adolescents through organized exposure to materials and information experiences related to this part of the life cycle, to help create the circumstances under which adolescents might begin to function as adults at home with themselves, their communities, and the world.

Measures:

1. Proportion of eligible served
2. Autonomous success rate
3. Collection appropriateness
4. Percentage of youth participation
5. Proportion of cross-age programs

Adapted from Mary K. Chelton, "Developmentally Based Performance Measures for Young Adult Services," *Top of the News.* (Fall 1984): 39.

7.5 MEASUREMENT AND EVALUATION

Finally, this chapter has mentioned measurement several times. Mary K. Chelton writes about the need for evaluation:

> [T]he ability to define and count precisely is an intrinsic skill necessary for good evaluation; the lack of such skill and resistance to learning it among young adult practitioners are, in combination, helping to maintain the invisibly of the adolescent client group, especially in public libraries . . . (evaluation) makes the invisible visible so that our decisions depend on information rather than intuition.[34]

Chelton then goes on to set up developmentally based performance measures. Although this article appeared over a decade ago, it is important to note how these measures evolved in the *Output Measures and More* document. Most YA librarians, even if they are not using formal performance measures, could now speak to all of these measures with some degree of knowledge for several reasons. First, because this article appeared in 1984, information about use is more readily available, thanks to automation. Second, YA librarians have, in order to justify their existence, found it more and more necessary to document what they do. Finally, the NCES survey gave librarians such important information to use (25 percent of all users, etc.) that many saw the advantages of collecting their own numbers and using them. They were not counting for the sake of counting, but gathering quantitative documentation on their programs of service.

Although libraries may not choose to complete all (or any) of the output measures for young adults, *Output Measures and More* provides insight into what is important in young adult services. For each measure, information is given on

- How to collect the data
- How to calculate the data
- How to interpret and use the data
- Further possibilities for measuring output

Throughout the book, there are samples of measurement techniques and the appendix contains reproducible forms for all the measures. The user surveys also appear in Spanish.

In addition to providing tools for quantitative research, *Output Measures and More* gives instruction on how to do qualitative research. Zollo also suggests both quantitative and qualitative research methods. Although the studies are much more detailed than most libraries could do (or afford), they give us a glimpse of how to organize and conduct this type of research. Qualitative research gives life to the numbers: it allows you to determine *why* things worked and *how* they positively affected the lives of your YA users. Measure the positive impact of connecting young adults and libraries; it seems like a waste to do all the work, and reap none of the rewards. Quantitative measurement tells you how many "fans" you have; qualitative measurement lets you know whether they are just casual fans or what you seek: raving fans.

ENDNOTES

1. Kenneth Blanchard and Sheldon Bowles, *Raving Fans*. New York: Morrow, 1993: 11–12.
2. Edwin Castagna, "YA Service on the Public Library Organization Chart," *Library Trends* (October 1968): 137–139.
3. JoAnn Rogers, ed., "Trends and Issues in Young Adult Services," *Libraries and Young Adults: Media, Services, and Librarianship.* Englewood: Libraries Unlimited, 1979.
4. Thomas Downen, "YA Services 1993," *Top of the News* (Fall 1979): 347–353.
5. Carolyn Caywood, "What the Market Will Bear," *School Library Journal* (April 1996): 46.
6. Patricia Muller, "YA Library Services Association President's Message," *Journal of Youth Services in Libraries* (Fall 1995): 15–17.
7. "School Enrollment Soars, Erases 1971 Bommer Mark, Strains Resources," *USA Today* (August 22, 1996): A1.
8. Peter Zollo, "Talking to Teens," *American Demographics* (November 1995): 22+.
9. "The Marketing Report on Youth Marketing," *Marketing* (July 8, 1996): 11–16.
10. Dorothy Broderick, "What (Most) Publishers and (Many) Librarians Need to Know, but Resist Learning," *Voice of Youth Advocates* (October 1996): 196.
11. Barbara Will Razzano, "Creating the Library Habit," *Library Journal* (March 1985): 111–114.
12. Mary K. Chelton, "The First National Survey of Services and Resources for YAs in Public Libraries," *Journal of Youth Services in Libraries* (Spring 1989): 227–231.
13. Suzanne Sullivan and Jody Stefansson, "The NCES Survey on YA Services in Public Libraries: Implications for Research," *Journal of Youth Services in Libraries* (Winter 1991): 155–157.
14. Mary Kay Chelton, "Three in Five Public Library Users Are Youth," *Public Libraries* (March/April 1997): 105.
15. *Services and Resources for Children and Young Adults in Public Libraries.* U.S. Dept. of Education, Office of Educational Research and Improvement, National Center for Education Statistics, 1995.
16. Chelton (1997), p. 108.
17. Susan E. Higgins, "Should Public Libraries Hire YA Specialists?" *Journal of Youth Services in Libraries* (Summer '94): 387–391.
18. Higgins, p. 390.
19. Virginia A. Walter, *Output Measures and More: Planning and Evaluating Public Library Services for Young Adults.* American Library Association, 1995.

20. Virginia A. Walter, *Output Measures for Public Library Services to Children: A Manual of Standardized Procedures.* American Library Association, 1997.
21. Nancy Van House, et al. *Output Measures for Public Libraries: A Manual of Standardized Procedures,* 2nd Edition. American Library Association, 1987.
22. Mary K. Chelton and James Rosinia, *Bare Bones: Young Adult Services Tips for Public Library Generalists.* Young Adult Library Services Association and Public Library Association, 1993.
23. *Excellence in Library Services to YAs: The Nation's Top Programs.* Mary K. Chelton, ed. American Library Association, 1994.
24. *Beyond Ephebiphobia: A Tool Chest for Customer Service to YAs.* American Library Association, 1994.
25. Kirk Astroth, "Beyond Ephebiphobia: Problem Adults or Problem Youths?" *Phi Delta Kappan* (January 1994): 30–34.
26. Margaret A. Edwards, *The Fair Garden and the Swarm of Beasts: The Library and the Young Adult.* Reprint ed. Commentary by Patty Campbell. American Library Association, 1994.
27. Patty Campbell, "Reconsidering Margaret Edwards," *Wilson Library Bulletin* (June 1994): 36.
28. Evie Wilson-Lingbloom, *Hangin' out at Rocky Creek: A Melodrama in Basic YA Services in Public Libraries.* Metuchen, NJ: Scarecrow Press, 1994.
29. *Directions for Library Service to Young Adults,* 2nd Edition. Young Adult Library Services Association, 1993.
30. Don Kenney and Linda Wilson, "From the Editors," *Journal of Youth Services in Libraries* (Winter 1995): 125–126.
31. Barbara Dimick, "Marketing Youth Services," *Library Trends* (Winter 1995): 467.
32. Dimick, p. 464.
33. Virginia Walter, "Research You Can Use: Marketing to Children," *Journal of Youth Services in Libraries* (Spring 1994): 287.
34. Mary K. Chelton, "Developmentally Based Performance Measures for Young Adult Services," *Top of the News* (Fall 1984): 41.

MARCH

Goal: Network locally, building support for YA services.

1. **Network with schools (part two):** You work with schools for practical reasons: to reduce frustration, get access to kids, and plan cooperative activities. Another reason, however, is to enlist schools as partners in support of serving YAs. Wouldn't it be great to have a class visit result in a teacher, principal, or a school superintendent communicating with your director on how wonderful your services for YAs are? When you tell your director this, you just work there and you have an agenda, but when the information comes from the outside, recommendations or encouragement for YA service have more impact. Follow up anything you do for a teacher with a letter to that teacher's principal, which tells the principal of your involvement. Or simply ask a teacher you have helped to write a letter to your director in support of the services.

2. **Get business cards made:** It is more important to print business cards than it is all those "how to cooperate" bookmarks. Those bookmarks will just get mailed—they are passive public relations items. But sticking business cards in a teacher's hand after a visit, and asking the teacher to "tell two friends" to call you for similar services—that is active promotion.

3. **Know thy network:** Who else in your community serves YAs? Who else wants to do it better? Who else does not have time to do big projects alone but might show interest in cooperating?

4. **Find parents:** Directors might enjoy getting a letter from a teen praising the library, but one from a parent is much better. Parents, after all, pay taxes. If you can get "off-desk" to do only one speaking engagement, make a trip to the middle school or junior high parent/teacher organization. Sell them on the good things libraries do or could do for YAs. Also look for "power parents." Most working librarians are removed from the Library Board of Directors or Friends group, but there might be YA connection. How many people on these boards have teenagers? If so, who are they and can you get them on your side?

5. **Community coalitions:** In addition to simple one-on-one networking, many communities have youth coalitions. For better or worse, most of these are springing up around the issue of youth/gang violence. The library needs positioning as an institution in the community that cares about its youth. If your library cares enough about youth to save lives, shouldn't they care enough about providing resources to make those lives better?

And are not most of the preventative measures against gang membership—providing other activities, keeping kids in school, fostering more connections between YAs and caring adults—things that libraries with YA services can accomplish?

8 ISSUES IN YA SERVICES

One thing that makes YA service unique is the constant "under attack" feeling many YA librarians experience. This feeling comes not only from within their own organizations but also from outside. Perhaps because adolescence is a time of transition and vulnerability, many social and professional issues revolve around YAs. Society and libraries vacillate between allowing YAs to behave responsibly and wanting to protect them. This vacillation presents larger philosophical questions about teenagers and their place in libraries and in society. In a time when teen curfews are all the rage, the answer to the "teen crisis" seems to be more restrictions, less access, and increased need for youth advocacy.

The issues concerning YAs boil down to a political question: who has what rights to what materials and services? It is all about access and restrictions. Simply quoting from the *Library Bill of Rights* falls short as a defense, because there are no easy answers to this question. I had a political science professor who used to say, "Where you stand depends on where you sit." I saw the truism of this when I moved from the "YA chair" to the "branch manager's chair." Issues I once saw as black and white now were shaded gray.

8.1 ACCESS

SCENARIO #1

You have decided to open Internet access to the public, but many people have expressed concern about youth accessing pornographic sites. A suggestion is made to put a filter (like Surfwatch) on all the machines. This will keep children (and adults) away from sites on the Internet whose titles contain certain keywords. Given the imperfect nature of such software, it also will keep them from some sights with no objectionable content. The choice is presented as an "either/or" decision. What is the best course of action for the YA advocate?

SCENARIO #2

Your library has a collection of *Playboy* magazines. It is held at the periodical desk and patrons have to ask for it. They also are required to leave behind some sort of identification. *Playboy* is not the only periodical treated this way: *Business Employment Weekly, Melody Maker,* and some investment newsletters also have limited access. A

YA patron asks for *Playboy.* The clerk at the desk isn't sure what to do.

Full access is a noble goal, but the tasks necessary to achieve it are difficult, the issues complex, and the day-to-day micro-decisions trying. In the first scenario, the goal obviously is for full Internet access for everyone, *sans* filters. But given a choice of no access or limited access, what is the best course of action? Is it best to accept limited access, and hope that patrons will complain loudly enough that the decision gets overturned? Or is it better to draw a line in the sand? The real enemy is not blocking software but policies within the library that block access by age. If the answer is blocking software only for children and YAs, that's a different problem. Access means equal access for everyone, even if it is limited access.

The second scenario presents similar issues, again balanced against real-world concerns. Often magazines are not kept on open stacks for good reasons: the loss or vandalism rate is just too high. After all, no one gets access if the item is stolen or mutilated. Protecting access again might mean limiting access. The problem with this scenario is twofold: first, many YAs don't have an identification source, including library cards; the second problem is differentiating between limits by material and limits by audience. In the scenario above, the reason the material is on limited access is the nature of the material, not the nature of the audience. If the 16–year-old wanted *Business Employment Weekly,* there would be no issue. If the library can't provide equal access, then perhaps collecting those materials in the first place requires discussion.

8.2 CONFIDENTIALITY

SCENARIO #1

An adult patron comes in with her YA son's overdue book notice—a laundry list of unreturned items. She says she wants to pay the fines for him, but she wants to know everything else he has checked out. She insists that because she is assuming financial responsibility, she has the right to know. Does this parent's "right" conflict with her son's right to confidentiality?

SCENARIO #2

A regular patron comes in and asks to pick up the materials on hold for everyone in her family. Her daughter has on hold a book you ordered for her on coping with an alcoholic parent. The circulation desk attendant says, "I know you have something on hold; so does your daughter." This is a case when you might make "special rules" for YAs to protect their confidentiality. In branches, the person picking up the book often is not the person who requested it. You may have policies against it, but in the real world, if Mr. Smith (who comes in every day) says he'll pick up his wife's books, you probably will check those books out to him. To have an "only the person" policy sounds good on an administrative level, but does not work well in reality.

Both of these scenarios present practical problems that policies can't really address. In the first, you are between the proverbial real rock and hard place: yes, everyone has confidentiality rights; but if the YA doesn't/can't/won't accept financial responsibility, can the person taking on this responsibility assume those rights? It is absurd to stand there and tell a parent, "Yes, I'll take your money; but, no, I won't tell you what you are paying for."

In the second scenario, a well-intentioned proactive staff member is "violating" a policy in order to provide good service—although, in this case, it backfires. The problem with most library policies is they are absolutes, and good customer service can't flourish in a straitjacket.

8.3 PRIVACY

Closely related to confidentiality are privacy rights. If we think of confidentiality as primarily relating to circulation records, privacy means everything else. A person's library use is a private matter, and YAs are the most private of people. Because many have, or at least feel they have, a secret life, their privacy is paramount.

SCENARIO #1

You've been working with a school principal to develop a cooperative library instruction program, and she has been great. The program is a success in part because this principal is so helpful. Now the same principal calls you up and asks for a favor. You want to help her, because she has been so accommodating and you want to nurture this relationship. She asks whether a certain student was in the library that day during school hours, and you say...what? Sometimes school officials feel you have an obligation to report to them students who are skipping school and hanging out in the library. If the school is a closed campus, they may want you to report students who visit the library during lunch hour or breaks. And if the school has rules of conduct involving smoking, for example, many administrators want you to enforce their rules for them. All of those situations, however, represent invasions of privacy. School officials need understand the right of privacy for everyone in a library.

SCENARIO #2

An adult patron who happens to be a friend of yours (or of the library) calls one day to ask about her teenage son. She wants to know whether he was in the library on a certain night. If a parent calls and asks if a son or daughter is in the building, would we page the YA? Does something so small have privacy implications?

Some of these questions relate to larger issues of privacy and confidentiality for everyone in the library setting. Others relate to the bizarre nature of YAs: they *are* old enough to have private lives, but their parents still have financial and legal responsibilities for what they do. Certainly if a YA's use of the library is to be a positive experience, knowing that use is a private matter is important.

8.4 SOCIAL RESPONSIBILITIES OF LIBRARIES AND LIBRARIANS

SCENARIO #1

A young woman comes into the library and asks for information on marriage. During your reference interview, the subject slowly shifts to spousal abuse and dating violence. She seems upset, and you can see a bruise on her face. Do you refer her to a battered women's shelter or a local hotline? Would you do more or less for a teenager than for another patron, or should you do anything at all? This question relates to privacy as well: would you contact a school counselor about this young woman and ask him or her to intervene? Is that your role?

SCENARIO #2

Did your library purchase tapes by Ice T or maybe 2 Live Crew? If so, did anyone on staff listen to them or read the lyrics? If we consider the sexism, racism, and outright "filth" to be social ills, are we promoting or sanctioning those ills by purchasing materials that exploit, advance, celebrate, or exemplify them? Again, this is a much larger question for all libraries: do you purchase *The Anarchist's Cookbook, The Satanist Bible,* Rush Limbaugh's latest tome, or the hundreds of other materials that advance causes or positions that you and the majority in your community reject? With YAs, the issue is even more intense because adolescence is the time of definition. Would you hand a copy of Brett Easton Ellis's *American Psycho* to a YA if he asked for it specifically, or if he asked for the "grossest" book out there? If we want the library to be a positive experience for YAs, do we fill it with negative examples?

SCENARIO #3

You know a YA who has been a patron for years; she has even volunteered from time to time. You notice that recently she's been moody, probably depressed. You want to say something or try to talk with her, but you never seem to find the time or place. She drops out of sight for a while, and the next time you see her she is standing in the check-out line, a copy of Derek Humphrey's *Dying with Dignity*: *Understanding Euthanasia* in her hands. Now, you've got questions. You are on record as fighting for YA access to all materials. Whenever discussion arises over buying controversial materials, you are on the side of "give 'em what they want—regardless." You would be the first person to discipline a checkout clerk who told a YA he or she "shouldn't" be checking out a certain item. But you have a real person standing in front of you now, and that policy and those positions might not seem so important.

Years ago I attended a program on how books could help people. Not many of us would argue with that. But isn't there a necessary flip side that says if books have the power to help, they also have the power to hurt? If a student uses the books we have given him to get an A on a paper and thanks us, we are happy to assume some measure of responsibility. If an adult patron uses our investment tools and strikes it rich, and then donates money to the library, we are happy to take it. But if someone leaves our building with materials that move them to an action which harms them or someone else, we want no responsibility. Just give us the credit; keep the blame.

8.5 CENSORSHIP

This is the big one. No issue of YA services is discussed more or is more important. The whole labeling of records and cassettes is still alive; and in school and public libraries across the country, YA books are still being challenged. There is not a lot to say that hasn't been said or written elsewhere: each library needs a collection development policy, a statement regarding intellectual freedom, and a procedure for handling complaints about materials. Examples of all of these can be found in the *Intellectual Freedom Manual*.[1] The battleground is now shifting to nonprint, for a variety of reasons:

Ratings: A YA certainly could go into any bookstore and purchase almost any reading material. The same YA, however, is prohibited from attending certain films and from renting or buying certain video tapes. There are examples outside our setting but within our own community of standards. It is a given that a library should reflect its community (why else would you do the community analysis assignment in library school?), but what if the community doesn't reflect library standards?

Nonprint problems: Opposition to popular teen music is not new, but it picked up steam in the 1980s and continues to do so as music pushes at the old boundaries and stakes out new bold (many would say offensive) territory. As certain forms (rap, primarily) gain in popularity, the move to censor them will increase. Unlike book media, we simply don't have the review media for nonprint. In addition, nonprint items sometimes have more of an impact and influence on behavior. White, suburban YAs are not walking around in LA Raider gear and talking down police because of something they read in a book.

The new bandwagon: Book banning or burning has a bad odor, but stopping YAs from listening to rap music doesn't seem to attract the same societal furor. Your community might be perfectly willing to stand up to book banners, but how many would join the crusade against rap music or slasher movies being inaccessible to YAs.

People in glass houses: It would be interesting if the *Newsletter on Intellectual Freedom* expanded its scope to cover censorship from the inside. Self-censorship is the only way to explain why many materials YAs need and want are not included in many collections. Under the guise of materials selection, many of the items challenged by community members fail to appear in our collections.

STORY #1

I was serving on the YALSA Reluctant Reader committee. One of the books up for discussion (which I nominated) was the *New Pictorial History of Wrestling*. Composed primarily of photos, with short readable biographies of professional wrestlers, the book was well-suited for reluctant readers: it was easy reading, had lots of photos, and covered a subject of high interest. Not only did it not make the RR list, it received only two votes. During the discussion, I heard statements such as "I couldn't (or wouldn't) have this book in my library." The point is not that the book didn't make the list (not every book can), but that these YA librarians would not select the book for their libraries because the subject matter offended them.

STORY #2

I worked in a large suburban library system during the fury over 2 Live Crew. The group's answer to their censorship challenge was a CD called *Banned in the USA* that quickly rose in the charts. It was even more graphic, sexist, and offensive than *Nasty as They Wanna Be* (which took some doing). In our system, only two branches purchased the tape. Because the primary selection tool for music in the system was supposed to be the *Billboard* charts, *Banned in the USA* certainly should have been selected, but it was not.

The line between selection and self-censorship gets very narrow in the nonbook field. Why don't libraries choose *Hustler*? Certainly, it would be popular. We draw lines based on a variety of factors; but when we draw lines based on our own agendas (or on fear of others), we are engaging in self-censorship. Librarians serving YAs face a challenge because many in the community want to draw the lines for us, and we often find them hard to draw ourselves.

8.6 RESTRICTED ACCESS TO SERVICES

In addition to limiting access to certain types of materials, many libraries have policies that limit access to services. Many of these policies ostensibly are age-neutral, but they are really aimed at youth. A policy mandating "no answering homework questions over the telephone" doesn't say anything about the age of the caller, but it seems clear that such a policy is aimed at children and YAs. Although there may not be a written policy on not doing Dialog searches for students, many libraries have informal understandings that librarians are not to do them. There are outrageous examples, such as labeling certain materials for "adults only," and various subtle ones. Librarians often think nothing of "breaking up" a group of students gathered at a table to study and talk, but many would hesitate to interrupt a group of adults doing the same thing. There is a touch of arrogance in our position on and mistrust of teenagers. Each library should take a look at the big and little things they do to restrict access. Figure 8–1 provides a self-evaluation you can use in your library to determine your policies on access restriction.

Figure 8–1 Self-Evaluation for Restricted Access

Restricting YA Access: A Self-Evaluation

[Yes]	[No]	Can YAs:
[ ]	[ ]	Hold their own library cards?
[ ]	[ ]	Check out non-YA books?
[ ]	[ ]	Check out all formats (including videos)?
[ ]	[ ]	Use all equipment?
[ ]	[ ]	Have database searches performed?
[ ]	[ ]	Have extended loan periods?
[ ]	[ ]	Get items through interlibrary loan?
[ ]	[ ]	Book meeting rooms?
[ ]	[ ]	Use special collections?
[ ]	[ ]	Find "labeled" materials?
[ ]	[ ]	Place reserves?
[ ]	[ ]	Attend board meetings?
[ ]	[ ]	Participate in friends' groups?
[ ]	[ ]	Get in-depth reference assistance?
[ ]	[ ]	Ask reference questions over the phone?
[ ]	[ ]	Find no YA limits on number of checkouts?
[ ]	[ ]	Have same access to the Internet as adult patrons?
[ ]	[ ]	Use OCLC and all information technology open to others?
[ ]	[ ]	Meet and study in groups?
[ ]	[ ]	Visit the library during school hours?
[ ]	[ ]	Find limits on number allowed in building?
[ ]	[ ]	Use telephones and fax machines?
[ ]	[ ]	Other:

SCENARIO #1

A YA comes in looking for Christopher Pike's book from the *Cheerleader* series called *Getting Even*. Like most libraries, your library doesn't have it in stock. It is also out of print. Would you think of offering interlibrary loan services to this YA?

SCENARIO #2

You're working at the desk with another reference librarian, a classic kid-hater. Already this morning you've heard him look up the winning Lotto numbers in *USA Today*, read off the top 10 ovens from *Consumer Reports*, and spend half an hour working on a grammar question for a secretary. You're helping another patron when your line rings. You excuse yourself and get ready to put the caller on hold, but before you can, the person—it sounds like a young person—asks for the monetary units for three countries. You ask the caller to hold and, seeing the other librarian is now free, reluctantly ask him to pick up the call. There's silence, a sigh, and then the question comes: "Is this for your homework?" A moment of silence; then "We don't do homework questions over the phone." The phone goes down and he mumbles quietly, "Damned kids."

8.7 LATCHKEY/HOMELESS

SCENARIO #1

During the summer, a young teen comes into your library every day when you open and stays until you close. From what you can tell, he doesn't bring a lunch with him, nor does he leave the building long enough to get something to eat. He doesn't cause any trouble: each day he reads, uses the computers, and sleeps. YA service is anxious to get YAs to use the library, and here is one who does—every day, five days a week, eight hours a day—and that is a problem. Is this a neglected child? Should you report him to child protection services? Should you try to contact his parents? If you don't do anything, you might be committing a crime (this varies by state). If that is the case, are you personally responsible or is the library? Where do you draw the line between the right to privacy and the need to protect children from harm?

SCENARIO #2

An older teen comes to your library every day in the winter when you open and stays until you close. She reads, sleeps, and smells bad. Do you call anyone? Do you intervene?

With the ever-increasing number of two-income and single-parent families, all libraries are facing the issue of latchkey children. But for some there is no such thing as a latchkey young adult. Once children reach 12, they are no longer considered "latchkey." And although homeless adults are a fact of library life, and each building deals with it in its own way, homeless teens and children present another question altogether: should intervention be attempted in such cases? This again ties in to questions of society responsibility and the right to privacy.

8.8 OUT-OF-SCHOOL AND NON-COLLEGE-BOUND YAs

If you develop a library instruction program, will it reach all classes? Or will the school send only certain classes; and isn't it a sure bet they will be honor classes? But what about the YAs taking shop? Can we develop programs that make the library important to these students, who might need our help more than the honor students?

ASSUMPTION #1

Most of us working in libraries didn't take shop, and we didn't hang around those who did. Our own kids don't take it, and we probably don't know people who do. Although it is a generalization, if one surveyed our profession one might find that we tend to serve the students we recognize in our own lives. The fact that we all went to college alienates us from students who aren't college-bound.

ASSUMPTION #2

When we work with schools, we tend to get caught up in their pretensions (and in our own pretensions) about YAs reading great literature or becoming independent scholars. Sometimes a school can give all noncollege-bound YAs a bad reputation, which the library easily buys into; we see only the bad kids and make no effort to meet the rest, because we figure they'll just be a headache too.

Another large group of YAs we miss are those no longer in school. Because so much goes into making school contacts, we almost default services to those YAs who have decided to leave school. We might do a GED program every now and them, but that's about it. This is one of the toughest groups to reach, for obvious reasons. Perhaps the best way to reach out-of-school YAs is to work with anti-dropout programs. Many of the services and resources libraries have to offer could be of use to at-risk students. The local library can identify the agencies within the community that target at-risk students and take some steps toward working together.

8.9 LACK OF DIVERSITY IN THE LITERATURE

When I was working in a community with a large Puerto Rican population, I was amazed at the lack of YA literature in English for this group. Although several articles have appeared recently about library services to Hispanics, there are few current YA novels available. Similar situations exist in YA literature for almost every ethnic minority group. There is little growth in books for African-American YAs. And although there have been a few titles of interest for Asian-Americans, the field is quite small. The only area that has seen much growth is books dealing with gay characters: there are plenty of new titles here, and they are much improved from earlier efforts. But overall, the literature for YAs remains white, suburban, straight, and middle-class. Again, it is a cyclical problem: because there is so little available, it is difficult to entice young people into the library and encourage them to read. If they don't read, there is no market and nothing new gets published. In *From Romance to Realism,* Michael Cart discusses the issue of diversity in literature in a chapter on "multicultural milieu."[2]

8.10 DEFINING YA SERVICES

Because the teen years are a time of confusion about identity, it seems only appropriate that libraries should suffer the same confusion about defining services to YAs. Librarians don't seem to know whether to call their collections YA areas, or teen areas, or anything at all. While many libraries focus services on older YAs, providing formal educational support through library instruction and reference materials, others focus on middle-school students, providing booktalking and "fun" library programs. As I said at the outset, YA is a time when young people don't want to consider themselves children, but they are not recognized as adults. Former YALSA president Christy Tyson writes:

> Libraries and their librarians use the term young adult in order to be able to plan, budget, and evaluate services for a specific age group, usually based on the configuration of their local schools. This has

left our specialty with a bewildering service range that spans ages from 10 to 21.[3]

Why do we have such a problem making a clear-cut definition of both YA and YA services?

Institutional reality: If a library has both a YA department and a children's department, it's a sure bet that grades 5 through 8 are a battleground. For a variety of reasons, many children's librarians don't serve these grades; yet, because of tradition, turf protection, and simple budget reality (the bigger your age range, the bigger your materials budget and your staff), they are not willing to "give up" these grades. Most students in this grade range are served not by children's but by YA librarians for both informational and recreational materials, but YA doesn't get the allocation or the credit for this.

Physical reality: If we match YA with the onset of puberty, we have to be aware of research showing that puberty has occurred earlier in every decade since 1940. Further, the same research has indicated that "biologically, today young adolescents are approximately two years in advance of the young people for whom the first junior high schools in America were established."[4]

Social reality: Our YA years don't match up with today's YA years. Noted YA commentator Audrey Eaglen has noted that libraries need to "recognize and accept that the world in which today's young people are living is a different one from that in which we grew up."[5] If we define YA by our own experience, maybe we'll remember that we weren't ready for books about sex when we were 12; but today's YAs are, if not ready, at least interested.

School reality: The Carnegie Council on Adolescent Development reported that middle and junior high schools "are potentially society's most powerful force to recapture millions of youth adrift."[6] The time to influence a child's identity is occurring much sooner.

Psychological reality: Psychologist David Elkind has detailed the variety of pressures on young adults today—pressures that are making them grow up too fast.[7] YAs are finding the pressures around them greater, occurring sooner in life, and more difficult to deal with.

Research reality: When it was time to redo the NCES YA survey, it was combined with the children's survey. Those of us involved in putting together the second survey were sure that the children's section agenda would dominate. It didn't, which was a delightful surprise; but even better were the results of the question on age definition. Of all the wonderful nuggets of information to come from the second NCES survey, this is one of the best:

The most common age range for children was from birth to 12 years, and for young adults from 12 to 18 years. [8]

This is something YA people have long known, even as they found it difficult to pry loose the children's departments' grips on middle-school students. Although this doesn't settle the issue, it provides hard evidence for a better definition of YA in a public library.

Because of these physical, social, and psychological realities, students in grades 5 and 6 often think of themselves as young adults and, when given the choice, will often choose YA materials. Cathy Hakala-Ausperk researched 5th and 6th graders' reading preferences and asked which section of the library (children's or YA) they would rather use. Her findings show a clear and strong preference in this age group for YA material: these students want to feel "grown up" and no longer be considered children (see Figure 8–2). Hakala-Ausperk concluded:

[W]hile many different arguments can be made as to why these youths feel so strongly about not wanting to use a children's room, only one thing really matters in the end—it *is* their choice. If librarians, in striving to protect the established service parameters of their areas, seek only to discount results such as these rather than face change, and perhaps, the surroundings of a piece of their audience, these patrons they are fighting over may simply leave and never come back…if the preferences of these youth are ignored, they might end up as patrons lost—from both rooms— for quite a while. [9]

If we redefine YA, how do we define YA services? What does it mean to reprioritize library roles to include YA? If we cannot or will not hire qualified, energetic YA librarians and give them support to implement a program of YA service, what levels of service can we provide? What is the base level that *all* libraries should provide, and how should services be prioritized beyond that? Each step represents more of a commitment on the part of the library

YA Services Levels Checklist

1. Materials meet formal educational support needs (in reference, nonfiction, and fiction).
2. Services meet basic formal educational support needs (reference service).
3. Materials meet basic informational needs (books about YA life and choices).
4. Materials meet basic recreational reading needs (fiction and magazines).
5. Space is provided for YA materials (separate YA collection).
6. YAs have access to the Internet and other library technology (fair library policies).
7. Space is provided for YAs to gather (separate YA area).
8. Staff is sensitive to the unique information needs of YAs (staff training/retraining).
9. Services meet basic formal educational support needs (library tours).
10. Services meet basic library literacy needs (library instruction).
11. Services encourage YA recreational reading (booktalking).
12. Opportunity is provided for YAs to contribute to the library (youth participation).
13. Services encourage library use (programming).
14. Materials meet YA nonreading recreational needs (nonprint collections).
15. Materials meet special needs (reluctant reader, rampant reader, homework collections, etc.).
16. Services meet special recreational, educational, or informational needs (cooperative programming).
17. Space is available to promote YA reading (merchandised YA collection).
18. Services increase use of library by YAs (marketing YA services).

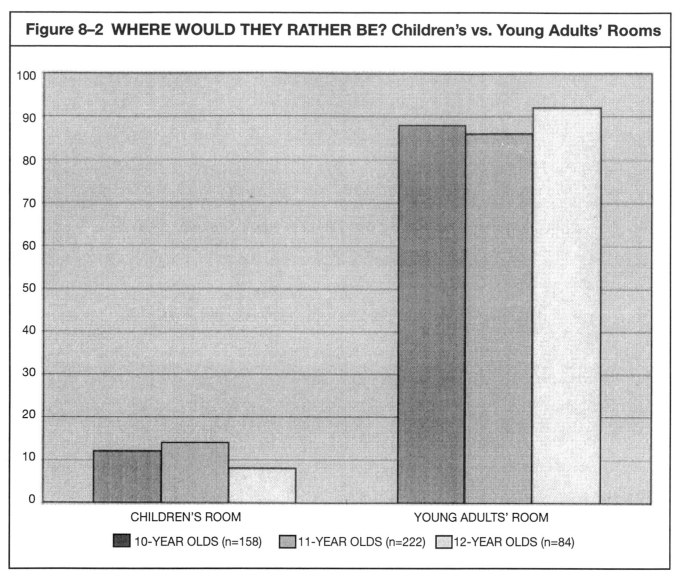

Figure 8–2 WHERE WOULD THEY RATHER BE? Children's vs. Young Adults' Rooms

Reprinted from Cathy Hakala-Ausperk, *Are Young Adults Getting Younger?* Master's Research Paper, Kent State University School of Library Science, 1991.

to the YA patron. Each is one step closer to providing 100 percent quality library service to help ensure that 25 percent of all patrons have a positive library experience.

ENDNOTES

1. *Intellectual Freedom Manual.* American Library Association, 1992.
2. Michael Cart, *From Romance to Realism: 50 Years of Growth and Change in Young Adult Literature.* New York: HarperCollins, 1996: 131.
3. Christy Tyson, "What's in a Name?" *School Library Journal* (December 1990): 47.
4. Joan Lipsitz, *Successful Schools for Young Adolescents.* New Brunswick, NJ: Transaction Publishers, 1984: 6.
5. Audrey Eaglen, "An Immodest Proposal," *School Library Journal* (August 1989): 92.
6. Carnegie Council on Adolescent Development, *Turning Points: Preparing Youth for the 21st Century.* Pittsburgh: Carnegie Corporation, 1989: 10.
7. David Elkind, *All Grown Up and No Place to Go.* Reading, MA: Addison-Wesley, 1984.
8. *Services and Resources for Children and Young Adults in Public Libraries.* U.S. Department of Education, National Center for Education Statistics, 1995: 4
9. Cathy Hakala-Ausperk, *Are Young Adults Getting Younger?* Master's research paper, Kent State University School of Library Science, 1991: 26.

APRIL

Goal: Network for YA services beyond the local level.

1. **Attend your state library conference:** April seems a big month for state library conferences. Does your state even have a YA group? If not, see whether you can organize a meeting time to hold a discussion group about YA issues. Don't be surprised at the number of people who show up looking to talk about YAs and how to serve them better.
2. **Get the message out:** Some states have district or chapter meetings that reach nonprofessional staff. This is another good networking opportunity, but also a place to listen and learn about nitty-gritty problems and practical solutions to those problems.
3. **Who else likes YAs:** Many states also have youth serving networks or agencies. It may be tough to justify the expense of attending these conferences, but at least get on the mailing lists for their newsletters or other documents.
4. **Make contacts:** Opportunities for one-on-one networking are tremendous for those with electronic mail. The big listservs like PUBYAC and LM-Net provide so much access not just by contributing to the list, but by contacting those who share an interest or who have solved a problem. This type of informal reaching out to people who share a similar interest can have tremendous professional as well as personal benefits.
5. **Look beyond library training:** Are there local opportunities to develop skills, gather information, and increase knowledge of serving YAs not directly related to libraries? Are customer service trainings available? What about school-sponsored training sessions on reaching out to at-risk kids? As an alternative, the training could be hands-on: Work for a day in a high school library or volunteer for a day at your local Boy's Club.

9 HIGH-SPEED CONNECTIONS— YAs AND THE INTERNET

Until a few years ago, for most of us, a gopher was a rodent, Veronica and Archie were characters in the comics, and the World Wide Web was a phrase from the days of McCarthyism. A bookmark was decorative, a Yahoo was a rube, and a spider was something to be squashed. Now, all those terms—and a lot more lingo—are part of everyday conversation. The Internet is changing our vocabulary, our workdays, and our interactions with YA patrons.

The Internet has forced renewed discussion about youth, access, and library policy. The questions are far-reaching, challenging some basic foundations of our profession. One foundation that is shaken is selection: for collections, librarians select materials from a long-established criterion; the Internet seems to defy selection. The information is simply there, and there is no accepted criterion for evaluating Internet content. Yet, in many ways, the Internet gives libraries a chance to do what libraries do best: provide order to the information chaos that multiplies daily. A lot of what is on the Internet is junk, shrapnel from the information explosion; the junk can crowd out some of the best the Internet has to offer for both YAs and YA librarians.

9.1 YOUTH, THE INTERNET, AND LIBRARY POLICY

When I began outlining this chapter, I knew I wanted to inform readers of the issues surrounding youth access to the Internet, both in macro (policy) and in micro (practical) terms. One of the best pages I found when I was putting together the YA Librarian's Help/Home Page was a document called "Youth: The Internet and Library Policy" (http://www.sils.umich.edu/~sbailey/723/723.html). The authors of the document had done an excellent job airing the essential issues of this topic. So, rather than reinvent the wheel, I asked the authors (Samantha Bailey, Josie Barnes Parker, and Mike Schmiedicke) for permission to include a revised version of the document as section 9.1, to serve as an introduction and overview of the various questions concerning youth, the Internet, and library policy.

LIBRARY POLICIES

Getting on the Internet has been likened to surfing. If that is an accurate metaphor, it can be said that this incredibly rich information resource is the fastest moving wave in the world today. For public libraries, this fact assumes a special importance. In providing access to a large population of users with a variety of interests and widely varying degrees of experience, orientation, or just plain curiosity, a pleasant cruise can easily become a treacherous battle simply to stay afloat. Trying to navigate the breakers of increasing patron demand, avoid the rocks of community opposition, and steer users away from the seamy backwaters can be a formidable challenge. Venturing into the surf without a policy is nothing short of leaving your board at home.

But getting on the Internet does not have to be a scary proposition; nor is writing a policy a fatalistic preparation for an inevitable collision. As with any new resource, a policy is the library's positive response to opportunity and an effort to tailor access to meet the needs of the community. Developing a policy is a means for the professional to better understand the medium in question, its potentials, and its hazards. Producing such a document presupposes an understanding of the resource and thus provides a perfect occasion for familiarization. As the library staff becomes increasingly accustomed to the Internet and its possibilities, their knowledge helps define the role they will play in relation to the needs and desires of their patrons.

No trip is ever without difficulty, but putting in the time and effort to develop a policy can greatly increase the likelihood of success. Not only can policy-writing be the starting place for dialogue that may well forestall trouble later, it can provide direction for future growth. Limited resources can be accurately dispensed according to well-thought-out priorities, and meaningful answers can be supplied to patron inquiries on the library's support of the new technology. Challenges can be dealt with in a consistent and judicious manner, to the benefit of all involved. But most importantly, the creation of an Internet policy puts the professional back in the driver's seat. Though at first glance seemingly impossible to control, an aggressive, knowledgeable policy that focuses on good selection, ongoing training, and intelligent guidance can harness the Internet and help librarians provide order to patrons' usage. It can enable librarians to use the skills they have always possessed, providing their users with an experience that is as productive, safe, and enjoyable as possible.

Currently, policies guiding Internet access focus largely on the concept of "acceptable use."[1] This approach can be problematic for several reasons. If we look at the acceptable use policies (AUPs) currently in force, we see that the majority are best suited for use in school systems. This poses a distinct conflict of interests for the public librarian looking for models on which to base an Internet policy. School librarians, like teachers, often must act *in loco parentis* for the children under their supervision. This being the case, policies dealing with Internet access in schools necessarily tend to focus mainly on guidelines for appropriate behavior and consequences for violations. Moreover, due to actual conflicts or anticipated troubles, many AUPs have a reactionary character, with language and prescriptions designed to avoid trouble as opposed to take advantage of a resource. To this end, most AUPs designed by school administrators aim at addressing their concerns, not those of librarians.

The consequences of this orientation are obvious. Although concerns over appropriate use of the medium and a desire to facilitate its application in a safe manner are necessarily high priorities, public librarians need to address other substantial issues as well. Unlike school professionals, public librarians cannot and should not act in a parental capacity toward youth. The AUP they adopt must anticipate the needs of a more diverse user group; librarians must determine what roles the technology will fill and formulate a strategy for the selection of sites. Thus, they need a model for an Internet access policy that is far more comprehensive than the average AUP; a model best approximated by the traditional concept of collection development.

In developing an access policy, we first must realize that the Internet, at its most basic level, is an information resource like any other information resource. It can be accessed for anything from entertainment to serious research. It is not self-explanatory. The extent of what is available is not intuitively obvious. It can be difficult to use. Different people will respond to it in different ways. Clearly, there is much more at stake than "acceptable use." A good collection development policy will take into consideration all these aspects. Two resources from the ALA—the *Guide for Written Collection Policy Statements*[2] and "Access to Electronic Information, Services, and Networks: An Interpretation of the Library Bill of Rights"[3]—provide a solid starting point, as well as general guidance throughout the process.

The library will want to focus particularly on three elements:

1. The mission and goals statement,
2. The selection criteria, and
3. The needs of special groups

By employing a mission statement, the specific needs of the community can be identified and clarified. The library staff should examine seriously and articulate clearly *why* they are providing access, *what* they hope to achieve by providing access, and *how* they intend to accomplish that. Access can then be responsibly structured in a manner that best meets these goals. An excellent resource for this is *Planning and Role Setting for Public Libraries,* which will help guide the planning committee in expressing "briefly and directly the library's purpose" in supporting the new service.[4]

Formulating selection criteria will serve two ends. First, it establishes an intelligent standard as to what constitutes a useful, usable, and appropriate Web site, based on definite parameters drawn from the librarian's experience with the resource. [5-6] But second, and more important, the act of selecting itself injects a modicum of professional control and order into an otherwise self-governing entity. The argument that, although "libraries can defend the selection criteria for the materials they have in their own collection, they can't do the same for the endless stream of information that is now accessible via the net," is terribly misleading and a poor excuse for not writing a definite policy.[7] No one is asking any single institution to defend the entirety of the Internet, just as no library attempts to justify the policies of all other libraries in its network, even though it may provide electronic access to their collections. Arranging Internet resources according to selection criteria that reflect the values and needs of the community is an achievable goal and a necessary, beneficial task. Organizing information has always been one of the librarian's most important skills; it is a skill people have come to rely on. It is no different now, but it requires a new level of commitment.

Public libraries must recognize the importance of the Internet as a major provider of information their patrons need, but recognize as well that it takes an investment of time and effort to use it well. Developing a home page that selects and organizes under topical headings the best of what the Internet has to offer is an excellent start. It can simplify the task of the information seeker, keep the librarian on top of the resource, and guide clients to reliable sites, helping to minimize misuse of the system.

The third essential element of the policy deals with discerning the needs of the many individuals who make use of the public library and their relation to this emerging technology. From businesspersons to single mothers, from entrepreneurs to the elderly, the needs are many and diverse, and all deserve attention. But of special concern are the needs of those who are the future of the library and whose lives will continue to be affected by this technology more than any others—the youth. The consequences of growing up in an electronically networked environment can scarcely be overrated. Today's young people are learning to accept global connectivity as nonchalantly as a previous generation accepted the telephone. In such a social milieu, it is difficult to imagine a scenario in which an information center that does not provide Internet usage will be judged relevant. Although our youth share many of the same general information needs as other library clients, they also have particular needs that should be considered when drafting an Internet policy.

Something we often hear about these days is the growing "social culture" on the Internet.[8] Young people are not only finding a broad electronic community of peers, they also find the navigation of the resource itself to be a "communal activity," where they can "huddle around the computer, share tactics, and urge each other on."[9] The importance of this activity should be recognized in a library's Internet usage policy, and time and space should be provided for it as much as possible. Young people are coming to expect that most, or even all, of their information needs can be met online.[10] Libraries failing to provide such a service will never even get the chance to educate these young people on the wealth of other resources available. In addition, given the prevalence of computers in the classroom and the increasing amount of homework students are expected to complete using network resources, the public library must be in a position to support this education initiative.[11] Expectations are running high, and they have to be met head on. A thoughtful development policy is the best way to approach these difficulties in a productive fashion.

Of course, there are other questions at stake as well. "Content filters" have received a great deal of attention in recent months, both positive and negative. Public librarians working with policy development owe it to themselves and to their communities to be familiar with the Internet screening tools available and the serious issues surrounding their use. Even though most of today's filters do not seem oriented for use in a public library—and can often act in a manner that shuts out important voices—those deciding whether or not to employ them should do so based on their own experience and not on the judgment of others.[12] There is also the law to consider. Site selectors need to be aware of how various state and federal statutes can affect their work and to what extent they may be responsible for links off their home pages.[13] Libraries may also want to write some statement of accountability into their policies that will help ensure a standard method for handling abuses of the system.

The Internet is the wave of the future; indeed, it is the wave of today. Librarians may not have had much to say about its growth as an information resource, but we stand in a position to have a great influence on its use in coming years. Learn about the Internet. Familiarize yourself with the issues. Some of the best information available, particularly on the topics discussed here, is available only online; so dive in. Organize a policy development committee. Put some teens and other concerned members of your community on the team. Difficulties inevitably will arise, but now is the time to face them. In the words of one insightful young person:

The Internet is exactly like real life, in regards to the availability of information. A student could, for instance, learn how to make a bomb from someone online—but he could gain the same knowl-edge from a chemistry book, so does that mean we have to ban books and stop teaching science, too? Of course not. It's just hu-man nature to fear and protect against something we don't under-stand. It's too bad that there are still so many who distrust the Internet, rather than being open to comprehending the advantages.[14]

SURFING HITS A BIG WAVE

In addition to the positive response of patrons who like having the chance to surf the Net, many libraries have encountered a huge wave of fear about what patrons—and, in particular, what children—were finding while they surfed. This manifested itself, along with concerns about the Internet in general, in the passing of the Communications Decency Act. Although key provisions of this Act were overturned by the United States Supreme Court in June of 1997, the political forces behind the legislation are very much alive.

Many public libraries started out with such broad Internet policies that, within a short time, they were forced to reconsider them. In some cases, this rethinking was the result of practical problems or staff is-sues; but in many cases, the rethinking was prompted by public com-plaint or, more often, by questions from a government official (a mayor, a city or county council, or the library board itself). In most cases, the rethinking occurred because of rising media interest in "kids and smut" and the wide availability of pornography to children via the Internet. Although most public library Internet workstations are not "digital peep shows," that is the image that seems to be sticking with people. This is, no doubt, due to a lot of misinformation about the Internet and about what public libraries do.

In airing this issue, Marilyn Gell Mason, the director of the Cleve-land Public Library, noted:

> They say that public libraries are no longer safe havens for chil-dren. They say that ALA has libraries peddling pornography. They say that librarians are unresponsive to the public's concern. They say that something must be done. The problem is a knotty one. How does a library provide free and open access to the 34 million sites now available through the Internet without inflaming parents and others in the community concern about children viewing pictures that most believe are pornographic?[15]

Resolution on the Use of Filtering Software in Libraries

WHEREAS, On June 26, 1997, the United States Supreme Court issued a sweeping re-affirmation of core First Amendment principles and held that communications over the Internet deserve the highest level of Constitutional protection; and

WHEREAS, The Court's most fundamental holding is that communications on the Internet deserve the same level of Constitutional protection as books, magazines, newspapers, and speakers on a street corner soapbox. The Court found that the Internet "constitutes a vast platform from which to address and hear from a world-wide audience of millions of readers, viewers, researchers, and buyers," and that "any person with a phone line can become a town crier with a voice that resonates farther than it could from any soapbox"; and

WHEREAS, For libraries, the most critical holding of the Supreme Court is that libraries that make content available on the Internet can continue to do so with the same Constitutional protections that apply to the books on libraries' shelves; and

WHEREAS, The Court's conclusion that "the vast democratic forum of the Internet" merits full constitutional protection will also serve to protect libraries that provide their patrons with access to the Internet; and

WHEREAS, The Court recognized the importance of enabling individuals to receive speech from the entire world and to speak to the entire world. Libraries provide those opportunities to many who would not otherwise have them; and

WHEREAS, The Supreme Court's decision will protect that access; and

WHEREAS, The use in libraries of software filters which block Constitutionally protected speech is inconsistent with the United States Constitution and federal law and may lead to legal exposure for the library and its governing authorities; now, therefore, be it

RESOLVED, That the American Library Association affirms that the use of filtering software by libraries to block access to constitutionally protected speech violates the Library Bill of Rights.

Source: Adopted by the ALA Council, July 2, 1997 (http://www.ala.org/oif.html)

Mason makes two points:

1. We won't be able to garner support to fund libraries and Internet access if the public sees us as "smut peddlers" allowing children to view pornography. This is, of course, merely a new riff on an old melody: how do we balance serving our communities against serving our professional values and core beliefs? Moreover, Mason suggests that if we don't have public support, funding will decrease and no one will have Internet access; thus, it is better to limit some access for some than to lose it all for everyone.

2. Mason suggests that filtering, while imperfect, is the answer. While noting the problems—both a technological and an intellectual freedom standpoint—she views filters as selection, not censorship, asking, "Is it any less valid to 'select out' material than it is to 'select in' material?"[16] Mason notes, however, that the ACLU has promised to sue libraries using filters.

The position of the American Library Association, adopted at the 1997 Annual Conference, is unequivocal: no filters. This follows from its early statement on electronic access that answered questions about filtering, as well as about youth access to electronic information.

Yet professional policy and individual libraries are not always harmonious. Although some libraries look to the ALA for guidance, each seems to be steering its own course based on its community, its resources, and its leadership. In reviewing the Internet policies of 75 public libraries, David Burt found great discrepancies:

Policies for Use of Public Internet Workstations in Public Libraries

Library not responsible for information found on the Internet	80%
Parents responsible for children's access	60%
Warns users they may find offensive material	57%
Warns users of loss of privileges for violation of policies	44%
Bars attempts to violate system security	36%
Bars illegal activity	36%
Bars violation of copyright or software licenses	32%
Has time limits	24%
Bars the use of user's own software	24%
Requires users to sign an acceptable use agreement	23%
Has sign-up sheets for use	21%
Bars use to harass others	20%
Has some limitations of printing	19%
Children may only use with parent's permission	15%
Supports ALA Bill of Rights	13%
Bars use of e-mail	13%
Offers training classes	12%
Bars viewing of pornography	12%
Limits to library card holders	9%
Bars commercial use	9%
Library respects privacy of user	8%
Bars misrepresentation	7%
Bars use of own disks	5%
Uses filtering software	4%
Charges fees	4%
Children may use only when accompanied by a parent	4%

Source: Adapted from David Burt, "Policies for the Use of Public Internet Workstations in Public Libraries," *Public Libraries* (May/June 1997): 156–159.

Burt concluded:

> Overall, the seventy-five public libraries agree on very little . . . The diversity in policies may be due to the newness of the Internet, and the fact that the Internet is not particularly analogous to any other library resource, service, or activity. Clearly, it will be some time before librarians agree on whether the Internet is a service or a resource, if it is more like a print medium or more like a broadcast medium, and what constitutes "selection" with regards to the Internet.[17]

Again, Burt notes this is merely "selection vs. censorship" in new clothes. It will be interesting to see how this issue develops as filtering

Access to Electronic Information, Services and Networks: Selected Questions & Answers

3. Why should libraries extend access to electronic information resources to minors?

Those libraries with a mission that includes service to minors should make available to them a full range of information necessary to become thinking adults and the informed electorate envisioned in the Constitution. The opportunity to participate responsibly in the electronic arena is also vital for nurturing the information literacy skills demanded by the Information Age. Only parents and legal guardians have the right and responsibility to restrict their children's and only their own children's access to any electronic resource.

11. Do libraries need an "acceptable use policy" for electronic information access? If so, what elements should be considered for inclusion?

Access questions are rooted in Constitutional mandates and a Library Bill of Rights that reach across all media. These should be professionally interpreted through general service policies that also relate to the specific mission and objectives of the institution. Such general policies can benefit from the legacy and precedents within the ALA's Intellectual Freedom Manual, including new interpretations for electronic resources. Reasonable restrictions placed on the time, place, and manner of library access should be used only when necessary to achieve substantial library managerial objectives and only in the least restrictive manner possible. In other words, libraries should focus on developing policies that ensure broad access to information resources of all kinds, citing as few restrictions as possible, rather than developing more limited "acceptable use" policies that seek to define limited ranges of what kinds of information can be accessed by which patrons and in what manner.

12. Why shouldn't parental permission be required for minor access to electronic information?

As with any other information format, parents are responsible for determining what they wish their own children to access electronically. Libraries may need to help parents understand their options during the evolving information revolution, but should not be in the policing position of enforcing parental restrictions within the library. In addition, libraries cannot use children as an excuse to violate their Constitutional duty to help provide for an educated adult electorate. The Library Bill of Rights—its various Interpretations . . . and ALA's Guidelines for the Development and Implementation of Policies, Regulations and Procedures Affecting Access to Library Materials, Services and Facilities—also endorse the rights of youth to library resources and information as part of their inalienable rights and the passage to informed adulthood. Electronic information access is no different in these regards.

Source: "Access to Electronic Information, Services and Networks: An Interpretation of the Library Bill of Rights," American Library Association, 1997.

software evolves and improves. There is little purity in this issue: a librarian who decries filters as censorship might regularly pass on buying rap tapes, graphic novels, or the like to avoid challenges. Or perhaps the selection takes place at a higher level when deciding which review sources to use: isn't selecting *not* to use *Feminist BookStore News* as a selection tool censoring gay/lesbian literature?

Many libraries are looking for a compromise, a way to "balance between providing Internet access to adults, protecting minors from pornographic images, and protecting staff from sexual harassment and legal liability."[18] I recently visited several public libraries in the Midwest, and each one had a different policy: some said no e-mail; others allowed it. Some wouldn't allow use of chat rooms; others did. Few had many plug-ins loaded, and many had the disk drive locked—to prevent computer viruses, no doubt, but it also prevents downloading. All of these are proactive measures libraries take to limit not so much access but use of the resource. One large urban library I visited had installed filters only on the Internet workstations in the children's room (they have no YA area). This does not preclude children from using those in the adult area, but it seemed a way to give the "public" what they wanted, while maintaining free access for adults. It is not a perfect solution, but it seems to be one that the governing body is agreeable to, and it should (for a while, anyway) stop the media hailstorm and public outrage.

Only one library—a major suburban system—required parental permission for use of the Internet by minors. This does not limit use of the resource, but it does limit access by restricting use for one particular user group. This is the line to hold: if you need to give in on other issues, even filters, stand firm on this one. It is what youth services—in particular YA adult services—is all about. Do we want our Internet workstations filled with 16–year-old boys surfing the Net for porn? Of course not. If libraries thought this was appropriate material for libraries, we'd be stocking XXX videos, books, and magazines, but we don't. Do we censor, or do we select? Either way, we draw a line. My concern is that the line is related to the material, *not to the user.*

Do we want that same 16–year-old boy to be able to search the Internet when he wants, how he wants, and for what he wants, without an additional barrier? Of course we do.

9.2 APPLYING THE POLICY

Policies are philosophical in nature, but the Internet presents librarians serving YAs with daily practical problems. Many of these might demand further policies or written procedures. The notable goal of Internet access for youth packs a lot of baggage, including this "dirty dozen":

More than the Web: Many libraries claim to offer Internet access, but instead they offer the ability to search the World Wide Web, which is certainly not the only resource available. Chat rooms, e-mail, Usenets, MUDS, and listservs are just a few of the other opportunities on the Internet. Libraries are hesitant to open these resources for three reasons. First, while the information on the Internet is unlimited, physical access (the number of terminals) is limited. Like most limited resources, libraries try to parcel out access in ways that serve what most see as our primary function: information, not entertainment. And although all of the resources above claim some informational value, the primary purpose of a MUD or chat room is entertainment. Second, it is much more likely for those monitoring a newsgroup to "plant" themselves at a terminal, which again is a problem because of the limited number of terminals. Finally, the contradiction of wanting to give youth access and responsibility crashes against our desire to protect them. The Internet reflects society as a whole, and there are plenty of people in society who prey on teenagers: chat rooms in particular seem to lend themselves to this sort of harassment.

"Paperless society": Isn't it interesting that, rather than creating a paperless society, the information age is creating one drowning in paper? Rather than the small scrap papers we used to leave beside the readers' guide and refill once a week, we now must stock the printer for Infotrac almost daily. If you own color printers, chances are the expensive inkjets get changed weekly, if not more often. Many library patrons, and not just youth, print everything because they are more comfortable using print format. If you provide e-mail access, chances are that some people do not read their mail online; they just print it. All the electronic encyclopedias have an easy-to-find print button, but not one for print preview. The Web is the same: students hit the print button, and only 75 pages later do they realize all of the information isn't necessary. This has serious cost implications—not so much for the paper as for the ink jets—as well as creating a high level of staff frustration. If you try to avoid the mess by allowing people to save on disk, you open yourself up not only to computer virus transmission but to another access issue: it doesn't do patrons any good to download information from the Internet if they don't have computers to upload it to eventually. If you don't allow printing at all, you're going to have a lot of unhappy customers (and rightly so).

Location: One very strong argument can be made against allowing unlimited Internet access: a user can bring up on the screen in a very visible public area pages filled with pornography. This is not just a nuisance; some staff consider it sexual harassment. If you put terminals in a public area, you have to deal with that issue. If you place them in a less public area, however, the chances of the machines being used for peep shows seem to increase. If libraries with YA areas have computers with Internet access, how do they keep those terminals free for YA use? The same dilemma arises with terminals in the children's room.

The vision meets reality: When a library decides to go forward with Internet access, it envisions users of all ages happily surfing for information, just like those happy people on the online services commercials. The real vision, in many public libraries, is quite different. It is one of terminals occupied endlessly by all those other regular patrons we "nickname." They are not cruising the information superhighway; they are bogged down in pornography, political conspiracy, and . . . well, you know the rest. Planting themselves firmly before the terminal, one finger poised to click the print button, and with no other place to go and nothing else to do, they monopolize your Internet access. Good liberal souls that most librarians are, we try setting limits on time or use, so we can have our cake ("access for all") and eat it too ("okay, but not for you"). The real issue isn't who is using the Internet (although there is that undercurrent), but that the supply can't meet the demand.

Keeping things clean: I'm not speaking of pornography here, but of viruses. There are several hoax viruses out there, and plenty of real ones, and your Internet access invites them onto your library's computers. In addition, the desktop itself must be maintained. Do you want to limit the ability of users to set bookmarks, change backgrounds, unzip files, and a hundred other small, nagging questions? Who is going to keep your machines clean and quick? A schedule for computer maintenance must be in place with your Internet access; if not, there won't be access for anyone if all the terminals are in the shop or hopelessly fouled up.

Technophobia: Just because we live in a world of computers doesn't mean our patrons do. There are many patrons, including some YAs, who just don't like computers. They view computers with stress, anguish, and frustration. The speed of computers and the ocean of information only makes it worse. We have to be sensitive to these patrons, especially when we don't have any other choices for them.

Staff technical knowledge: So, a YA has found a great 75–page document on the Internet, and she wants to print only selected parts of several pages. Do you know how? Do you know how to change the options to allow her to print a page with white ink on a black background? Do you know how to save images and then manipulate them? In other words, can you and your staff really be reliable and credible with YAs using the Internet?

YA technical knowledge: Although the word *hacker* is overused, it seems a good term to describe those people who, for the thrill of it, screw up someone else's computer system. Many YAs know how to do this (as do adults): can you prevent it? Are your computers set up so that patrons can't delete or change operating system files?

"The best": Many YAs think the Internet is Yahoo, but most librarians know better. In addition to being able to solve problems, is the staff reliable and credible about the core function of retrieving information from the Internet?

"The worst": Is your staff trained on what to say—and what *not* to say—when dealing with YAs and the Internet? If a YA brings up a pornographic site, how is that handled? What about a page of filthy jokes? Again, it is one thing to have policies, but it is quite another to have staff with the knowledge, skills, and attitudes to apply these policies in day-to-day interactions.

"Who's in charge here?" A staff of any size really needs a *cybrarian*—a librarian whose job description is doing Internet collection development. With great new Web sites added every minute, it is impossible for an entire staff to keep up. In fact, it is impossible for one person to

Web Sites Evaluating Web Sites/Internet Information Sources

http://www.ucla.edu/campus/computing/bruinonline/trainers/critical.html
Thinking Critically about World Wide Web Resources, by Esther Grassian, UCLA College Library

http://duckdock.acic.com/carolyn/criteria.html
Library Selection Criteria for WWW Resources, by Carolyn Caywood

http://www.science.widener.edu/~withers/Webeval.htm
Widener University / Wolfgram Memorial Library's Teaching Critical Evaluation Skills for World Wide Web Resources

http://thorplus.lib.purdue.edu/research/classes/gs175/3gs175/evaluation.html
"Evaluating World Wide Web Information," by Ann Scholz

http://www.vuw.ac.nz/~agsmith/evaln/index.htm
Criteria for Evaluation of Internet Information Resources, by Alastair Smith, VUW Department of Library and Information Studies, New Zealand

http://www.library.cornell.edu/okuref/research/skill26.htm
"How to Critically Analyze Information Sources," by Joan Ormondroyd, Michael Engle, and Tony Cosgrave

http://mbln.lib.ma.us/emrls/Webeval.htm
Eastern MA Regional Library System Guidelines

http://milton.mse.jhu.edu:8001/research/education/net.html
Evaluating Information Found on the Internet, by Elizabeth E. Kirk

http://www.lib.lehigh.edu/evaluating.Web.html
Evaluating Scholarly/Information Sites on the Web, from Lehigh University

http://www.ups.edu/library/research/handouts/eval.htm
by Lori Ricigliano, Collins Memorial Library at University of Puget Sound

do so, but it seems more efficient and effective to assign the task of disseminating information about new sites and issues to a few rather than to the many.

"Who's in charge here?" part two: One of the primary sources of tension in many libraries isn't between staff and patrons over content, but between public services staff and support staff over broken printers, damaged software, and the hundreds of other irritants of the computer age. If the printer hooked up to your Internet search stations goes down on a Friday evening, who can fix it? It doesn't do much good for youth advocates to gain access if the library can't or won't support access with public-service-minded technical staff.

These are just a few of the practical issues that someone—normally the "front line" librarian—has to deal with on a daily basis. Instant access to information creates tension tidal waves. Yes, the Internet is great and, yes, libraries should have it; but it is a limited resource. Like other limited resources, from typewriters to bestsellers, the only solution is to limit use.

Our concern, however, is that the limiting is not done based on age but on other criteria. At the same time we are thinking about criteria for use or limiting the use of the Internet, librarians are trying to figure out criteria for evaluating the information they find on the Infobahn.

9.3 ALPHABET OF CRITERIA

Several excellent sites are available that offer criteria for evaluating World Wide Web sites and Internet resources. Because the field is so new, however, there isn't yet an established method of thinking about sites. Most of the review journals mention sites; some actually provide, if not reviews, at least annotations.[19] There are Web search services that review sites, but how well do they perform this function?[20] In addition, the sites reviewed are not all of interest to libraries, let alone to YAs. The best method for evaluating sites for YA use, of course, is to let YAs do it themselves.

I would like to advance a list of questions, from A to Z, that librarians should consider when evaluating sites or developing Web pages. This list is based on the criteria found on other sites as well as on my experience developing Web pages and working with YAs in using Web pages. Although every page won't score a perfect "52," the criteria offered does attempt to define quality on the World Wide Web:

A Audience
 1. Does the page state that its intended audience is youth?
 2. Does the content—both links and text—match the intended audience?

B Background
 3. Does the background color or image detract from viewing the page?
 4. Does the background color or image cause problems when printing?

C Criteria
 5. Are there stated criteria for choosing what goes on the page?
 6. Does the page follow the stated criteria?

D Dead ends
 7. Do all the external links work?
 8. Do all the internal links work?

E E-mail
 9. Is the author's e-mail address visible and "clickable"?
 10. Can users submit e-mail even without having e-mail (using form submission)?

F Frames
 11. Are both frames and nonframes versions available?
 12. Do the frames add to the experience of the page?

G Graphics
 13. Are the graphics attractive, proportioned, and appropriate?
 14. Do the graphics add to content of the page?

H Hypertext links
 15. Does the page provide ample links to other pages?
 16. Are the links appropriate for the audience of the page?

I   Interactivity
17.   What, if anything, does the page state about the confidentiality or safety of information submitted online?
18.   Are there surveys, polls, or chat opportunities?

J   Justify
19.   Why does the page exist?
20.   Does the page present a purpose or goal for its existence?

K   Knowledge
21.   Does the page add to human knowledge?
22.   Whose knowledge is it? Does the page contain copyright information?

L   Layout
23.   Is the page layout and organization attractive yet practical?
24.   Does the page use lists, horizontal rules, paragraphs, and other methods to make information easy to find and read?

M   Multiple access points
25.   Is there more than one way to find information on the page?
26.   Does the page provide an index or table of contents?

N   Navigating
27.   Can you easily navigate within the page?
28.   Are there buttons to return, go back, or jump to another page?

O   Objectivity
29.   Is the page without bias?
30.   Is the purpose of the page to inform rather than persuade or sell?

P   Publisher
31.   Is the page backed by an organization, corporation, or educational institution?
32.   Does the page allow you to go to other pages by the same publisher?

Q   Query
33.   Does the page itself have a search engine?
34.   Does the page search function provide instruction?

R   Reliable
35.   Is the page normally accessible (server not down)?
36.   Is the information on the page correct and accurate?

S   Summary
37.   Does the page begin with a paragraph explaining the *who*, *what*, and *why* of the page?
38.   Does the abstract or summary discovered on the search engine accurately reflect the actual content of the page?

T Text

39. Is the page free of typographical errors and misspellings?
40. Is the text clear, concise, and free of grammatical errors?

U Up-to-date

41. Is the date the page was created and last updated noted?
42. Is the frequency of updating sufficient and satisfactory?

V Viewers

43. Can the page support different viewers and browsers?
44. Is there a link to download the "best" browser for the page?

W Web only

45. Does the page contain information, or is it merely an index of links?
46. Does the page annotate these links rather than merely listing them?

"X" Expertise

47. Is it immediately apparent who authored the page?
48. Is there a link to the author's resume/vita, to present his or her expertise in the area?

Y Youth

49. If the page is intended for youth, is the age range too broad?
50. If it is for teens, are the majority of the links of interest and appropriate?

Z ZZZZZ

51. Does the page take too long to download?
52. Is the page too big for its own good?

These 26 areas and 52 questions don't take in everything, but they create a semi-objective "scorecard" for rating Web pages.

9.4 PUBLIC LIBRARY YA WEB SITES

As more public libraries offer Internet access, build Web pages, and become energized in their emerging cyber-role, the most exciting collections are often those being developed on Web pages.[21] Unfortunately, the pattern in cyberspace mirrors that of physical space: most public library Web environments don't have separate YA Web pages. And many of those that have YA links keep them as part of a large "youth" page. The percentage of public libraries with separate YA pages is small—nowhere near 58 percent. It is closer to the same small percentage of libraries staffing a YA librarian—11 percent.[22]

Table 9.1. Directory of Public Library YA Pages

Allen County Public Library (IN)	http://www.acpl.lib.in.us/ Young_Adults/yarespla.html
Berkeley Public Library (CA)	http://www.cl.berkeley.ca.us:80/bpl/ teen/
Boston Public Library (MA)	http://www.bpl.org/WWW/KIDS/ TeenLounge.html
Boulder Public Library (CO)	http://bcn.boulder.co.us./library/bpl/ ya.html
Carmel Clay Public Library (IN)	http://www.carmel.lib.in.us/ya/ yamain.htm
Carnegie Library of Pittsburgh (PA)	http://www.clpgh.org/ein/ya/
Cedar Falls Public Library (IA)	http://www.iren.net/cfpl/yadept/ nletter3.html
Cedar Rapids Public Library (IA)	http://www.cedar-rapids.lib.ia.us/ crpl/ya/crpl-ya.html
Central Rappahannock Regional Library (VA)	http://www.crrl.org/services/ya/ index.htm
Danbury Public Library (CT)	http://www.danbury.lib.ct.us/org/dpl/ yasite.htm
Dayton/ Montgomery County Public Library (OH)	http://www.dayton.lib.oh.us/ ~ya_james/index.html
Escondido Public Library (CA)	http://www.ci.escondido.ca.us/ library/teen
Farmington Community Library (MI)	http://metronet.lib.mi.us/FCL/ yapage.html
Fort Collins Public Library (CO)	http://www.ci.fort-collins.co.us/ C_LIBRARY/teen.htm
Internet Public Library (MI)	http://ipl.sils.umich. edu:80%2fclassroom/teen/
Jefferson-Madison Regional Library (VA)	http://monticello.avenue.gen.va.us/ Library/JMRL/Teen/
Kent District Library (MI)	http://www.kentlibrary.lib.mi.us/ teens.html
King County Library System (WA)	http://www.kcls.org/newya/ya.html
Lake Oswego Public Library (OR)	http://www.ci.oswego.or.us/library/ teen2in.htm
Lakewood Public Library (OH)	http://www.lkwdpl.org/teenconn.htm
Littleton Bemis Public Library (CO)	http://www.littleton.org/LCN/ Governme/Library/GOteens.htm
Liverpool Public Library (NY)	http://www.lpl.org/ya.html
Livonia Civic Center Library (MI)	http://tln.lib.mi.us/~lvcc/ya.htm

Los Angeles Public Library (CA)	http://www.lapl.org/central/tnscp.html
The Mid-Hudson Library System (NY)	http://midhudson.org/services/children/hotteens.htm
Mount Vernon/Knox County Public Library (OH)	http://www.knox.net/knox/library/ya.htm
Multnomah County Public Library (OR)	http://www.multnomah.lib.or.us/lib/outer/index.html
New York Public Library (NY)	http://www.nypl.org/branch/teen/teenlink.html
Newington Public Library (CT)	http://www.newington.lib.ct.us/Web1.html
Oak Park Public Library (IL)	http://www.math.uic.edu:80/oakpark/oppl/ya.html
Orion Township Public Library (MI)	http://www.orion.lib.mi.us/teen.htm
Pasco County Library System (FL)	http://power.pasco.lib.fl.us/tab.html
Prescott Public Library (AZ)	http://yavanet.prescottlib.lib.az.us/libteen.htm
Quincy Public Library (MA)	http://ci.quincy.ma.us:80/tcpl/htm/teen.htm
Richmond Public Library (BC)	http://www.rpl.richmond.bc.ca/teen/
Rocky River Public Library (OH)	http://www.ne-ohio.net/rrpl/rrpl_ya.html
Salem Public Library (OR)	http://www.open.org/library/teen.html
San Francisco Public Library (CA)	http://sfpl.lib.ca.us/edc/teenpage.htm
San Jose Public Library (CA)	http://www.sjpl.lib.ca.us./sjplhome/teens.htm
Santa Clara County Library System (CA)	http://www-lib.co.santa-clara.ca.us/ya.html
Santa Cruz Public Library (CA)	http://www.garfieldlib.com/
Seattle Public Library (WA)	http://www.spl.lib.wa.us/youngad/ya.html
Somerset County Library System (NJ)	http://somerset.lib.nj.us/teensWeb.htm"
Southfield Public Library (MI)	http://metronet.lib.mi.us/SFLD/yaframe.html
Springfield-Greene County Library District (MO)	http://www.orion.org/library/sgcl/teens/teens.htm
St. Charles City County Library District (MO)	http://www.win.org/library/services/yas/yapage.htm
St. Louis County Library (MO)	http://www.slcl.lib.mo.us/services/bkreviews/
Stockton—San Joaquin County Public Library (CA)	http://www.stockton.lib.ca.us/intplace.htm

Tempe Public Library (AZ)	http://www.tempe.gov/library/yabibs.htm
Timberland Regional Library (WA)	http://timber20.timberland.lib.wa.us/teens.htm
Upper Arlington Public Library (OH)	http://www.uapl.lib.oh.us/young
Warren-Trumbull County Public Library (OH)	http://www.wtcpl.lib.oh.us:80/teen.htm
West Babylon Public Library (NY)	http://199.173.91.20/libraries/wbab/young.htm
West Bloomfield Township Public Library (MI)	http://metronet.lib.mi.us/WEST/teenland.html

Updates to this list can be found at http://members.aol.com/naughyde/publibya.htm

Survey of YA Webpages in February 1997

	Over 2 years	1 to 2 years	Six months to 1 year	Under 6 months
How long has your YA Web page been available?	0	3	12	5

	Daily	Weekly	Biweeky	Monthly	As needed
How often is the page updated?	0	1	2	7	10

	Library's Webmaster	YA librarian	Other
Who has overall responsibility of the Web page?	11	6	3

	YES	NO
Are teens involved in creating, designing or maintaining the page?	10	10

	Using search engines	Internet Public Library, Teen Division	Other public library YA sites	YA suggestions	Other
How have you found most of the links of your page	11	2	2	1	4

	YES	NO
Have you experienced any intellectual freedom challenges related to your Web page?	1	19

Table 9.1 lists models of virtual YA areas from libraries of all sizes. This list (http://members.aol.com/naughyde/publibya.htm) was developed from the YA Librarian's Help/Home page (http://www.kcpl.lib.mo.us/ya) and via use of Internet search engines. These virtual YA areas resemble their physical counterparts in several ways:

- They're easy to spot on entering the library's Web environment.
- They reside on a separate page from those with information about other collections.
- They include information and links to other formats in addition to books.
- They post announcements and flyers of local interest.
- They contain booklists or other finding aids.
- They house information links to materials of YA interest.

The elements of success for a YA area seem to be the same in physical and cyberspace: load it with high-interest materials, make it attractive, involve YAs in the process, and make it easily identifiable from other parts of the library by having a clearly defined audience, collection, appearance, and scope.

In February of 1997, I surveyed the creators of YA Web pages (http://members.aol.com/naughyde/plsurvey.htm). The results of this survey, which you see in the margins, indicate that YA Web pages are a young but growing field; most have been in existence for under one year. Even though most Web page developers start out with good intentions, the onslaught of other demands precludes the type of constant feeding and weeding a Web page needs. The survey results show that only half of YA Web pages are updated at least monthly. Although overall responsibility for most of the Web pages remains with the library's Webmaster, almost every library reported strong participation of the YA or youth librarian with assistance from other staff and YA patrons. Only half of the libraries reported teen involvement, but the other half are planning to engage teens. Most of the links on pages came through use of search engines, although a few libraries reported using YA suggestions as their starting point. Despite the initial fears reported by some librarians about the "controversial" links YAs might provide, only one librarian reported facing an intellectual freedom challenge.

CONTENT

Although the content varies, most YA Web pages consist of five elements: book reviews, hypertext links, lists of resources, information about programs, and information about services. There is a wide variety of combination of these elements, from pages that merely list a few links to those containing all five elements. Each element is important: users of Web pages expect to find hypertext links, users of libraries expect to find information about programs and services, and YA librarians routinely provide lists and reviews of library materials. Obviously, each library's ability to have all five elements represented on its Web page will depend upon its staff, its resources, and its goals for the page.

Some libraries are already moving beyond these five elements. Much as public libraries have clearly defined roles, so do Web pages. Most YA Web pages support the roles of reference center, formal educational support, and popular materials center, but a few pages (for example, Lakewood) show another role at work—that of community information center. Other local networking takes place (such as Littleton) where the public library Web page provides links to local school Web pages. Finally, some Web pages (for example, Allen County) do internal networking by providing access to YA resources for all library locations, not just the main library.

Some Web pages do it all. The Web pages at Berkeley and Santa Clara look a lot alike—each using a table format to organize a great deal of information, including upcoming programs, reviews of books and music, reading lists and links, lists of magazines, subjects arranged by Internet link, links to local high schools and community information, links to chat rooms and e-mail services, and college information. Multnomah's page, while not quite as comprehensive, has the most interesting graphic look.

New York Public Library, not surprisingly, is the vanguard in the virtual YA world as it is in the YA field with its Teen Link page, which it describes this way:

> [A] home page created to connect you with hotlines where you can get answers to problems; to other Internet sites for homework help; sports information; fun & games; and to Web pages that teens have posted. . . . There will be a Cool Site of the Week to acquaint you with the variety at your fingertips, and opportunities to submit your

creative writing to our electronic anthology. This is your page and we want . . . your opinion.[23]

A call for teen input is present on most pages, but some libraries go beyond that. Some (such as Carmel Clay) feature teen reviews from their advisory boards. The St. Charles page features the Cybernauts, a YA group that meets to evaluate and suggest links.

The Internet Public Library (IPL) had extended this approach by organizing a teen board not just to provide content, but to be involved in the decision-making process. The IPL's teen division has a simple mission:

> [T]o make the Internet a more useful place for teenagers, by collecting and creating information resources of interest, and by giving teenagers the opportunity to shape the direction of the Division by serving on our Advisory Board. The Teen Division . . . treats teenagers as people, not as a market to be exploited or a problem to be solved.[24]

IPL lives up to that mission with its basic subject arrangement (Arts and Entertainment, Books and Writing, Career and College, Clubs and Organizations, Health, Issues and Conflicts, Math and Science, Politics and History, and Sports), a solid but not overwhelming collection of annotated links, and easily navigable pages. Any public library that does not have its own YA page should consider linking to IPL's quality page.

The impact of YA Web pages on library services to YAs is still unknown—the field is too new—but every library that involved youth groups in the effort documented positive results. Most librarians have ambitious plans for their pages, almost all include involving YAs. Libraries like Boulder Public Library in Colorado have given over most of the Web page responsibility to teens, while other libraries involve teens in providing reviews. Most of the pages featuring quality content, the best and most links, and the best designs are those put together by or with YAs. Librarians have long known the value of youth participation, but it has never been more obvious than on YA Web pages. YAs involved in Web page projects can be the key to making the pages useful, interesting, and attractive—the goals for any Web page. By allowing youth to become involved, not only does the quality of the page increase, the value of the library's overall service to YAs is enhanced.

The YAs in libraries now, and the record numbers emerging, are the first wired generation. Computers are not tools or toys to them; they are everyday artifacts, like television sets. So librarians serving YAs need to work toward the smooth integration of the Internet with

> **" Librarians have long known the value of youth participation, but it has never been more obvious than on YA Web pages. "**

our traditional roles. We do this by following the same principles that have always guided YA librarians: access, participation, equality, and advocacy. With these beliefs as a launching pad, our expeditions into cyberspace and virtual YA areas will soar.

9.5 THE YA LIBRARIAN'S HELP/HOME PAGE

The YA Librarian's Help/Home page—also known as the YA Web—(http://www.kcpl.lib.mo.us/ya) began in December 1995 as a simple attempt to fill a vacuum. Even though there were World Wide Web home pages like the Children's Literature Web and the Youth and Children's Resource Net, a home page designed just for librarians serving YAs was not available. At this time, YALSA, like many other ALA divisions, didn't have a home page, nor were there many public libraries with servers supporting professional or YA home pages.

The first edition of the YA Web consisted primarily of sites gleaned from the Children's Literature Web and subject searches on topics such as "young adult reading" or "adolescent behavior" in Web search engines like Yahoo. The first YA Web was divided into two main sections: resources about young adults and resources for young adults. The purpose of the home page was to provide links to professional resources like book lists and to give those compiling home pages for YAs suggested sites. The emphasis was on general sites for teens containing lists of links, but also sites of teen special interests, such as skateboarding. Ezines and cybermags of interest to teenagers also were included.

The special interest sites had to be limited. Otherwise, the page would have been unmanageable. Besides, if YAs can search Yahoo, they can find the sites they want on their favorite movie stars, sports, and music groups. Because the audience of the page was primarily librarians, the YA sites were those of general interest (more indexes than anything else) or those that a YA might not find. For example, we linked to Fishnet, a terrific site that a YA probably would not seek out but would be delighted to find. Finally, the page acted as a current awareness service by listing and linking to new pages as they were discovered.

More than just a list of links, however, the YA Web also contained documents. Some were handouts used at library conferences, like "Magazines of Interest to Young Adults." Others were booklists that appeared on the PUBYAC listserv (for example, "Adventure Books for Young Adults") or entire Web pages submitted by users (such as "Links to Comic Book and Graphic Novel Sites"). Although it is not an official home page of YALSA, several YALSA documents (such as the "YALSA Vision Statement") have been featured on the YA Web. Documents such as bibliographies, which were not perhaps best suited for Webbery, allowed users to download, then cut and paste for projects they were developing. Because none of the documents carried copyright information, all were intended to be accessed, and then reproduced.

As more links were discovered, the YA Web was reorganized into a dozen subject categories. By April 1996, the YA Web was given a makeover and split from one page into six and from one long list into several shorter lists. This made the YA Web easier to use by putting new links, documents, and the introduction on one page and the subject areas on other pages. An introduction, which explains the basics of the YA Web (when it is updated, why it exists, etc.) was expanded and included the following disclaimer:

> The Young Adult Librarian's Help/Home page is a micro index to the vast amount of resources available on the World Wide Web. It is not a review, recommendation, or endorsement of these links/pages, but only a finding tool to be used by librarians for professional development and/or used by those putting together pages for young adults in their libraries. Users are strongly urged to inspect each link/page on the Young Adult Librarian's Help/Home page completely before adding it to their own documents/pages.

This disclaimer should have been included in the first edition, but it was only after working on the home page that it became obvious such a statement was needed. The disclaimer also focused on this question: what is a Web page? Is it an index (somewhat objective) or a review source (very subjective)? As the YA Web has developed, we have tried to be more selective about sites, resulting in more reviewing and less indexing. The primary criterion for listing a site is practicality. Graphics and other bells and whistles are nice, but the ticket for inclusion is that the information presented can be used by librarians to improve their YA services or their YA home pages.

The practical applications of such a page are many. For example, during a readers' advisory interview, a high school student spoke of her interest in time travel books. Using the YA Web, a link to a list of such titles was located. Another student was interested in information about a private school her friend attended. A print source was not available, but the YA Web linked to Peterson's site, which provided the information. Several librarians have used the page to set up their own YA pages, and the YA Web is now linked on public library, school library, and professional organization pages. Finally, the documents on the page have provided users with handouts from conferences they could not attend, such as one entitled "The Care and Reading of Young Adults."

An issue that is behind every YA selection is age appropriateness. The problem with many Internet sites for youth is that they are "kids' pages," and they mix links to science museums and toy stores with sites like the "Internet Public Library Teen Division." Deciding to "spin a Web" is just that—creating a thread among other interconnected threads which can't be controlled. Trying to design a home page without links that might link to something "offensive" is virtually impossible. The direct link must be evaluated like any other material for youth, but the only sure way to avoid linking to a site that might link directly (or indirectly) to an "objectionable" page is to skip having links at all.

Selectivity is the key. A Web page should not just reproduce the results of a Yahoo search, nor can it contain everything. Yet, at the same time, a Web page with little content and few links isn't going to be satisfactory to most users. Finding the right balance and maintaining it is essential. Weeding is necessary to remove sites that are no longer relevant, practical, or current. Addresses are constantly changing and need correction, and sometimes sites just disappear. The elements of a strong Web site are the same as those of a successful collection: proper needing, feeding, and weeding.

The best sources for feeding the home page are teen Web pages, not search engines. The Web is loaded with personal home pages, and many of them are produced by YAs. These home pages are gold mines of links and information about YA life and times. Involving YAs in creating home pages is the best case scenario, as many school librarian Webmasters have discovered; but if that is not an option, then visiting teen-created home pages will plug librarians in to how teenagers are using the Internet.

Several other tools are available for finding new sites. Most of the major search engines have a "what's new" section. There are entire indices of nothing but new Web pages. In addition, current awareness listservs like "The Scout Report" are invaluable, and the sites mentioned on the listservs PUBYAC and LM_NET often are outstanding. As you became more sophisticated in your knowledge of how search engines work, you'll have much better results finding pages fast. Magazines like *NetGuide, Internet World,* and *Classroom Connect* also contain articles not just listing sites but including annotations and reviews. Finding information is no problem—deciding what to include is the challenge. But that is always the challenge in this profession: infinite resources available and finite facilities (time, staff, space) to house them.

Even though many YA librarians view hosting a Web page as a new thing, it is really something quite traditional. Librarians have always

> Even though many YA librarians view hosting a Web page as a new thing, it is really something quite traditional. Librarians have always been about connecting information and users.

been about connecting information and users. The skills and knowledge of the "language" might be new, but the YA librarian's roles as youth advocate, collection developer, and teen trend follower are perfectly suited to this new environment.

9.6 ANNOTATED BEST SITES

In putting together the YA Web (and a new column for *Voice of Youth Advocates*), I had the chance to examine a couple hundred Web pages. What follows is a list of 60 of the best sites (the top five in 12 categories) available for YA librarians as of July 1997. These represent some of the best in terms of content, presentation, ease of use, and practical application. This list obviously does not include every site of interest of teenagers, but rather professional resources and sites teens might like or need but probably wouldn't find on their own. Information about "popular" teens sites is lacking, with only one article appearing on the subject so far.[25] First, a caveat: Putting Web addresses and pages in print is iffy—there's a good chance some of these pages will no longer exist or will be at different addresses by the time this book is in print. Updates can be found at this book's Web site, http://members. aol.com/naughyde/connecting/index.htm. If they do still live at the same address, they might have changed focus, scope, or content. Yet, given the sheer number of sites out there—more than 300 on the YA Web page alone—it is equally iffy not to provide some information about which pages are good. For the most part, I have let the pages speak for themselves, by quoting directly from the source as to its scope and purpose.

STARTING POINTS

1. *Thinking Critically about World Wide Web Resources*
   http://www.ucla.edu/campus/computing/bruinonline/
   trainers/critical.html
   Prepared by Esther Grassian, at the UCLA College Library, this page presents evaluation criteria, noting that "the World Wide Web has a lot to offer, but not all sources are equally valuable or reliable." Using a series of questions, Grassian allows users to think about the differences between print and electronic resources.

2. *Youth: Library and Internet Policy*
   http://www.sils.umich.edu/~slbailey/723/723.html
   This is the page that supplied the text for the first part of this

chapter. In addition to the text article, there are links to "professional viewpoints, legal aspects and resources, acceptable use policies, public library policies, young adult services, content filters, library selection criteria for Internet resources," and an extensive bibliography. The mix of content and links to documents (such as library policies) make this page essential reading.

3. *Internet Public Library Teen Division*
   http://aristotle.sils.umich.edu/teen/
   Sections here include information on "colleges and universities, entertainment, extracurricular activities, fine art and literature, and social service (including sexuality, drugs and alcohol, violence, and more)." An indispensable page because of its authority, organization, and pertinence.

4. *Electronic Resources for Youth Services*
   http://www.ccn.cs.dal.ca/~aa331/childlit.html
   This Web site is dedicated to reviewing WWW resources related to children's literature and youth services. These resources are aimed toward school librarians, children's writers, illustrators, book reviewers, storytellers, parents, and others interested in this area.

5. *The Children's Literature Web Guide*
   http://www.ucalgary.ca/~dkbrown/
   The Children's Literature Web Guide is an attempt to gather together and categorize the growing number of Internet resources related to books for Children and Young Adults. Much of the information that you can find through these pages is provided by others: fans, schools, libraries, and commercial enterprises involved in the book world.

   There is no better source on the World Wide Web for links to lists, awards, authors, and publishers of YA books.

SCHOOL LIBRARY LINKS

1. *LM_NET on the Web*
   http://ericir.syr.edu/lm_net/inde.html
   LM_NET is a discussion group open to school library media specialists worldwide, and to people involved with the school library media field. It is not for general librarians or educators. [The page includes] the Web LM_NET Archives, The LM_NET FAQ and Answers, Etiquette on LM_NET, and LM_NET Librarian Links.

2. *LION: Librarians' Online Information Network*
http://www.libertynet.org/education/schools/lion/lion.html
LION is sponsored by Library Services of the School District of Philadelphia as an information resource for school librarians in Philadelphia and throughout the nation. [Sections include] cataloging resources for school libraries, CD-ROMs for school libraries, Internet mailing lists and newsgroups for school librarians, lesson plans & teaching activities, LION Bookmarks, LION Forums, LION Reading Room, professional resources, and a Who's Who in School Librarianship.

3. *Peter Milbury's School Librarian Web Pages*
http://wombat.cusd.chico.k12.ca.us/~pmilbury/lib.html
School librarians are among the most active users of the Internet and World Wide Web. They are especially involved in bringing these resources to students and staff. [The links here are for] Web Pages created or maintained by school librarians. Some of these Web Pages are for entire schools, while others are simply for their school libraries. Some are personal, professional and other interesting Web creations by individual school librarians. Also included are a few related resources and helpful links for Web Page creation.

4. *School Libraries on the Web: A Directory*
http://www.voicenet.com/~bertland/libs.html
This is a list of library Web pages maintained by K-12 school libraries in the United States and in countries around the world. This directory is limited to listing pages which focus on the school library/media center. The content of these pages is quite varied and displays the marvelous creativity of school librarians around the world.

5. *School Library Hot Spots*
http://www.mbnet.mb.ca:80/~mstimson/text/hotspots.html
From Australia comes a huge index of school library sites, including sites on "instruction, materials sources and reviews, reference literature, and other recommended library links."

READING LINKS

1. *St. Louis County Public Library*
http://www.slcl.lib.mo.us/services/bkreviews/
A collection of "books reviewed by teens for teens. These reviews are written by St. Louis County Library's Teen Book Reviewers."

2. *YA-zine, from HarperCollins*

http://www.harpercollins.com/kids/yazine.htm
Each issue of YA-zine features the words, sights, and sounds of the authors that we highlight [which have included Chris Lynch and Francesca Lia Block. Other features include] digital galleries of cover art & design, free sample chapters from new books—plus complete booklists for each author, words and music from each author, latest news and reviews of YA authors.

3. *Young Adult Reading*
http://www.docker.com/~whiteheadm/yaread.html
[L]ists and reviews of young adult literature suitable for teenagers. They have been compiled by Murray Whitehead, a language arts teacher working with middle years students.

4. *Vandergrift's YA Literature Page*
http://www.scils.rutgers.edu/special/kay/yalit.html
A long essay with plenty of embedded links concerning the YA and society, YA problems and concerns, YA literature and reader-response criticism, YA literature and feminist criticism, traditional literature for YAs, biographical and informational works for YAs, visual and electronic media and the YA, and research relating to YAs.

5. *Adolescent Literature Quick Author List*
http://www.epas.utoronto.ca:8080/~tfulk/authors.html
Attention all secondary education English/Language Arts teachers! This fall have your students do biographical research on their favorite authors. Then have them create a Web Page for that author. Send me the URL or give me the info and I'll create the Web Page.

LIST LINKS

1. *Literary Prizes: Fiction*
http://compstat.wharton.upenn.edu:8001/~siler/litlists.html
Includes lists for American Fiction Awards and Nobel Prize Winners in Literature.

2. *Contemporary and Modern Classics to Teach*
http://www.econoclad.com:80/whatsnew/contemp.html
A page from the late great Mike Printz, who writes:

Having served as a school librarian for 36 years, I know that language arts teachers are always searching for different titles to teach. The following two lists are compiled as a result of consulting some of the teachers with whom I worked and other veteran teachers that I have surveyed in different parts of the country. I hope these bibliographies are helpful.

3. *ALA "Best" Lists*
   http://www.ala.org/booklist/best.html
   All the lists fit to print, including Notable Books, Best Books for Young Adults, Notable Children's Books, Quick Picks for Reluctant Young Adult Readers, Notable Children's Computer Software. and Selected Videos for Young Adults.

4. *Literature for Teens: Writers' Recommendations*
   http://www.bookwire.com/hmr/Review/recom.html
   Put together by the *Hungry Mind Review*, this page is based on project in which the editor "approached a number of writers and asked each of them to select a book that strongly influenced them at that time in their own life, or a book that they have read subsequently, which they feel would have strong appeal for contemporary teenage readers."

5. *Vandergrift's 100: List of Young Adult Authors and Titles*
   http://www.scils.rutgers.edu/special/kay/100list.html
   This list, which changes each year, is a very small portion of the wealth of literature published for young adults. Some books of historical significance stay on the list while some new titles are added. Many of the titles are in paperback, and almost all will be in public libraries. This list is intended to provide guidance for those unfamiliar with literature for young adults, but it is certainly not exhaustive.

PUBLISHING LINKS

1. *Econoclad*
   http://www.econoclad.com:80/
   Welcome to our new Web site, our most recent addition to quality service. We invite you to browse our online electronic catalog of more than 19,000 titles, download a Redi-Notes teacher's guide, check out new products, or read an article in Noteworthy, the Econo-Clad quarterly newsletter.

   This site is worth visiting for its numerous booklists.

2. *Ingram Book Group*
   http://www.ingrambook.com/

   [Information from jobber about] Ingram and its services, bestseller lists, new titles recently received, & much more, Web Site for Librarians, press releases, Internet gateway to the World Wide Web of the Book Industry.

3. *The Multicultural Publishing and Education Council Home Page*
   http://www.quiknet.com/mbt/mpec/mpec.html
   The Multicultural Publishing and Education Council (MPEC) is a national networking and support organization for independent publishers, authors, educators, and librarians fostering authentic multicultural books and materials. [Web site includes information about] What Is an Authentic Multicultural Book? Multicultural News Update; News of Multicultural Publishers and Educational Networks; Multicultural Publishers and Resources; and MPEC Multicultural Recommended Book List & Awards.

4. *The BookWire Index Children's Publishers*
   http://www.bookwire.com/index/Childrens-Publishers.html
   No more than an index, this is a regularly updated list to publishers. Many of the houses that do children's books also have YA lines, so this is one of the better lists. Annotated with direct links, a must for everyone trying to keep up with publishers' home pages on the Net.

5. *Scholastic Central*
   http://www.scholastic.com/
   A page that is just loaded—there are book clubs, magazines for both teens and teachers, plus a variety of other resources. Some parts of the page are free, others requiring "joining a club." Still, a good page demonstrating probably where publishers pages are heading: you didn't think they were going to continue to give it away, did you?

PROFESSIONAL LINKS

1. *American Library Association*
   http://www.ala.org/
   Web site containing links to AASL, YALSA, plus a host of other information resources.

2. *The Assembly on Literature for Adolescents*
   http://english.byu.edu/alan.html
   Information about the history of this association, its convention, award, foundation, and publications, plus links to other sites on YA literature.

3. *Booklist*
   http://www.ala.org/booklist/index.html

This Web site is designed to introduce *Booklist* to a new group of readers and to provide current subscribers with additional services and points of access. By clicking on the appropriate text below, you can examine a current selection of reviews, enjoy a wealth of feature articles, or consult a newly developed cumulative index not available in the print *Booklist*.

4. *School Library Media Research*
http://copper.ucs.indiana.edu/~callison/home.html
School Library Media Research is intended to be a cross-disciplinary and refereed journal devoted to the study of information literacy for children and young adults. Manuscripts are based on original research and are usually constructed on methods which are experimental, theoretical, or naturalistic. Survey and descriptive studies will be considered, provided they represent a substantial population. Content of accepted manuscripts should provide better understanding for the application of inquiry methods, library collections, and information services to youth, and the use of information in all formats to a wide variety of learning environments.

5. *Wisconsin Division for Libraries and Community Learning's Library Resource List*
http://www.state.wi.us/agencies/dpi/www/lib_res.html
This is primarily a meta-listing of "over 450 Internet resources that will be of interest to the library community." It is divided into several basic sections, including information about search engines, reference sites, education resources, and library sites.

EDUCATIONAL LINKS

1. *Big Six*
http://edWeb.sdsu.edu/edfirst/bigsix/bigsix.html
The Big Six Skills is a product of Mike Eisenberg and Bob Berkowitz. This Web page includes a basic overview of the Big Six Skills, actual Instructional Units, a glossary of terms, additional resources of interest to Big Six users and informational specialists, a directory of Big Six users and institutions, and finally, information about the folks who made the site possible.

2. *National Center for Education Statistics*
http://www.ed.gov/NCES/
The National Center for Education Statistics fulfills a Congressional mandate to collect, collate, analyze, and report complete statistics on the condition of American education; conduct and publish reports; and review and report on education activities internationally.

3. *Kathy Schrock's Guide for Educators*
http://www.capecod.net/Wixon/wixon.htm
A classified list of sites on the Internet found to be useful for enhancing curriculum and teacher professional growth. It is updated daily to keep up with the tremendous number of new World Wide Web sites. Also links to Internet tutorials, authoring tools, and even a slide show explaining the difference between search engines and directories.

4. *Michigan Electronic Library—Education Section*
http://mel.lib.mi.us/education/education-index.html
Here is a huge list of education-related sites, including a list of "What's New?" followed by "All Sites Listed Alphabetically" and a "Subject Index." Subjects include "Education Associations and Organizations, Education Journals and News, Hot Topics in Education, Research in Education, Resources for Educators, State Education Departments, and U.S. Department of Education."

5. *Ask ERIC*
http://ericir.syr.edu/
AskERIC is . . . the award-winning Internet-based education information service of the ERIC System, headquartered at the ERIC Clearinghouse on Information & Technology at Syracuse University. Because AskERIC is also a Sun SITE repository, AskERIC is able to expand the quality and quantity of its resources and services to the education community. AskERIC is composed of three major components: AskERIC Q & A Service, AskERIC Virtual Library and AskERIC R&D.

ADOLESCENCE LINKS

1. *Youth Indicators*
http://www.ed.gov/NCES/pubs/yi/
This edition of Youth Indicators marks the fourth edition of a series that was first issued in 1988. Youth Indicators is a statistical compilation of data on family structure, jobs, education, and other elements that comprise the world of young people. The report includes chapters on the home environment, including demographics, family composition, and family income; the school environment, including school descriptions, outcomes, and out-of-school experiences; health; citizenship and values; and students' futures.

2. *Center for Adolescent Studies Home Page*
http://education.indiana.edu/cas/cashmpg.html
The Center for Adolescent Studies focuses on meeting the social

and emotional growth and development needs of adolescents through providing support to adults working with youth, investigating current social issues, and providing tools for teens to learn and practice new, healthy behaviors.

This site includes the *Adolescence Directory Online (ADOL)* (http://education.indiana.edu/cas/adol/adol.html)

3 *Great Transitions: Preparing Adolescents for a New Century*
http://www.carnegie.org/reports/great_transitions/gr_intro.html
Selected sections for the concluding report of the Carnegie Council on Adolescent Development:

[A] key lesson from its experience is the importance of careful examination of the facts, nonpartisan analysis, broad dissemination with the involvement of key sectors, and sustained commitment over a period of years. Above all, a long-term view is essential if there is to be any progress in bringing about the difficult yet fundamental changes necessary to improve the life chances of all our young people.

4. *YouthInfo*
http://youth.os.dhhs.gov/
A new information resource developed by the U.S. Department of Health and Human Services to provide you with the latest information about America's adolescents. YouthInfo currently includes the following: a statistical profile of America's teenagers; new reports and publications about adolescents; information for parents of teens; speeches by federal officials on youth topics; and links to youth-related Web sites at HHS, other federal agencies, private foundations, and research organizations.

5. *Welcome to MiddleWeb*
http://www.middleWeb.com/
A World Wide Web site exploring the challenges of middle grades' reform, with a special focus on urban middle schools.

TEEN LINKS: GENERAL

1. *Teen Hangout*
http://www.Webcom.com/searay/
The Teen Hangout is a Web site for teens made only by teens. As the Web grows in size and confusion, the Teen Hangout staff is dedicated to starting innovative projects that we can participate in around the Net. No gimmicks. No cheap tricks. All we are trying to accomplish is to be the "center" for teens on the Net.

2. *Cyberteens*
   http://www.cyberteens.com/
   Our goal is to create and promote youth community worldwide, and give teens a voice and an interactive place to express their creativity. Young people all over the world make Cyberteens a sharing, caring space. When a teen posts a message on the Cyberteens b-board about a problem he or she is having, the Cyberteen community jumps in with support and helpful information. For example, when someone asked what to do about a friend afflicted with an eating disorder, many teens gave advice from their own experiences, and the editors published links to anorexia and bulimia Web sites.

3. *Cyberspace Middle School*
   http://www.scri.fsu.edu/~dennisl/
   Cyberspace Middle School is designed for students in the 6th, 7th, 8th, and 9th grades who are using the World Wide Web to help get an education and work on science fair projects.

4. *High School Central*
   http://www.azc.com/client/enn2/hscentral.htm
   A cool gathering environment for high school students. As we progress, you'll find everything you could possibly think of and more.

5. *The Student Center*
   http://studentcenter.infomall.org/
   An organization for college students, high school students, and teenagers. There's plenty of serious information, lots of entertainment, and an entire section dedicated to students communicating with each other.

TEEN LINKS: SPECIAL

1. *Teen Advice Online*
   http://www.winternet.com/~tfenner/advice/
   A group of intelligent and caring teens volunteering our time and effort toward helping resolve your teenage dilemmas. Can't figure out what to buy your sister for her birthday? Having relationship troubles? Problems with your parents? If you are trapped in a predicament that you need settled, feel free to give Teen Advice a try. We'll offer a variety of possible solutions to aid you in making the right decision.

2. *CollegeNET*
   http://www.collegenet.com/

CollegeNET lets you conveniently browse institutions by various criteria including geography, tuition, and enrollment. Note that each list you generate bubbles "checked" colleges to the top. Checked schools are profiled by CollegeNET's colorful, easy-to-read "AT-A-GLANCE" pages. Becoming familiar with the "AT-A-GLANCE" page format enables you to quickly locate key information about a school and to easily compare one college to another.

3. *College Board Online*
   http://www.collegeboard.org/
   The authoritative educational and information resources of the College Board into homes and offices around the world via the World Wide Web. Here students and parents will find the Web's most comprehensive menu of information to aid in the transition from school to college. Educators will find an expanding array of up-to-date information about familiar College Board tests, programs, and services.

4. *The Vegetarian Youth Network*
   http://www.geocities.com/RodeoDrive/1154/
   An informal, grassroots, nonprofessional organization run entirely by, and for, teenagers who support compassionate, healthy, globally aware, vegetarian/vegan living. The Network is committed to providing support and encouragement to vegetarian youth through programs that emphasize communication (by mail, phone, and e-mail).

5. *Society for Creative Anachronism*
   http://www.sca.org/
   The Society for Creative Anachronism (SCA), is an international organization dedicated to researching and recreating pre-17th-century European history. All persons interested in such study are invited to use these pages to obtain information about the SCA.

TEEN-EZINES

1. *Writes of Passage*
   http://www.writes.org/index.htm
   Writes of Passage is the outlet for teens who are creative, talented, and have something to say. It is the literary organization that takes young writers seriously and provides opportunities for them to showcase their work. By providing a forum for topics important to teens, *Writes of Passage* inspires creativity and communication. It features poems and stories that reveal the

truth, fears, confusion, excitement, controversy, and reality of teenage life. And it offers educators an exciting new way to encourage their students to write.

2. *The Edge at Fishnet*
http://www.jayi.com/Open.html
Just an excellent example of an ezine: sophisticated, timely, and on-target. The ezine is part of the large Fishnet environment, which contains information on colleges and universities and weird facts, among other content.

3. *Virtually React*
http://www.react.com/
Produced by *Parade* magazine, this site allows users to interact with other teens, answer polls, find sites of interest, and shop. In addition, a user can "download the react sound sensation."

4. *Troom*
http://www.troom.com/index2.html
Ezine featuring " My Diary, Cooltunes, Reflections, Top Drawer, Looking Good, Sports and Fitness, Answer Girl, Calendar, Pen Pal Club, and Gameline." Sponsored by Tampax, the page's motto is, "A Place You'll Want to Visit More Than Once a Month."

5. *XX Empowered Young Females*
http://www.eyf.com/
This magazine is about the strength, intelligence, love, and power that girls have to offer. *XX Empowered Young Females* is for girls of all colors, shapes, sizes, and styles.

The number of people using the Internet increases daily and dramatically, and a lot of these users are teenagers. Many get their first exposure in a school setting for research purposes, but they soon find the recreational options as well. The information available, likewise, changes daily: the Internet transforms itself every year it seems, at first a place to "gopher" into university computers, then filled with pages of organizations, next loaded down with personal pages, and now being consumed by commercial pages. Concerns about the amount of traffic and the lack of filters, not to mention the overall impact of the Internet on learning, get hashed out daily. More people are getting connected, more information is becoming available, and libraries must be part of it to stay relevant.

Libraries didn't die out when the radio appeared, or television, or book clubs. Libraries didn't die when every mall got a bookstore and then a "super" bookstore. Libraries didn't die when the card catalogs, *Reader's Guide,* and shelf lists vanished. Libraries have not died because they perform an important, traditional, even indispensable function: they connect people and information. The world is not yet digitized, nor is every magazine online; traditional print sources will remain with us for some time. And the role of librarians remains the same: going out into the world of information available, selecting from it, organizing it, and making it easily accessible.

ENDNOTES

1. Dave Kinnaman, "Critiquing Acceptable Use Policies," 1995. URL:http://gnn.com/gnn/meta/edu/features/archive/aup.html

2. *Guide for Written Collection Policy Statements*. Collection Management and Development Guides, No. 3. American Library Association, 1989.

3. *Access to Electronic Information, Services, and Networks: An Interpretation of the Library Bill of Rights*. American Library Association, 1996.

4. Charles McClure, et al., *Planning and Role Setting for Public Libraries: A Manual of Operations and Procedures*. American Library Association, 1987: 43.

5. Carolyn Caywood, "Selection Criteria for WWW Resources," 1995. URL:http://duckdock.acic.com/carolyn/criteria.htm

6. G. Edward Evans, *Developing Library and Information Center Collections*, 3rd ed. Englewood: Libraries Unlimited, 1995: 260–292.

7. Bette Ann Hubbard, et al., "Newest Members of the Net Set," *Library Journal* (February 1, 1996): 44–46.

8. Scott McCartney, "Society's Subcultures Meet by Modem: For Teens, Chatting on Internet Offers Comfort of Anonymity," *Wall Street Journal* (Eastern Edition, December 8, 1994): B1+.

9. Frances F. Jacobson, "What Students Expect of the Internet," *American Libraries* (November 1995): 1030.

10. John Markoff, "The Keyboard Becomes a Hangout for a Computer-Savvy Generation," *New York Times* (Late New York Edition, August 31, 1993): A1+.

11. *Ibid*.

12. Carolyn Caywood, "Narrow Searches, Narrow Minds," *School Library Journal* (November, 1995): 38.

13. "Censorship Watch," *American Libraries* (March, 1996): 15.

14. Kinnaman, 1995.

15. Marilyn Gell Mason., "Sex, Kids, and the Public Library," *American Libraries* (June/July 1997): 104.

16. Mason, p. 106.

17. David Burt, "Policies for the Use of Public Internet Workstations in Public Libraries," *Public Libraries* (May/June 1997): 159.

18. "To Filter or Not To Filter?" *American Libraries* (June/July 1997): 100–102.

19. Julie Todaro, "New Tools of the Trade: 48 Essential Net Resources for Librarians," *School Library Journal* (November 1996): 24–29.

20. Gus Venditto, "Critic's Choice: Six Sites that Rate Web Sites," *Internet World* (January 1997): 83–96.
21. Kate Murphy, "Moving from the Card Catalogue to the Internet: To Control the Information Glut, Librarians Become More Technologically Oriented," *New York Times* (January 6, 1997): C15.
22. *Services and Resources for Children and YAs in Public Libraries*, U.S. Dept. of Education, Office of Educational Research and Improvement, National Center for Education Statistics, p. 10.
23. New York Public Library, "Teen Links," http://www.nypl.org/branch/teen/teenlink.html (February 7, 1997).
24. Sara Ryan, "The Internet Public Library Teen Division," *The Internet Trend Watch for Libraries* (January 1997).
25. Andrew Kantor and Michael Neubearth, "Off the Charts: State of the Internet 1996," *Internet World* (December 1996): 45+.

MAY

Goal: To train other staff on quality services to YAs.

1. **Make an investment:** We're back to that same logical base; it is a poor investment of a library's resources not to serve YAs well. That means, everyone serves them well. If you have done many of the things listed in this book, it will all be for nothing if the YAs coming into the library meet up with the "desk clerk from hell." Make your director realize that unless all staff gets YA training, then all the money spent on youth services is simply wasted.

2. **Find someone else:** Remember that you just work there—you are not an expert. For YA training, bring in an outsider. This does not mean you must blow $1,000 on some motivational speaker; instead, try calling some of those people you met in March and April. A librarian from another system, a guidance counselor, a minister in charge of youth groups, or anyone else who can help provide insight into the YA world can do a successful training for your staff. Finally (and best), consider working with a group of YAs (you know, that group you put together last February) on some training. They could do role playing or simply state their concerns. In particular, consider asking a high school librarian to talk with staff about not just reference work with YAs, but about solutions to problems of mass assignments and other horrors. This could also be a *quid-pro-quo* because by inviting the school librarian to talk at "your" library, it might be easier now to address a teacher or department about coming in to speak to their school.

3. **Read the literature:** The new edition of *Youth Participation in Libraries* has great stuff on staff training. It has a wonderful section with lots of exercises. There are also many easy-to-use/out-of-the-box training activities in this book as well (see 10.4).

4. **Set high expectations of quality:** Let others know what makes a good YA librarian and provide ample praise when they hit the mark. Unless staff know your expectations of them, then they cannot really give quality service. Building support emerges from building quality.

5. **Model behavior:** Some learn by doing; others by watching. One of the most effective training techniques in your toolkit is your behavior: demonstrate day-in and day-out how to do it right.

10 YA TRAINING

"Those damned kids" is a good starting point. The continued frustration and constant complaining of some staff members in dealing with YAs should alert you to the fact that something is amiss. We become frustrated with things we don't understand, that we don't know how to deal with, and that we are a little afraid of.

So there's a problem regarding knowledge, skills, and attitudes. Deficiencies in any of these areas negatively affect YA services and demonstrate a need for training. But if there is a need for training, what needs to be learned? Setting clear and measurable learning objectives directly tied to these needs and recognizing the unique traits of the adult learner will increase the quality of training. Finally, training should not just be lectures: using active learning exercises means training not only has a better chance of "sticking"; it also is more interesting, enjoyable, and memorable.

10.1 THE NEED FOR TRAINING

The NCES surveys revealed two major and contradictory facts: many public library users are YAs, and few public librarians are YA librarians. This is a vacuum that training can fill. Although there are staff who will never learn to work well with YAs (the classic kid-haters), many would like to, but don't have the tools. This book (along with documents like *Bare Bones* and *Output Measures*) is a good starting point. The problem with the book approach, however, is twofold. First, using this book in the first place indicates some self-motivating behavior. Second, not everyone learns best by reading. Some people learn best by doing, some by seeing. Some learn best alone, some in small groups, others only in large groups. Regardless, training is a key to improving YA services. Everyone in the building should be trained on the *who, what, when, where, why,* and *how* of serving YAs.

One of the outgrowths of the first NCES survey and *Bare Bones* was YALSA's "Training the Trainer" program. Writing about the program in *American Libraries*, YALSA member Karen Sipos noted:

> [R]ecognizing the dearth of young adult service specialists, and admitting the reality that probably won't change in that in the near future, YALSA decided in 1994 that it was time to give everyone a chance who works with teens—generalists, children's librarians, adults' services staff—the tools they need to do a good job. Toward

that end, ALA staff and member leaders created a group of "on call" trainers, committed YA specialists who were leaders in the field.[1]

The YA specialists receiving training agreed to return to their home libraries, regions, or states and provide training sessions aimed at generalists. The types and sizes of workshops have varied, from small groups to large auditoriums filled of people. In most cases, the YALSA trainer tried to impart a little knowledge and teach a few skills, but primarily worked at changing the attitudes of trainees toward YAs.

10.2 THE GOALS OF TRAINING

The goals of YA training workshops will be different, considering the time allotted and the needs of the hosting library. A generic training might cover the core of YA services generalists need to know. Of course, there are many things not listed here: serving YAs requires character traits like those listed in the quality-for-quality services section. Some of these traits can be learned; others perhaps are innate. There are two methods of transforming work behaviors (getting people unstuck). The first is changing people's goals or convincing them their current strategies won't allow them to reach their goals. If the librarian's goal is simply to be less frustrated, the answer is *not* expecting YAs to change their behavior; the librarian needs to change the goal. The second method is to provide skills, knowledge, and a YAttitude. This allows a change in strategies for serving YAs. This "image theory" also can work at the organizational level.[2] If the library's overall goal is to be a provider of quality service, *not* serving YAs won't get the library to that goal.

Yet the key to effective training isn't teaching, but learning. Learning "happens when a concept, an aptitude, or a body of knowledge is understood, assimilated and mastered by the learner."[3] Trainers need to try to get into the heads of their learners by asking themselves, "If I were attending this workshop, what would I need to know, and what would be the best way to learn it?" That is why I use the genealogist as an example of my own bias: if there was a workshop called "Connecting Genealogists and Libraries," what type of information would change my attitude? One of the big differences between training adults and teaching youth is who drives the training: it is not the teacher's but the learner's agenda that matters most.

What Generalists Need to Know About

YA Psychology
1. Developmental tasks
2. Behaviors
3. Redirecting behavior

YAs in Libraries
1. How YAs use libraries
2. Why YAs use libraries
3. Why YAs need libraries
4. Why libraries should serve YAs

Services
1. Planning/evaluating
2. Staffing skills (YALSA competencies/YALSA vision)
3. Issues: intellectual freedom, confidentiality, etc.

Collections
1. What to buy; what's best (subjects/formats)
2. How to buy it (resources)
3. Why to buy it (justifying popular materials)

Homework Support
1. Reference interview
2. Proactive reference
3. Why help with homework (justifying educational support role)

Promoting Services
1. Merchandising/marketing
2. Booktalking
3. Outreach

Programming
1. How to plan
2. What works
3. YA advisory boards

Other
1. Technology
2. Readers' advisory
3. Teen volunteers

10.3 TIPS AND TOOLS FOR TRAINING

What follows is a list of the elements of success. These 26 strategies are general concepts applicable to the training of adult learners and adapted to YA training—an A-to-Z approach to training.

A **Anecdotes:** As any good writer will tell you, "Don't just tell me, *show me*." Illustrate important points with personal experiences, examples in short anecdotes, or slogans. Give participants an image or memory to hang a concept on in order to increase retention.

B **Brainstorming:** Action learning requires participants to act by thinking. Brainstorming sessions get participants thinking and acting.

C **Closing:** The last thing you do as a presenter is have the participants take the first step in transferring the training: ask them to write action plans or sign pledges.

D **Discussion/dialogue:** Participants will often learn more from each other than from you if you provide them chances for discussion and dialogue.

E **Experiences, practical:** Everyone in training wants to know the same thing: "What's in it for me?" So part of training is demonstrating practical application of the ideas to your own work experiences and allowing participants to share their own success stories.

F **Flip charts:** In groups of fewer than 50 participants, use flip charts to record main points, make lists, and so on. Either prepare these beforehand or make them up on-site. For larger groups, consider using an overhead projector or a computer with PowerPoint and a projector.

G **Group work:** Because people are social animals, allow participants many chances to work together. Consider changing groups (use colored name tags) or varying group sizes.

H **Handouts:** Librarians love handouts. They always want documentation, bibliographies, and examples. Handouts should supplement material, not replace the presentation. Consider using different colors, page numbers, or three-ring binders to make handouts easy for participants to use during and after training. Most generalists want bibliographies, sample forms, and lists of resources (magazines, review sources, etc.).

I **Involve everyone:** Not everyone will ask questions or speak in small groups, so look for ways to involve everyone. You might accomplish this by using small groups or teams, or a question to large group for which everyone provides a short answer.

J **Jobs, during breakouts:** To make things more efficient, in small groups assign or ask participants to assume various jobs, such as recorder, presenter, or facilitator.

K **Kickstart beginnings:** Get participants' attention by using a booktalk, a quiz, or perhaps a statistic. Don't just leap into training. Classic icebreakers work as well.

L **List making:** Let participants leave with a variety of lists: five things to do, 10 magazines to buy, and so on. Organize information in lists to increase retention.

M **Mix up a variety of techniques:** Use more than one technique in training. It keeps participants interested and involved if each segment is a little different.

N **Nonverbal:** Presenters communicate with more than words. Movement adds to the learning experience and forces participants to do something (move their eyes to follow you). It also lets you "belong" to different sections of the room at various times.

O **Outlines:** Participants need to know *what* they are going to learn, *when* they are going to learn it, and *how* they are going to learn it. Providing an outline lets them follow along and chart progress.

P **Play games:** Training doesn't have to be all work: training games are fun and reinforce points along the way. You might include role-playing, cooperation exercises, or other activities that involve the learner in doing (and thus learning) something.

Q **Questions throughout:** Answer and record questions throughout: let participants get information when they need it. If you don't know the answer, don't try to fake it; instead, see whether anyone else in the audience has ideas.

R **Repetition:** Training sessions should have themes, and you should revisit those themes throughout and review them after each segment. For example, after introducing "developmental needs of young adolescents" return to the list often to relate information back to the core idea.

S **Synthesizing:** Adult learners need time to process information. They need to think about what they've learned and how it relates to their experience and their situation.

T **To-dos:** Ask participants to develop lists of actions they intend to take based on their learning. Then ask each one to share one item with the group.

U **Utility—stress the practical:** Always stress the transfer of training by outlining practical steps participants can take after each segment.

V **Visual aids:** Most participants learn visually, so use overheads, charts, videos, multimedia (such as PowerPoint presentations), or other aids to make and reinforce points.

W **Wit and humor:** Participants are more likely to believe what you say if they like you; they are more likely to apply what they've learned if they leave feeling good about the training. A little bit of humor goes a long way to achieve both of these goals.

eX **Expectations—discover and deliver:** Ask the organizer to give you an idea of the group's expectations. Outline what you understand these to be early in the training, and be flexible about modifying to accommodate new expectations. Expectations are questions; learning objectives provide the answers.

Y **Yakking/lecture:** For many content areas, the best way to train is to lecture. Participants do expect lectures, but using many of the techniques listed here turns something passive into something more active and enjoyable.

Z **ZZZ:** Participants need opportunities for breaks (it might even be in their union contracts); not just for bathroom trips, but to recharge, visit, and process information.

These elements of success run throughout the literature on training, which is plentiful. Before conducting a training session, consult some of the tools of the trade and learn some sound presentation strategies. Knowing the content area is not enough; you must understand your audience, their needs, and how they learn.

Most training sessions are divided into three segments: the opening, the content, and the closing. For each of these segments there are different types of learning activities that work best. The type of learning method you choose will depend on the size of your audience (you can't do a lot of these in a group of 200), their knowledge, and your own training style. As with booktalking, training involves adapting techniques to your own particular performance style to make for a successful venture. Training and booktalking are similar also in that the purpose of both is to get your audience to *do* something: in booktalking, it is to read; in training, it is to transfer the learning to their environment. How well they transfer learning depends not just on what they learn but on how they learn it.

Top Training Tools: Bib Squib

Tom Bourner, *Workshops That Work: 100 Ideas to Make Your Training Events More Effective.* New York: McGraw-Hill, 1995.

Douglas Fleming and Barbara Fleming, *Tactics for Trainers: A Workshop Leader's Guide.* Lunenberg, MA: School Strategies & Options, n.d.

Lois Hart, *Training Methods That Work.* Los Altos, CA: Crisp Publications, 1991.

Robert Jolles, *How to Run Seminars and Workshops: Presentation Skills for Consultants, Trainers, and Teachers.* New York: John Wiley & Sons, 1993.

Ken Jones, *Imaginative Events for Training: A Trainer's Sourcebook of Games, Simulations, and Role-Play Exercises.* New York: McGraw-Hill, 1993.

Gary Kroehnert, *100 Training Games.* New York: McGraw-Hill, 1994.

Lawrence S. Munson, *How to Conduct Training Seminars: A Complete Reference Guide for Training Managers and Professionals.* New York: McGraw-Hill, 1992.

Carolyn Nilson, *Games That Drive Change.* New York: McGraw-Hill, 1995.

Tony Pont, *Developing Effective Training Skills: A Practical Guide to Designing and Delivering Group Training,* 2nd ed. New York: McGraw-Hill, 1996.

Edward E. Scannell and John W. Newstrom, *The Complete Games Trainers Play: Experiential Learning Exercises.* New York: McGraw-Hill, 1995.

Effective Openings
1. Anecdote
2. Audience survey
3. Challenge questions
4. Icebreakers
5. Quotations/cartoons
6. Reading poems, letters, etc.
7. Analogies, metaphors
8. Starting statistics
9. True-false quiz
10. Word games/puzzles

Source: Adapted from Douglas Fleming and Barbara Fleming, *Tactics for Trainers: A Workshop Leader's Guide.* School Strategies & Options, n.d.

10.4 TRAINING EXERCISES

The following represent some of the most successful training exercises I've used. For each exercise, you will find:

- The exercise title
- The subject and section of this book to which the exercise pertains
- Learning objectives
- Strategies (with variations)
- The time and materials needed

Most of these exercises involve small-group work (four to five people). Although they represent different types of active learning exercises, most are based on simple problem-solving models.

EXERCISE #1: YA FAMILY FEUD

See also: By the Numbers (7.2)

Objectives:
1. Create awareness of YAs and their world
2. Provide information on statistics related to YA trends
3. Develop strategies for libraries to respond

Training Tips and Strategies

The Learning Cycle
1. Presentation of learning activity
2. Participants' response
3. Applications/transfer of training

Characteristics of Adult Learners
1. Decide for themselves what is important
2. Need to validate information based on beliefs
3. Expect learning to be of immediate use
4. Have many past experiences to draw upon
5. Are problem-centered
6. Will actively participate
7. Function best in collaborative environment

Does Your Training:
1. Focus on practical problems?
2. Emphasize practical application?
3. Relate learning to stated objectives?
4. Relate learning to past or present experiences?
5. Allow for debate, challenge, and exchange?
6. Encourage members to share information?

Introducing an Activity
1. State purpose
2. Rearrange furniture and participants
3. Elicit information on participants' knowledge and experience
4. Provide definitions
5. Give directions: explain *what* exactly will be done now and after
6. Distribute printed instructions and handouts
7. Ask for and answer questions
8. Demonstrate
9. Provide structure (time; who does what)
10. Review

Conducting the Activity
1. Circulate around the room; be available
2. Call group together if the same question on process recurs
3. Be alert to time
4. Observe interaction problems
5. Be ready to answer questions

Processing the Activity
1. Plan as much time to process as to conduct
2. Record participants' feedback and ideas
3. Expect differences; moderate discussion
4. Relate activity back to objectives
5. Relate activity to practical applications

Source: Adapted from Lois Hart, *Training Methods That Work.* Los Altos, CA: Crisp Publications, 1991.

Effective Active Learning Approaches

1. Behavior inventory
2. Brainstorming
3. Carousel brainstorming
4. Case studies
5. Mock game shows
6. Problem-solving
7. Role-playing
8. Scavenger hunt
9. Skit
10. Small group discussion and surveys

Source: Adapted from Douglas Fleming and Barbara Fleming, *Tactics for Trainers: A Workshop Leader's Guide.* School Strategies & Options, n.d.

Effective Closings

1. Answering challenge questions
2. Contracts/pledges
3. Emotional appeals
4. List-making
5. Objective review
6. Personal action plans
7. Remembrance
8. Ten commandments
9. Making and sharing to-do lists
10. Trend-telling

Source: Adapted from Douglas Fleming and Barbara Fleming, *Tactics for Trainers: A Workshop Leader's Guide.* School Strategies & Options, n.d.

Strategies:

1. Choose 10 people from the group, divide into two teams of five. Choose an emcee; the presenter acts as scorekeeper. Ask three other people to act as judges.
2. Invite one person from each team to come to the front of the room.
3. Ask one of the survey questions.
4. Contestants must guess other top answers; if they miss three, the question goes to the other team.
5. If the answer is correct, the scorekeeper writes it down on a pad and gives the team points based on the number of teens who provided that answer. If the answer is close, ask the judges to decide.
6. At the end of each round, use the overhead (see Figure 10–1) to show the complete survey.
7. Do as many rounds as possible.
8. The "winner" is the team with the most points.
9. Discuss the implications for libraries and develop strategies based on the discussion.
10. Play the same game, but use statistics from the NCES survey.

Time: 15 - 30 minutes

Materials: "Family Feud" overhead (Figure 10.1), flip chart, markers, overheads with statistics, prizes

EXERCISE #2: ACTION PLAN 2000

See also: Trends in YA Services (Chapter 1)

Strategies:

1. Discuss trends in services, provide overview of *why* the trends exist.
2. Assign each group one trend, and distribute large sheets of paper.
3. Ask each group to develop an action plan for its trend.
4. Action plans should include statements of goals, objectives, and tasks.
5. Action plans also should estimate cost in dollars, staff, and other resources.
6. Post the sheets and ask each group to explain its action plan.
7. Assign each group to come up with list of obstacles for another group's plan.
8. Share obstacles with groups (write them on large sheets and post them).
9. Ask third group to come up with solutions to obstacles on a third sheet.
10. Share these solutions with the group.

Figure 10–1 Family Feud Overheads

Top Leisure Activity of High School Seniors (1990 poll)

1.	Watch TV	72%
2.	Hang out	49%
3.	Read	47%
4.	Sports/exercise	46%
5.	Be alone	41%
6.	Work around the house	28%
7.	Cruise	28%
8.	Play or listen to music	28%

Best Time Teenagers Say They've Had
So Far (high school seniors)

1.	Getting driver's license	12%
2.	Winning sports championship	11%
3.	Starting high school	9%
4.	Sneaking out at night	8%
5.	Losing virginity	8%
6.	Academic achievement	8%
7.	First party without parents	7%
8.	Prom	6%

Top Concerns Facing the United States (1993)

1.	AIDS	21%
2.	Crime/gangs	15%
3.	Education	13%
4.	Racism/intolerance	6%
5.	Environment	5%
6.	Homelessness	3%
7.	Guns	2%

Reasons Teens Attempt Suicide (1991)

1.	Family problems	47%
2.	Depression	23%
3.	Problems with friends	22%
4.	Low self-esteem	18%
5.	Boy/girl relationships	16%

Source: Adapted from "The American Teenager:
By the Numbers," *Scholastic Update* (January 14, 1994): 2–10.

Time: 30 minutes or more

Materials: Flip chart paper, markers, tape

EXERCISE #3: TOP 10 STEREOTYPES

See also: Contradictions/Stereotypes (2.1)

Objectives:

1. Sensitize participants to the contradictions between young adults and libraries
2. Demonstrate that many "issues" are institutional in nature, rather than personal
3. Develop strategies to bridge these contradictions

Strategies:

1. Divide group into small groups and distribute flip chart paper.
2. Ask each group to make a list of 10 stereotypes about teenagers.
3. Ask each group to make a list of 10 stereotypes about libraries and librarians.
4. Have small groups post their lists and report on their discussions. Make a common list of answers.
5. Compare the two lists, pointing out similarities and differences.
6. Suggest solutions in areas of knowledge, skills, and attitudes.
7. As a variation, do stereotypes of YA librarians and library administrators.

Time: 10 - 30 minutes

Materials: Flip chart papers, markers

EXERCISE #4: TASKS FOR TASKS

See also: Developmental Tasks (2.2)

Objectives:

1. Inform participants about developmental tasks—why kids act and react the way they do
2. Provide practical solutions/to-do items
3. Establish that quality library services for YAs must be responsive to real needs

Strategies:

1. Distribute developmental needs handout (use Figure 10–2).
2. Divide into four small groups. Assign each group one of the needs.
3. Ask each group to come up with three negative behaviors associated with the developmental need and three positive.

4. List at least three practical things libraries can do to meet each need.
5. Report back and discuss.

Time: 10 - 20 minutes

Materials: "Tasks for Tasks" handout (see Figure 10–2), flip chart papers, markers

EXERCISE #5: THAT WAS THEN, THIS IS NOW

See also: YA Lives and Times (2.5)

Objectives:

1. Provide information on emotional experience of adolescence
2. Provide information on current trends in the lives of young adults
3. Examine similarities and differences between "then" and "now"

Strategies:

1. Divide group into pairs: one person acts as the adult, the other as the teenager.
2. Give each adult and teen the appropriate survey (use Figures 10–3 and 10–4).
3. Ask each to fill out then share the survey.
4. Ask them to switch roles and do survey as the other person.
5. Have them share information again.
6. Ask pairs to share information with the large group.

Time: 15 - 30 minutes

Materials: "That Was Then, This Is Now" handouts (see Figures 10–3 and 10–4), flip charts, markers, handouts

EXERCISE #6: A DAY IN THE LIFE

See also: YA Lives and Times (2.5)

Objectives:

1. Create awareness of YAs and their world
2. Provide information on research related to YA psychology
3. Develop strategies for libraries to respond

Strategies:

1. Provide each person with a handout containing nothing but a large circle in the middle.
2. Ask participants to make the circle into a pie chart, showing percentages of time they think teens spend in leisure, productive, and maintenance activities.
3. Divide into small groups.

Figure 10–2 Tasks for Tasks Handout

Tasks for Tasks Handout

Directions: For each developmental need of young adolescents, think of three concrete to-do items a library can pursue.

Physical activity: Boundless energy and dreamy lethargy; growing bodies need time to move and relax
1.
2.
3.

Competence and achievement: Self-conscious about themselves; need to do something well and receive admiration; need chances to prove themselves
1.
2.
3.

Self-definition: Need opportunities to explore the widening world and reflect upon new experiences and their roles
1.
2.
3.

Creative expression: Need to express new feelings and interests; need to understand and accept themselves
1.
2.
3.

Positive social interaction with peers and adults: Need support, companionship, and criticism; relationships with those willing to share
1.
2.
3.

Structure and clear limits: Need to know and understand rules of the system; search for security is helped by boundaries
1.
2.
3.

Meaningful participation: Need to express social and intellectual skills; gain a sense of responsibility
1.
2.
3.

Source: Task statements adapted from Leah Lefstein and Joan Lipsitz, *3:00 to 6:00 PM: Program for Young Adolescents.* Carrboro, NC: Center for Early Adolescence, 1991.

Figure 10–3 That Was Then, This Is Now (Adult)

When I was a teenager:

1. My favorite athlete was:
2. My favorite musical performer was:
3. My favorite type of music was:
4. My favorite activity was:
5. I spent the most time:
6. My favorite TV show was:
7. My favorite section of the newspaper was:
8. The word that was "in" was:
9. The word that just went "out" was:
10. The "in" clothes to wear were:
11. The "out" clothes to wear were:
12. The biggest problem facing me and other teens was:
13. My favorite book was:
14. My favorite movie was:
15. My favorite magazine was:
16. My favorite place to shop was:
17. The worst thing about being a teenager was:
18. The best thing about being a teenager was:

---

4. Give each group a large sheet of paper, also with a circle on it.
5. Ask each group for percentages for each activity, then subdivide each activity on handout (use Figure 10–5).
6. Ask them to "draw" this proportionally in pie chart form on the sheet of paper.
7. Display charts; note differences and discuss.
8. List strategies libraries could develop to respond to each activity.

Time: 15 - 30 minutes

Materials: "A Day in the Life" handout (use Figure 10–5), flip charts, tape, markers

---

Figure 10–4 That Was Then, This Is Now (Teen)

That Was Then, This Is Now (Teen)

1. My favorite athlete is:
2. My favorite musical performer is:
3. My favorite type of music is:
4. My favorite activity is:
5. I spend the most time:
6. My favorite TV show is:
7. My favorite section of the newspaper is:
8. The word that is "in" is:
9. The word that just went "out" is:
10. The "in" clothes to wear are:
11. The "out" clothes to wear are:
12. The biggest problem facing me and other teens is:
13. My favorite book is:
14. My favorite movie is:
15. My favorite magazine is:
16. My favorite place to shop is:
17. The worst thing about being a teenager is:
18. The best thing about being a teenager is

EXERCISE #7: BUILDING THE PERFECT YA LIBRARIAN

See also: Qualities for Quality Service (5.1)

Objectives:

1. Determine the traits of a successful YA librarian
2. Identify the most important traits
3. Introduce YALSA's *Young Adults Deserve the Best* document

Strategies:

1. Break into small groups.
2. Give participants a sheet listing skills, knowledge, and attitudes for YA librarian and a large sheet of paper.
3. Ask participants to choose the 10 most important traits for librarians serving young adults. They should prioritize traits from 1 to 10.
4. Each group will record its top 10 and post its sheet on the wall.
5. Ask one member of the group to discuss why the group ranked traits as it did.
6. Discuss in the large group a "model" for successful service.
7. Distribute YALSA document; compare to traits listed.
8. Keep results posted and refer back to them when discussing reference service.

Figure 10–5 A Day in the Life

A Day in the Life

Divide into percentages the amount of time you think YAs spend doing the following during their waking hours.

1. Leisure activities
2. Productive activities
3. Maintenance activities

Now, for each divide the percentage by the following specific activities.

1. Leisure activities
   A. Socializing
   B. Sports/games
   C. Watching TV
   D. Listening to music
   E. Arts/hobbies
   F. Thinking
   G. Napping/resting
   H. Nonschool reading
   I. Other (list)
2. Productive activities
   A. Classwork
   B. Studying
   C. Jobs/volunteering
   D. Other (list)
3. Maintenance activities
   A. Eating
   B. Personal care
   C. Transportation
   D. Other (list)

Now, represent these numbers on your sheet of paper in pie-chart form. Use blue markers for leisure, red markers for productive activity, and black markers for maintenance activity.

Time: 15 - 30 minutes

Materials: Handout (Figure 10–6), tape, markers, flip chart, transparency or handout of YALSA document

---

Figure 10–6 Building the Perfect YA Librarian

Building the Perfect YA Librarian

Energetic	Problem solver
Articulate	Complaint handler
Evaluative	Knowledge of computers
Planning minded	Intellectual freedom fighter
Ethical	Interior designer
Respectful	Reviewer
Disciplinarian	Merchandiser
Encouraging	Booktalker
Knows YA psychology	Discussion leader
Knows YA literature	Instructor
Knows YA pop culture	Organizer
Communicator	Reference librarian
Research minded	Politically skilled
Creative	Youth involver
Promoter	Empathetic
Budget minded	Rule breaker/risk taker
Sense of humor	Statistician
Fund raiser	Enthusiastic
Nonjudgmental	Patient/persistent
Cooperative	Approachable

EXERCISE #8: COOKIE CUTTER

See also: Reading Interests (4.3)

Objectives:

1. Relate popular reading to YA developmental tasks
2. Explore reasons for popularity of certain YA genres and formats
3. Discuss issues in YA collection development

Strategies:

1. Ask participants to bring in one YA book they have read.
2. Provide a checklist of emotional needs kids meet through books.
3. Ask several volunteers to run their books through the checklist.
4. Run an R.L. Stine, V.C. Andrews, or Stephen King title through the list.

Time: 10 - 20 minutes

Materials: Flip chart, markers, handout (Figure 10–7)

Figure 10–7 Meeting the Needs of YAs through Fiction

Fiction meets the emotional needs of YAs in these ways:

1. Reassures them that they are normal physically, mentally, emotionally, and socially
2. Presents opportunities for emotional independence from adults
3. Shows YAs how to resolve problems
4. Allow YAs to experience success
5. Enables them to picture satisfying relationships
6. Provides help establishing roles
7. Supports development of socially responsible behaviors
8. Helps YAs work out their personal philosophies
9. Furnishes opportunities for emotional engagement, pleasure, and relaxation

Adapted from "Meeting Kids' Emotional Needs Through Books" by Pat Scales (handout, Reading Connections conference) Indiana Dept. of Education, 1993.

EXERCISE #9: PRIORITIES!

See also: Setting Collection Priorities (4.5)

Objectives:

1. Create awareness for need to prioritize within YA collections
2. Demonstrate practical budgeting exercise
3. Encourage discussion of different collection development philosophies and practices

Strategies:

1. Divide into small groups.
2. Give each group $5,000 in play money.
3. Consider the following circumstances to be true:
   A. Adult librarian buys reference.
   B. Adult librarian hates kids.
   C. Adult librarian buys music.
   D. Adult librarian hates rap.
   E. YA collection is separate.
   F. YA collection is new.
4. Ask groups to complete the priorities document (see Figure 4–2) by dividing the $5,000 into various budget lines.
5. Ask groups to report on their budgets, including their discussion of choices.

Time: 15 - 30 minutes

Materials: Play money, flip chart, markers, priorities document

EXERCISE #10: LISTMANIA

See also: Fiction Collections (see 4.6)

Objectives:

1. Explore what YAs like in genre fiction.
2. Develop practical reading lists to use with YAs.
3. Make links between YA genre fiction and other media.

Strategies:

1. Divide group by reading interests or fiction genres.
2. Ask each group to list five things a YA might like about that genre.
3. Ask each group to list five authors who represent the genre.
4. Ask each group to list five titles that represent the genre.
5. Ask each group to list five nonfiction areas related to the genre.
6. Ask each group to list five movies or TV shows that represent the genre.
7. Ask each group to list the top element, top author, top title, top nonfiction area, and top movie or TV show that represent the very best of the genre.
8. As a variation, divide by age levels and come up with the best title for middle school, junior high, senior high, rampant reader, and reluctant reader.

Time: 30 minutes or more

Materials: Flip chart, markers, tape

EXERCISE #11: NEWSSTAND

See also: Periodical Collections (4.8)

Objectives:

1. Learn about different magazines for YAs
2. Learn why these magazines are of interest to YAs
3. List best magazines for teens

Strategies:

1. Divide into small groups.
2. Provide each group with a stack of YA magazines.
3. Ask each group to examine all magazines.
4. Ask each group to concentrate on certain magazines.
5. Discuss for each magazine:
   A. Intended audience
   B. Reading level
   C. Reasons for popularity
   D. Primary subject

    E.   Types of articles/regular features
    F.   "Problems"
6. After discussion, give each person magazine subscription cards for each title
7. Ask them to "vote" by handing in cards for their favorite magazines. Each person gets three votes. Report totals and discuss.

Time: 30 minutes or more

Materials: Lots of YA magazines and subscription cards

EXERCISE #12: WHO HAS THE PROBLEM?

See also: Reference Services (see 5.2)

Objectives:

1. Demonstrate common communication problems between YAs and librarians.
2. Learn from "negative" role models' positive reference skills.
3. Problem-solve training of staff with poor YA skills.

Strategies:

1. During break or lunch, recruit 10 participants.
2. Announce that the audience will be asked to identify the problem behavior and provide solutions.
3. Flash overhead of stereotypes of YA librarians and of YAs (refer to Chapter 2 for lists of stereotypes).
4. Choose two people to start, one playing a librarian, the other a YA.
5. Provide them with a broad outline of a reference scenario.
6. Tell participants they should attempt to role-play the stereotypes listed. You may ask participants to make it harder or easier on each other.
7. If the role-play seems to be lagging, yell, "Switch," and rotate in two new players. At this point, give more instruction on how each person should behave. Also allow the audience to provide direction.
8. Continue until everyone has rotated in at least once.
9. Afterward, ask participants to divide into small groups and figure out who had the problem, what the problem was, and what might be possible solutions.

Time: 30 minutes or more

Materials: Furniture to serve as reference desk, overhead of stereotypes (see 2.1).

Note: This exercise is based on a script written by *Bare Bones* co-author Jim Rosinia entitled, "What's Wrong With This Picture?"

EXERCISE #13: BLAMING THE VICTIM

See also: Reference/Cooperation (see 5.2 and 5.5)

Objectives:

1. Explore common problems in school and public library cooperation
2. Develop solutions to these problems
3. Learn how to organize information and time to better cooperate

Strategies:

1. Divide into small groups. Distribute "Blame the Victim" handout (Figure 10–10), listing examples of vexing homework problems in the form of reference questions.
2. For each question, ask small groups to determine the problem and list solutions.
3. Develop a list of the best solutions and strategies.

Time: 15 - 30 minutes

Materials: Questions, flip chart, markers, "Blame the Victim" handout (use Figure 10–8)

EXERCISE #14: "SWORDFISH"

See also: Schools and Library Cooperation (5.5)

Objectives:

1. Develop awareness of other agencies or organizations that serve YAs
2. Develop ideas on cooperative projects
3. Provide solutions to common problems related to networking

Strategies:

1. Divide into small groups.
2. Provide each group with a large sheet of paper and one of these topics:
   A. Educational
   B. Recreational
   C. Cultural
   D. Social/Political
   E. Business
   F. Local
3. Ask each group to brainstorm and list within their subject area names or types of organizations that serve youth. Ask for at least 10.
4. Ask a person from each group to come to the front of room and read the group's list.

Figure 10–8 Blame the Victim

- Do you have a copy of *The Scarlet Letter?* Everyone in the 10th grade has to read it.
- Do you have anything on Ponce De Leon? Everyone in my class is doing a report on him.
- I need magazines with pictures for my Current Events scrapbook. Do you have scissors?
- I need a fiction book set in Ancient Rome that is interesting and more than 200 pages.
- I need three newspaper articles on Chaucer.
- My teacher told me to find articles using the *Reader's Digest Guide.* Where is it?
- Which of these books on my summer reading list is good?
- I need original sources about the U.S. Constitution.
- Why are all the science project books on making a volcano checked out?
- My teacher won't let me read R.L. Stine for a book report. What else is good?
- How do you do an outline?
- Where can I buy a term paper?
- Is there an encyclopedia that would print out my report on Brazil for me?
- My teacher says you can tell me over the phone all the presidents in U.S. history.
- Who is Roy G. Biv?
- Why can I never find any books here about euthanasia?
- **Parent, with child:** He's doing a report about Lincoln that is due tomorrow. He has waited until the last minute, and now we need to find as much information as possible.
- **Parent, without child:** My daughter is doing a report on Lincoln that is due tomorrow. She has waited until the last minute, and now I need to find as much information as possible.

---

5. For each organization listed, ask the group to list at least two cooperative projects a library could do in cooperation with the organization. Put this on another big sheet.
6. Ask another person from each group to come to the front of room and post or read the group's list.
7. Ask groups to post their lists so that words are facing inward, leaving a blank sheet of paper facing the audience.
8. Draw a doorknob on a blank sheet of paper; tell the audience that all of these are great ideas. Ask why they aren't happening? Ask the small groups to come up with "passwords" or solutions to the problem of locked doors. They need to give specific solutions, not generic answers like, "Communicate better." Have them describe a strategy for cooperation.
9. Write these strategies down, then "open the door."
10. Distribute the "Programming Tapestry" handout (use Figure 10–9).

Time: 15– 30 minutes

Materials: Flip chart, markers, tape, "Programming Tapestry" handout (use Figure 10.9)

10.5 A TRAINING CHECKLIST

Training provides answers to asked and unasked questions. What follows is a training outline/checklist called "Young Adults 101: A (Real) Crash Course in Basic Library Service to Teens." I developed this outline with Stella Baker of the Allen County Public Library in Fort Wayne, IN. It is a training outline in the broadest sense: These all are questions you would want someone working with YAs to be able to answer.

PHILOSOPHY
- Why serve YAs?
- Who are they?
- What are they here for?
- Why don't they come?
- What are the YA roles of a public library?
- "What about all those damned noisy kids?"
- What is a service plan?
- Why are kids the way they are?
- Am I part of the problem or part of the solution?
- Should YAs have access to everything?

COLLECTIONS
- What should I weed?
- Should we buy magazines for YAs?
- What are the best selection tools?
- How do I know what to buy?
- What authors and what genres should I buy?
- What about nonfiction?
- What about nonprint?
- What about those R.L. Stine books?
- "But I don't have time to do selection!"
- Do I need a collection development policy?

PHYSICAL AREA
- What is a YA area?
- What is a YA collection?

Figure 10–9 Programming Tapestry

School-Related
student councils
class councils
social clubs
academic clubs
political clubs
cultural clubs
academic departments
parent organizations
advising departments
counseling services
school library

Youth Services
group homes
boys/girls clubs
YMCA/YWCA
Junior Achievement
youth counseling services
substance abuse programs
free clinic or health service
scholarship services
employment services
legal services
adolescent psychologists
social services

Youth-Related Businesses
exercise studios
gyms
bike shop
skateboard shops
hair salons
clothing stores
model shops
sporting goods stores
cable TV channels
radio stations

Community Contacts
martial arts schools
sports card stores
comic book stores
amusement parks
neighborhood centers
Red Cross

Cultural Agencies
museum
theater groups
musical groups
film societies
zoo or parks departments
colleges and universities
dance groups
photography studios
storytellers' guilds
writers' workshops
gaming groups

Agencies within the Library
children's department
reference/adult department
AV department
Friends of the Library
homebound services
subject specialists
other branches/libraries
consortiums
special services
nationwide programs
volunteer programs
colleagues

Big Business
publishers/author visits
national programs
magazine contests
foundations
national associations
game companies
software companies
chain bookstores
chain computer stores
fast food/teen employers

- What is merchandising?
- Why should we do it?
- How do we do it?
- What attracts kids to materials?
- What types of materials go in a YA area?
- What types of equipment go in a YA area?
- What is a perfect YA area?
- How can I use space creatively?
- How do I make it look attractive?
- "Shouldn't everything be where it belongs?

REFERENCE AND READERS' ADVISORY

- What is a homework center?
- What books are good for term papers?
- Why do a readers' advisory?
- How do you do a readers' advisory?
- What are the best readers' advisory tools?
- What "passive" techniques can be used?
- What makes a good YA booklist?
- Where can I find other YA booklists?
- What makes YA reference "different"?
- "That's not a toy!"

COOPERATION

- Whom do I talk to at a school?
- When is the best time to contact schools?
- How do I make contacts?
- How do I convince teachers to listen?
- Should teachers get special privileges?
- "Where did all these kids come from?"
- What organizations can we cooperate with?
- What types of services can we offer?
- Can cooperation be too successful?
- Why should we cooperate?

CLASS VISITS

- How do I schedule class visits?
- What should I include in a class visit?
- Are there things I should exclude from a class visit?
- How do I begin the visit?
- How do I communicate with teachers?
- "Why are all these kids here now?"
- How do I time things so a class visit goes smoothly?
- How do I know if my class visits are working well?

- How do I promote class visits?
- Are there handouts that can help?

EVALUATION
- How do I evaluate my services to YAs? (the big picture)
- How do I evaluate my services to YAs? (the local picture)
- "Why does this library suck?"
- "Why is this library so awesome?"
- Can teachers help?
- What does the staff say?
- Is it broke, and do I need to fix it?
- When do I know if I've succeeded?
- What would a user survey look like?
- How do I use circulation statistics?
- What other statistics might help measure success?

REDIRECTING BEHAVIOR
- Whose job is it anyway?
- How should I approach disruptive teens?
- How should I *not* approach disruptive teens?
- Is consistency "the hobgoblin of little minds"?
- What are responsible limits?
- What rules should I post?
- What if the staff have bad attitudes?
- Is every patron treated fairly?
- How do I train staff about YAs?

ENDNOTES

1. Karen Sipos, "Training Trainers in Teen Service," *American Libraries* (November 1996): 54–55.
2. T. R. Mitchell and W. F. Silver, "Image Theory and Organizational Decision Making," in *The Thinking Organization*, H. P. Sims, ed. San Francisco: Jossey-Bass, 1986: 293–316.
3. Frank O'Meara, "The Pedagogue's Decalogue: Techniques for Effective Training Sessions," *Training* (January 1993): 43.

JUNE

Goal: Evaluate formal educational support activities.

1. **Count the results:** If you put together a planning document, how well did you meet your own objectives? Measure in pure numbers how many class visits there were to and from the library; how many teacher meetings you attended, etc.

2. **Get input:** Ask other staff—maybe even do a survey—about their perceptions of how well the library met the needs of students. Because this is the "high profile" role, it is one that requires heavy-duty attention and evaluation by anyone involved. If staff has complaints or concerns, stress what solutions are available, with the bottom line always being the need for support from administration.

3. **Send thank-you notes:** Much like you sent thank-you notes to people in your own building, send one to every person in schools who helped you—from the principal to the school secretary. Let them know you appreciate their assistance—on the behalf of the kids who got the real benefit—and wish them a nice summer, reminding them that you will see them next year.

4. **Do collection development:** Go through the folder you have on each school. Study the assignments that gave the library the most trouble or those for which you had the fewest resources. Order now for next year, and think about multiple copies.

5. **Promote summer reading:** If you made contacts during the year with teachers, here is your payoff. You probably started this in May, but you will finish here. Promote the summer reading program, especially in the middle grades, by making school visits. There is no sense planning a program if you cannot take time to promote. Yes, the desk requires your presence, and working on the desk from 9:00 a.m until 3:00 p.m. will give you interaction with zero YAs; the same time spent at a school will let you encounter 300—so which is the better use of your and the library's time? Booktalk a few titles, but spend most of the time showing off different formats—tapes, CDs, magazines, videos, etc. The only contact many kids have with any library is to run in, photocopy the encyclopedia article, and leave. How can they check stuff out if they don't even know what the library has? Also, show off prizes. Don't say the prizes are "cool" because probably that's the wrong temperature, and they will figure it out for themselves. When you are at the school, make sure to snag summer reading lists: Did you collect these from schools? If not, this is your last chance. Do you have copies of the books on the list—multiple copies? Are copies of the list available for other staff?

APPENDIX A: YA PUBLISHERS DIRECTORY

SOURCES

The Children's Book Council, <http://www.CBCBooks.org>
Books in Print 1996–97, Volume 9. New Providence, NJ: R.R. Bowker, 1996.

ABC-CLIO
P.O. Box 1911
Santa Barbara, CA 93116
{nonfiction}
<http://www.abc-clio.com/>

ACE
(A division of Berkley Publishing Group)
200 Madison Avenue
New York, NY 10016
{science fiction}

AERIAL FICTION
(An imprint of Farrar, Straus and Giroux)
19 Union Square West
New York, NY 10003
{paperbacks}

ALYSON PUBLICATIONS
P.O. Box 4371
Los Angeles, CA 90078
{Gay & lesbian fiction/nonfiction}

ANDREWS & MCMEEL
4900 Main Street, 9th floor
Kansas City, MO 64112
{comics}

ARCHWAY PRESS
(An imprint of Simon and Schuster)
1230 Avenue of the Americas
New York, NY 10020
{paperbacks/series}

ARCO BOOKS
(An imprint of Macmillan)
1230 Avenue of the Americas
New York, NY 10020
{nonfiction}
<http://www.mcp.com/mgr/arco/>

ATHENEUM BOOKS FOR CHILDREN
(An imprint of Simon and Schuster)
1230 Avenue of the Americas, 4th Floor
New York, NY 10020
{fiction/nonfiction}

AVONOVA
(An imprint of William Morrow)
1350 Avenue of the Americas
New York, NY 10019
{science fiction}

AVON BOOKS
1350 Avenue of the Americas
New York, NY 10019
{paperbacks}
<http://www.avonbooks.com/">

BAEN PUBLISHING
(A division of Simon and Schuster)
P.O. Box 1403
Riverdale, NY 10471
{science fiction}
<http://www.baen.com/">

BALLANTINE BOOKS

(A division of Random House)
201 East 50th Street
New York, NY 10022
{paperbacks}

BANTAM BOOKS

(An imprint of Bantam Doubleday Dell)
1540 Broadway
New York, NY 10036
{fiction/nonfiction}

BANTAM DOUBLEDAY DELL BOOKS FOR YOUNG READERS

1540 Broadway
New York, NY 10036
{fiction/nonfiction}
<http://www.bdd.com/">

BARRON'S EDUCATIONAL

250 Wireless Blvd.
Hauppauge, NY 11788
{nonfiction}
<http://ads.barrons.com/>

BERKLEY/PACER

(An imprint of the Putnam Berkley Publishing Group)
200 Madison Avenue
New York, NY 10016
{paperbacks}

BETHANY HOUSE

11300 Hampshire Avenue S.
Minneapolis, MN 55438
{Christian fiction/nonfiction}

BLACKBIRCH PRESS

260 Amity Road
Woodbridge, CT 06525
{nonfiction}
<http://www.blackbirch.com/bbphtml/
blackbirch.html">

BRADBURY PRESS

(An imprint of Simon and Schuster)
1230 Avenue of the Americas
New York, NY 10020
{fiction}

BROWNDEER PRESS

(An imprint of Harcourt Brace and Company)
9 Monroe Parkway, Suite 240
Lake Oswego, OR 97035–1487
{fiction}

CANDLEWICK PRESS

2067 Massachusetts Avenue
Cambridge, MA 02140
{nonfiction}

CHELSEA HOUSE

1974 Sproul Rd, Suite #400
Broomall, PA 19008
{nonfiction}
<http://www.chelseahouse.com/">

CHRONICLE BOOKS

275 Fifth Street
San Francisco, CA 94103
{nonfiction}
<http://www.chronbooks.com">

CLARION BOOKS

215 Park Avenue South
New York, NY 10003
{fiction/nonfiction}

CLASSICS ILLUSTRATED

(An imprint of the Putnam Berkley Publishing Group)
200 Madison Avenue
New York, NY 10016
{paperbacks/comics}

CLIFF'S NOTES

P.O. Box 80728
Lincoln, NE 68501
<http://www.cliffs.com/>

COBBLEHILL BOOKS

(An affiliate of Dutton Children's Books/Penguin USA)
375 Hudson Street
New York, NY 10014
{fiction/nonfiction}

COLLIER BOOKS FOR YOUNG ADULTS

(An imprint of Simon and Schuster)
1230 Avenue of the Americas
New York, NY 10020
{fiction/nonfiction}

CRESTWOOD HOUSE

(An imprint of Silver Burdett)
299 Jefferson Rd.
Parisippany, NJ 07054
{nonfiction}

CROSSWAY BOOKS

(A division of Good News Publications)
1300 Crescent Street
Wheaton, IL 60817
{fiction/nonfiction}

CROWN BOOKS FOR YOUNG READERS

(A division of Random House)
201 East 50th Street
New York, NY 10022
{fiction/nonfiction}

DARK HORSE COMICS

10956 SE Main Street
Milwaukee, WI 97222
{comics/graphic novels}
<http://www.dhorse.com/>

DAW BOOKS

375 Hudson Street
New York, NY 10014
{science fiction}
<http://www.tadwilliams.com/daw.html">

DC COMICS

(A division of TimeWarner)
1700 Broadway
New York, NY 10019
{comics/graphic novels}
<http://www.dccomics.com/>

DEL REY

(An imprint of Ballantine Books)
201 East 50th Street
New York, NY 10022
{science fiction}
<http://www.randomhouse.com/delrey/">

DELACORTE BOOKS

(An imprint of Bantam Doubleday Dell)
1540 Broadway
New York, NY 10036
{fiction/nonfiction}

DIAL BOOKS FOR YOUNG READERS

(A division of Penguin USA)
375 Hudson Street
New York, NY 10014
{fiction/nonfiction}

DILLON PRESS

(An imprint of Silver Burdett)
299 Jefferson Rd.
Parisippany, NJ 07054
{nonfiction}

DK PUBLISHING, INC.

95 Madison Avenue
New York, NY 10016
{nonfiction}
<http://www.dk.com/">

DOUBLEDAY BOOKS FOR YOUNG READERS

(An imprint of Bantam Doubleday Dell)
1540 Broadway
New York, NY 10036
{fiction/nonfiction}

DUTTON CHILDREN'S BOOKS

(A division of Penguin USA)
375 Hudson Street
New York, NY 10014
{fiction/nonfiction}

ENSLOW PUBLISHERS, INC.

44 Fadem Road
Box 699
Springfield, NJ 07081–0699
{nonfiction}
<http://www.enslow.com/">

FACTS ON FILE

11 Penn Plaza
New York, NY 10001
{fiction/nonfiction}

FANTAGRAPHICS BOOKS

7563 Lake City Way
Seattle, WA 98115
{comics/graphic novels}

FARRAR, STRAUS & GIROUX, INC.

19 Union Square West
New York, NY 10003
{fiction/nonfiction}

FAWCETT

(An imprint of Ballantine Books)
201 East 50th Street
New York, NY 10022
{paperbacks}

FOCUS ON THE FAMILY

8605 Explorer Drive
Colorado Springs, CO 80920
{Christian fiction/nonfiction}

FOUR WINDS PRESS

(An imprint of Simon and Schuster)
1230 Avenue of the Americas
New York, NY 10020
{fiction}

FRANKLIN WATTS

(A division of Grolier Inc.)
Sherman Turnpike
Danbury, CT 06813
{nonfiction}
<http://intl.grolier.com/publishing/fw/>

FREE SPIRIT PRESS

400 First Avenue N., Suite 616
Minneapolis, MN 55401
{nonfiction}

GREENHAVEN PRESS

P.O. Box 289009
San Diego, CA 92198
{nonfiction}

GREENWILLOW BOOKS

(A division of William Morrow)
1350 Avenue of the Americas
New York, NY 10019
{fiction}

GULLIVER BOOKS

(An imprint of Harcourt Brace and Company)
525 B Street, Suite 1900
San Diego, CA 92101
{fiction}

HARCOURT BRACE AND COMPANY

525 B Street, Suite 1900
San Diego, CA 92101
{fiction/nonfiction}
<http://www.harcourtbrace.com">

HARPERCOLLINS CHILDREN'S BOOKS

10 East 53rd Street
New York, NY 10022
{fiction/nonfiction}
<http://www.harpercollins.com/">

HARPER TROPHY

(An imprint of HarperCollins Children's Books)
10 East 53rd Street
New York, NY 10022
{paperbacks}

HOLIDAY HOUSE

425 Madison Avenue
New York, NY 10017
{fiction/nonfiction}

HENRY HOLT AND COMPANY, INC.

115 West 18th Street
New York, NY 10011
{fiction/nonfiction}
<http://www.obs-us.com/obs/english/books/holt/
index.htm">

HOUGHTON MIFFLIN CHILDREN'S BOOK DEPARTMENT

222 Berkeley Street
Boston, MA 02116
{fiction/nonfiction}
<http://www.hmco.com/">

HYPERION BOOKS FOR CHILDREN

114 Fifth Avenue
New York, NY 10011
{fiction/nonfiction}

INFORMATION PLUS

2812 Exchange Street
Wylie, TX 75098
{nonfiction}

KITCHEN SINK PRESS

320 Riverside Drive
Northampton, MA 01060
{comics/graphic novels}

KNOPF, INC.

201 East 50th Street
New York, NY 10022
{fiction/nonfiction}
<http://www.randomhouse.com/knopf/">

LAUREL LEAF BOOKS

(An imprint of Bantam Doubleday Dell)
1540 Broadway
New York, NY 10036
{paperbacks}

LERNER PUBLICATIONS COMPANY

241 First Avenue North
Minneapolis, MN 55401
{nonfiction}

LITTLE, BROWN & CO.

34 Beacon Street
Boston, MA 02108
{fiction/nonfiction}
<http://www.pathfinder.com/twep/Little_Brown/
Little_Brown.html">

LODESTAR BOOKS

(An affiliate of Penguin USA)
375 Hudson Street
New York, NY 10014
{fiction}

LOTHROP, LEE & SHEPARD BOOKS

1350 Avenue of the Americas
New York, NY 10019
{fiction}

LUCENT BOOKS

(An imprint of Greenhaven Press)
P.O. Box 289009
San Diego, CA 92198
{nonfiction}

MACMILLAN BOOKS FOR YOUNG READERS

(An imprint of Simon and Schuster)
1230 Avenue of the Americas
New York, NY 10020
{fiction/nonfiction}
<http://www.mcp.com/">

MARGARET K. MCELDERRY BOOKS

(An imprint of Simon and Schuster)
1230 Avenue of the Americas
New York, NY 10020
{fiction}

MARVEL COMICS

387 Park Avenue S.
New York, NY 10016
{comics/graphic novels}
<http://www.marvelcomics.com/>

MESSNER

(An imprint of Silver Burdett)
299 Jefferson Rd.
Parisippany, NJ 07054
{fiction}

THE MILLBROOK PRESS, INC.

2 Old New Milford Road
Brookfield, CT 06804
{nonfiction}
<http://www.neca.com/mall/millbrook">

MORNING GLORY PRESS

6595 San Haroldo Way
Buena Park, CA
{fiction/nonfiction}

MORROW JUNIOR BOOKS

1350 Avenue of the Americas
New York, NY 10019
{fiction/nonfiction}
<http://www.tumble.com/hearst/bpub2.html">

THOMAS NELSON PUBLISHING

P.O. Box 1410000
Nashville, TN 37214
{Christian fiction/nonfiction}

NEW AMERICAN LIBRARY

(A division of Penguin USA)
375 Hudson Street
New York, NY 10014
{paperbacks}

NEW DISCOVERY BOOKS

(An imprint of Silver Burdett)
299 Jefferson Rd.
Parisippany, NJ 07054
{nonfiction}

NTC PUBLISHING GROUP

4255 West Touhy Avenue
Lincolnwood, IL 50646
{career books}

OLIVER PRESS

2709 Lyndale Avenue, S.
Minneapolis, MN 55408
{nonfiction}

ORCHARD BOOKS

95 Madison Ave, 7th floor
New York, NY 10016
{fiction/nonfiction}

PARACHUTE PRESS, INC.

156 Fifth Avenue
New York, NY 10010
{paperbacks}

PARADOX PRESS

(An imprint of DC Comics)
1700 Broadway
New York, NY 10019
{comics/graphic novels}

PENGUIN USA

375 Hudson Street
New York, NY 10014
{nonfiction}
<http://www.penguin.com/usa/">

PERSA BOOKS

171 Madison Avenue
New York, NY 10016
{fiction/nonfiction}

PETERSON'S GUIDES

P.O. Box 2123
Princeton, NJ 08543
{nonfiction}
<http://www.petersons.com/>

PHILOMEL BOOKS

(An imprint of The Putnam & Grosset Group)
200 Madison Avenue
New York, NY 10016
{fiction/nonfiction}

POCKET BOOKS

(A division of Simon and Schuster)
1230 Avenue of the Americas
New York, NY 10020
{paperbacks}

PUFFIN BOOKS

(A division of Penguin USA)
375 Hudson Street
New York, NY 10014
{paperbacks}

G.P. PUTNAM'S SONS

(The Putnam & Grosset Group)
200 Madison Avenue
New York, NY 10016
{fiction/nonfiction}
<http://www.mca.com/putnam/">

RAINTREE STECK-VAUGHN

466 Southern Blvd.
Chatham, NJ 07928
{nonfiction}
<http://www.steck-vaughn.com/>

RANDOM HOUSE

201 East 50th Street
New York, NY 10022
{fiction/nonfiction}
<http://www.randomhouse.com/">

ROC

(An imprint of New American Library)
375 Hudson Street
New York, NY 10014
{science fiction}

ROSEN

29 E. 21st Street
New York, NY 10010
{nonfiction}

ROURKE PRESS

P.O. Box 3328
Vero Beach, FL 32964
{nonfiction}

SCHOLASTIC, INC.

555 Broadway
New York, NY 10012–3999
{fiction/nonfiction}
<http://www.scholastic.com/">

SCRIBNER'S

(An imprint of Simon and Schuster)
1230 Avenue of the Americas
New York, NY 10020
{fiction/nonfiction}
<http://w3.mlr.com/mlr/scribner/">

SIGNET BOOKS/SIGNET CLASSICS

(An imprint of New American Library)
375 Hudson Street
New York, NY 10014
{paperbacks}

SILVER BURDETT

(A division of Simon and Schuster)
299 Jefferson Rd.
Parisippany, NJ 07054
{nonfiction}

SIMON AND SCHUSTER BOOKS FOR YOUNG READERS

1230 Avenue of the Americas
New York, NY 10020
{fiction/nonfiction}
<http://www.SimonSays.com/">

SOCIAL ISSUES RESOURCES PRESS

P.O. Box 2348
Boca Raton, FL 33427
{reference}
<http://www.sirs.com/>

SPECTRA

(An imprint of Bantam Doubleday Dell Books)
1540 Broadway
New York, NY 10036
{science fiction}

SPORTS ILLUSTRATED FOR KIDS

(An imprint of Bantam Doubleday Dell)
1540 Broadway
New York, NY 10036
{nonfiction}

STARFIRE BOOKS

(An imprint of Bantam Doubleday Dell Books
for Young Readers)
1540 Broadway
New York, NY 10036
{paperbacks}

TICKNOR & FIELDS

(An affiliate of Houghton Mifflin)
215 Park Ave. S., 10th floor
New York , NY 10003
{fiction}

TOR BOOKS

(A division of Tom Doherty Assocs., Inc & St.
Martin's Press)
175 Fifth Avenue
New York, NY 10010
{science fiction}
<http://www.tor.com/">

TWENTY-FIRST CENTURY BOOKS

(A division of Henry Holt)
115 W. 18th Street
New York, NY 10011
{nonfiction}

U*X*L

(An imprint of Gale Research)
835 Penobscot Bldg.
Detroit, MI 48226
{nonfiction}
<http://www.thomson.com/uxl.html">

VIKING

(A division of Penguin USA)
375 Hudson Street
New York, NY 10014
{fiction/nonfiction}

WALKER AND COMPANY

435 Hudson Street
New York, NY 10014
{fiction/nonfiction}

WARNER BOOKS

(A division of Time Warner)
1271 Avenue of the Americas
New York, NY 10020
{fiction/nonfiction/graphic novels}
<http://www.pathfinder.com/twep/
Warner_Books/">

WORKMAN

708 Broadway
New York, NY 10003
{nonfiction}

JANE YOLEN BOOKS

(An imprint of Harcourt Brace and Company)
525 B Street, Suite 1900
San Diego, CA 92101
{fantasy/science fiction}

ZONDERVAN PUBLISHING HOUSE

(A division of HarperCollins)
5300 Patterson Ave. SE
Grand Rapids, MI 49530
{Christian fiction/nonfiction}
<http://www.zondervan.com/>

APPENDIX B: YA MAGAZINES DIRECTORY

Source: *Standard Periodical Directory 1996*

BECKETT BASEBALL CARD MONTHLY
15850 Dallas Parkway
Dallas, TX 75248 [$20.00]
{sports}

BLACK BEAT
Sterling/McFadden
232 Park Ave S.
New York, NY 10003 [$20.00]
{music}

BOP
3500 W Olive Avenue #850
Burbank, CA 91505 [$15.00]
{fanzine}

BREAKAWAY
351 Executive Drive
Carol Stream, IL 60188 [$15.00]
{religious}

BRIO
351 Executive Drive
Carol Stream, IL 60188 [$15.00]
{religious}

CIRCUS
6 18th Street, 2nd floor
New York, NY 10011 [$19.00]
{music}

COMICS SCENE
475 Park Avenue S.
New York, NY 10016 [$30.00]
{comics industry}

CRACKED
441 Lexington Avenue, 2nd floor
New York, NY 10017 [$9.00]
{humor}

DISCOVER
114 Fifth Avenue
New York, NY 10011 [$30.00]
{science}

DRAGON
201 E. Sheridan-Springs Rd #11
Lake Geneva, WI 53147 [$30.00]
{games}

ELECTRONIC GAMING MONTHLY
Sendi Publications
1920 Highland Ave, Suite #222
Lombard, IL 60148 [$28.00]
{games}

ENTERTAINMENT WEEKLY
Time Warner
1271 Avenue of the Americas
New York, NY 10020 [$51.00]
{general interest}

FANGORIA
Starlog Group
475 Park Avenue S.
New York, NY 10016 [$29.00]
{horror/sci fi movies}

FRESH
19431 Business Center Drive #27
Northridge, CA 91324 [$30.00]
{music}

HERO ILLUSTRATED
Warrior Publications
1920 Highland Ave, Suite #222
Lombard, IL 60148 [$20.00]
{comics industry}

HIT PARADER

40 Violet Avenue
Poughkeepsie, NY 12601 [$30.00]
{music}

INSIDE OUT

P.O. Box 460268
San Francisco, CA 94146 [$12.00]
{gay/lesbian youth}

MAD

DC Comics
1700 Broadway
New York, NY 10019 [$15.00]
{humor}

MERLYN'S PEN

P.O. Box 1058
East Greenwich, RI 02818 [$21.00]
{literary}

METAL EDGE

Sterling/McFadden
233 Park Avenue S.
New York, NY 10003 [$20.00]
{music}

NERVE

235 Park Ave
New York, NY 10003 [$18.00]
{music}

NICKELODEON

1515 Broadway
New York, NY 10036 [$17.00]
{humor}

NINTENDO POWER

P.O. Box 97043
Redmond, WA 98073 [$40.00]
{games}

PRO WRESTLING

London Publications
7002 W Butler Pike
Ambler, PA 19002 [$20.00]
{sports}

RAP PAGES

Larry Flynt Publications
9171 Wilshire Blvd, Suite #300
Beverly Hills, CA 90210 [$18.00]
{music}

RIGHT ON

Sterling/McFadden
233 Park Avenue S.
New York, NY 10003 [$10.00]
{music}

RIP

Larry Flynt Publications
9171 Whilshire Blvd, #300
Beverly Hills, CA 90210 [$18.00]
{music}

ROLLING STONE

Werner Media
1290 Avenue of the Americas
New York, NY 10104 [$26.00]
{music}

SCHOLASTIC UPDATE

555 Broadway
New York, NY 10012 [$19.00]
{general interest}

SEVENTEEN

850 Third Avenue
New York, NY 10022 [$16.00]
{general interest}

SIXTEEN

Sterling/McFadden
233 Park Avenue S.
New York, NY 10003 [$17.00]
{fanzine}

SLAM

1115 Broadway , 8th floor
New York, NY 10010 [$25.00]
{sports}

THE SOURCE

594 Broadway
New York, NY 10012 [$20.00]
{music}

SPIN

6 West 18th Street
New York, NY 10011 [$18.00]
{music}

SPORTS ILLUSTRATED FOR KIDS

Time Warner
1271 Avenue of the Americas
New York, NY 10020 [$18.00]
{sports}

SPY

49 E 21st St
New York, NY 10010 [$24.00]
{humor}

STARLOG

Starlog Group
475 Park Avenue S.
New York, NY 10006 [$40.00]
{movies/science fiction}

SUPERTEEN

Sterling/McFadden
233 Park Avenue S.
New York, NY 10003 [$15.00]
{fanzine}

TEEN

Peterson Publishing
6420 Wilshire Blvd
Los Angeles, CA 90048 [$16.00]
{general interest}

TEEN BEAT

Sterling/McFadden
233 Park Avenue S.
New York, NY 10003 [$21.00]
{fanzine}

TEEN MACHINE

Sterling/McFadden
233 Park Avenue S.
New York, NY 10003 [$15.00]
{fanzine}

THRASHER

High Speed Productions
1303 Underwood Avenue
San Francisco, CA 94124 [$17.00]
{sports}

TIGER BEAT

Sterling/McFadden
233 Park Avenue S.
New York, NY 10003 [$15.00]
{fanzine}

TRANSWORLD SKATEBOARDING

Imprimatur Inc.
353 Airport Road
Oceanside, CA 92054 [$20.00]
{sports}

VIBE

205 Lexington Ave
New York, NY 10016 [$18.00]
{music}

WARP

Imprimatur Inc.
353 Airport Rd
Oceanside, CA 92054 [$12.00]
{sports}

WCW MAGAZINE

London Publications
7002 W. Butler Pike
Ambler, PA 19002 [$20.00]
{sports}

WORD UP

63 Grand Ave #230
River Edge, NJ 07661 [$20.00]
{music}

WRITES OF PASSAGE

817 Broadway
New York, NY 10003 [$12.00]
{literary}

WWF MAGAZINE

Box 3857
Stamford, CT 06905 [$20.00]
{sports}

YM

Gruner & Jahr
685 Third Avenue, 30th floor
New York, NY 10017 [$18.00]
{general interest}

YOUTHWALK

351 Executive Drive
Carol Stream, IL 60188 [$15.00]
{religious}

YSB

Paige Publications
1700 W. Pine
Washington, DC 20018 [$20.00]
{general interest}

ZILLIONS

Consumers Union
101 Truman Avenue
Yonkers, NY 10703 [$16.00]
{consumer}

APPENDIX C: YA PROFESSIONAL PERIODICALS DIRECTORY

Source: *Standard Periodical Directory, 1996.*

ALAN REVIEW

National Council of Teachers of English
1 University Heights
Ashville, NC 28804 [$15.00]

APPRAISAL: SCIENCE BOOKS FOR YOUNG PEOPLE

605 Commonwealth Avenue
Boston, MA 02215 [$42.00]

THE BOOK REPORT

Linworth Publishing
480 E. Wilson Bridge Rd., Suite L
Worthington, OH 43085 [$39.00]
{junior/senior high school librarians}

BOOKLIST

50 E Huron St.
Chicago, IL 60611[$56.00]

BOOKSTORE JOURNAL

Christian Booksellers Association
2620 Venetucci Blvd.
Colorado Springs, CO [$29.00]
{Christian books}

BULLETIN OF THE CENTER FOR CHILDREN'S BOOKS

University of Illinois Press
1325 S Oak Street
Champaign, IL 61820 [$29.00]

CLASSROOM CONNECTION

Wentworth Worldwide Media
1866 Colonial Village Lane
Lancaster, PA 17605 [$39.00]
{technology/web sites}

CM: A REVIEWING JOURNAL OF CANADIAN MATERIALS FOR YOUNG PEOPLE

200 Elgin Street, Suite 602
Ottawa, CA K2P 1L5 [$42.00]

EMERGENCY LIBRARIAN

Ken Hancock & Associates
Box 34069, Dept. 349
Seattle, WA 98124 [$49.00]

ENGLISH JOURNAL

National Council of Teachers of English
1111 W Kenyon Road
Urbana, IL 61801 [$35.00]

FREE MATERIALS FOR SCHOOLS AND LIBRARIES

Box 34069, Dept. 349
Seattle, WA 98124 [$20.00]

HORN BOOK GUIDE

11 Beacon Street, Suite #1000
Boston, MA 02108 [$50.00]

HORN BOOK MAGAZINE

11 Beacon Street, Suite #1000
Boston, MA 02108 [$42.00]

JOURNAL OF READING

Box 8139
Newark, DE 19711 [$50.00]

JOURNAL OF YOUTH SERVICES IN LIBRARIES

50 E. Huron Street
Chicago, IL 60611 [$40.00]

KLIATT

33 Bay State Road
Wellesley, MA 02181 [$36.00]
{paperbacks, audiobooks, and software}

LOCUS

P.O. Box 13305
Oakland, CA 94661 [$35.00]
{science fiction}

MEDIA AND METHODS

1429 Walnut St.
Philadelphia, PA 19102 [$30.00]
{technology}

THE NEW ADVOCATE

Christopher-Gordon Publishers
480 Washington Street
Norwood, MA 02062 [$45.00]

SCHOOL LIBRARIAN'S WORKSHOP

Library Learning Resources
61 Greenbriar Drive
Berkeley Heights, NJ 079222 [$40.00]

SCHOOL LIBRARY JOURNAL

249 W. 17th Street
New York, NY 10011 [$75.00]

SCHOOL LIBRARY MEDIA ACTIVITIES MONTHLY

17 E. Henrietta Street
Baltimore, MD 21230 [$49.00]

SCHOOL LIBRARY MEDIA QUARTERLY

50 E. Huron Street
Chicago, IL 60611 [$40.00]

SCIENCE BOOKS & FILMS

American Association for the Advancement of
Science
1333 H Street
Washington, DC 20005 [$35.00]

SOURCE

Search Institute
Thresher Square West, Suite #210
Minneapolis, MN 55415
{youth issues/at-risk students}

VOICE OF YOUTH ADVOCATES

Scarecrow Press
4720A Boston Way
Lanham, MD 20706 [$38.50]

YA HOTLINE

School of Library Service
Dalhousie University
Halifax, Nova Scotia, Canada B3H 4H8
[$9.50]

BIBLIOGRAPHY

INTRODUCTION

Blanchard, Ken and Sheldon Bowles. *Raving Fans: A Revolutionary Approach to Customer Service.* New York: Morrow, 1992.

LeBoeuf, Michael. *How to Win Customers and Keep Them For Life.* New York: Berkley, 1987.

Services and Resources for Children and Young Adults in Public Libraries. U.S. Dept. of Education, Office of Educational Research and Improvement, National Center for Education Statistics, 1995

"Young Adult Library Services Association Vision Statement" *Journal of Youth Services in Libraries* (Fall 1994): 108–109.

Zollo, Peter. *Wise Up to Teens: Insight into Marketing and Advertising to Teenagers.* Ithaca, NY: New Strategist Publications, 1995

CHAPTER 1: TRENDS IN YA SERVICES

Broderick, Dorothy. "Building the Bridge to Adult Literacy," *Voice of Youth Advocates* (April 1995): 6

Carlson, Pam. "Books, Books, Books—Let Us Read: A Library Serving Sheltered and Incarcerated Youth." *Voice of Youth Advocates* (August 1994): 137–139.

Carnegie Council on Adolescent Development. *A Matter of Time: Risk and Opportunities in the Nonschool Hours.* Carnegie Corporation, 1992.

———. *Great Transitions: Preparing Adolescents for a New Century.* Carnegie Corporation, 1995.

———. *Consultation on Afterschool Programs.* Carnegie Corporation, 1994.

Caywood, Caroline A.; Young Adults Library Services Association. *Youth Participation Committee. Youth Participation in School and Public Libraries: It Works.* American Library Association, 1995 .

———. "What the Market Will Bear," *School Library Journal* (April 1996): 46.

Chelton, Mary Kay. "Three in Five Public Library Users Are Youth," *Public Libraries* (March/April 1997): 104–108.

Craver, Kathleen W. *School Library Media Centers in the 21st Century.* Westport, CT: Greenwood, 1994.

Edelman, Margaret Wright. *The Measure of Our Success.* Boston, MA: Beacon, 1992.

Flum, Judith G.; Weisner, Stan. "America's Youth Are at Risk: Developing Models for Action in the Nation's Public Libraries," *Journal of Youth Services in Libraries* (Spring 1993): 271–282.

Howard, Beth. "Class of 2001," *Omni* (September 1992): 34–39.

"In Service to Youth: Reflections on the Past; Goals for the Future," *School Library Journal* (July 1994): 23–29.

Lerner, Richard, and Doris Entwisle, and Stuart Hauser. "The Crisis among Contemporary American Adolescents: A Call for Integration of Research, Policies, and Programs," *Journal of Research on Adolescence,* no. 4 (1994): 1–4.

Mark, Linda. "Trouble with a Capital T: Teens in Troubled Times," *Wilson Library Bulletin* (November 1994): 11+.

Olson, Renee. "A Safe Haven for Teens in Trouble," *School Library Journal* (March 1997): 90.

"President Franklin Recognizes Outstanding Youth Programs," *American Libraries* (April 1994): 370.

Prothrow-Stith, Deborah. *Deadly Consequences: How Violence Is Destroying Our Teenage Population and a Plan to Begin Solving the Problem.* New York: HarperCollins, 1991.

Sadowski, Michael. "The Power to Grow: Success Stories from the National Library Power Program," *School Library Journal* (July 1994): 30–35.

Scales, Peter. *A Portrait of Young Adolescents in the 1990s: Implications for Promoting Healthy Growth and Development.* Center for Early Adolescence, 1991.

Stripling, Barbara. *Libraries for the National Education Goals.* ERIC, 1992.

"Today's Teens: Dissed, Mythed and Totally Pissed," *Utne Reader* (July/August 1994).

VanHemert, Shannon L. "PUBYAC: Yacking It Up on the Internet," *Journal of Youth Services in Libraries* (Fall 1995): 79–85.

CHAPTER 2: INVESTIGATING THE AUDIENCE

WORKS IN PROGRESS/YA LIVES AND TIMES

Benson, Peter, Judy Galbraith, and Pamela Espeland. *What Kids Need to Succeed.* Search Institute, 1994.

"Changing Middle Schools for the Future," The Carnegie Council on Adolescent Development. *The Education Digest.* (January 1990): 12–14.

Early Adolescence: Perspectives on Research, Policy, and Intervention. Richard M. Lerner, ed. Lawrence Erlbaum Associates, 1993.

Fenwick, Elizabeth and Dr. Tony Smith. *Adolescence: The Survival Guide for Parents and Teenagers.* New York: Dorling-Kindersley, 1993.

Hechinger, Fred. *Fateful Choices: Healthy Youth for the 21st Century.* Carnegie Council on Adolescent Development, 1992.

Howe, Neil and Bill Strauss. *13th Gen: Abort, Retry, Ignore, Fail?* New York:Vintage, 1993.

"In Her Own Words: From ages 10 through 14, what kids need most is supervision, says Dr. Ruby Takanishi of the Carnegie Council on Adolescent Development." *People* (November 13, 1995): 13+.

Johnson, Heather Moors. "The Secret Life of Teens," *The Ladies' Home Journal* (September 1, 1996): 96+.

Kaktani, Michiko. "Adolescence Rules," *The New York Times Magazine* (May 11, 1997): 22.

Lefstein, Leah and Joan Lipsitz. *3:00 to 6:00 PM: Programs for Young Adolescents.* 2nd Edition. Center for Early Adolescence, 1986.

Lewis, Anne C. "Youth Well-Being," *Education Digest* (December 1996): 73.

Lewis, Sydney. *'A Totally Alien Life-Form': Teenagers.* New York: New Press, 1996.

Lipsitz, Joan. *After School: Young Adolescents on Their Own.* Center for Early Adolescence, 1986.

Males, Mike A. *The Scapegoat Generation: America's War on Adolescents.* Common Courage Press, 1996.

National Research Council. Losing Generations: Adolescents in High Risk Settings. National Academy Press, 1993.

Palladino, Grace. *Teenagers: An American History.* New York: HarperCollins, 1997.

"Risk Taking: Why Teens Take Risks," *Scholastic Choices.* (October 1, 1996): 6+.

Scales, Peter C. *A Portrait of Young Adolescents in the 1990s: Implications for Promoting Healthy Growth and Development.* Center for Early Adolescence 1991.

Smith, Chris. "My Generation, Third Verse," *New York* (May 23, 1994): 30+.

Stephens, Gene. "Youth at Risk: Saving the World's Most Precious Resource," *The Futurist* (March/April 1997): 31–38.

Whitman, David. "The Youth Crisis," *U.S. News and World Report* (May 5, 1997): 24–27.

Wice, Nathaniel. *Alt.Culture.* New York: HarperCollins, 1996.

OPPOSITES ATTRACT

Arterburn, Tom R. "Librarians: Caretakers or Crimefighters?" *American Libraries* (August 1996): 32–34.

Caywood, Carolyn. "Managed Conversation; Management Theory Offers Some Clues to Cutting Down Excess Library Noise," *School Library Journal* (July 1993): 37.

Chadbourne, Robert D. "Disorderly Conduct: Crime and Disruptive Behavior in the Library." *Wilson Library Bulletin* (March 1994): 23–25.

Comstock-Gay, Stuart. "Disruptive Behavior: Protecting People, Protecting Rights," *Wilson Library Bulletin* (February 1995): 33–35.

Kollasch, Matthew. "School Media Matters: D 'n' A," *Wilson Library Bulletin* (January 1991): 67–71.

Patron Behavior in Libraries: A Handbook of Positive Approaches to Negative Situations. Beth McNeil and Denise Johnson, eds. American Library Association., 1996.

Turner, Anne M. *It Comes with the Territory: Handling Problem Situations in Libraries.* McFarland, 1993.

Williamson, Leann. "Discipline in the School Library Media Center: Strategies for Beginning Media Specialists," *Indiana Media Journal* (Winter 1991): 3–6.

CHAPTER 3: MAKING THE CASE

WHY KIDS NEEDS LIBRARIES/WHY LIBRARIES NEED KIDS

Chelton, Mary K. "Youth's Right to Know: Societal Necessity or National Oxymoron?" in *Your Right to Know: Libraries Can Make It Happen.* American Library Association, 1993.

Cooke, Eileen D. "The Political Viability of Youth Services: A Bit of Legislative History." *The Bottom Line* (Winter/Spring 1994): 21–5.

Kuhlthau, Carol Collier. "Bringing up an Information Literate Generation: Dynamic Roles for School and Public Libraries," *Information Literacy.* McFarland & Co., 1991.

Library Services for Children and Youth: Dollars and Sense. Virginia Matthews, ed. New York: Neal-Schuman, 1993.

Mathews, Virginia. "Kids Can't Wait...Library Advocacy Now!" *School Library Journal* (March 1997): 97–102.

Matthews, Virginia, et al. "Kids Need Libraries: School and Public Libraries Preparing the Youth of Today for the World of Tomorrow," *Journal of Youth Services in Libraries* (Spring 1990): 197–207.

Rosenzweig, Sue. "Leading by Example," *School Library Journal* (October 1995): 58.

School Library Journal's Best: A Reader for Children's, Young Adult, and School Libraries . New York: Neal-Schuman Publishers, 1996.

Staerkel, Kathleen, Mary Fellows and Sue McCleaf Nespeca. *Youth Librarians as Managers*. American Library Association, 1994.

The VOYA Reader. Dorothy M. Broderick, ed. Metuchen, NJ: Scarecrow Press, 1990.

Wemet, Lisa. "Librarians as Advocates for Young Adults," *Journal of Youth Services in Libraries* (Winter 1997): 168–176.

"What Kids Can't Wait For," *American Libraries* (June/July 1997): 82–89.

CREATING SUPPORT/FULFILLING THE ROLES

Caywood, Carolyn. "Role Play: A Complicated Game," *School Library Journal* (December 1993): 49.

Durrance, Joan C. and Catherine Allen. "WHCLIS Goals vs PLA Roles," *Library Journal* (June 15, 1991): 37–43.

D'Elia, George and Eleanor Jo Rodger. "Customer Satisfaction with Public Libraries," *Public Libraries* (September/October 1996): 292–297.

———. "Public Opinion about the Roles of the Public Library in the Community: The Results of a Recent Gallup Poll." *Public Libraries* (January/February 1994): 23–28.

———. "Public Library Roles and Patron Use: Why Patrons Use the Library," *Public Libraries* (May/June 1994): 135–144.

———. "The Roles of the Public Library in the Community; The Results of a Gallup Poll of Community Opinion Leaders," *Public Libraries* (March/April 1995): 94–101.

Jones, Patrick. "Role-Playing: YAs as Independent Learners," *Voice of Youth Advocates* (August 1993): 136–140.

McClure, Charles R. "Updating Planning and Role Setting for Public Libraries: A Manual of Options and Procedures," *Public Libraries* (July/August 1993): 198–199.

Planning and Role Setting for Public Libraries: A Manual of Operations and Procedures. American Library Association, 1987.

Shearer, Kenneth. "Confusing What Is Most Wanted with What Is Most Used: A Crisis in Public Library Priorities Today," *Public Libraries* (July/August 1993): 193–197.

Starr, Leah K. "The Future of Public Libraries: Divided They Serve," *Public Libraries* (March/April 1995): 102–104.

PLANNING YA SERVICES AND PROGRAMS

Carey, Cathy and Sylvia C. Mitchell. "The It's Not Totally Dreamland Quiz: Public Library Teen Area Self-Evaluation." *Voice of Youth Advocates* (August 1995): 150–151.

Farmer, Lesley S.J. *Young Adult Services in the Small Library*. Library Administration and Management Association, 1992.

Hultz, Karen and Lisa C. Wemett. "A Dozen Ways to Reach Young

Adults When You Are Short on Space, Staff, and Time," *Voice of Youth Advocates* (December 1991): 298.

Reese, Laurie B. "Space Planning for Young Adults," *Voice of Youth Advocates* (October 1991): 213–216.

Sprince, Leila J. "For Young Adults Only: Tried and True Youth Participation Manual," *Voice of Youth Advocates* (October 1994): 197–199.

Wallace, Mildred G. "Tips for Successful Young Adult Programming," *Journal of Youth Services in Libraries* (Summer 1993): 387–90.

Wisconsin Library Association. Children's and Young Adult Services Section. YA Task Force. *Young Adult Program Idea Booklet.* Wisconsin Library Association, 1991.

CHAPTER 4: YA COLLECTIONS

YA LITERATURE

Abrahamson, Richard F. "Collected Wisdom: The Best Articles Ever Written on Young Adult Literature and Teen Reading," *English Journal* (March 1997): 363–370.

Adolescent Literature as a Complement to the Classics. Norwood, MA: Christopher-Gordon Publishers, 1995.

Aronson, Marc. "The Betrayal of Teenagers," *School Library Journal.* (May 1996): 23+.

———. "The Challenge and the Glory of Young Adult Literature," *Booklist* (April 15, 1997): 1418.

———. "The YA Novel Is Dead, and Other Fairly Stupid Tales." *School Library Journal* (January 1995): 36–37.

Best Books for Young Adult Readers (1997 Edition). Stephen J. Calvert, ed. New Providence, NJ: R.R. Bowker, 1997.

Brown, Jean E. *Teaching Young Adult Literature: Sharing the Connection.* Belmont, CA: Wadsworth Publishing, 1995.

Bushman, John H. *Using Young Adult Literature in the English Classroom.* New York: Maxwell Macmillan International, 1993.

Bushman, Kay Parks. *A Thematic Guide to Young Adult Literature: Annotation, Critiques and Sources.* The Writing Conference, 1993.

Campbell, Patty. "Perplexing Young Adult Books: A Retrospective," *Wilson Library Bulletin* (April 1988): 20–26.

———. "Rescuing Young Adult Literature," *The Horn Book* (May/ June 197): 363–369.

Carroll, Pamela Sissi. "Today's Teens, Their Problems, and Their Literature," *English Journal* (March 1997): 25–35.

Cart, Michael. "Carte Blanche: Young Adult Literature—Past and Future," *Booklist* (October 15, 1994): 411.

———. *From Romance to Realism: 50 Years of Growth and Change in Young Adult Literature*. New York: HarperCollins, 1996.

———. "Of Risk and Revelation: The Current State of Young Adult Literature," *Journal of Youth Services in Libraries* (Winter 1995): 151–164.

Carter, Betty. *Best Books for Young Adults: The Selections, the History, the Romance*. American Library Association, 1994.

Chelton, Mary K. "YAs Don't Need 'Best Book'," *School Library Journal* (December 1996): 52.

Cockett, Lynn S. "Best Books for Young Adults, Real Young Adult Opinions of the List, the Process, and the 1995 Selections," *Voice of Youth Advocates* (December 1995): 284–287.

Coffey, Rosemary K. and Elizabeth F. Howard. *America As Story: Historical Fiction for Middle and Secondary Schools*, 2nd Edition. American Library Association, 1997.

Collins, Carol Jones. "A Tool for Change: Young Adult Literature in the Lives of Young Adult African-Americans," *Library Trends* (Winter 1993): 378–392.

Cueso, Allan. *Homosexual Characters in YA Novels: A Literary Analysis, 1969–1982*. Metuchen, NJ: Scarecrow Press, 1993.

Donelson, Ken. "Honoring the Best YA Books of the Year: 1964–1995," *English Journal* (March 1997): 41–48.

——— and Alleen Pace Nilsen. *Literature for Today's Young Adults*, 5th Edition. New York: Scott Foresman, 1996.

Gallagher, Mary Elizabeth. *Young Adult Literature: Issues and Perspectives*, Revised Edition. Catholic Library Association, 1990.

Herz, Sarah K. *From Hinton to Hamlet: Building Bridges between Young Adult Literature and the Classics*. Westport, CT: Greenwood Press, 1996.

Hiple, Ted. "Young Adult Literature and the Test of Time," *Publishing Research Quarterly* (Vol 8, no. 1): 5–13.

Krickeberg, Sandra K. *A National Survey on Young Adult Literature*. Thesis (Ed. D.)—Northern Illinois University, 1995.

Lenz, Millicent. *Young Adult Literature and Nonprint Materials: Resources for Selection*. Metuchen, NJ: Scarecrow Press, 1994.

Literature for Teenagers: New Books, New Approaches. Don Gallo, ed. Connecticut Council of Teachers of English, 1993.

Lomax, Earl Dean. *Contemporary Issues in Young Adult Literature*, 2nd Edition. Needham, MA: Ginn Press, 1992

Lukens, Rebecca J. *A Critical Handbook of Literature for Young Adults*. New York: HarperCollins College Pubs., 1995.

Lynch, Chris. "Today's YA Writers-Pulling No Punches," *School Library Journal* (January 1994): 37–38.

Monseau, Virginia R. *Responding to Young Adult Literature.* Portsmouth, NJ: Boynton/Cook Publishers, 1996 .

Mosaics of Meaning: Enhancing the Intellectual Life of Young Adults through Story. Kay E. Vandergrift, ed. Metuchen, NJ: Scarecrow Press, 1996.

November, Sharyn. "We're Not 'Young Adults'—We're Prisoners for Life," *Voice of Youth Advocates* (August 1997): 169–172.

Peck, Richard. *Love and Death at the Mall: Teaching and Writing for the Literate Young.* New York: Delacorte, 1994.

———. "The Silver Anniversary of Young Adult Books," *Journal of Youth Services in Libraries* (Fall 1993): 19–23.

Poe, Elizabeth, et al. "Past Perspectives and Future Directions: An Interim Analysis of Twenty-Five Years of Research on Young Adult Literature," *ALAN Review* (Winter 1995): 46–50.

Printz, Mike. "A Big Fat Hen; A Couple of Ducks," *Voice of Youth Advocates* (June 1992): 85–88.

Reed, Arthea J.S. *Comics to Classics.* International Reading Association, 1988.

———. *Reaching Adolescents: The Young Adult Book and the School.* New York: Maxwell Macmillan, 1994

Rollins, Deborah and Donna Helmer. *Reference Sources for Children's and Young Adult Literature.* American Library Association, 1996.

Small, Robert. "The Literary Value of the YA Novel," *Journal of Youth Services in Libraries* (Spring 1992): 227–285.

Snodgrass, Mary Ellen. *Characters from Young Adult Literature.* Englewood, CO: Libraries Unlimited, 1991.

———. *Literary Maps for Young Adult Literature.* Englewood, CO: Libraries Unlimited, 1995.

Stover, Lois T. *Young Adult Literature: The Heart of the Middle School Curriculum.* Portsmouth, NH: Boynton/Cook Publishers, 1996.

Stringer, Sharon A. *Conflict and Connection: The Psychology of Young Adult Literature (Young Adult Literature Series)* Portsmouth, NH: Boynton/Cook, 1997.

Woodson, Jacqueline. "A Sign of Having Been Here," *The Horn Book* (November/December 1995): 711–715.

READING RESEARCH/INTERESTS

Abrahamson, Richard F. and Eleanor Tyson. "What Every English Teacher Should Know about Free Reading," *The ALAN Review* (Vol. 14, no. 1): 54–58.

Burroughs, Robert. "Supporting Successful Literature Programs: Lessons from a New National Survey," *School Library Media Quarterly* (Spring 1993): 159–163.

Carter, Betty. "Readers' Choices: A Comparison of Critical Comments from Young Adults and Professional Reviewers," *ALAN Review* (Spring 1993): 52–55.

Culp, Mary Beth and Jamee Osborn Sosa. "The Influence of Nonfiction on Attitudes, Values, and Behavior," *English Journal* (December 1993):60–64.

Davidson, Judith and David Koppenhaver. *Adolescent Literacy: What Works and Why.* 2nd Edition. New York: Garland, 1993.

Ediger, Marlow. "The Middle School Student and Interest in Reading," *Reading Improvement.* (Fall 1992): 171–173.

Fronius, Sandra K. *Reading Interests of Young Adults in Medina County, Ohio.* (October 1993) ERIC, ED367337.

Glassner, Sid S. "I Am What I Read Survey," *Teaching and Learning Literature with Children and Young Adults* (September/October 1995): 60–61.

Humphrey, Jack W. "A Study of Reading in Indiana Middle, Junior, and Senior High Schools," *Indiana Media Journal.* (Fall 1992): 1–48.

———. "Becoming a Community of Readers: A Blueprint for Indiana," *Indiana Media Journal* (Summer 1995): 1–17.

Isaacs, Kathleen T. "Go Ask Alice: What Middle Schoolers Choose to Read," *New Advocate* (Spring 1992): 129–143.

Kaiser, Marjorie. "The Young Adult Literature Course: Young Readers Teach Prospective Teachers about Reading Interests and Reader Response," *ALAN Review* (Winter 1995): 32–35.

Krashen, Stephen. *The Power of Reading.* Englewood, CO: Libraries Unlimited, 1993.

Ley, Terry C. "Longitudinal Study of the Reading Attitudes and Behaviors of Middle School Students," *Reading Psychology* (January-March 1994): 11–38.

——— and Terry Mitchell. "Reading Attitudes and Behaviors of High School Students," *Reading Psychology* (January-March 1996): 65–92.

McKenna, Michael C., et al. "Children's Attitudes toward Reading: A National Survey," *Reading Research Quarterly* (October-December 1995): 934–956.

Mitchell, Connie. "Once upon a Time...an Examination of the Decline in Recreational Reading as Students Progress through School," *Indiana Media Journal* (Fall 1992): 54–78.

Moffitt, Mary Anne S. and Ellen Wartella. "Youth and Reading: A Survey of Leisure Reading Pursuits of Female and Male Adolescents," *Reading Research and Instruction* (Winter 1992): 1–17.

Rinehart, Steven D. "Choosing a Book: Are BOB Summaries Helpful?" *Reading Psychology* (July-September 1994): 139–153.

Russikoff, Karen A. and Janice L. Pilgreen. "Shaking the Tree of Forbidden Fruit: A Study of Light Reading," *Reading Improvement* (Summer 1994): 122–124.

Traw, Rick. *Nothing in the Middle: What Middle Schoolers Are Reading.* (1993) ERIC: ED384864.

Virgil, Sharon. "More Time and Choices Overcome Students' Resistance to Reading," *Clearing House* (September -October 1994): 52–54.

"Vocabulary Study Reveals Books Most Often Recommended for High School," *The College Board Review* (Winter 1994–1995): 30.

PROMOTING READING

Bloestein, Fay. *Invitations, Celebrations: Ideas and Techniques for Promoting Reading in Junior and Senior High School.* New York: Neal-Schuman, 1993.

Clary, Linda Mixon. "Getting Adolescents to Read," *Journal of Reading* (February 1991): 40–45.

Conlon, Alice. "Unleashing the Power of Reading in Your School and Library," *Catholic Library World* (December 1995): 22–23.

Cooper, Cathie E. "Thirteen Ways to Promote Books," *Book Report* v. 10 (January/February 1992): 19–20.

Farnan, Nancy. "Connecting Adolescents and Reading: Goals at the Middle Level," *Journal of Adolescent & Adult Literacy* (March 1996): 436–445.

Hunt, Gladys M. and Barbara Hampton. *Read for Your Life: Turning Teens into Readers.* Grand Rapids: Zondervan Publishing House, 1992.

Kollasch, Matthew. "School Media Matters: Books R Us," *Wilson Library Bulletin* (March 1992): 59–60+.

Leonhardt, Mary. *Parents Who Love Reading, Kids Who Don't: How It Happens and What You Can Do About It.* New York: Crown, 1993.

Lesesne, Teri S. "Developing Lifetime Readers: Suggestions from Fifty Years of Research," *English Journal* (October 1991): 61–64.

Loertscher, David V. "You Can Count on Reading! Library Media Specialists Make a Difference," *Indiana Media Journal* (Fall 1994): 62–70.

Oldfather, Penny. "What's Needed to Maintain and Extend Motivation for Literacy in the Middle Grades," *Journal of Reading* (March 1995): 420–422.

Parcell, Kit. "REACHing for Books: Promoting Leisure Reading at the High School Level," *Indiana Media Journal* (Fall 1993): 15–18.

Podl, Jody Brown. "Introducing Teens to the Pleasures of Reading," *Educational Leadership* (September 1995): 56–57.

Rasinski, Timothy V. "Inertia and Reading: Stimulating Interest in Books and Reading," *Middle School Journal* (May 1991): 30–33.

Sanacore, Joseph. "Encouraging the Lifetime Reading Habit," *Journal of Reading* (March 1992): 474–477.

Walston, Ellen R. "Enticing Titles," *The School Librarian's Workshop* (March 1995): 14+.

Yesner, Bernice and M. Mary Murray. *Developing Literature-Based Reading Programs: A How To Do It Manual.* New York: Neal-Schuman, 1993.

YA POPULAR LITERATURE/AUTHORS/PUBLISHING

Ammon, Bette D. amd Gale Sherman. *Worth a Thousand Words: An Annotated Guide to Picture Books for Older Readers.* Englewood, CO: Libraries Unlimited, 1996.

Arts, Chandra Kaye Massner. *An Exploratory Study of Young Adult Popular Literature: The Mass Medium Influence of Paperbacks on Female Adolescents.* Thesis. University of Kentucky, 1993.

Authors and Artists for Young Adults. New York: Gale, 1989.

Bruggeman, Lora. "Zap! Whoosh! Kerplow!" *School Library Journal* (January 1997): 22–28.

Carlsen, G. Robert, and Anne Sherrill. *Voice of Readers: How We Come to Love Books.* Urbana, Ill.: National Council for Teachers of English, 1988.

Carter, Betty; Abrahamson, Richard F. *Nonfiction for Young Adults: From Delight to Wisdom.* Oryx Press, 1990.

Caywood, Carolyn. "Judge a Book by Its Cover," *School Library Journal* (August 1993): 58.

———. "Series Fiction." *School Library Journal* (August 1992): 94.

Cornog, Martha, and Timothy Pepper. *For Sex Education, See Librarian.* Westport, CT: Greenwood, 1996.

Dunleavey, M. "Books That Go Bump in the Night," *Publishers Weekly* v. 240 (July 5, 1993): 30–31.

Engelhardt, Tom. "Reading May Be Harmful to Your Kids," *Harpers* (June 1991): 55+.

Genco, Barbara A. "Juggling Popularity and Quality: Literary Excellence vs. Popular Culture," *School Library Journal* (March 1991): 115–119.

Greenlee, Adele A., Dianne L. Monson, and Barbara M. Taylor. "The Lure of Series Books: Does It Affect Appreciation for Recommended Literature?" *Reading Teacher* (November 1996): 216–225.

Hodges, Jane. "Publishers Persist in Troubled Teens Field," *Advertising Age* (August 28, 1995): 34.

Huntwork, Mary M. "Why Girls Flock to Sweet Valley High," *School Library Journal* (March 1990): 137–140.

Hutchison, Allison Rogers. "Pay More, Get Less: The New World of Publishing," *Voice of Youth Advocates* (February 1993): 331+.

Kies,Cosette. "Eeeck! They Just Keep Coming! YA Horror Series," *Voice of Youth Advocates.* (April 1994): 17–19.

———. "Horror Fiction in School Library Media Centers," *School Library Media Activities Monthly* (May 1993): 29–30+.

Lodge, Sally. "Life after Goosebumps." *Publishers Weekly* (December 2, 1996): 24–27.

Makowski, Silk. "Series About Series: Selection Criteria for a Neglected Genre," *Voice of Youth Advocates* (February 1994): 349–351.

Nilsen, Allen Pace. "Big Business, Young-Adult Literature and the Boston Pops," *English Journal* (February 1993):70–75.

Opening Doors for Middle-Grades Readers. Recommended Paperback Books for 10– to 15–Year-Olds: A Compilation Including Annotations, Booklist Sources, Booktalks and Bookmarks. Indiana Library Federation/Opening Doors Project, 1993.

Rosenberg, Judith K. *Young People's Books in Series: Fiction and Nonfiction, 1975–1991.* Englewood, CO: Libraries Unlimited, 1992.

Ross, Catherine Sheldrick. "If They Read Nancy Drew, So What? Series Book Readers Talk Back," *Library & Information Science Research* (Summer 1995): 201–236.

———. "Reading Series Books: What Readers Say," *School Library Media Quarterly* (Spring 1996): 165–171.

Shapiro, Lillian and Barbara L. Stein. *Fiction for Youth: A Guide to Recommended Books.* 3rd Edition. New York: Neal-Schuman, 1992.

Shipley, Roberta Gail. *Teaching Guides for 50 Young Adult Novels.* New York: Neal-Schuman, 1995.

Speaking for Ourselves: Autobiographical Sketches by Notable Authors of Books for Young Adults. Donald R. Gallo, ed. National Council of Teachers of English, 1990.

Speaking for Ourselves, Too: More Autobiographical Sketches by Notable Authors of Books for Young Adults. Donald R. Gallo, ed. National Council of Teachers of English, 1993

Suelain, Moy. "To Shock Is the System: Teen Thriller Novels," *Entertainment Weekly* (January 31, 1992): 68.

Twentieth-Century Young Adult Writers. Chicago, IL: St. James Press, 1994.

Writers on Writing for Young Adults: Exploring the Authors, the Genre, the Readers, the Issues, and the Critics of Young-Adult Literature: Together with Checklists of the Featured Writers. Detroit, MI: Omnigraphics, 1991

Youth Services Section, Wisconsin Library Association. *Middle Readers Handbook.* Wisconsin Library Association, 1993.

PERIODICALS

Buboltz, Dale and Ruby Ling-Louie. "A Treeful of Good Reading," *The Book Report* (January/February 1992).

Carmody, Deirde. "Competition for Young Readers Has Magazines Totally Psyched," *New York Times* (January 18, 1993).

Chepesiuk, Ron. "The Zine Scene: Libraries Preserve the Latest Trend in Publishing," *American Libraries* (February 1997): 68–70.

Cockett, Lynn S.; Kleinberg, Janet R. "Periodical Literature for African-American Young Adults: A Neglected Resource," in *African-American Voices in Young Adult Literature*. Metuchen, NJ: Scarecrow Press, 1994.

Evans, Ellis. "Content Analysis of Contemporary Teen Magazines for Adolescent Females," *Youth & Society* (September 1991).

Fine, Jana. "Teen 'Zines: Magazines and Webzines for the Way Cool Set," *School Library Journal* (November 1996): 34–37.

Gunderloy, Mike and Cari Janice Goldberg. *The World of Zines: A Guide to the Independent Magazine Revolution*. New York: Penguin Press, 1992.

Huhn, Mary. "At Seventeen, Teens Look a Little Older," *Mediaweek* (June 15, 1992).

Jensen, Jeff. "A New Read on How to Reach Boys," *Advertising Age* (August 23, 1993).

Jones, Patrick. "A to Z and In-Between: New Magazines for Young Adults," *Voice of Youth Advocates* (February 1994): 352–358.

———. "Spy!, The Source, and Son of Sassy: New YA Magazines," *Voice of Youth Advocates* (October 1992): 219–220.

Katz, Bill. *Magazines for Libraries*. 7th Edition. New Providence, NJ: R.R. Bowker, 1992.

Katz, Bill and Linda Sternberg Katz. *Magazines for Young People*. New Providence, NJ: R.R. Bowker, 1991.

Kerwin, Ann Marie. "Forget Dual Audiences: New Teen Magazines Go Girl Crazy," *Advertising Age* (May 19, 1997): 10–11.

"Magazines for Young Adults," *Emergency Librarian* (March/April 1994): 67–68.

"Magazines for Young Adults," *Journal of Youth Services in Libraries* (Fall 1993): 97–103.

Manly, Lorne. "Is There a Market Where the Boys Are?" *Folio* (May 15, 1993).

Massey, Judy. "Girl Talk Mags," *School Library Journal* (October 1992).

McCann, Paul "Teen Titles Stoke Magazine War," *Marketing Week*. (April 26, 1996): 16.

Pratt, Jane. "Just Say KNOW: Magazine Publishing; the Sassy Approach," *Journal of Youth Services in Libraries* (Summer 1991): 383–388.

Rosch, Leah. "Not So Sweet Seventeen," *Folio* (June 1, 1993).

Stoll, Donald R.; Walsh, Russell. "Skill Builders: Mad about Magazines," *Learning* (April-May 1995): 82–84.

"Teen Magazines Plan 'Guidelines' Over Sex," *Marketing* (February 29, 1996): 3.

AUDIO VISUAL

Chance, Rosemary. "Literature-Based Videos for Young Adults," *Journal of Youth Services in Libraries* (Fall 1994): 94 -100.

Harris, Karen H. "Growing up Listening," *Booklist* (Apr. 15, 1994): 1548.

Kliatt Audiobook Guide. Jean Palmer, ed. Englewood, CO: Libraries Unlimited, 1994.

Weisbard, Eric. *The Spin Magazine Alternative Record Guide.* New York: Vintage, 1995.

Wynne, John. *The Listener's Guide to Audiobooks.* New York: Fireside, 1995.

TECHNOLOGY

Berger, Pam. "Spinning the Hits: The Best CD-ROMs," *Information Searcher* (March 1994): 1+.

——— and Susan Kinnell. *CD-ROM for Schools.* Eight Bit Books, 1994.

Bradburn, Frances. "Thinking about CD-ROMS," *Booklist* (November 1, 1996): 486–487.

Clements, Jim and Paul Nicholls. "A Comparative Survey of Multimedia CD-ROM Encyclopedias," *Computers in Libraries* (Sept. 1995): 53–59.

Collicutt, Cathy. "Technology, Young People, and the Library," *North Carolina Libraries* (Summer 1993): 75–76.

Dewey, Patrick R. *303 CD-ROMs to Use in Your Library: Descriptions, Evaluations, and Practical Advice.* American Library Association, 1996.

Echler, Nikki; Olson, Rebecca. "Top Spins: 50 New CD-ROMs—You'll Laugh, You'll Cry—but Mostly You'll Thank Us for Wading through Hundreds of CD-ROM Titles to Bring You the Very Best 50," *MacUser.* (October 1995): 106 +.

"Fast Reference Facts." *Booklist* (May 15, 1996): 1606+.

Gillespie, Thom. "Best Buys: What to Collect in Multimedia," *Library Journal.* (February 1, 1995): 40–43.

Herther, Nancy K. " CD-ROM for Your Home—Today's 50 Best Bets," *Database* (May 1996): 26.

Hoffert, Barbara. "The Encyclopedia Wars: CD-ROM or Online? Illustration or Information? Search or Browse? Don't Expect Easy Answers from Publishers," *Library Journal* (September 1, 1994): 142–145.

———. "Reinventing Reference for a New Age," *Library Journal* (November 15, 1996): S4–S7.

Jacso, Peter. "The Hardware Helper: Taking the Guesswork out of Multimedia Systems," *School Library Journal* (November 1996): 30–33.

———. "The Hardware Helper II," *School Library Journal* (January 1997): 30–33.

———. "Long Live Books on Paper...and Their Directories and Reviews on CD-ROM," *Computers in Libraries* (September 1995): 60–62.

———. "State-of-the-Art Multimedia in 1996: The "Big Four" General Encyclopedias on CD-ROM," *Computers in Libraries* (April 1996): 26–32.

Jody, Marilyn and Marianne Saccardi. *Computer Conversations: Readers and Books Online*. National Council of Teachers of English, 1996.

Juhl, Beth. "Ex machina: Electronic Resources for the Classics," *Choice* (April 1995): 1249–1261.

Koutnik, Chuck. "The World Wide Web Is Here: Is the End of Printed Reference Sources Next?" *RQ* (Spring 1997): 422–429.

LaGuardia, Cheryl M. and Ed Tallent. "Best CD-ROMs of 1995," *Library Journal* (April 15, 1996): 41+.

———. *The CD-ROM Primer: the ABCs of CD-ROM*. New York: Neal-Schuman, 1994.

Newman, Marilyn D. "Stepping into CD-ROM," *The School Librarian's Workshop* (November 1994): 7+.

Nicholls, Paul. "CD-ROM and Multimedia Trends: The Year in Review," *Computers in Libraries* (November/December 1995): 56–60.

Oliver, Ronald Gerard. "The Influence of Instruction and Activity on the Development of Skills in the Usage of Interactive Information Systems," *Education for Information* (March 1996): 7–17.

Pappas, Marjorie L.; Geitgey, Gayle. "Observing Student Searches in an Electronic Encyclopedia," *Book Report* (March/April 1994): 13–14.

Powers, Joan C. "CD-ROM in Schools," *The Reference Librarian* no. 49–50 (1995): 335–346.

Richards, Trevor and Lynne McKechnie. "CD-ROM Encyclopedias," *OCLC Systems & Services* (Winter 1994): 26–30.

Safford, Barbara Rip. "The Death of a Book: The Dictionary," *School Library Media Activities Monthly* (December 1995): 46–47.

Sorrow, Babara Head, and Betty S. Lumpkin. *CD-ROM for Librarians and Educators*. 2nd Edition. McFarland, 1996.

"Top 10 CD-ROM Titles in All Categories," *CD-ROM Professional* (December 1995): 28.

MULTICULTURAL LITERATURE/SERVICES

Alire, Camila and Orlando Archibeque. *Serving Latin Communities: A How-To-Do-It Manual*. New York: Neal-Schuman, 1997.

Dame, Melvina Azar. *Serving Linguistically and Culturally Diverse Students: Strategies for the School Library Media Specialist*. New York: Neal-Schuman, 1993.

Dealing with Diversity through Multicultural Fiction: Library Classroom Partnerships. Lauri Johnson and Sally Smith, eds. American Library Association, 1993.

Gallagher, Mary Elizabeth. "History and Heritage: Multicultural Books for Young Adults," *Catholic Library World* (July-September 1994): 19–27.

Many Faces, Many Voices: Multicultural Literary Experiences for Youth. Anthony L. Manna and Carolyn S. Brodie, eds. Fort Atkinson, WI: Highsmith, 1992.

Miller, Lynda, Theresa Steinlage and Mike Printz. *Cultural Cobblestones; Teaching Cultural Diversity.* Metuchen, NJ: Scarecrow Press, 1994.

Multicultural Aspects of Library Media Program. Kathy Howard Latrobe and Mildred Knight Laughlin, comps. Englewood, CO: Libraries Unlimited, 1992.

Rochman, Hazel. *Against Borders: Promoting Books for a Multicultural World.* American Library Association, 1993.

Sages, Judy. "Connections—YA Publishers, YA Librarians, YA Readers: Linking Multicultural Needs," *Journal of Youth Services in Libraries* (Winter 1993): 166–170.

Totten, Herman L. *Culturally Diverse Library Collections for Youth.* New York: Neal-Schuman Publishers, 1996.

Writers of Multicultural Fiction for Young Adults: A Bio-Critical Sourcebook. Westport, CT: Greenwood Press, 1996.

RELUCTANT READERS

Baines, Lawrence. "Cool Books for Tough Guys: 50 Books out of the Mainstream of Adolescent Literature That Will Appeal to Males Who Do Not Enjoy Reading," *ALAN Review* (Fall 1994): 43–46.

Beers, G. Kylene. "No Time, No Interest, No Way! The Three Voices of Aliteracy," *School Library Journal* (February 1996): 30–33.

———. "No Time, No Interest, No Way! Part 2," *School Library Journal* (March 1996): 110–113.

Grimes, Marijo. "Finding Hooks to Catch Reluctant Readers," *English Journal* (January 1991): 45–47.

Miller, Frances A. "Books to Read When You Hate to Read: Recommended by Reluctant YA Readers in Grades 7–12," *Booklist* (February 15, 1992): 1100–1101.

Moniuszko, Linda K. "Motivation: Reaching Reluctant Readers Age 14–17," *Journal of Reading* (September 1992): 32–34.

Rosenzweig, Sue. "Books that Hooked 'em: Reluctant Readers Shine as Critics," *American Libraries* (June/July 1996): 74–76.

Sherman, Gale W. and Bette D. Ammon. *Rip-Roaring Reads for Reluctant Teen Readers.* Englewood, CO: Libraries Unlimited, 1993.

Turner, Gwendolyn Y. "Motivating Reluctant Readers: What Can Educators Do?" *Reading Improvement* (Spring 1992): 50–55.

Turner, Pat W. "Wrestling with Reluctant Readers," *School Library Journal* (December 1994): 42.

CHAPTER 5: REFERENCE, READERS' ADVISORY, AND INSTRUCTION

RAVING FANS/CUSTOMER SERVICE

Sandy, John H. "By Any Other Name, They're Still Our Customers," *American Libraries* (August 1997): 43–45.

Smith, Kitty. *Serving the Difficult Customer: A How-to-Do-It Manual*. New York: Neal-Schuman, 1993.

Walters, Suzanne. *Customer Service: A How-to-Do-It Manual*. New York: Neal-Schuman, 1994.

Weingand, Darlene E. *Customer Service Excellence: A Concise Guide for Librarians*. American Library Association, 1996.

REFERENCE

Albsmeyer, Betty. "Barriers to Good Reference Service," *Illinois Libraries* (November 1991): 529–531.

Banks, Linda. "Small School Libraries Can Be Reference Centers," *Illinois Libraries* (November 1991): 565–566.

Bell, Anita C. "A Term Paper Resource Center," *School Library Journal* (January 1992): 34–36.

Benton, Bleue J. "Throw It All Together: Integrating Adult and Youth Nonfiction and Reference," *Illinois Libraries* (November 1991): 523.

Boardman, Edna M. "How to Help Students Deal with 'Too Much Information'," *Book Report* (September/October 1995): 23–24.

Borne, Barbara Wood. *100 Research Topic Guides for Students*. Westport, CT: Greenwood, 1996.

Brewer, Rosellen. "Help Youth at Risk: A Case for Starting a Public Library Homework Center," *Public Libraries* (July/August 1992): 208–212.

Bunge, Charles Albert. "Responsive Reference Service: Breaking Down Age Barriers," *School Library Journal* (March 1994): 142+.

Crosson, Vicky L. "Hey! Kids Are Patrons, Too!," *Texas Libraries* (Summer 1991): 48–50.

Del Vecchio, Rosemary A. "Privacy and Accountability at the Reference Desk," *The Reference Librarian* no. 38 (1992): 133–140.

Durrance, Joan C. "Factors that Influence Reference Success: What Makes Questioners Willing to Return?" *The Reference Librarian* no. 49–50 (1995): 243–265.

Grover, Robert J. and Janet Carabell. "Diagnosing Information Needs in a School Library Media Center." *School Library Media Activities Monthly* (January 1995): 32–36+.

Isenstein, Laura J. "Get Your Reference Staff on the STAR (System Training for Accurate Reference) Track." *Library Journal* (April 15, 1992): 34–37.

Job, Amy G. and MaryKay W. Schnare. *Reference Work in School Library Media Centers: A Book of Case Studies*. Metuchen, NJ: Scarecrow, 1996.

Johnson, Doug. "The Changing Face of Student Research," *Technology Connection* (April 1997): 48–49.

Kuhlthau, Carol Collier. "Students and the Information Search Process: Zones of Intervention for Librarians," in *Advances in Librarianship*, v18. Academic Press, 1994.

Latrobe, Kathy Howard.; Havener, W. Michael. "Addressing School Library Media Reference Services: Guidelines for Success," *The Reference Librarian* no. 44 (1994): 161–172.

———. "The Information Seeking Behavior of High School Honor Students," *Journal of Youth Services in Libraries* (Winter 1997): 188–200.

Loorie, Nancy S. "Whose Homework Is It, Anyway? Helping Parents at the Reference Desk," *New Jersey Libraries* (February 1993): 15–17.

McDougald, Dana, and Melvin Bowie. *Information Services for Secondary Schools*. Westport, CT: Greenwood Press, 1997.

Patrick, Gay D. *Building the Reference Collection: A How-to-Do-It Manual for School and Public Librarians*. New York: Neal-Schuman, 1992.

Pobanz, Becky L. "Reference in a School Media Center," *Illinois Libraries* (November 1991): 563–564.

Riechel, Rosemarie. *Reference Services for Children and Young Adults*. Library Professional Publications, 1991.

Ross, Catherine Sheldrick and Patricia Dewdney. "Best Practices: An Analysis of the Best (and Worst) in Fifty-Two Public Library Reference Transactions," *Public Libraries* (September/October 1994): 261–266.

Safford, Barbara Rip. "The Once and Future Role of the Internet in Reference Service and Information Retrieval," *School Library Media Activities Monthly* (June 1996): 39+.

School Library Reference Services in the 90s: Where We Are, Where We're Heading. Carol Truett, ed. Binghampton, NY: Haworth Press, 1994.

Schwartz, Vanette M. "The Reference Interview: Including Instruction?" *Illinois Libraries* (November 1991): 535–536.

Shontz, Marilyn L. "Measuring Reference Transactions in School Library Media Programs," *The Reference Librarian* no. 44 (1994): 145–160.

Small, Ruth V. and Sueli M. Ferreira. "Multimedia Technology and the Changing Nature of Research in the School Library," *The Reference Librarian* no. 44 (1994): 95–106.

Sutton, Ellen D. and Leslie Edmonds Holt. "The Reference Interview," in *Reference and Information Services,* 2nd Edition. Englewood, CO: Libraries Unlimited, 1995.

Swanson, Constance L. "Is This a Homework Question? Coping with the Information Needs of Young Library Patrons," *New Jersey Libraries* (Winter 1995): 18–20.

Thompson, Elizabeth. *Reference and Collection Development on the Internet: A How-to-Do-It Manual.* New York: Neal-Schuman, 1996.

Truett, Carol. "New Technologies in Reference Services for School Libraries," *The Reference Librarian* no. 44 (1994): 123–144.

Using the Internet, Online Services, and CD-ROMs for Writing Research and Term Papers. Charles Harmon, ed. New York: Neal-Schuman Publishers, 1996.

READERS' ADVISORY

Abdullahi, Ismail. "Multicultural Issues for Readers' Advisory Services," *Collection Building* v. 12 no. 3–4(1993): 85–88.

Baker, Sharon L. "Readers' Advisory Services: A Call for More Research." *RQ* (Winter 1992): 166–169.

Carruth, Gorton. *The Young Reader's Companion.* New Providence, NJ: R.R. Bowker, 1993.

Chelton, Mary K. "Books for the Beast: a Maryland How-We-Did-It-Good Self-Training Success Story!" *Voice of Youth Advocates* (August 1993): 141–144+.

———. "Read Any Good Books Lately? Helping Patrons Find What They Want," *Library Journal* (May 1, 1993): 33–37.

Herald, Diana Tixier. *Genreflecting: A Guide to Reading Interest in Genre Fiction.* Englewood, CO: Libraries Unlimited, 1995.

Iacono, Pauline. "Fabulous Fiction Finders," *Public Libraries* (November/December 1995): 342–346.

Lundin, Anne H. "The Company We Keep: Advisory Service for Youth," *Collection Building* v. 12 no. 3–4 (1993): 45–56.

McCook, Kathleen de la Pena. "Considerations of Theoretical Bases for Readers' Advisory Services," *Collection Building* v. 12 no. 3–4(1993): 7–12.

———. "The First Virtual Reality," *American Libraries* (July/August 1993): 626–628.

———— and Gary Rolstad. "Developing Readers' Advisory Services: Concepts and Commitments." (special issue) *Collection Building* v. 12 no. 3–4 (1993): 5–117.

Ross, Catherine Sheldrick. "Readers' Advisory Service: New Directions," *RQ* (Summer 1991): 503–518.

Saricks, Joyce G. and Nancy Brown. *Readers' Advisory Service in the Public Library.* 2nd Edition. American Library Association, 1997.

Sasges, Judy. "Read My Genre: A Reader's Advisory Workshop," *Voice of Youth Advocates* (June 1993): 79+.

Smith, Duncan F. "Reconstructing the Reader: Educating Readers' Advisors," *Collection Building* v. 12 no. 3–4 (1993): 21–30.

Spencer, Pam. *What Do Young Adults Read Next?: A Reader's Guide to Fiction for Young Adults.* New York: Gale Research, 1994.

White, Dorothy J. "Tools for Readers' Advisory: An Annotated and Selected Bibliography," *Collection Building* v. 12 no. 3–4 (1993): 37–38

The Young Adult Reader's Adviser. New Providence, NJ: R.R. Bowker, 1992.

LIBRARY INSTRUCTION/ORIENTATION

Bleakly, Ann and Jackie L. Carrigan. *Resource Based Learning Activities: Information Literacy for High School Students.* American Library Association, 1994.

Callison, Daniel. "The Impact of New Technologies on School Library Media Center Facilities and Instruction," *Journal of Youth Services in Libraries* (Summer 1993): 414–419.

Eadie, Tom. "User Education Does Not Work," *Library Journal* (October 15, 1990): 42–45.

Eisenberg, Michael B. and Robert E. Berkowitz. "The Six Habits of Highly Effective Students; Using the Big Six to Link Parents, Students, and Homework," *School Library Journal* (August 1995): 22–25.

Evaluating Library Instruction; Sample Questions, Forms, and Strategies for Practical Use. Diana Schonack, ed. American Library Association, 1995.

Farmer, Lesley S.J. "Information Literacy: More Than Pushbutton Printouts," *Book Report* (November/December 1995): 11–12.

————. *Informing Young Women: Gender Equity Through Literacy Skills.* McFarland, 1996.

Garret, Linda and JoAnne Moore. *Teaching Library Skills in Middle and High School: A How-To-Do-It Manual.* New York: Neal-Schuman, 1993.

Information Literacy: Learning How to Learn. American Library Association, 1991.

Jones, Patrick and Candace B. Morse. "What to Do When the World Book Is Missing; A Program of Pubic Library Instruction for High School Students," *RQ* (Fall 1985) 31–34.

Kuhlthau, Carol. "The Information Search Process of High-, Middle-, and Low-Achieving High School Seniors," *School Library Media Quarterly* (Summer 1989): 224 - 226.

———. "Information Search Process: A Summary of Research and Implications for School Library Media Programs," *School Library Media Quarterly* (Fall 1989): 19–25.

———. *Teaching the Library Research Process*. 2nd Edition. Metuchen, NJ: Scarecrow Press, 1994.

Library Lessons for Grades 7–9. Arden Drusc, cd. Mctuchen, NJ: Scarecrow.

Stripling, Barbara and Judy M. Pitts. *Brainstorms and Blueprints: Teaching Library Research as a Thinking Process*. Englewood, CO: Libraries Unlimited, 1988.

Teaching Information Literacy Using Electronic Resources for Grades 6–12. Mary Alice Anderson, ed. Linworth, 1996.

SCHOOLS AND LIBRARY COOPERATION

Brown, Margaret and Pat Muller. "TAB: A Middle School/Public Library Success Story," *Voice of Youth Advocates* (December 1994): 255–258.

Callison, Daniel. "A National Survey on Public Library and Secondary Library Cooperation: Do They Know Each Other?" *Indiana Media Journal* (Summer 1991): 17–21

Douglas, Janice. "The Public Library and the School System: Partner in Lifelong Education," *Emergency Librarian* (February 1990): 9–13.

Handy, Lynne. "Serving Youth through Cooperative Efforts," *Illinois Libraries* (January 1992): 24–25.

Miller, Carol L. and Lynn Presley-Clarke. "School and Public Libraries: A Popular Collaboration," *The School Librarian's Workshop* (June 1994): 15+.

Schuyler, Michael. "Libraries and Schools—the Technology of Cooperation; Plus, Whose Responsibility Is the Data?" *Computers in Libraries* (January 1996): 43–45.

Shannon, Donna M. "Cooperation between School and Public Libraries: A Study of One North Carolina County," *North Carolina Libraries* (Summer 1991): 67–70.

Vandergrift, Kay. "Cooperative Dialogue: Using an Instrument to Empower," *Voice of Youth Advocates* (June 1994): 73–77.

Vollrath, Elizabeth. "The Junior High Comes to the Public Library," *Voice of Youth Advocates* (October 1996): 197–198.

CHAPTER 6: BOOKTALKING

Bodart-Talbot, Joni. *The Effect of a Booktalk Presentation of Selected Titles on the Attitude toward Reading of Senior High School Students and on the Circulation of These Titles in the High School Library.* Thesis (Ph. D.)—Texas Woman's University, 1985

Dahl, Pamela Kay. *The Effects of Booktalks on Self-Selected Reading.* Thesis (M.S.)—Moorhead State University, 1988.

Gillespie, John T. *JuniorPlots 4: A Booktalk Guide for Use with Readers Ages 12–16.* New Providence, NJ: R.R. Bowker, 1993.

———. *MiddlePlots 4: A Booktalk Guide for Use with Readers Ages 8–12.* New Providence, NJ: R.R. Bowker, 1994.

———. *SeniorPlots: A Booktalk Guide for Use with Readers Ages 16–18.* New Providence, NJ: R.R. Bowker, 1995.

Graham, Kent W. "Dramatic Booktalks (for the Untheatrical)," *Voice of Youth Advocates* (December 1993): 282–283.

Herald, Diana Tixier. "Booktalking to a Captive Audience," *School Library Journal* (May 1995): 35–36.

Nollen, Terrence David. *The Effect of Booktalks on the Development of Reading Attitudes and the Promotion of Individual Reading Choices.* Thesis (Ph. D.)—University of Nebraska—Lincoln, 1992.

Reeder, Gail. *Effect of Booktalks on Adolescent Reading Attitudes.* Thesis (Ph. D.)—University of Nebraska, 1991.

CHAPTER 7: SURVEYING THE FIELD

Broderick, Dorothy. "What (Most) Publishers and (Many) Librarians Need to Know but Resist Learning," *Voice of Youth Advocates* (October 1996): 196.

Levere, Jane L. "A New Survey Charts the Habits of Teen-agers around the World," *New York Times* (June 11, 1996): D8.

"The Marketing Report on Youth Marketing," *Marketing* (July 8, 1996): 11–16.

Marney, Jo. " The Wherefores and Whys of Generation Y: The Younger Siblings of the Ge-Xers Are Now Coming into Marketers' Sights," *Marketing* (April 1, 1996): 15.

"Special Report: Marketing to Teens," *Advertising Age* (August 23, 1993): S1–S14.

Zollo, Peter "Focus on Teens," *American Demographics* (Marketing Tools Supplement). (January/February 1996): 10–17.

———. "Talking to Teens," *American Demographics.* (November 1995): 22+.

————. *Wise Up to Teens: Insights into Marketing and Advertising to Teenagers.* Ithaca, NY: New Strategist Press, 1995.

BY THE NUMBERS

Brightman, Joan. "What Smells Like Teen Spirit?" *American Demographics.* (November 1994): 10+.

Chelton, Mary K. "Developmentally Based Performance Measures for Young Adult Services," *Top of the News* (Fall 1984): 39–52.

————. "The First National Survey of Services and Resources for Young Adults in Public Libraries," *Journal of Youth Services in Libraries* (Spring 1989): 224–231.

Dunn, William. "Hanging out with American Youth," *American Demographics.* (February 1992): 24–35.

Fisher, Phyllis Jean Dansbery. *An Analysis of the Resources Allocated to Young Adults in Public Libraries in the Thirty Eight Largest Standard Metropolitan Statistical Areas in the United States.* Dissertation, University of Texas at Austin, 1992.

Higgins, Susan E. *A Study of the Effectiveness of Public Library Service to Young Adults.* Dissertation, Florida State University, 1992.

————. "Should Public Libraries Hire Young Adult Specialists?" *Journal of Youth Services in Libraries* (Summer 1994): 382–391.

Latrobe, Kathy Howard. "Report on the Young Adult Library Services Association's membership survey." *Journal of Youth Services in Libraries* (Spring 1994): 237–253.

Population projects of the United States by age, sex, race, and Hispanic origin, 1993–2050. U.S. Bureau of the Census, Current Population Reports, 1993.

Public School Library Media Centers in 12 States: Report of the NCLIS/ALA Survey. National Commission on Libraries and Information Science, 1994.

Razzano, Barbara "Creating the Library Habit," *Library Journal* (March 1985): 111–114.

Rice, James. "Library Awareness Survey," *Public Libraries* (November/December 1992): 347–350.

Services and Resources for Young Adults in Public Libraries. U.S. Dept. of Education, Office of Educational Research and Improvement, National Center for Education Statistics, 1988.

State of America's Children Yearbook–1995. Children's Defense Fund, 1995.

Sullivan, Suzanne.; Stefansson, Jody. "The NCES Survey on Young Adult Services in Public Libraries: Implications for Research," *Journal of Youth Services in Libraries* (Winter 1991):155–157.

Van House, Nancy, et al. *Output Measures for Public Libraries: A Manual of Standardized Procedures.* 2nd Edition. American Library Association, 1987.

———— and Thomas A. Childers. *The Public Library Effectiveness Study: A Complete Report.* American Library Association, 1993.

Waity, Gloria. "A Look at the YALSA Research Agneda. ADE, and the Current OERI/FRSS Survey." *Journal of Youth Services in Libraries* (Summer 1997): 418–422.

Walter, Virginia A. *Output Measures and More: Planning and Evaluating Public Library Services for Young Adults.* American Library Association, 1995.

————. *Output Measures for Public Library Services to Children: A Manual of Standardized Procedures.* American Library Association, 1992.

Welch, Alicia J. and Christine N. Donohue. "Awareness, Use and Satisfaction with Public Libraries," *Public Libraries* (May/June 1994): 149–154.

Youth Indicators 1996: Trends in the Well-Being of American Youth. National Center for Education Statistics, 1996.

Zinn, Laura. "Teens: They're Back," *Business Week* (April 11, 1994): 1+.

BY THE BOOKS

Astroth, Kirk "Beyond Ephebiphobia: Problem Adults or Problem Youths?" *Phi Delta Kappan* (January 1994): 28–33.

Beyond Ephebiphobia: A Tool Chest for Customer Service to Young Adults. American Library Association, 1994.

Book Beat, A Young Adult Services Manual for Louisiana's Libraries. State Library of Louisiana, 1992.

Bridging the Gap: Young Adult Services in the Library. Missouri State Library, 1992.

Campbell, Patty. "Reconsidering Margaret Edwards," *Wilson Library Bulletin* (June 1994): 20+.

Chelton, Mary K. and James Rosinia. *Bare Bones: Young Adult Services Tips for Public Library Generalists.* Public Library Association/Young Adult Library Services Association, 1993.

Developing Public Library Services for Young Adults. Division of Library and Information Services, Florida Dept. of State, 1994.

Directions for Library Service to Young Adults, 2nd Edition. Young Adult Library Services Association, 1993.

Edwards, Margaret A. *The Fair Garden and the Swarm of Beasts: The Library and the Young Adult.* Reprint Edition. Commentary by Patty Campbell. American Library Association, 1994.

Excellence in Library Services to Young Adults: The Nation's Top Programs. Mary Kay Chelton, ed. American Library Association, 1994.

Excellence in Library Services to Young Adults: The Nation's Top Programs. 2nd Edition. Mary Kay Chelton, ed. American Library Association, 1997.

Wilson-Lingbloom, Evie. *Hangin' Out at Rocky Creek: A Melodrama in Basic Young Adult Services in Public Libraries.* Metuchen, NJ: Scarecrow Press, 1994.

SHORT HISTORY

Atkinson, Joan. "Pioneers in Public Library Services to Young Adults," *Top of the News* (Fall 1986): 27–44.

Castagna, Edward. "Young Adult Service on the Public Library Organization Chart," *Library Trends* (October 1968): 132–139.

Downen, Thomas "YA Services: 1993," *Top of the News.* (Fall 1979): 347–353.

"Imagination and Scholarship: The Contributions of Women to American Youth Services and Literature" in *Library Trends* ; vol. 44, no 4. (1996).

Rogers, JoAnn. "Trends and Issues in Young Adult Services," in *Libraries and Young Adults: Media, Services, and Librarianship:* Englewood, CO: Libraries Unlimited, 1979.

Weisner, Stan. *Information in Empowering: Developing Public Library Services for Youth at Risk.* 2nd Edition. Bay Area Library and Information System, 1992.

"Young Adult Services in the Public Library," *Library Trends* (October 1968): 115–220.

MARKETING TO YOUNG ADULTS

Dimick, Barbara. "Marketing Youth Services," *Library Trends* (Winter 1995): 463–477.

Strickland, Charlene. "You Sell—They Buy!" *Wilson Library Bulletin* (October 1992): 58–59.

Walter, Virginia A. "Research You Can Use: Marketing to Children," *Journal of Youth Services in Libraries* (Spring 1994): 283–288.

MEASUREMENT

Assessment and the School Library Media Center. Carol Kuhlthau, ed. Englewood, CO: Libraries Unlimited, 1994.

Caywood, Carolyn. "Counting Beans," *School Library Journal* (June 1995): 48.

Childers, Thomas A. and Nancy A. Van House. *What's Good? Describing Your Public Library's Effectiveness.* American Library Association, 1993.

Franklin, Barbara and Margaret Hamil. "Youth Services Evaluation in the Small Library: A Case Study." *Public Libraries* (September./October 1992): 278–283.

Making Data Work for You: A Guide to Resources for Program Developers and Youth Advocates. Indiana Youth Institute, 1995.

Yesner, Bernice and Hilda Jay. *Operating and Evaluating School Library Media Programs: A Handbook for Administrators and Librarians.* New York: Neal-Schuman, 1998.

Zweizig, Douglas L., Debra Wilcox Johnson, Jane Robbins, and Amy Owen. *Evaluating Library Programs and Services: Tell It!* School of Library and Information Studies. University of Wisconsin-Madison, 1993.

DEVELOPING A VISION/STANDARDS & GUIDELINES

Bryson, Susan A. and Marilyn L. Shontz. "Young Adult Services for the Year 2000," *North Carolina Libraries* (Summer 1991): 58–63.

Building, Books, and Bytes: A Report on the Public's Opinion of Library Leaders' Visions for the Future. Benton Foundation, 1996.

Crowley, John D. *Developing a Vision: Strategic Planning and the Library Media Specialist.* Westport, CT: Greenwood, 1991.

Illinois Library Association. *Managing Change: Directions for Youth Services in Illinois Public Libraries.* Illinois Library Association, 1993.

Kids Welcome Here! Writing Public Library Policies that Promote Use by Young People. Anne E. Simon, ed. New York Library Association, 1990.

MacRae, Cathi Dunn. "A Library Where Silence Is Banned," *Voice of Youth Advocates* (April 1996): 7 -12.

Marcoux, Betty and Delia Neuman. "Into the Twenty-First Century: New Guidelines and Standards for Library Media Programs," *School Library Media Quarterly* (Summer 1996): 213–216.

Marshall, Philip. "Children and Young People: Guidelines for Public Library Services," *International Review of Children's Literature and Librarianship* v. 6 no. 3 (1991): 201–209.

Mellon, Constance A. and Emily S. Boyce. "School Library Standards: A Force for Changes in Library Services for Children and Young Adults," *Journal of Youth Services in Libraries* (Winter 1993): 128–137.

New Jersey Department of Education. *Guidelines for Young Adult Services in Public Libraries in New Jersey.* New Jersey State Library, 1987.

———. *Guidelines for Young Adult Services in Public Libraries in New Jersey and Analysis: Follow-up Survey of 1990 - Guidelines for Children's and Young Adult Services in Public Libraries of New Jersey.* New Jersey Dept. of Education, 1990.

New York Library Association. Youth Services Section. *The Key to the Future: Revised Minimum Standards for Youth Services in Public Libraries of New York State.* New York Library Association, 1994.

Ruth, Lindsay D. and Sari Feldman. "The Whole Service Approach: Plugging the Holes in Your YA Service," *School Library Journal* (May 1994): 28–31.

Tello, Jerry and Laura Weber. *Developing Public Library Service for Youth.* Los Angeles Public Library, 1993.

Vandergrift, Kay. *Power Teaching: A Primary Role of the School Library Media Specialist.* American Library Association, 1994.

Willett, Holly. *Public Library Youth Services: A Public Policy Approach.* Ablex, 1995.

Wisconsin Public Library Youth Services Guidelines. Madison, WI: Youth Service Section, Wisconsin Library Association, 1995.

"Young Adult Library Services Association Vision," *Journal of Youth Services in Libraries*, (Fall 1994): 108–109.

CHAPTER 8: ISSUES IN YA SERVICES

American Library Association, Office for Intellectual Freedom. *Intellectual Freedom Manual.* 5th ed. American Library Association, 1996.

Anderson, Arthur James. "Two Thumbs Down: Children's Access to Videos," *Library Journal* (December 1995): 70+.

Avi. "Young People, Books and the Right to Read," *Journal of Youth Services in Libraries* (Spring 1993): 245–256.

Boardman, Edna M. *Censorship: The Problem That Won't Go Away.* Linworth, 1993.

Bradburn, Frances Bryant. "The Policeman within: Library Access Issues for Children and Young Adults," *North Carolina Libraries* (Summer 1993): 69.

Cart, Michael. "Carte Blanche: Winning One for the First Amendment," *Booklist* (April 15, 1996): 1431.

Caywood, Carolyn. "The Courage to Trust," *School Library Journal* (August 1995): 43.

———. "What's a Teen?" *School Library Journal* (February 1993): 42.

———. "YA Confidential," *School Library Journal* (August 1996): 11.

Dixon, Judith. "Are We Childproofing Our Public Libraries? Identifying the Barriers That Limit Library Use by Children," *Public Libraries* (January/February 1996): 50–56.

Dowd, Frances Smardo. "Homeless Children in Public Libraries: A National Survey of Large Systems," *Journal of Youth Services in Libraries* (Winter 1996): 155–166.

———. "Public Library Programs for Latchkey Children: A Status Report," *Public Libraries* (September/October 1995): 291–295.

Eaglen, Audrey. "An Immodest Proposal," *School Library Journal* (August 1989): 92.

Foerstel, Herbert. *Banned in the USA: A Reference Guide to Book Censorship in Schools and Public Libraries.* Westport, CT: Greenwood, 1994.

———. "Conflict and Compromise over Homosexual Literature," *Emergency Librarian* (November/December 1994): 28–30.

Garden, Nancy. "Annie on Trial: How It Feels to Be the Author of a Challenged Book," *Voice of Youth Advocates* (June 1996): 79+.

Gerhardt, Lillian. "Been There, Done That: Freedom of Access for Children," *School Library Journal* (December 1995): 4.

———. "Loco Video Law." *School Library Journal* (April 1996): 4.

Glunt, Cynthia. "Guidance to Go," *School Library Journal* (October 1995): 56.

Gordon, Ruth I. "I Helped Children Lie," *School Library Journal* (February 1995): 42.

Hakala-Ausperk, Cathy. *Are Young Adults Getting Younger?* Master's Research Paper. Kent State University School of Library Science, 1991.

Hawkins, Helma. "Opening the Closet Door: Public Library Services for Gay, Lesbian, & Bisexual Teens," *Colorado Libraries* (Spring 1994): 28–31.

Hildebrand, Janet. "Is Privacy Reserved for Adults? Children's Rights at the Public Library." *School Library Journal* (January 1991): 21–25.

Intellectual Freedom Committee of the Young Adult Library Services Association. *Hit list II: Frequently Challenged Books for Young Adults.* American Library Association, 1996.

Intellectual Freedom Manual. American Library Association, 1992.

MacDonald, Frances Beck. *Censorship and Intellectual Freedom: A Survey of School Librarians' Attitudes and Moral Reasoning.* Metuchen, NJ: Scarecrow Press, 1993.

MacRae, Cathi Dunn. "Watch Out for "Don't read this!" How a Library Youth Participation Group Was Silenced by Schools Yet Made Its Voice Heard," *Voice of Youth Advocates* (June 1995): 80–87.

Mason, Marilyn Gell. "Sex, Kids, and the Public Library," *American Libraries* (June/July 1997): 104–106.

Meyer, Randy. "Furor over R-Rated Videos Sparks Library Legislation," *School Library Journal* (April 1996): 11.

Nyfeler, Suzan. "Kids and Confidentiality; Balancing Privacy with Parents' Rights," *Texas Libraries* (Fall 1993): 103.

Palmer, Lee, Janine Givens, and Jean B. Palmer. "Equal Access to Library Materials," *Wilson Library Bulletin* (September 1991): 38–40.

Reichman, Henry. *Censorship and Selection: Issues and Answers for Schools*. American Library Association, 1993.

Sadker, Myra and David Sadker. *Failing at Fairness: How America's Schools Cheat Girls*. New York: Scribners, 1994.

Symons, Ann and Charles Harmon. *Protecting the Right to Read: A How-to-Do-It Manual*. New York: Neal-Schuman, 1996.

Tyson, Christy. "What's in a Name?" *School Library Journal* (December 1990): 47.

Vandergrift, Kay E. "Privacy, Schooling, and Minors," *School Library Journal* (January 1991): 26–30.

White, Herbert S. *Ethical Dilemmas in Libraries: A Collection of Case Studies*. G.K. Hall, 1992.

CHAPTER 9: HIGH-SPEED CONNECTIONS

Amey, Larry and Stephen Elliot. "Serving the Cyberteen: Library Service for the 21st Century Adolescent." *Voice of Youth Advocates* (April 1997): 21–22.

Anderson, Arthur James. "Minor Altercation on the World Wide Web," *Library Journal* (June 1, 1996): 68+.

Anderson, Mary Alice. "The Impact of the Internet," *Book Report* (May/June 1997): 27–28.

Barron, Daniel D. "Haven't We Been Here Before? Children, Schools, Pornography, Intellectual Freedom, and the Internet," *School Library Media Activities Monthly* (April 1996): 47–50.

———. "Keeping Current: School Library Media Specialists and the Internet - Road Kill or Road Warriors?" *School Library Media Activities Monthly* (May 1994): 48–50.

Benson, Allen C. and Linda Fodemski. *Connecting Kids and the Internet: A Handbook for Librarians, Teachers and Parents*. New York: Neal-Schuman, 1996.

Boehring, Julie C. "Should Libraries Have the Ability to Block Internet Sites?" *Library Journal* (August 1995): 12.

Bradburn, Frances Bryant. "alt.sex: Detour Off the Information Highway," *North Carolina Libraries* (Summer 1995): 56–57.

Burt, David. "In Defense of Filtering," *American Libraries* (August 1997): 46–48.

———. "Policies for the Use of Public Internet Workstations in Public Libraries," *Public Libraries* (May/June 1996): 156–158.

Carrigan, Jackie L. "Evaluating Internet Resources," *Journal of Youth Services in Libraries* (Summer 1997): 423–425.

Caywood, Carolyn. "Guide and Seek," *School Library Journal* (July 1996): 35.

———. "Narrow Searches, Narrow Minds," *School Library Journal* (November 1995): 38.

———. "Raising Net.citizens," *School Library Journal* (January 1995): 44.

Collins, Boyd. "Beyond Cruising; Reviewing," *Library Journal* (February 15, 1996): 122–124.

"CyberSites," *Journal of Youth Services in Libraries* (Summer 1996): 395.

Eisenberg, Michael B. and Peter Millbury. "LM_NET: Where Media Specialists Meet in Cyperspace," *School Library Journal* (November 1994): 31–33.

Farmer, Lesley S.J. "Library Home Pages: A New Knowledge Environment," *Technology Connection* (December 1996): 23–26.

Flanders, Bruce L. "A Delicate Balance," *School Library Journal* (October 1994): 32–35.

Gainor, Larry. "Let Teens Talk," *School Library Journal* (December 1996): 50.

Hubbard, Bette Ann, et al. "Newest Members of the Net Set," *Library Journal* (February 1, 1996): 44–46.

Hyman, Karen. "Sex at the Library: Film at 11," *Library Journal* (November 1, 1996): 35–36.

The Internet for Teachers and School Library Media Specialists: Today's Applications, Tomorrow's Prospects. Edward J. Valaukas and Monica Ertel, ed. New York: Neal-Schuman, 1996.

Jacobson, Frances F. "Children and the Internet," *Journal of Youth Services in Libraries* (Winter 1996): 185–189.

———. "Road Scholar: A School Librarian Sets Out in Search of High-tech Success," *School Library Journal* (November 1995): 20–23.

———. "What Students Expect of the Internet," *American Libraries* (November 1995): 1030.

Johnson, Douglas A. "Student Access to Internet: Librarians and Teachers Working Together to Teach Higher Level Survival Skills," *Emergency Librarian* (January/February 1995): 8–12.

Johnson, Yvette. "Notes from a Reluctant Cybernaut," *Journal of Youth Services in Libraries* (Winter 1996): 195–198.

Jones, Corie. "Virtual Reference Desks: Finding Your Answers Online," *Technology Connection* (March 1997): 24–25.

Junion-Metz, Gail. "Internet Access for Kids and Young Adults," *Public Libraries* (January/February 1997): 30–31.

———. *K-12 Resources on the Internet.* Berkeley, CA: Library Solutions Press, 1996.

Kennedy, Shirley Duglin. *Best Best Internet: Reference and Research When You Don't Have Time to Fool Around.* American Library Association, 1997.

Kniffel, Leonard. "In the Name of the Children," *American Libraries* (September 1995): 768.

LaRue, James. "Censorship and the Internet," *Colorado Libraries* (Fall 1995): 31–35.

"Libraries Nationwide Pressured to Install Internet Filters," *American Libraries* (April 1997): 14.

Markoff, John. "The Keyboard Becomes a Hangout for a Computer Savvy Generation," New York Times, (Late New York Edition, August 31, 1993): A1+.

Matsco, Sandra and Sharon Campbell. "Writing a Library Home Page," *Public Libraries* (September/October 1996) 284–287.

McCartney, Scott. "Society's Subcultures Meet by Modem: For Teens, Chatting on Internet Offers Comfort of Anonymity," *Wall Street Journal.* (Eastern Edition, December 8, 1994): B1+.

McDonald, Janice T. "Gender Differences in Computer Use," (causes and solutions for parents and schools) *Ohio Media Spectrum* v. 45 (Fall 1993): 19–20+.

Metz, Roy and Gail Junion-Metz. *Using the World Wide Web and Creating Home Pages: A How-to-Do-It Manual.* New York: Neal-Schuman, 1996.

Milbury, Peter G. "K-12 Schools in the Global Village: Teachers and Kids Cruise the Information Superhighway," (special issue) *Internet Research* v. 5 no. 1 (1995): 1–88.

Minkel, Walter. "BlenderWeb? Nerd World?" *School Library Journal* (July 1997): 24–28.

———. "Lost (&found) in Cyberspace," *School Library Journal* (March 1997): 102–106.

———. "Web Rebellion." *School Library Journal* (September 1996): 142.

Mondowney, JoAnn G. "Licensed to Learn: Drivers' Training for the Internet," (Enoch Pratt Free Library Tutors at-Risk Youth) *School Library Journal* v. 42 (January 1996): 32–34.

National Commission on Libraries and Information Science. *1996 National Survey of Public Libraries and the Internet: Progress and Issues.* Government Printing Office, 1996.

Olson, Renee. "Blocking Software Not Yet Widespread, SLJ Tech Survey Shows," *School Library Journal* (April 1997): 16.

Palgi, Rebecca D. "Rules of the Road: Why You Need an Acceptable Use Policy," (teaching students to be responsible on-line) *School Library Journal* v. 42 (August 1996): 32–33.

Parker, Josie Barnes. "Internet Public Library Youth Division," *Journal of Youth Services in Libraries* (Spring 1996) 270–278.

Rotenberg, Marc and Janet Murray. "Intellectual Freedom on the Information Highway," (presented at the IFRT program at the 1995 ALA Conference) *Newsletter on Intellectual Freedom* v. 44 (September 1995): 126–127+.

Schneider, Karen G. "A Garden of Earthly Delights," (Internet Resources for Children's and Young Adult Library Services) *American Libraries* v. 27 (May 1996): 70+.

———. "Fears of Filth Foster Filtering Follies," *American Libraries* v. 26 (September 1995): 798.

Serim, Ferdi. *NetLearning: Why Teachers Use the Internet.* Berkeley, CA: Osborne, 1996.

"Sex on the Internet," (ALA Intellectual Freedom Round Table program "Intellectual Freedom: Will It Become Roadkill on the Information Superhighway?") *American Libraries* v. 26 (July/August 1995): 671.

Schrock, Kathleen. "It Must be True. I Found It on the Internet!" *Technology Connection* (September 1996): 12–15.

Symons, Anne. "Sizing up Sites: How to Judge What You Find on the Web," *School Library Journal* (April 197): 22–25.

"Teenagers and Technology," *Newsweek* (April 28, 1997): 86.

"To Filter or Not to Filter?," *American Libraries* (June/July 1997): 100–103.

Todaro, Julie. "New Tools of the Trade: 48 Essential Net Resources for Librarians," *School Library Journal* (November 1996): 24–29.

"Who Uses the Internet and How Do They Use It?" *Book Report* (May/June 1997): 20.

CHAPTER 10: YA TRAINING

Bessler, Joanne M. *Putting Service into Library Staff Training: A Patron-Centered Guide (LAMA occasional papers).* American Library Association, 1994.

Developing Library Staff for the 21st Century. Maureen Sullivan, ed. Haworth, 1992.

Doll, Carol A. "Smart Training; Smart Learning: The Role of Cooperative Learning in Training for Youth Services." *Journal of Youth Services in Libraries* (Winter 1997): 183–187.

Hart, Lois B. *Training Methods That Work: A Handbook for Trainers.* Los Altos, CA: Crisp Publications, 1991.

Lester, June. "Competency Colloquium: Developing the Competency Statement." *Public Libraries* (Mar/April 1994): 81–91.

Nichols, C. Allen. "Get on Board the YA Train," *Voice of Youth Advocates* (February 1995): 333–335.

Ohles, Judith K. and Julie Ann McDaniel. *Training Paraprofessionals for Reference Service.* New York: Neal-Schuman, 1993.

O'Meara, Frank. "The Pedagogue's Decalogue: Techniques for Effective Training Sessions," *Training* (January 1993): 43+.

Sipos, Karen. "Training Trainers in Teen Service," *American Libraries* (November 1996): 54–55.

Staff Development: A Practical Guide. 2nd Edition. American Library Association, 1992.

JULY

Goal: Take a vacation already!

It is hard enough to get through every day's "to do" list without adding the tasks listed here. Yet, to create support for serving YAs, you must be proactive. Listed in the earlier monthly calendars were over 70 "to dos"—read this, count this, etc.—which is more than one year's worth of work. What do you need to do now? Prioritize. You know your director, your organization, and what works. You also know the obstacles that are facing you. But remember the biggest obstacle, in most cases, is not lack of staff, time, money, or resources but the failure of libraries to dedicate these things to serving YAs because YA is not a priority. With over 50 idea and strategies to choose from, the odds are in your favor that one (or some) of the ideas in this book will push the right buttons at the right time with the right people. This is even more likely if the idea is coupled with the right attitude—a Yattitude—dedicated to connecting young adults and libraries.

INDEX

Adolescence (Fenwick and Smith), 30–31
Acceptable use policies (AUPs), 334–335
Access to Electronic Information, Services and Networks (ALA), 335, 341
Against Borders (Rochman), 127
ALAN Review, 202
American Library Association, Annual Conference (Summer 1994), 5, 15
American Library Association, Annual Conference (Summer 1995), 12
American Library Association, Annual Conference (Summer 1996), 154
American Library Association, Annual Conference (Summer 1997), 339
Athletic Shorts (Crutcher), 269–270
Audio books, SEE Non-print
Austin (TX) Public Library, 15

Baker, Stella, 396–399
Bare Bones: Young Adult Services Tips for Public Library Generalists (Chelton and Rosinia), 1, 14, 80, 111, 180, 301, 375
Berkeley (CA) Public Library, 353
Best Years of Their Lives (Zvirin), 43
Beyond Ephebiphobia (ALA), 5, 301–302
Bib Squibs,
    Body image, 124
    Comic novels, 126
    Death and Dying, 123
    Fun fast facts, 196
    Genre of style, 131
    Historical fiction, 125
    Horror novels, 119
    Informational nonfiction, 134
    Life and death, 123
    Mysteries and thrillers, 124
    Parenting young adults, 42
    Picture books for young adults, 170
    Programming, 35
    Romance, 125
    Sex and sexuality, 120
    Social Issues, 122
    Substance abuse, 121,
    Teen Volunteers, 32
    Training Tools, 380

    Underground classics, 130
    Violence, 122
    Young adult literature, 98
    Young Adult lives and times, 59
    Youth Participation, 33
Big Six (Eisenberg and Berkowitz), 31, 218–221, 364
Bodart, Joni Richards, 243–244, 246
Book discussion groups, 45
Booklists. *see also* Bib Squibs.
    annual lists, 160–161.
    creating, 202–206.
    Internet access to, 361–362
    from *Booklist,* 162.
    other lists, 163
    reference books, 164
Booktalking, 243–273
    assumptions, 247–248
    elements of success, 258–259.
    evaluating, 262–266.
    examples, 256–257, 266–273
    forms, 250, 263–265
    models, 248–249
    policies, 247
    presentations, 260–262.
    research, 243–245
    resources, 244
    rules, 245–247, 251
    strategies, 253–256
    writing, 249–253.
Boulder (CO) Public Library, 12, 354
Breaking the Fall (Cadnum), 267–268
Broderick, Dorothy, 283
Burt, David, 339–340

Campbell, Patty, 5, 99, 302
Carnegie Council on Adolescent Development, 8–9, 11, 25, 28, 29, 34, 39–46, 121, 281, 283, 326, 366
CD-ROMs, 156–159.
Censorship, 11, 319–321
Chelton, Mary Kay, *see also Bare Bones, Excellence in Library Services,* 8, 10, 14, 31, 72, 76, 193, 285, 289, 298, 307, 309
Children of the River (Crew), 268

Children's Literature Web Guide (Brown), 359
Collection development, 82–83, 95–171, 175, 396, 401
   see also fiction, Internet, non-fiction, non-print, periodicals, choices, 108–112, 114–115.
   concerns, 160, 165–167, 296
   merchandising, 116
      priorities, 112–114
      training exercise, 391
   selection tools, 159–164
   statistics, 292
   tools, 161–164.
   weeding, 160, 175
   youth participation, 152, 175
Comic books, 128, 140–141
Confidentiality, *see also* privacy, 316–317
Customer service, 37–38, 65–66, 179–186
   training exercise, 393
Cuyahoga County (OH) Public Library, 13

Delacorte Press Prize for Best First YA Novel, 131–132
Dimick, Barbara, 303–304.
Directions for Library Service to Young Adults (YALSA), 1, 111, 303, 311
Dyson, Lillie Seward, 186, 187

Eaglen, Audrey, 326
Edwards, Margaret, 5, 6, 301–302
Enoch Pratt (MD) Public Library, 15
Ephebiphobia, 69
Excellence in Library Services to Young Adults (Chelton, ed.), 5, 9, 13, 183, 194, 301

Fair Garden and the Swarm of Beasts (Edwards), 5, 302–303
Fiction, 114–132.
   adult authors, 100, 166–167
   classics, 127–130
   emotional needs met through reading, 112, 391
   genres, 119–132
   science fiction and fantasy, 126
   series, 110–112, 115, 117–119, 165–166

   thrillers, 119
   training exercise, 392

Fine, Jana, 143, 146, 147
Fleming, Douglas and Barbara, 380, 382
Formal educational support. *See* Homework assignments, reference services,
From Romance to Realism (Cart), 99, 325

Giver (Lowrey), 272–273
Graphic novels, 130
Great Transitions: Preparing Adolescents for a New Century (Carnegie Council), 28–29, 39–46, 281, 366
Greenhaven Press, 136–137

Hakala-Ausperk, Cathy, 327–328
Hangin' Out at Rocky Creek (Wilson-Lingbloom), 303
Hart, Lois, 381
Higgins, Susan, 299–300
Hit List (YALSA), 11
Houston (TX) Public Library, 9
How to Win Customers and Keep Them for Life (LeBoeuf), 183, 185–186
Homework centers, 9, 15, 194
Homework collections, 193
Homework assignments, 66, 72, 80–81, 83, 136–137, 187–192, 225–231, 323, 401
   training exercise, 394, 395

I Know What You Did Last Summer (Duncan), 256–257
Illinois Goals for Youth Services, 74, 77
Information, access to, 9–10, 315–316, 321–323, 341, 334–346
Information Power (AASL), 234
Intellectual freedom, 11, 142, 319–321
Internet, 333–369
   access to, 9–10, 315–316, 321–323, 341, 334–346
   adolescence web sites, 365–366
   booklists web sites, 361–362
   collection development, 158, 357–369
   educational web sites, 364–365

ezines, 143, 368–369
evaluating resources, 336, 345–348, 356–357
filtering, 10, 315–316, 337–342
policies, 333–342
professional resources, 93, 355–366
public library YA web sites, 348–354
publisher's web sites, 362–363
reading web sites, 360–361
school library web sites, 359–360
starting points, 358–359
teen sites, 366–369
use 35, 137, 336, 339–340, 342–345.
youth participation, 12, 45, 353–355
youth views toward, 337–338
Internet Public Library, Teen Division, 12, 353–354, 358

"Kids Can't Wait" (ALA), 16
Kids Need Libraries (ALA), 2, 16, 71, 90
Kies, Cosette, 111

Latchkey, 323–324
Latrobe, Kathy Howard, 299–300
Librarians, training. see Young adult library services, training.
Library cards, 31
Library Power, 16
Library instruction, 31, 206–208, 216–223, 191, 192, 398
  evaluation, 223
  strategies, 216–218, 223
Library literacy, 207
Library orientation, 206–216, 398
  evaluating, 212–216
  forms, 213–215
  planning, 208–209
  strategies, 209–212, 216
Lincoln (NB) Public Library, 15
Literature for Today's Young Adult (Doneleson and Nilsen), 99

Magazines, *see* Periodicals
Makowski, Sylvia (Silk), 111
Margaret Edwards Lifetime Achievement Award, 128

Marketing, 304–307
  forms, 308
  market segments, 305
  planning, 306–307
  using surveys, 306
Mason, Marilyn Gell, 338–338
Mass homework assignments. *see* Homework assignments
Matter of Time: Risk and Opportunities in the Nonschool Hours (Carnegie Council), 34
Merchandising, 116
Michigan Electronic Library—Education Section, 365
Middle Readers Handbook, 12
Middle school students, 12–13, 42–43, 326–328
Milbury, Peter, 359
Music, 32–33, 151–152

National Education Goals, 15–16, 73–74
Networking, 41, 44–45, 49, 78–80, 313–314, 331, 397
  training exercise, 394–395, 397
New York (NY) Public Library, 353
New York Standards for YA Services, 74, 76
Non-fiction, 132–138
  educational, 133
  informational, 43–44, 134
  issues, 138
  priorities, 133
  ready reference, 196
  series, 43, 135–137
Non-print, 153–155, 319–321

Opening Doors for Middle Grade Readers, 12
Output Measures and More (Walter), 7, 76, 300–301, 304, 309

Paperbacks, 44, 81, 109–112,115–132, 165–166, 204
  Thrillers, 118
Periodicals, 35, 81, 138–151
  best for young adults, 143–151

ezines, 368–369
disadvantages, 141–142.
training exercise, 392–393
Planning and Role Setting for Public Libraries, 79, 335
The Power of Reading (Krashen), 101, 128
Printz, Mike, 361
Privacy, 80, 188, 189, 317–318. *see also* confidentiality
Programming, 9, 34–37, 41, 79, 397
Public libraries,
excellence in, 179–180
indispensability of, 90
roles 79–84
users, 286
Public relations, 65–66, 77, 78, 140, 207, 241
Public School Library Media Centers in 12 States, 7

Rampant readers, 166–167
Raving Fans (Blanchard), 183–186
Readers' advisory services, 36, 136, 195–206, 398
forms, 199, 203,
goals, 196
strategies, 197–198, 201–202
tools, 162–164, 200
Reading promotion strategies, 168–171
Reading research, 100–108, 165–166
Reference books, 137–138, 164, 193, 195
Reference services, 83–84, 184–195, 398, 401
behaviors for successful, 187
goals, 186–187
proactive, 194
strategies, 187–192
Ten commandments of, 184–185
training exercise, 393–394
transactions, best, 186
transactions, worst, 186
Reluctant readers, 139–140, 168–171
Resolution of the Use of Filtering Software in Libraries (ALA), 339
Rosinia, James, 393. *see also Bare Bones*
Ross, Catherine Sheldrick, 165–166, 186

San Diego (CA) Public Library, 9, 15
Santa Clara (CA) Public Library, 353
School and public library cooperation, 211, 223–239, 313, 397, 398
advantages of, 223–224
barriers to, 224–225
elements of success, 238–239
forms, 227–230, 235–236
initiating, 232–233
marketing, 236–238
statistics, 293
strategies, 225–231
training exercise, 394–395, 397
Services and Resources for Young Adults in Public Library-1988 (National Center for Education Statistics), 283, 296, 298, 300, 375
Services and Resources for Children and Young Adults-1995 (National Center for Education Statistics), 7, 8, 21–22, 26, 27, 53, 69, 80, 84, 87, 283–300, 309, 326–327
Silver Kiss (Klause), 271–272
Sipos, Karen, 375–376
Social responsibility, 318–319
Staying Fat for Sarah Brynes (Crutcher), 270–271
Stine, R.L. , 118, 119, 165–166, 260
Summer reading lists, 231
Summer reading programs, 275–276, 401
Surveys,
reading interests, 107
restricting access, 322
self-evaluation, 87
user survey, 85
using, 305–306

Teachers, 231. *see also* school public library cooperation
Technology, *see also* Internet, CD-ROMs,
access to, 9–10, 333–345
collection development, 156–159
instruction, 222–223
planning, 93
Training, 375–399. *see also* Young adult library services, training

content, 377, 396, 398–399
exercises, 380–396
goals of, 376
need for, 375–376
strategies, 377–379, 380, 382
Tyson, Christy, 325–326

Vandergrfit, Kay, 360, 361
Videos, *see* Non-print
Voice of Youth Advocates, 1, 93, 126, 135, 136, 160, 202

Walter, Virginia, 300, 304. *see also Output Measures and More*
Weetzie Bat (Bloch), 198, 266–267
White House Conference on Libraries, Second, 71
Wise Up to Teens: Insights into Marketing and Advertising to Teenagers (Zollo), 33, 35, 53–61, 144, 180, 182, 184

Young adult advisory groups, *see* Youth Participation.
Young adult areas, SEE Young Adult Library Services, Space Planning
Young adult librarians, 297–300
  need for, 299–300
  needs facing, 299
  statistics, 284, 285, 297
  traits, 180–186, 187, 299, 390
  training exercise, 388–390
Young Adult Librarians' Help/Home Page, 93, 354–357
Young Adult Library Services Association, 1, 241, 281
  Best Books, 99,
  Best of the Best, 128–129
  competencies for YA Librarians, 181
  goals, 78
  history, 301
  membership survey, 299, 300
  Quick Picks Committee, 168–169
  "Serving the Underserved" seminars, 14–15, 375–376
  vision statement, 90, 111

web site, 1
youth participation in, 12

Young adult library services
  availability of services, 294, 321, 327
  barriers to, 16, 284, 287–290, 321
  contradictions, 25–27
  creating support for, 69–90, 313–314
  defining, 325–329
  defining quality, 179–186
  documents, 1, 300–303
  goals and objectives, 70–75, 84–90
  history, 279–281,301–303
  issues, 315–329
  levels of service, 290, 291, 327
  marketing, 237–238, 303–307, 308
  measurement and evaluation, 7, 21–22, 76, 87, 212–216, 223, 262–266,300, 307–309, 399, 401
  need for, 70–75, 396
  outreach services, 13–14, 38
  outreach, 38
  planning, 1–2, 21–22, 65–66, 75–78, 84–90, 93, 175, 241, 275–276, 313–314, 331, 373
  service plans, 84–86
  space planning, 34–35, 89, 116, 175, 194, 396, 398
  staffing, 88, 285, 289, 297, 299–300
  standards, 1, 74, 76, 77, 78, 181
  statistics, 21–22, 285–298.
  training, 14–15, 83, 331, 373, 375–399
  trends, 5–16
    training exercise 382

Young adult literature, 97–100, 127–128
  authors, 103, 115, 128
  best books, 129, 201
  lack of diversity, 325
  reference books, 164
Young adult volunteers, 31–32

Young adults,
  ages of, 53–54, 55
  attracted to in advertisements, 182.

as independent learners, 81–82
as library customers, 180–186, 284
at risk, 5–6, 8–9, 25, 72, 73–75, 323–325
demographics, 7–8, 12–13, 280, 281–284, 295
developmental tasks, 30–38, 140, 275
    training exercise, 384–385, 386
disruptive behavior, 36, 38, 46–53, 66, 399
health, 28–29, 36–38, 43–44, 282
Internet web sites about, 365–366
leisure time activities, 56–58, 383
    training exercise, 385, 387, 388
library needs, 84
myths and misconceptions, 27–28, 61
    training exercise, 284
parenting, 42
psychological aspects, 30–46, 53–61
reading interests, 100–108

training exercise, 390–391
self-perception, 53–55, 59–61
social life and customs, 53–61.
    training exercises, 385
statistics, 54–61, 282, 284, 295

Young Adults Deserve the Best (YALSA), 181
Youth, the Internet, and Library Policy, 333–338, 358
Youth Indicators 1996, 282, 365
Youth participation, 11–12, 31–33, 45, 152, 353–354
Youth Participation in Libraries (Caywood, ed.), 12, 373

Zero to the Bone(Cadnum), 268–269
Zollo, Peter, 53, 99, 124, 127, 180, 248, 309
    see also Wise Up to Teens

ABOUT THE AUTHOR

Patrick Jones is a librarian in Houston, Texas. He is the author of *What's So Scary About R.L. Stine?* (Scarecrow Press, 1998). Jones has written over forty articles for such library professional publications as *The Horn Book, School Library Journal, Voice of Youth Advocates*, and *The Journal of Popular Culture in Libraries* as well as essays for reference books such as *Children's Books and Their Creators* (Houghton Mifflin, 1995). He is a frequent speaker at library conferences across the United States, as well as in Canada and New Zealand. He created the Young Adult Librarian's Help/Homepage (http://www.kcpl.lib.mo.us/ya). He currently edits a column for *The Voice of Youth Advocates* called "YA Clicks" about Internet sites for teenagers. He is also working on a young adult novel, *Things Change*.